SEARCH FOR
HOLOGRAPHIC
MIND
THEORY OF FRAGMENTATION

CHESTER LITVIN, PHD

Order this book online at www.trafford.com
or email orders@trafford.com

Most Trafford titles are also available at major online book retailers.

Print information available on the last page.

ISBN: 978-1-4907-9834-9 (sc)
ISBN: 978-1-4907-9835-6 (e)

Trafford rev. 02/29/2020

 www.trafford.com
North America & international
toll-free: 1 888 232 4444 (USA & Canada)
fax: 812 355 4082

*In the memory of my late
mother, Polina Gimelfarb, and
father, Max Ltvinov*

HOLOGRAPHIC IMAGES

I am an emigrant from the soviet collective, and my hero is a sailor and a mind traveler. I want to believe that all my fellow emigrants are sailors. My hero was fighting the pressure of the soviet collective to have his mind free. I grew up in a country with a rigid structure of the radical collective. To suppress our individuality, the radical collectives were using dreadfully destructive power. They used brutal force to make us compliant. They were torturing and killing. They fabricated a lot of justification for their unkindness. They were imposing their way of thinking, which we were obliged to follow. They claimed that they were straightening our minds and making us happy. In reality, they built a society of criminals and the naïve. To accommodate their goals of dominance, they altered our minds. Not so many inside the radical collective were able to resist the structural damages inflicted on them. The sailor is one who was able to keep his psyche solid despite pressure to become analogous. He is dealing with his internal and external foes and building his individuality.

The great philosopher Martin Buber in his book I and Thou proposed a new type of interaction between individuals. To be happy he proposed to bring our relationships to a higher level, which included meetings through dialog. At the same time, psychologist Heinz Kohut introduced the model of self, and the psychologist Melanie Kline talked about interactions inside our psyche. Neuro-linguistic programming with groups of words developed a power to open our experiences and change our behavior. In the meantime the many unique characters in the books of the great writer Fyodor Dostoevsky seemed to want unification, but were influenced not to connect and were splitting and suffering.

Having the mind of sailors, we want to connect. We are discovering and unifying all parts of our psyche, and are having genuine dialogs and real meetings. In the past we were forced to become part of the collective, where the ideologists were acting as crooked preachers to lure the naïve. The ideologists were enlisting us to live a life of monks. In return they promised happiness and a heaven on earth. In contrast to the radical collective, who created the rigid structure of compliance and ignored our subconscious feelings, sailors decided to enjoy flexible interactions between all parts of the psyche. To be happy we are altering connections between our fragments. The plasticity of self is a big advantage. It includes the cooperation of consciousness and subconsciousness. We do not suppress our thoughts and feelings and are treating them with respect. We are not rejecting any subconscious messages regardless of how unlike they are. Only when our fragments are respectful of each other does genuine dialog exist; then our identity is solid and does not fall apart under the stress.

As emigrants we made a tremendous voyage inside our psyches. I believed that our sailor's spirit would never die. We are not afraid to sail away from the radical settings and be happy. By being sailors we are changing the reactions of chemicals in our brain. We are opposite to any radical collective, which is also changing our brain's chemistry with the goal to control us. The radical collective wants to make us analogues and easy to manipulate. Many sailors resisted the power of the collective. Being individuals, they have collections of diverse fragments. I am introducing a character, Professor Kryvoruchko that represents my own alter ego, the holographic fragment, who has the spirit of sailor. Any resemblances to any one real are accidental.

The mind work is enchanting. The psyche creates variety of fragments with many holograms that are notions of particular times of life or situations. The holograms about our suffering, trauma and embarrassment somehow build without our conscious awareness. The psyche that contains the unidentified fragments looked like a library without catalog. We are using our imaginative power to discover our fragments and we need to identify to what theme they belong. When we ascertain our fragments we bring our subconscious dreams to conscious awareness. When we understood our fragments we better understand our self. The positive holograms required some effort from our part. With some training the psyche can activate images that are nicely formed and have some degree of the opacity, density and can appear as the paintings and photos.

To connect our fragments we always can use holographic projector built in our mind by nature. Our goal is to unite holograms in mutual system that is a real Collective. By using his imagination Sailor binds together many positive holographic fragments. Sailor creates holographic collectivism in his consciousness and builds the solid psyche.

Chester Litvin, PhD
Psychologist

CONTENTS

The Individual and Collective Identities are Not Alike

The collective identity is one that was imposed on us by ideology, lifestyle, or circumstances, which come from outside our psyche world. It is pressuring all our responses to be attached to the outside world. Unrelated groups such as liberals, peasants, aristocrats, and guerilla fighters are assuming that they have collective identities. Some societies provide us with a collective identity by displaying an external standard mirror designed by the set of collective rules, and want every member to adjust their psyche accordingly. The leaders of collectives are controlling the followers through audio, visual, and kinesthetic slogans. They have visual slogans in the form of big constructions, paintings, and posters. The kinesthetic slogans are in the form of meetings, parades, and demonstrations. The audio slogans are in speeches and music. All slogans use pathos and grandeur, because they exploit our desire to be important and belong to something bigger. Some collectives are old-style, peaceful, flexible, and democratic, and we voluntarily become part of the big collective, where we may well keep some degree of individuality and *selfishness*. Some collectives take us by force and do not let us go. Those collectives are radicalized and very punitive, demanding complete obedience. They are unwilling to negotiate, and use confrontation and manipulation. They are forcing us by the threat of death to create a standardized psyche. They are talking about the special design they were granted by a legacy of being a selected group.

Some psyches have a natural resistance to the virus of radicalization. Some leaders, for example Oliver Cromwell, Giuseppe Garibaldi, and Abraham Lincoln, had a strong identity and were immune to the virus of radicalization, which did not affect their brain cells. For many the exposure to the virus of radicalization is changing the configuration of their brain cells, and in a certain way, without their conscious awareness, they are becoming a part of the collective. The secret is why some collectives get radicalized and how to avoid it. Right now we know only that the radicalization of our minds is comparable to a computer virus. With excessive research in anthropology we probably would be able to understand where this virus gets started. Further, we will talk only about radicalized collectives and try to understand them.

The common trend of the radicalized collective is that the virus represents *self* in an infliction in our minds. The main symptom is that we are emotionally numb and disregard those who are not part of our group. The virus of radicalization narcotizes us against the discomfort of being a butcher of the individuality and *self*. The radicalized collective is making promises that surely will not be fulfilled. By bringing a reward in the form of feelings of camaraderie the virus is luring us into the trap of radicalization. The virus is providing the illusion of unification by putting in front the unreachable goals. It actually made the infected proud because of illusion that they are participating in something big. The fictitious goals are luring members to think they are building a solid identity. In reality the members are only brainwashed. Their identity is still fragmented.

Some collectives are promising lots of food for a country that was always starving. The collectives are talking about Valhalla and the victory of the great spirit, when, contradictory to the high spirits, they were pushing their subjects to get rotten in the trenches and completely out of style for the superhuman, pushing civilians to their death in the gas chambers. Some collectives are promising innocent children, who have never had intercourse, that after their death, for promoting a collective's cause, they will reside in a heavenly environment with many concubines around them. Because of future expectations, the brains, affected by a virus, are developing feelings of emotional numbness to their surroundings and unfounded feelings of superiority. Unfortunately for many of us the radicalized collective is creating a new organization in our minds by using pretension together with brutal force. The radicalization of our psyche by the forceful approach is creating a lot of resentment and producing a split in our identity.

Less demanding collectives are attractive to us because they use more sophisticated slogans. But, those collectives also do not survive the tests of time, because eventually, they too become bloody and vicious. The ideologists, the same as computer hackers, are brainwashing the minds of the crowd and lowering resistance to their messages. Their stereotypes imply that the collective mind is better than the individual. The agitators pushed us into believing that in the big structures of the collective we are not important, and we are supposed to forget our own thoughts and desires and just obey the collective.

Many of us honestly fall for these slogans of the radicals. We think the collective mirror is reflecting very safe responses, which were approved by the majority, and that the collective knows better what is good for us. Unfortunately, the primitive stereotypes are very appealing and we easily absorb many of them, provided by ideologists of the radicalized collective, and are ready to give up our *self*. Many of us with a big hole and defects in our individual mirror find that it is very attractive to be a part of the collective, because the collective mirror immediately covers the damage in our psyche and gives the illusion of the unordinary identity.

In a few radicalized collectives the ideologists implied that if we have a working class background, we are inherently smart, which is very inviting. In some collectives the propaganda was that all belonging to the same ethnicity, or having the same religious background, are superior. This is the easiest way to avoid dissent, because if the messenger does not appear equal to other members, the message is not accepted. When we are killing an insignificant mosquito, we do not think about his message. The radicalized collective would not accept the individual messenger as a partner, because the individual messenger is not equal to the collective. In the same way the radicalized collective mind would never accept from an individual a quest for peace and a dialog.

The internal process in the individual mind is poles apart from the collective mind. Because we are living without any ideology and ideologists, it is harder to depend on our own *self* than on the collective. The collective, who is dominated by ideologies, gives a simplified solution to any of our problems. Shrewd individuals with aggressive and violent tendencies easily take advantage of the system of the collective, which is covering a split in the psyche, and they skillfully manipulate a myth to satisfy their own wishes.

Fortunately, until now, that type of organization, which was based on false promises, was not strong enough to survive for long. After the crash of doctrines the members are trying to understand the reason why their collective image was easily defeated. After the crash of a myth of being unordinary, we, as disillusioned members, are eventually realizing that external mirror authority would not bring a congruency between the parts of our psyche. Under the force and lies we are not allowed to see inside our psyches. In other words, we are admitting to *self* that our own internal mirror has a big hole in the middle and creates a lot of confusion by reflecting strange images.

Now we understand the truth: that our identity was exhibiting our own damages by showing us how we were responding to the situation. Our broken identity is contained inside the mirror, which operates as if it had been broken with a hammer. All the pieces of the broken mirror are loosely connected and provide us with unstable pictures of the outside world. It is similar to when we have bad musical memory and cannot reproduce a tune. Because of damage in our ear, we cannot hear correctly and as a result cannot memorize the tune. That psycho-virus, when it infects territory, is affecting our minds and then leaving us and moving to new territory. When the virus is leaving, some radicalized collectives understand that they are morally defeated, and as a last attempt, they try to embrace lost individuality. We are regaining our lost inside thinking. We are restructuring *self* to the pre-morbid condition. Our psyches do the refiguring of the brain cells. We are recognizing that the theories that we followed were only a myth. In the beginning the process of cleaning *self* from the virus of radicalization also includes blaming others for being misled. Only later, when we are getting healthier, does it become clear to us that our collective image was defeated by the lack of congruence in our responses. Because of the lack of our *self*-confidence or other reasons, it was easier to have scapegoats to unify against perceived danger and to point fingers at invented enemies.

Building a solid identity is not easy. The process of putting the pieces of the individual mirror together is a very delicate one, because the pieces are very fragile. We ought to be sure that we do not force the pieces but are gentle when assembling them. All the pieces of our psyche share the same physical body and need to be understood and respected. In our internal world we do not have any insignificant parts, and are striving for congruency between all components in our psyche. We are responding to stimulation by presenting the internal and external connections between our responses. Our reflection of the outside world depends on our internal logic. When we have congruency in our responses, we are feeling good about *self*. We have strength to resist stress and we are sure about the quality of our responses. We have a high level of *self*-esteem and know our *self*-worth; in other words, we have a solid psyche that contains the reflection of the solid mirror, which is built from the connected pieces. The solid identity is the collection of life experiences and beliefs. It reflects the outside world, which is congruent with our experiences and images.

Stepan Kryvoruchko is A Hero of Our Time

Stepan Kryvoruchko, later in life Professor Kryvoruchko, was born in a country that called with a sick humor a "workers' paradise". The biggest achievement proclaimed by pseudo-Collective was Communal living.

The Communal apartment had fifteen not-related families living together with only one rest-room and one kitchen. The kitchen had one stove with four gas-burners. There were enormous fights whose turn was cooking food and constant line to use restroom. It was shortage of toilet paper and every tenant was bringing for wiping own newspaper. On the top, everyone was suspecting others of being informers and hated them. The life was far away from academic definition of Communal. It came from word Community, where small group of people pursuing common interest and values, sharing responsibility with peace, love and security. Instead the Communal life was ugly.

The characters in the book made everything possible to withstand the pseudo-Communal setting. They were fighting the evil of depersonalization. As a result of their fight, they were able to keep their individuality. They were sailing out of pseudo-Collective and are in search of real Collective.

Professor Kryvoruchko represents author's holographic fragment of the Sailor, who is very positive, really nice and honest. He is a hero of our time, and one with solid identity. As an individual with solid identity he feels good about *self* and is loved. Even if he is a fictional and cumulative character, he represents a psyche that was able to recover from many splits and become whole.

Stepan's psyche was suffering from many ruptures, and he was on the verge of completely losing his identity. His domineering fragment was able to solidify the dissimilar fragments under his original name and, despite the danger to *self* and with many sacrifices, was able to bring together all the fragments. He has the genes of warriors and heroes and was capable of preserving the original name and establishing a stable identity. He was a confused boy in the beginning of his life, then a fighter, and eventually a wise man. His psyche was able to have many dialogs with his dissimilar fragments.

The real hero of our time is one who puts scattered little pieces of his identity together and is able to build a solid psyche and become a complete one. Despite the fact that he inherited a shattered identity, Stepan's achievement was very impressive in the area of *self*-growth, which is not having any materialistic gains. Many may perceive it as foolishness. His identity is injecting positive energy into relationships to the point that they too are able to have a dialog. He was able to do the impossible. He unified his parts and got them together in a solid identity. He feels comfortable in any place and has the strength to interact with anyone with dignity and confidence.

Life in the radical collective, where he was born, created a big split in his identity. When he left the collective, his identity was fragmented. The first significant experience for him outside of the collective was in Israel. In Israel he was circumcised, had basic Jewish education, and went through the process of conversion to Judaism. Very soon he became a soldier. His new homeland was in crisis, and he was doing his best to help his country get out of the crisis.

He was able to comprehend that his country was under siege and put aside his own issues. He also realized that, when the survival of a state is at stake, it is not a good time to get in touch with internal feelings. This was a time when his thoughts were only about his country and doing his soldier's duty. When his nation had a period of truce and life was safer, he knew the time had come to take care of the splits and fragmentations in his own psyche and build a solid identity.

The split was created by his heritage, because his mother is a Gentile woman, and technically he is not a Jew. This internal discord created a lot of splits. In the worker's paradise he refused to be part of the collective. In Israel he was poles apart from the collective and felt good, but he also was under tremendous stress to defend his new homeland. He was busy dealing with external enemies and not able to resolve his internal splits. Because of external threats to their survival, his fragments appeared to be together. Unfortunately, they were not unified by internal dialogs. Their unification was an act of negotiation to put aside all internal problems until a safe time would come.

The difference between negotiation and dialog is very big. The act of negotiation is when we are trying to understand someone else, or do something for the benefit of someone else even if it means sacrificing our own feelings. The dialog is a state of mind when we are having complete understanding of our own internal feelings. Stepan was aware which fragment was providing what kind of responses, because all his fragments share the same body and he did not have lost memories. He also felt that he needed to go to a place where without external stress and disruptions he might engage his fragments in a dialog. When he fell in love with his Canadian wife, he realized that Canada was a perfect country in which to feel safe and to engage in a process of building a solid identity. Canada had split between French and English parts and was looking for dialog. The quietness and long distance from all hot spots in the world made Canada a perfect place for *self*-actualization. Stepan knew that as soon as he could possibly unify his fragments and build a solid identity, he would be able to live anywhere on the globe and feel good.

He had a tricky task in front of him that sometimes appeared impossible. He wanted to build a solid identity. He was able to succeed. He moved to a new country and was able to solidify all his fragments through internal meetings and dialogs. As a result of his effort, Stepan is feeling good about *self* and about his actions. The individuals in his surroundings are feeling the same way about him. He is proudly looking ahead to represent *self* as one who achieved equilibrium and is congruent in his beliefs and choices. We are presenting a few from the many fragments, which are mainly congruent and belong to our hero, who spent many years of his life building up his solid identity. The biggest gain for his effort in solidifying his identity is living a stable life without the recurrent turbulence that creates the storms and hurricanes in *self*. Professor Stepan Kryvoruchko is able to live the rest of his life with dignity and respect.

Below are fragments that are parts of Professor Kryvoruchko's psyche. Fragment contains subconscious and conscious imagery. Our psyche has variety of fragments that are the storages of holograms. Stepan Kryvoruchko is a Sailor - the mind traveler, who wanted to explore his psyche to find the holographic collectivism. There is not place for false dogma and cheating. Sailor is identifying the purposed fragments in his psyche and unites them in solid entity. Sailor does not accept the pseudo collectivism that killing individuality. Inside of his psyche he is creating individual holographic collectivism.

Andrusha was An Innocent Victim

Andrusha was a very nice, young, and innocent victim who was killed by a vicious assassination. He represents honesty and nobility. He enjoyed a life and beautiful things, with which he wanted to be surrounded. He was a naive man who was treacherously destroyed by a greedy mind. He lived in sheltered surroundings as the son of a powerful father. From childhood he enjoyed luxury that ordinary kids did not have. He was like a beautiful flower brought into this world for pleasure and admiration.

Andrusha generated the feeling of freshness, youthful enthusiasm, and optimism. He was admired by everyone who was close to him. Andrusha was not a fighter and lacked the dominance to offend anyone, but he became the target of a deception. As happens to many innocent minds, he was unknowingly crossing someone's path. He did not do any harm to anyone. He knew the meaning of the good life and was impressed with nice things that the Western lifestyle gives, and was impatient to enjoy it. He dreamed about the comfortable life and adored luxury. He did not mind working hard to have comfort around him. He did not want to be part of a generation of sacrifices. He was smart, intelligent, and not afraid to apply his talents to any field. He spoke five languages fluently. He was good-looking. He completed a sailor's academy with honors. He would be an asset to any place where he would apply his gifts. He did not want to grab anything from anyone, but unfortunately, his life was taken from him. He was assassinated, because a vicious one denied him his future and ignored his human feelings. He was treated as an object that needed to be removed from someone's way, an obstacle. He was an obstruction in a treacherous game. The light of his life was closed. The heartless gambler killed him. Everyone who knew Andrusha had feelings of sorrow about his terrible fate.

Ivan Represents a Fragment, Which Can Change

Ivan is a fragment that represents the hope for change, an honest man who is changing his devotion when he sees treason from the leader. He is an honest policeman who has fidelity, loyalty, dedication, and love for his country. He is one who believes in the rules and defends them with his life. He is a protector and is very serious about his duties.

He grew up poor. He had a very hard childhood, did not have anything nice or beautiful around him, and suffered a lot. He wanted his family to have many exquisite things and to enjoy a prosperous life. He did not need anything for *self*, because he was trained to sacrifice his needs. He came from a family of givers, which did not express *self* very well. Takers are more verbal because they need verbal skills to solicit.

Ivan also was the son of an honest policeman, and he too became a policeman. He was devoted to his country. He had the capability to give up his life for his motherland without second thoughts. He had a tremendous amount of fatherly love for his only son, but his son, Andrusha, did not understand him. Ivan was not a role model for his son. His son possibly did not accept his roughness, straightforwardness, and obedience, or his strict following of rules and regulations. His son kept it a secret and did not want to disclose to his friends that his father was a policeman. In workers' paradise a policeman had a stigma of brutality. Ivan never tried to explain to his son any of his struggles. He assumed that his son understood that the motherland needed someone to do a dirty job and that he did not mind being in dirt and blood. He did this job for everyone, including his son, and was spending his life between serial killers and drug addicts.

Ivan did not talk much with his son and did not tell Andrusha that he did not feel any shame doing the job of protecting his country. He also did not have time to tell his son how much he loved him. His son was assassinated and died without knowing how much his father loved him. His son did not leave him a grandson and any hope of continuation of his bloodline. Ivan was heartbroken.

In his life Ivan lived through tremendous losses and despair, but his son's death made a dramatic change in Ivan's character. He was transformed from a dry bureaucrat to a sensitive one. He started to appreciate the difference. Sam Kaufman was his informer and a confused man. Ivan was able to create a father-son relationship with Sam and became a father figure to him. Under Ivan's supervision, Sam became a better man. Ivan was not able to save his son's life, but together with Sam, Ivan saved someone else's grandson. He saved someone whom he never met.

Sam Kaufman Intended to Be The Antihero

Sam Kaufman represents the antihero, who suffered from the split of his psyche, loneliness, confusion, and internal turmoil around him. His life was affected by loneliness, the lack of proper parenting, the absence of a father figure, an abusive mother, and bullies at school. Sam badly needed a role model, because his father had a fragmented identity and was more confusing than directing. His mother was a frustrated woman who had no power to find her place in the universe. Sam's father was a convicted felon, and Sam was accused by a woman of date rape. Sam was young and naïve and the accuser did not present any evidence of rape, but only a naïve attempt at seduction. He felt guilty and miserable. Sam was ashamed and admitted to the police that he had done it. By the law of the collective, Sam, as a confessed rapist, had two choices to avoid prison. His first choice was to marry his accuser. The second was to take an offer from a policeman named Ivan, who needed him as an informer. Sam became an informer for the secret police. Suddenly, the rude but honest policeman became Sam's island of stability and his connection to the collective.

Sam's identity did not have anything heroic in it, and no one would possibly expect him to do something heroic. The passwords for his life were misery and fears. He was afraid and was capable only of cowardice. He was a victim, then accused violator, and then informer. Sam accepted Ivan as a role model and Ivan helped him form a courageous identity. Unexpectedly, Sam did some heroic actions. Despite his unattractive image and misdeeds he was able to save the life and honor of two individuals. This act turned his life around. He was able to regain his own *self*-confidence and purpose in life. He was very grateful to Ivan for the leadership. He gave his son the name Andrusha, which was the name of Ivan's son, who was assassinated by evil forces. The individuals whose lives Sam saved feel great appreciation and share their lives with him. Sam always feels welcome and enjoys their company. He is very close to them. He is also happily married, not lonely, and not split anymore. At the same time, Sam continues his longstanding relationship with Ivan. Ivan is his son's godfather.

Stepan Luchko is Characterizing a Soldier

Stepan Luchko represents a fragment that is a soldier. He lacked the dominance to disobey orders from his superior. Without a second thought, he was willing to risk his life at the first request of his superiors. He swore to defend his country and was serious about fulfilling his commitment. He was loyal and proving it with his life. He respected his authorities and did not question their intentions. He sacrificed everything, including his whole life, for his homeland. Despite a very pleasant side of his character, he had the strength to act as a heartless machine if he believed he was acting for the good of his country. He was captured by enemies and presumed dead during the war. He was tortured but survived. He was able to endure all the horrors because of his enormous physical strength.

He also was tragically misinformed that his family was dead. Being in distress, he accepted an assignment from the military agency of the collective to work as a security agent in the Western countries. Because of his honesty, dedication to a cause, and respect for authority, he was not able to recognize that his superior was a criminal who used his position as an agent of national security to skillfully manipulate innocent ones by tricking him into taking part in his scam. Boris tricked everyone, but only one meeting helped Luchko understand how wrong he was and how far from reality his beliefs were.

Luchko unexpectedly found out that his family was alive. He met his grandson, Stepan Kryvoruchko, who was in danger, and was protecting him with his life. The meeting with his grandson opened Luchko's eyes. He also showed strength of character, because as soon as he realized what was really going on, he stopped obeying orders from his superior and refused to have any part in the criminal affairs. Stepan Luchko, without second thoughts, was putting his life in danger to save his grandson from harm. To save his grandson he would go to extremes and tell everything about *self* to the Canadian authorities. He was ready to do it, but suddenly he got help from antihero Sam Kaufman and from a policeman, Ivan. Sam and Ivan were able to save him and his grandson. They saved the soldier's honor and his grandson's life. Now the soldier is learning how to enjoy his present role as a great-grandfather and is spending a lot of time in the company of Stepan Kryvoruchko, Sam Kaufman, and their children. He eventually met Ivan, a man who helped him at a crucial moment of his life, and was able to express his gratitude.

Rivka Signifies The Sacrifice

Rivka, the grandmother of Stepan Kryvoruchko, is the fragment of a victim who sacrificed her life to be with her baby daughter, Lizochka, and her elderly father, Hershel. She is the one who ended her life in a sacrifice. She, her baby, and her father were killed by monsters that were so angry and insensitive that they did not mind that in front of them were a helpless woman with a little baby and a sick old man, and they killed them in cold blood. Rivka was not killed by a bullet but hit with a crowbar and dropped into a ravine. The woman of this terrible fate was the grandmother of our hero, Stepan Kryvoruchko.

In a moment of danger Rivka split from her son, Lyonya, who became the father of our hero. She did it only to protect her son, to give him the gifts of life and joy. Lyonya continues his bloodline through his children and grandchildren. Rivka represents the fragment of the mother who, at the most critical time made her choice to sacrifice her life for her family. She was with them to the end. She was comforting her daughter and her father when they were told to strip off their clothes and belongings, and pushed into a pit by the bunch of beasts, which may even call *self* the humans. Those beasts hit them with a crowbar on the head and buried them alive and cut their throats with shawls.

It is not easy to imagine that human mothers can give birth to those monsters. Only a few of the victims were lucky to be killed by bullets. They needed all their luck to be killed by bullets instead of crowbars and shovels. Rivka chose to die rather than run away and leave behind her sick daughter and elderly father. Her fate was horrible. If she had not had the strength to let her son go, nothing would have been left after her. Stepan Kryvoruchko is living proof that her life was not wasted and the beasts did not succeed in erasing her from the face of the earth. The monument built in Ukraine, Babiy Yar, is in memory of savagely murdered Ukrainian citizens. Monuments to Babiy Yar's victims were built in many cities around the world from donations given by immigrants of the former USSR. One of those monuments was built in Los Angeles, California, in Plummer Park, where, in addition to the Kryvoruchko family, many immigrants visit.

Lyonya Represents The Survivor

Lyonya, father of Stepan Kryvoruchko, is a fragment of the survivor, who received from both his parents a most valuable present, the gift of life. He is the father of our hero, Stepan Kryvoruchko, and he was exceptionally lucky. If his mother had not split from him on the road to death, he would have ended up with a broken scalp in a ravine. In the capital of Ukraine, Kiev, where those atrocities happened for many years, not even one monument was built in memory of the innocents killed by beasts. To our shame, the beasts were our own, Ukrainian males who volunteered to do these ugly atrocities. The beasts would not repent until the end of their lives. They continued to poison the atmosphere of the Ukraine with the venom of prejudice toward the citizens of their land. The authorities, who were infected with hate, did not have any compassion for the victims. They decided to build a housing complex on the site of the massacre, but the ground gave way and opened up to reveal the bodies of the killed, and the houses fell down to cover the bodies. The dead reminded the living of their horrible fate.

Lyonya was fortunate that his mother saved him from her tragic destiny and spared him from a vicious death. Then his father was able to save him from hunger and physical pain. His father came to his rescue at a moment when Lyonya least expected it. When his father came into his life, Lyonya was dying from hunger, cold, and physical pain. His father was able to protect his son by providing shelter, food, and hope for the future. Apparently, Lyonya by his presence saved his father from the anger and hate of the soldier blinded by grief, who would kill anyone just obeying questionable orders. Because of Lyonya's influence, his father was able to keep human dignity.

Lyonya's father was not a coward hiding from a fight, or a killing machine. He was able to keep his humanity and build a comfortable nest for his son and the family of his friend, who was presumed dead. Lyonya thoughtfully used his good fortune, received from his parents: the gift of life. First of all, he built a strong identity and lived a happy life. He became an educated man, was able to share his life with a beautiful woman, and raised a family.

Alexander Kryvoruchko is Supporting Humanity

Alexander Kryvoruchko, grandfather of Stepan Kryvoruchko, represents humanity. He is another grandfather of our hero and father of Lyonya. To achieve security for his family he split his identity. In later times his grandson, Stepan Kryvoruchko, was able to unify fragments to the new solid identity. Alexander was a soldier, but was dissimilar from the mechanical type of soldier. He was a smart fighter. He fought many fights, but he never killed on someone else's order. He was a professional soldier and was well trained about how to kill. With his training he could kill too, but he fought only enemies who threatened his life. He may perhaps become a vigilante, because he lost his wife, his daughter, and his father in atrocities, but he was not an angry and bloodthirsty person, and he chose a contradictory path. He did lose his family to the atrocities of the war, but was able to keep his humanity. He felt that he was spared for a reason that was far removed from being a killing machine. He was a trained soldier, but without enormous luck, he would not have been able to save his life and the life of his son. He just took many chances, and luck was on his side.

Alexander was a pragmatic man and not a very emotional one, but he was supporting his grandson's quest for identity. He lost many. He was not a religious man, but he understood there was a reason why he might have died many times but lived instead. He grieved after the death of his wife, daughter, father, and friend. He believed that the presence of a surviving son and hope for the future saved him from physical and moral death. He took responsibility for the family of his friend, who was presumed dead. He proved that he was a responsible human being. From his tragedy he learned how to survive. He knew how to masquerade to avoid being a target. He had an obligation to provide safety for his son and the family of his friend. He was able to revive *self*, his son, and the family of his friend. In his actions he focused on his responsibilities to build a new life.

He did not become a vigilante, who condones all monsters and their families to death by the rules of *self*-justice. He was not driven away from his goal by the temptations of destruction. He thoughtfully understood that his identity was a very fragile one and may be the cause of future troubles. He was a wise man, and was able to foresee the future. He had had enough sacrifices in his life and did not want any more. Alexander decided to split in order to protect. He was correct, because if he had continued with his previous identity, he would have brought a lot of struggles and discomfort on *self* and his son. To provide safety for his son and the family of his friend he split from his previous identity to save more. In a safe place, Alexander was able to build a family, provide for his son, his new wife, and his stepdaughter, and to have grandchildren. He built his new life from the broken pieces and is happy and proud of his achievement. He did not want any sacrifices and wanted to have an easy life, but he never sold out his humanity.

Marinka is a Symbol of Love

Marinka is a mother of *Stepan Kryvoruchko*, our hero. *Marinka* was her nickname, but on her ID she had the name *Maria*, which is the same as the name of Jesus' mother. *Marinka* let her son go to find his way. Before her, Rivka too let her son go and saved his life. *Lyonya* became a respected engineer and happy father of our hero. *Marinka* loved her son, but also understood his struggles. Because of her love, she sacrificed her needs to keep her son near her. She allowed her son to leave her and travel the world to follow his quest and find his identity.

Marinka is a medical doctor and surrounded by pain and suffering, but for Stepan she represents a mother's love and high regard. She also has support and admiration from all of *Kryvoruchko's* family. She is very lovable. She married Lyonya

Kryvoruchko, a man who had a tragic childhood. She was doing everything to keep him happy. She symbolizes love, friendship, and a positive attitude. She is a bright and powerful part of her son's life.

As a little girl, she lost her father, who worshipped her, in the war. The tragic loss at such an early age was very traumatic. She grieved for him. Her father, after his presumed death, was highly regarded and revered by many and decorated with honors as a hero of the war. As the daughter of a hero, she had respect. She was fortunate that right away another one became a father figure for her and, together with her mother, took good care of her. She did not suffer from poverty. She did not know how hard it was to be without a father in the ruined, post-war country. She was provided with everything she needed. She was able to live a happy life and become a medical doctor and was proud of her achievements. She with her daughter stayed in workers' paradise and helped raise her daughter's children. She was a very powerful fragment in her son's psyche. Even though physically her son was far away from her, he always felt her presence. Because of her love, her son was able to solidify his identity.

Galena Signifies Comfort

Galena represents the comfort of the family home. She is the mother of *Marinka* and is *Stepan Luchko's* first wife. Her first husband, whom she loved with all her heart and was presumed dead, was a war hero. *Stepan Luchko* was decorated posthumously as a hero of the war, but decorations did not relieve *Galena's* pain. *Her* second husband, *Kryvoruchko Sr.,* was a good friend, very nice, and a responsible man. He lost his wife to the Holocaust but did not become angry and callous. *Galina* was lucky to have two distinguished men as her husbands.

During World War II she lived, as a partisan, in a Ukrainian forest with her first husband and daughter. They lived in a mud hut, but *Galena* was able to create a relaxed and somehow pleasant atmosphere. When *Kryvoruchko Sr.* and his son *Lyonya* joined the partisans' unit, they were assigned to live in *Galena's* hut. After all the suffering of running away from the enemies, and being on the verge of extermination, they eventually found peace, love, and tranquility. Instant relief from the pain and suffering was brought about by *Galena's* hospitality. She was able to create a very marginal but still comfortable dugout. The Kryvoruchko family was very thankful to *Galena* for everything. In the comfort of the partisan's hut they felt as if they were regaining control of their lives.

When *Galena* lost her first husband, who was a brave partisan and was captured by the enemies, the Kryvoruchkos were her main support in getting over her loss and having the energy to continue with her life. She took her loss very hard. She was completely lost in her suffering. Only time and the knowledge that she had a small daughter to take care of were healing her wounds. Her daughter was all she had left after the death of her first husband.

Alexander Kryvoruchko was a widower and understood her pain. She was grateful to Alexander for his support. After many years of friendship they got married. Her second husband was a family man who was good to her and to her children, *Lyonya* and *Marinka*.

The Icons are The Ancient Art and Religious Artifacts

Icons are ancient paintings on wood with a lacquer. In the radical collective they were considered religious artifacts, and according to ideology they had to be destroyed. The ideologists did not care that icons represent the supreme beauty, spiritual beauty, and are ultimately a reflection of deity. Despite the brainwashing of the ideology many wished to be purified by the icons' spiritual beauty. They believed that icons cleansed them from sin, and saved the icons from ideologists. For many artists the icons were freeing. They revered them and committed to this mode of painting, which a lot of us admire also. For many years the icons were appreciated as beautiful art and presented in big museums and private collections. For many around the world icons are the Divine Beauty. Many were destroyed by the collective, but some individuals were less brainwashed and preserved icons as paintings of distinct spiritual beings.

The price of icons became very high at the end of the twentieth century. When the ideologists got a wakeup call and realized that icons needed to be preserved as national treasures, many of the icons were lost. Countless art dealers made a fortune selling icons. The icons that survived the ideological persecution of radicals became very hot commodities. They were smuggled out of the collective in big quantities and were depleting the national treasury.

Boris Represents Defiance and Viciousness

Boris represents viciousness. He is intended to be a troublemaker and his function is to create a split. He is an egocentric criminal. The troublemaker is always testing the solidity of our psyche. We need to have the villain, who is defeated by the hero. The hero does not exist without a bad fragment. Every victory makes a hero stronger. The task of overpowering a baddie in our psyche is sometimes more challenging than defeating the real one. He, like a worm, is continually digging his holes in our psyche and like a spider creates a web of deception and cruelty. He will do everything to manipulate everyone in his swindle. His goal is exactly opposite of the goal of the hero. He is using brutality and treachery to keep his con going. He is the one who ordered the killing of *Andrusha*, the innocent young man. He is a criminal sociopath, who believes that he is above the law. He does not stop in front of any obstacles and is using killing to advance his con. He is a very skillful splitter and creates a big turmoil in others. His viciousness wants confusion and instability around him. His primary function is to create splitting, dividing and eliminating anyone who is an obstacle to his selfish ambitions. We must be consciously aware that viciousness may well be part of our psyche too and would create ambushes to take over our psyche.

In contrast to the villain, the hero wants to unify and create stability. The domineering fragment, *Stepan Kryvoruchko*, was able to mobilize his fragments, which included *Stepan Luchko, Sam Kaufman*, and *Ivan* to restrain this fragment. The domineering fragment is dealing with *Boris* in a delicate way, because they share the same body. If he hurts *Boris*, he will hurt *self*. He deals with *Boris* by using negotiation and awareness of *Boris*'s capacities to split. He prevented the split and kept his identity solid. He, as the domineering fragment, was winning over the forces of splitting.

This time *Boris* lost, but he would never give up his future attempts to split. If we are recognizing viciousness in us, we are resisting the splitting forces to take over control of our psyche, and feeling good when we are able to intercept the viciousness in our behavior. The domineering fragment, *Stepan Kryvoruchko,* was able to recognize *Boris's* tricks and was resisting the *Boris* influence by being fearless and alert. He was neutralizing *Boris's* use of violence and splitting. He was negotiating the ways of dealing with *Boris,* to be ahead of *Boris's* game, and avoiding the split of his psyche.

The Scientist Splits on His Visual Sensor

The scientist had the fixated fragments on his visual sensor and his identity was fragmented. The scientist disclosed that when he was a teenager, he masturbated a few times when looking at his mother through the door crack. The scientist's childhood experience haunted him all his life. He ran away from life. He relieved sexual tension by using adult publications. He read many books. The biggest part of his upbringing was acquiring knowledge, which included books of great philosophers, scientists, and writers. His identity incorporated the information from the books, life experiences, emotional losses, traumas, relationships, and stories, which embellished his life and became parts of his identity. He has big success in science but experienced emptiness in his relationships.

General Vlasov is A Traitor

General Vlasov and his army were traitors who betrayed their oath to the collective and surrendered to fascists. He organized the ROA (Russian Liberation Army) from prisoners of war, who fought on the fascists' side. Perhaps we have the last word to challenge the lies fabricated by the collective about the ROA. The Soviet collective did not sign the Geneva Conventions about treatment of prisoners of war. The collective betrayed their soldiers and let them die from hunger and infections. Because of General Vlasov the surviving soldiers, who did not return to the collective, were able to live, have families, and raise children. General Vlasov saved more than a million soldiers from death in prison camps. Vlasov's soldiers were brave and did not commit any atrocities against civilians. Nevertheless, to everyone they are traitors. After the war the collective was killing and sending them to prisons.

In the first place the soldiers ended up in the fascists' camps because they lacked certainty to get back to their side and be alive. Those coming back were killed by military police officers of the collective, who killed in the hot battles more of their own than the fascist soldiers. Before the war the leaders of the collective had many dealings with fascists but were not prepared for war. It was their fault that they did not win the war sooner and without many losses. Before the war the leaders of the collective tortured and killed in their prisons their best soldiers and paralyzed their army. The leaders betrayed their own members. The military police of the soviet collective committed many atrocities against civilians on occupied territory. During the war the soldiers of the collective were getting alcohol daily and were drunk during the military operations. Many were rough with civilians in occupied territories, and some were looting, marauding, and getting rich. After the war they presented *self* as defender of civilians and as heroes.

The Polizies are Scary Characters

The polizies were the local collaborator groups associated with fascists. They were given the power by fascist secret police to be the killers' tool. They had carte blanche to torture Jews, kill them with crowbars, and burn them alive. They killed, tortured, burned alive, and raped their neighbors. They killed many civilians in punitive actions to scare the partisans. Before the war the polizies were regular members of collective, who used an opportunity and became monsters. After the war the polizies changed their names and were hiding in big cities that were not occupied by fascists. They brought fascist ideology to big cities, which included hatred toward Jews and the intelligentsia.

Lola Splits on Her Kinesthetic Sensor

Lola felt freeze-like sensations all over her body that blocked her from responding kinesthetically to danger as well as to pleasure. One of her fixated fragments belonged to the sexually abused little girl, who was very frightened and experienced the freeze-like sensation when she was in front of the perceived danger. To overcome her unpleasant responses she needed to empower her mind to use her sensors. By using the link between body and mind she perhaps did get relief from the freeze-like kinesthetic sensation.

Ola is Detaching from His Feelings

Ola was born into a wealthy family in a northern European country, where East European women were working as domestics. His mother was an East European woman. As a child he was ashamed that his mother was talking in accented language and was illiterate. He kept his mother's origin a secret and pretended that his mother was poles apart. He never tried to defend his mother, and ran away when someone was laughing at his mother's accent. By detaching from his feelings Ola was pretending that nothing terrible happened in his life.

Arthur's Visual Sensor Retains The Abused Little Child

Arthur was physically abused as a child by an alcoholic father. He had sudden flashbacks. He was a target of his father's rage. In Arthur's knowledge the alcohol was only one escape from reality. He would drink and get drunk so that he would not have his terrible flashbacks. He said he was seeing many horrible images. To get rid of his flashbacks, instead of drinking, he needs to learn to translate his visual experiences to various sensors. His translation of visual experiences is unpleasant and tough, but he needs to do it to get relief.

Clara Splits on The Audio Sensor

Clara had split on her audio sensor. Clara had intrusive thoughts, and was hearing the terrible noises of suffering and dying. In her life she had many losses. Many around her died. She was also frightened in a collective's airport for taking her jewelry out of the country. She was threatened with arrest and detained. She was separated from her son, who at that time was a young boy. She remembers his cry and how he was calling for her. To stop the splitting of her psyche Clara needs to translate the audio responses to the divergent manners of representation.

Our Identity

Our identity has many pieces tied together in a complicated architectural design, which includes flexible, fixed, and domineering fragments. Our identity is always responding to forces of unification and splitting. The process of building our identity is a dynamic one. Our identity is not static but always dynamic, and depends on interaction between fragments. Our psyche is a place where a lot of parts are located. The construction, which is built from those parts, we call an identity. Our identity is also the organization of our psyche and the internal logic, which is operating our psyche.

The logic of our psyche together with the construction of the psyche is a composition of our identity. We are seeing dissimilar identities because of the unrelated proposals and logics of their psyches, which is partly hereditary and partly learned. Our identity is our unique quality that characterizes us by our ability to respond to the stresses and pleasures of life. When we are sure about our identity, we, first of all, are aware of who we are, and know how to face the outside world. We are satisfied with our own reactions to the world while being comfortable with the world's reaction to our presence.

Our solid identity is a single entity but with many components. When all parts of the identity are built in a solid construction, we see a solid identity. Some of our identities have loose parts, which may perhaps be mixed and, suddenly, end up in places on the construction where they were not assigned. The spontaneous dislocation of the parts of the psyche creates big discomfort and chaos. Such discomfort may be compared with paradoxical situations, such as preparing food in the bedroom instead of the kitchen, and eating dinner in the garage instead of the dining room.

When we are enduring stress, we must be aware that the logic of our psyche may be distorted. When the psyche is falling apart, we feel physical discomfort. There are many reports that in times of stress we feel as if something is physically breaking apart inside of our heads. With a fractured identity we are fragmented and broken. We are not all together. Others around us may well detect that something is wrong with us. In contrast, we are all together with a solid identity and have everything in the right places. It is a big pleasure to have a solid identity. Usually, carriers of a solid identity are happy with *self*. The solid identities are the magnets that attract us to them. They are the most responsible members of any society.

Our identity is an indication of how we feel about *self* and how others feel about us, and is an important part of our existence. Our psyche is like a mirror trying to reflect the world around us, but what we see in our mirror is not an exact replica of our surroundings. The *self* is becoming an image of our identity in the imaginative mirror. We have the ability to put meanings to the images in the mirror and to change the view. When we are dealing with the outside world, we are distinguishing between who treats us as an object and wants to patronize and humiliate us, and who is open for negotiations and even for a dialog. Dialog is possible only when two of us see the same picture in front of us and share similar feelings. During dialog we are expressing our feelings freely and enjoying a real meeting of souls. Negotiation happens when we are seeing the pictures in front of us and want to help our opponent understand what we see. Real negotiation is an attempt to change the opponent's view but is done without manipulation and confrontation. The negotiation is based on the condition that the conciliations benefit the opponents. By providing evidence for compromises, we are also disclosing our desire to avoid confrontation and manipulation. The process of negotiation is done only to benefit our opponent, because during the process of negotiation only his feelings are important. We do not want to intimidate our opponent with our feelings.

When we have a solid identity, we are open to negotiating with anyone who is willing to deal with us as equals. Our solid identity is strong enough to ignore someone fragmented who is looking for confrontation and wants to humiliate. When our solid identity is objectified by others, it must attempt to resolve conflict peacefully, not to be hurt, and not to hurt. If this is not possible, we fight others back by all available means, including splitting. In contrast, when we are interacting within our *self*, where all our fragments are sharing the same body, our identity becomes solid only if we are able to have dialogs between our fragments. Our psyche has our internal parts, and we have a responsibility to find a way to facilitate a dialog between them.

An identity has a destructor, which is our own fragment challenging the stability of the psyche. We experience the presence of a destructor when we are suddenly facing an internal attack directed on *self*, when suddenly we are calling *self* by derogatory names, exhibiting negativity toward self, acting upon uncontrollable impulses, having outbursts of anger, and attempting to hurt *self*. A solid identity is able to recognize a destructor and have distinct options to persuade the destructor to stop his challenges. In hurting the fragments the destructor does not realize that he is hurting *self*.

Our psyche has the continuous task of keeping our identity solid and safe. Our identity is not cracking under the pressure. A few benefits of solid identity are the feelings of *self*-respect as well as the respect from others surrounding us.

The Utopian Collective

In the Utopian collective, which may be only in our fantasy, relationships are based on complete understanding and acceptance between unrelated individuals. A Utopian collective is based on the mutual respect of all members, which we perhaps may not find in real life. It is built on compassion, because in Utopia we do not have any enemies. The Utopian collective, which is built on constant meetings and dialogs, is in our imagination and does not need any sacrifices.

In the Utopian collective the individual truth does not exist. All truths are justified and fair for everyone and are accepted by all members of the collective. This supremacy would happen only in Utopia, because only in Utopia may we agree with everything. In real life it is impossible for all fragments of diverse individuals to accept all common truths. The Utopian collective takes away from us the right to disagree. It is our own choice to give up our right to disagree. If someone has voluntarily chosen to join a collective and wants to give up his individual right to disagree, then this choice is suitable, but enrollment by force is not acceptable.

In reality, many collectives were built by force and were suppressive. They were not built on dialog and negotiation. The collectives were created to protect and unite against adversaries. The collective is a part of the protective structure that creates rules and selective procedures for admission. The most dangerous is a radical collective. The members to be a part of radical collective need to completely give up something very important, which is their individuality or *self*. Radical collectives are fragmenting our identities. They always insist that many are more forceful than one. When we are part of any collective, we have a hard time keeping our individuality or *self*, because the outside threats push us to sacrifice and give up our identity. In contrast to the collective, our individuality keeps intact our right to disagree. The collection of fragments, which are unique for us, we are calling an identity. Only in solid identity or *self* do all our fragments accept their own truth, which is important for our well-being. To defend our *self* we do not need confrontation, so the unique psyche organization may be well built.

The decision to accept came after struggle and sacrifices. It takes a lot of work before we welcome our individual fragments to our own collective. Eventually we understand that our psyche is a collection of fragments that share the same memory and physiology. All our fragments are sharing one body and need to be together to care for it. By hurting our fragments we are hurting *self*. The last word is that we must not patronize, ignore, and humiliate any of our fragments. Our internal organization does not need to use confrontation, manipulation, pretension, and persuasion. We are supposed to be compassionate about our fragments, because they are parts of us.

The agreement in collection of our fragments creates harmony, *self*-respect, and *self*-esteem inside of our psyche. Every time we get angry, upset, and frightened, we are identifying which fragment is taking over our psyche, and we are having a dialog with a domineering fragment to restore our good feeling. Only our solid identities possibly will organize our psyche in a way that our own Utopian collective becomes possible. When our psyche is built on mutual respect between fragments, our psyche is an ideal place for a Utopian collective. The failure to maintain a solid identity leaves us with splits. It is a weakness and a big obstacle to our happiness and satisfaction with life. We understand that the reason for becoming emotional and out of control is not a result of others, but is a consequence of the action of one of our fragments that is taking over our psyche. The denial of our responsibility for our failures is a sign of fragmented identity. Fragmented identity does not take responsibility for failures, attributing problems to unfriendly forces and blaming them. With a fragmented identity the fragments are working against each other and are causing the internal split and hate.

Some psyches adjust well to the split and appear to be in harmony. Their structure is not solid, but strong, because they are building a coalition of fragments to hate other fragments. This psyche organization is an exact resemblance to the radical collective, which is built on hatred of adversaries. The goal is splitting and is fabricating the need for protection against enemies. To mislead us radical ideologists were presenting a style of Utopian collective. They were trying to convince us that the Utopian collective can be positioned outside our psyche. It is not yet built outside our psyche because we are all dissimilar. Many of us do not have a solid identity and are suffering from splits. We are not having many dialogs and meetings outside our psyche. The agitators deceived many innocent minds. Presently, our solid psyche is the only place where we may have all the benefits of our own Utopian collective without any abuses.

The Fragments

The fragments are small parts of our psyche. They are identified by our responses, which are formed as a result of our emotional experiences. Our identity is a construction, which is built from the fragments by using internal logic. Each fragment is carrying a particular response, and is a small part of a psyche.

A fragment may perhaps be compared with the growth rings on a tree, which we see on the stump. We can analyze rings and fragments. The difference with the tree is that on the tree the rings correspond to the longevity but in psyche the fragments track emotional experiences. On the tree one ring represents one year of the tree's life. By exploring the ring on the stump we can see how good the particular year was.

Our fragment represents the emotional experience associated with our age, and by evaluating our fragment, we can understand the extent of struggle triggered by the experience. In our psyche the fragment exists in unity or as split from the other fragments. The fragment's responses are a result of our life experience, and also learned from distinct movies or books. The unification of our fragments is a positive process that includes the meeting and dialog between fragments when, as a result, we are experiencing the good feelings about *self*.

Our psyche contains many fragments or responses. Our responses are congruent or incongruent with our fragments. Our congruent responses are the result of an internal dialog between fragments. The congruency of our responses is a sign of solid identity. When our psyche is providing us with congruent responses that are satisfying our desirable *self*-image, then our psyche has congruency in its logic. The congruence in the responses allows us to be in control of our feelings, and to project to the surroundings our feeling of stability. The fully developed identity is based on our feelings of acceptance, dignity, and respect of our *self*-presentation to the world. Every human being in our lives and every book we read affect our responses to life's demands and becomes part of our identity.

When we are talking to a distinguished individual, we may consider the fact that he is becoming a fragment in our psyche, because subconsciously we are copying many of his appealing and valuable responses. We are also assuming that his responses will not change, because we cannot correctly predict his future responses. This assumption is wrong and leads to incongruence in our responses, because the responses of others are constantly changing. In our internal world, we are always talking to the unchangeable images but not to the real one. Even when we spend a lifetime learning someone else's responses, we still end up with the imaginative one, which is based on our own life experiences and might have nothing to do with the real one.

The process of development of the internal image is comparable to the process of how a blind individual creates the image of someone by touching his face. The feelings that the blind person has about others are based on his life experiences, the sensitivity of his hand, and his bio-energetic tune. Similarly, our relationships depend on our internal logic, which provides us with the needed responses. Our common sense is shaping responses to the limit of our experiences, sensitivity, and bio-energetic tune. We are dealing with others by depending on our internal logic and intuition. If our psyche has a consistent logic and good intuition, then our relationships are stable. When the internal logic of our psyche is changing, then our relationships are changing because our assumptions are changing. Our fragments are providing us with the responses, but only our inside judgment is functioning as a manager, which is completely responsible for choices of which fragment to use in the particular situation.

The decision of our internal logic to join the splitting is a negative process in our psyche and a sign of instability. Our splitting has been characterized by loosely connected parts of our psyche's construction, when our fragments are generating feelings of fear, anxiety, and anger, and are in a state of disarray. Our incongruence in responses is a sign of fragmented identity, and the internal rationale is unstable and suffers from the split. We copy the real individual as images in our psyche, but then they become a product of our imagination, and we can only guess what kind of responses they would have to diverse situations. Because we do not know for sure who they were meeting, what books they read, the places they visited, and the experiences they had, we do not know about them.

Suppose we spend a lot of time learning about someone's past and that eventually, we learn many things about him. Because, in the meantime, he continues to meet and avoid, read books, and see movies, he is acquiring experiences unknown to us and again becomes diverse from the one whose past we studied. We have the potential to learn something about someone, but to know everything is an unattainable task, so we are filling up the rest with our imagination. We possibly will not win a race of knowing everything about him and being able to predict his responses. As a result we are creating in our psyche his image, which is based on many of our own assumptions. His image is distorted and rooted in our own life experiences. In many instances we are under the wrong impression that we are using other individual responses, but it is not true, because those responses are modified by our own experiences. Our psyche has many fragments, and some fragments are congruent and some are not. Our incongruent fragments are continuing to generate responses that are dissimilar in similar life events, and we are mistakenly attributing those responses to the influences of others.

Great Writer Fyodor Dostoevsky

Everyone who knew about the life of the great writer Fyodor Dostoevsky was surprised at how many aspects there were to his own character. He was opposed to any collectives. In his books the characters are his own fragments, but apparently, they all are suffering. They are disturbed individuals, and he expressed his feelings through them. In his stories they represent his own feelings. He probably had many conflicting fragments that had strived for unification but were not able to have dialogs and meetings. He wrote about relationships between his fragments and their unaccomplished desire to have dialog. He was the first of the writers who expressed in his books the incredible desire of his characters to unify and described the obstacles to unification. His characters operate on diverse manners of articulations. He enlightened their incongruousness, because they have dissimilar styles of representation and possibly may never have dialog.

In *The Idiot,* Count Mishkin, Rogojin, and Nastasia may be fragments of the same psyche. Dostoevsky's stories are sad, because he illustrated the fragments, which may well not have integration but honestly want to. They operate on divergent styles of responses and are blocked in their understanding of others. Apparently, Dostoevsky was writing about insurmountable obstacles, which were in the way of his fragments and preventing meetings and dialogs. Count Mishkin has very sophisticated audio responses but restricted kinesthetic and visual responses when all his emotions are boiling. He has a very naïve and distorted vision of reality, but he expresses *self* well in the audio form. He acts as a perfect gentleman. He is very logical but appears boring. In contrast to Count Mishkin, Rogojin has exaggerated hyper-kinesthetic responses and a sociopathic vision of reality. His responses are very impressive. Nastasia Philipovna has the capacity to be responsive to the audio and kinesthetic trigger, but she produces mainly visual responses, which are very dramatic. All those characters are influenced by the incongruent fragments of one psyche, the author. Dostoevsky had lived all his life in internal turmoil and perhaps was not able eased his discomfort by translating the unrelated responses to one approach. He did not find common ground and had not met divergent fragments.

The radical collectives knew the strength of distinct ways of illustration and were using them to brainwash their members. They were successfully using audio slogans, visual effects in the form of portraits of leaders, and visual art, which were glorifying their ideas and polluting the members' consciousness. They were also using kinesthetic manner in the form of parades, demonstrations, and marches. All the forms had one goal: to suppress individuality. The radical collectives in many instances used the notion of unification for splitting. They pretended they wanted unification by covering up their brutality. They compromised the meaning of unification.

In our psyche the dialog between unrelated manners is complicated and sometimes impossible, because of a divergent chemistry behind them. Our responses in divergent manners are unrelated. Our style is a carrier of our unifying energy. We are not accepted by various approaches and, as a result, are not increasing the unifying energy. Nastasia Philipovna expresses a range of visual responses. Her relationship with Count Mishkin is in the audio category, but her bond with Rogojin is of a kinesthetic nature. She may not overcome the materialistic trigger and powerlessness in front of the attractiveness of common sense. The responses of Count Mishkin and Rogojin are completely incomparable. They both, in distinct ways, are responsive to the visual connection. It is Nastasia Philipovna who accepts both stimulations. She may stimulate the dialog between Count Mishkin and Rogojin. She is a force to be the intermediary between them because of her links. She understands both men and is able to translate their responses. Unfortunately she is a splitting force, because she has the ability to understand them but is not able to initiate dialog and meeting.

Nastasia Philipovna, Count Mishkin, and Rogojin are ready to have a meeting and dialog. They want to build the Utopian collective, which does not have a place for greediness, impulsivity, and meanness, but they perhaps may not influence or communicate with others. They are not able to have a genuine dialog, because they cannot meet. To have dialog we need to have the transfer of responses back and forth: from audio connection to visual and kinesthetic, from visual to audio and kinesthetic, and from kinesthetic to audio and visual. The first step of a dialog is to understand the meaning of having a meeting. When we have never had a dialog before and do not know what it is about, we need to have an intuitive goal to at least have unification. Only when we have a meeting do we know what the biggest benefit of having interconnection of the fragments in our psyche is. On a conscious level if we understand someone who does not speak our language, we are using a common language of gestures and sounds, visual, kinesthetic, and other responses. To unify fragments, we are translating the incongruent fragments to the one manner. To have cohesive presentations in styles that are poles apart, they have been translated to one approach. The translation without the goal of unification does not make any sense. To have unification we need the conscious awareness of our subconscious feeling. Consciously, Dostoevsky did not know how to translate responses and to achieve a dialog and to have a meeting, but he was the one who had pointed to the problem.

Our Psyche or Self

The psyche, or self, has a collection of the fragments, which consist of our inherited responses, learned from significant figures, from the individuals we met, the movies we saw, and the books we read. The unified fragments represent a *solid identity, or solid self.* The fragments, which are splitting, feuding, and sabotaging each other, are not solid and are part of *fragmented identity, or fragmented self.*

Our psyche has three ways of managing its fragments: splitting, unification, or being neutral. We have complexity to understand consciously the process of splitting, unification, and indecisiveness or neutrality, because the operations of our psyche depend on subconscious logic. Our fully developed identity is represented by the solid psyche, which possibly will sustain a significant amount of stress and discomfort and is not falling apart under duress. Normally our psyche strives for unification to create the solid identity, but often this task is impossible, because unfortunately, many psyches are not sustaining stress and discomfort. They are splitting and their responses become incongruent. Under pressure some psyches fall apart, and become a collection of isolated fragments, which are loosely connected and do not have a consistency in their replies. The psyche, which suffers from the incongruence, is representing a fragmented identity and making unpredictable the interaction within self and with others.

The individuals and things in our own world influence our psyche in two opposite ways: to split or to unite. The biggest influence on our responses come from our parents, our teachers, books we read, movies, stage performances, and the society we live in. The distinction between solid and fragmented identity is in the internal and external feelings, which are the outcome of our relationships with others and with the fragments inside of *self.* We have more troubles in our relationships when we are operating with inconsistent logic and fragmented identity; then our psyche contains many loosely connected parts.

Childhood trauma, which comes at a time when our mind is not very strong, becomes one of the obstacles to our developing a solid identity. Childhood trauma is a reason that in later life our psyche loses clear perspective and has negative or aggressive responses in nonthreatening circumstances. Not only in childhood, but at any age we are powerlessness in front of physical or psychological trauma, which came from stress, or illnesses, and is causing a split. When we live in a very sheltered environment where we are overprotected, we encompass the stumbling blocks of growing up and having a fully developed solid identity. To remedy the damages our fragments need to be unified in a solid identity by using genuine dialog.

Our fragments are presenting dissimilar life experiences. In the same way as anyone who is learning from analyzing the diverse stages of his life, our fragments have the power of learning how to have internal dialogs. Dialog comes from understanding the importance of the divergent fragments in our responses. The self-growth process includes the unification of the same loosely connected fragments. When we are initiating genuine internal dialog between our fragments, the process cannot stop. The desire to have a solid identity also motivates us to express the real feelings to our fragments. Authentic dialog is achieved when the fragments, the same way as we do, are interacting honestly and openly. Further, we want to present two types of individuals. One is able to resist a virus of radicalization, but the other is completely taken by a virus.

Utopian Collective May Be Achieved in Our Psyche

We have the strength to achieve the Utopian collective in our psyche, where our fragments are sharing only one physical body. Nevertheless, the Utopian collective is the ultimate human hope to have understanding, loving and carrying relations between members of collective. The Utopia is that all individuals, who are acting as a group, may enjoy a state of constant dialog.

The Autopsy Without Using Chirurgic Interventions

We may do an autopsy on our dysfunctional psyche without using chirurgical interventions. An autopsy is a post-mortem examination done by medical professionals to determine the cause and manner of death. The autopsy of the psyche is a procedure when we are analyzing what is wrong with it. This examination is not a post-mortem and does not require a presence of any dead bodies. The goal of psyche autopsy is to determine how severely brutality is resisting unification and keeping away our solid identity.

The Psyche's Anatomy

The psyche is an imaginable and complex system and has an anatomy. As any functional system our psyche can be defined from various perspectives and provides information about how and why the system functions. To understand how and why the psyche functions we need to know the psyche anatomy. We are identifying and labeling our fragments, which are components of our psyche. The rigid fragments bring roughness, and unbendable and inflexible interactions. We are achieving plasticity in interaction between our fragments. Our interactions become gentle, flexible, and soft.

The Congruence in Responses

The congruence in our responses is helping the psyche overcome our deficits in comprehension, in the adaptive functioning and the social interactions. The lack of our adaptive functioning is related to the lack of the correct translations of stimulations and responses. Our impairments, which are blocking the audio, visual, and kinesthetic translations, prevent us from forming the balanced responses.

We are receiving comparable information by translating responses into kinesthetic, audio, and visual areas of the brain. In the meantime our brain is creating many new neurons by transferring various stimulations, and is using the various parts of our brain to understand more deeply the same information. The new data increases our attention to detail and helps us sustain maximum mental effort within the psyche. When our psyche is producing the kinesthetic response of fighting, we know it is presenting the behavior of one of our fragments, including aggression and overreaction. The translation of our responses is the more optimal way of increasing plasticity. By transferring the stimulations to be processed in the dissimilar part of the brain we are organizing and planning our activities better and are focused on the task. The deeper understanding of the stimulations is helping us stabilize our feelings and avoid overreaction.

Our adaptive functioning relies mainly on the correct translation from one to the other area of our brain. Underneath those exchanges, the neurological circuits of the firing neurons are being laid. The translation allows the balanced release of the chemistry in the diverse parts of the brain. With correct conversion of the response we get feelings of social and emotional reciprocity, which help increase our effectiveness in our communications and our ability to control our emotions. By using congruent translation of responses to kinesthetic areas we are increasing the motor coordination, and breaking the patterns of stereotyped and repetitive motor mannerisms. If, as children, we were abused by bullies and grew up as fearful, our psyche organization built a structure that avoids dangerous stimulations.

Let us call a fragment, which had precedent in the fearfulness, by a made-up name; then we have the capacity to do our analysis of the patterns of fearfulness by using this name. We are translating the childish visual fears of Sam to more age-appropriate reactions. In our psyche we are storing the unrelated processes of our brain function. Those processes are not concrete but, nevertheless, are very useful. The oppositional aggressive behavior was built up to protect Sam from bullies and is forming responses through the many neurological passes of the brain. The oppositional responses we are calling Boris and Ivan, where Boris is antisocial and is acting up. He is selfish and his actions are unlawful, and he is the opposite of Sam. For his part Ivan does everything by the book. Ivan is Sam's protector, but he is, at the same time, a defender of law and order and does everything by the law. It is very demanding to follow the physiological processes in the brain and the brain's neurological passes. It is not easy to talk about symbioses between fragments of Sam, Boris, and Ivan, but the neurological passes are much more complicated.

In contrast to Sam and poles apart are Boris and Ivan, who are always ready to attack. They are not as helpless as Sam. The dialog between Sam, Ivan, and Boris makes responses more flexible. It is tricky to understand how our complicated brain circuitry is working and to follow the divergent passes of our brain, which are transporting the signals and building our responses. Instead, we are putting a label on our whole circuitry. We are creating a systematic approach. Under every label we have the real system with diverse responses.

First, we are observing how our fragments are responding to stimulation. When our fragments are forming incongruent responses, we give to the fragments a label to identify the divergent behaviors. We are not concerned about the physiological function of our brain, but interested only in psychological responses of our labeled psyche. Our responses are the result of our brain functioning. Our fearful responses are developed as a result of childhood intimidation. To a fixated fragment, which is representing childish fears, we give the name. The name includes the behavior of fearfulness, avoidance, and continuous feelings of intimidation after nonthreatening stimulations. At the same time as we give a name to our protector, our flexible fragment is providing us with more congruent responses.

We are studying the anatomy of Sam's psyche. Sam had a frightened character. He sees danger everywhere, because he is a weak child. He does not know the difference between right and wrong. Sam, as child, is depending on other fragments to defend him. By knowing his characteristics, we possibly will detect when this character is taking over the whole psyche. We are alerted to the influence of distinct fragments and know by name which fragment is taking over our psyche. To make the interaction more effective we are providing the fictional fragments with many details. To analyze the fragment, we are cutting it from our psyche. This process might remind us of the process of an autopsy. We are translating a fixated fragment, which has more of the visual responses, to more appropriate kinesthetic and audio responses.

The Transformation of Our Fixated Fragment to The Flexible

Through dialog we have the power to achieve the transformation of our fixated fragment to the flexible. Our psyche, which struggles with attention, concentration, and planning, may be restructured by using dialog to overcome the psychological convolutions. We are dealing with fixated fragments, which are preventing the completion of the desired task. The process of transformation from the fixation to plasticity is involving the dialog between our fragments. With dialogs we are establishing the reciprocity between our fragments to understand correctly and interpret the stimulations.

We are keeping all of our approaches ready to provide the correct responses. We are emphasizing that the dialog between our fragments is possible because the fragments are sharing our body and perfectly aware of the feelings each of them are experiencing. When we are dealing with interpretation of the versatile data, we are facing the complexity of the neurological processes in our brain. The benefit of the dialog is that in the process of psychological restructuring our fragments we are avoiding a direct involvement with the deepest neuropsychological processes and the neurological passes. We are just labeling our fixated responses and restructuring them to the flexible.

This process requires preparation. In a situation when we are deciding to lift a heavy weight with our hands, we need to have all the muscle groups, including legs, adequately prepared to handle the weights. We do not lift anything very heavy until we are ready. Similarly, in our psyche we are resolving our psychological complications by increasing our knowledge in analysis of our psyche. In preparation, we are emphasizing the importance of timing. We also do not want to use tools; they are too complicated, and we do not know how to handle them. When we are converting our fixated fragments to flexible, we are using a dialog. We are dealing with our problems on the psychological level, instead of being surrounded by physiological configurations.

Our fixated and flexible fragments are from diverse psychological structures. The structure, which does not have *self*-regulatory tools, has a very low probability of forming a congruent response. The fixated fragments have the structure, which is not able to balance our responses, is poorly equipped, and lacks tools to handle the complicated tasks. The other systems, the flexible fragments, are well equipped with tools, can function in distinct areas, and form balanced responses. In the second structure we mobilize our audio, kinesthetic, and visual skills to do the needed task and do a good job of translating the audio stimulations to visual and kinesthetic. If we are not able to express our feelings in disparate modalities, we may not complete the required task of balancing our emotions. We advocate taking time to see the problem from poles apart and then to balance our emotions. We do not want our approach to sound primitive because simple is not primitive.

The psychological approach is simpler than the physiological but is far away from the primitive one. Behind the many fragments are the divergent neurological passes of the incoming signals and their processors in the disparate areas of the brain. Our approach would identify the audio, visual, kinesthetic, and olfactory obscurity. After the completion of the main goal to be in the state of internal dialog, we become solid. All the fragments of our psyche have transformed to plasticity. During the state of dialog, the roads of communication in our psyche are accessible and fragments understand others. They are honestly validating their feelings, and may well find solutions that are satisfactory for all of them. This procedure is similar to the situation when we are sloppy and put off organizing things in our rooms. We possibly will not find anything we need. If we would start organizing one corner at a time, we would bring order to our house.

When we are dealing with the fragments of individuals, we do not have any idea how our feelings are affecting them. They might not feel the same joy and misery. We may never know, but intuitively we can feel. Some of us assume how the opponents are feeling, because we have guessing capacities. Nevertheless, we cannot be sure how the stimulations affect fragments of various individuals. We are not completely aware of what is going on in others. The best method of interaction with others is negotiation. During negotiation we are sending small probes to others to understand their feelings. We are practicing negotiation with others, but it is dissimilar to dialog.

The external dialog is still dialog within our *self*, because during the external dialog we become united with our partner. External dialog is possible when the other individual psyche becomes our extension. Only after we transform our rigid fragments to flexible and after extensively practicing the inside dialogs may we engage in external dialogs.

Overdevelopment in The Kinesthetic Area

Overdevelopment in the kinesthetic area is responsible for complexity in understanding the audio and visual stimulations and, as a result, is causing convolution in negotiations with others. Our psyche with its domineering kinesthetic fragment is splitting from the audio and visual fragments. When our fragments cannot properly translate our visual and audio responses to kinesthetic, the negotiations between our psyche and others get down to the kinesthetic level, which is the more primitive level and usually ends in a split. Overdevelopment in our kinesthetic area leads to feelings of grandiosity and superiority. It accounts for our more primitive view of the world.

Our disturbance in attention and concentration is related to kinesthetic overdevelopment, because the chemicals are distributed in only one or two areas of our brain, which are overworked. As a result, it minimizes our audio and visual queues and ignores reality probes, which are coming from our visual and audio sources. When we are splitting from verbal and visual negotiations, we are left only with the kinesthetic way to solve our grievances. When our negotiations are on the kinesthetic level and our opponents are functioning on the audio and visual level, we do not understand others. Our negotiators on the kinesthetic level show our strength when we do some movements. Sometimes we use kinesthetic superiority just as an attempt to show our strengths.

We do know our strengths but do everything in accordance with our honorable agreements and never physically hurt others. The bullies too are usually overdeveloped in the kinesthetic area, but they always want to hurt. They challenge everyone. It is up to their opponents to take a challenge or not. If we do not feel like fighting and the aggressor wants to split from us, we are still holding up and hoping for unification even if the bullies are not leaving us alone.

Our nonviolent psyches face a predicament on how to avoid fighting and prevent a split. We are using negotiations with others. At the end of the negotiations we expect a successful agreement, which prevents fighting and splitting. We do not want to fight, because a fight is not a negotiation, but a confrontation. A fight also is a split, which includes force. Behind every split is unhappiness, because parties are displeased and disagree on values of confrontation. In every negotiation a dilemma is present: stop negotiations and continue to fight, or negotiate and not fight. It means that in negotiations with others we are not sure whether we will succeed.

The clash starts when one of the arguing parts refuses to bargain. Some of us do not believe that a bad peace is better than a good war. Others with kinesthetic strength are rarely dealing with reality because they are relying on their kinesthetic abilities. Very soon their psyche would split from negotiations and settle the differences with brutal force. Interesting that in the animal kingdom many animals are trying to negotiate before a fight. They make some sound to caution the opposite side about the consequences of the fight. They try to show body postures to the opponents to demonstrate that they are fit and determined. When the differences are not resolved and negotiators are stopped, the struggles start. For everyone the failure to compromise results in confrontation.

The opponents are driven by splitting. They forget all previous agreements and soon the confrontation starts. It often happens that between the fighting parties, one is not the initiator of the fight and is driven in. The attackers, who are hurting others, do not have empathy and show clear signs of emotional instability. The fight always includes anger and aggression. The other feelings are of pain and hurt, but the fighters detach from those feelings. The worst scenario happens when one opponent is fighting but the other is running away. During the chase things may get bloody. In many instances, when a weak part asks for help and no one wants to help, the weak survives in any way he can and may well use illegal tricks and concealed weapons.

By continuing to fight without the proper strength the losing fighter may be destroyed. The best solution is to surrender. If during the fight one opponent is appearing much stronger, then the feeble one needs to surrender or prepare to get serious injuries or die. When the end is the grave anyway, it is better to end life by fighting than by being slaughtered. The fight, when the opponents want to hurt others, is a split on all levels of functioning. The winner is the one who finds a way to hurt his opponent more.

After the scuffle, when no one is winning, some negotiations may start again. The more solid psyche is inclined to sit for negotiation. Opposite, the psyche with an internal split is more driven to fight. The negotiating psyches need to achieve congruency in perceptions by learning new ways of interaction. In the negotiation between two psyches, the psyches send probes to understand each other's intention. The one psyche needs to be aware of whether the opposite psyche is ready for agreement or wants only manipulation and confrontation. To negotiate agreement both psyches must have a sincere desire to work together. If one psyche is pretending negotiation and taking time to restructure its forces, then negotiations will fail. If the other psyche categorically refuses to negotiate, then in the end we will not see any agreement, but another fight.

Sometimes it appears that the parts are reaching an agreement, but this agreement is only "on paper," and in reality, the future split is not resolved. Even if both psyches have a written agreement, the peace may not last long. The part with the better negotiating skills does not care about the turmoil in the other psyche. It is just enjoying better terms and getting pleasure from winning. This negotiator is a gambler. If it turns out that the opponent does not agree to the terms, then the split resurfaces again and leads to confrontation.

When we identify that the neurological passes are impaired in our kinesthetic area of the brain, we are focusing on unrelated areas and emphasizing the audio and visual experiences. These areas of our brain may be intact. When in our negotiation we focus on audio and visual processors, we are relying on many verbal or previous written agreements. Our real negotiators are not seeking a short-term solution but aiming for long-term understanding. The modification of our psyche to become a better negotiator is effectively helping us when we are experiencing resistance in recognizing and identifying our feelings, which are affected by emotional instability and attention deficit.

The restructuring of our psyche by using fragments is helping our brain achieve a balance without wasting time on the physiology. We do not need excessive knowledge about the neurological passes through which the brain's chemistry is moving. By restructuring the overdeveloped kinesthetic area of the brain we are transferring the kinesthetic responses to the audio and visual areas. We are exploring visual and audio feelings about all kinesthetic activities, including tactile experiences, and are having free associations about the audio and visual capacities and how to resolve our grievances without a fight.

Diverse Forces are Affecting Our Identity.

To understand the process of building a solid identity we need to understand the dynamic forces behind this process. Inside of our psyche during organization and maintenance of solid identity we are responding to the forces of unification and splitting. We are unifying fragments to get a solid identity and to have congruent responses. The work of unification is completely disparate from expansion. We do not want to incorporate our fragments by all available means, because they are sharing the same physical body. Forceful incorporation leaves resentments and hatred between them, and our body will be subjected to unpleasant feelings.

Unhappiness, the main sign of splitting, includes the offensive *self* name calling, and feelings of anger and irritation. When our psyche is involved in the process of splitting, our body also experiences feelings, which include fears, worry, anxiety, despair, and obsession. We feel as if we are in the operating room, because the splitting brings feelings of danger, despair, abandonment, and regret. The splitting may perhaps present when we are building a solid identity. Sometime we need to overcome unpleasant feelings during the process of unification.

As paradoxical as it is, but within reasonable limits, splitting helps solidify our identity. With splitting we test whether we are in the process of unification. We need to be sure that the positive feelings about *self* are not associated with *selfishness*, putting others down, or enjoyment of distraction and chaos. The interpretation of splitting and unification is very individual and is crucial for us to be clear about the forces that are affecting our identity. In the process of building a solid identity it may happen that the unification process is interpreted as a splitting and contrary. Sometimes, because of fears of getting soft and appearing weak, we are giving up our fundamental beliefs—the rejection of violence. As a result, we are unifying with violence, impulsive urges, deviant behavior, and many other things, which actually are against our nature. For the fragmented identity the splitting sometimes brings false feelings of satisfaction and victory.

The main indicator, which helps us understand what process we are involved in, is our positive or negative feelings about *self*. If after the splitting we have positive feelings about *self,* that is an indication of fragmented identity. A solid identity would never feel good about splitting, except when we are splitting to survive. The psyche in the dynamic interactions is modeling the relationships between individuals. It is not always possible, because the interactions between our fragments are dissimilar to the interaction outside our psyche. We are aware that our fragments are sharing the same physical body, and we must be very gentle in the interactions with our fragments. In our internal interactions we do not want to harm our *self.* It is very important that we be aware of what forces are in control of our psyche. When the process of unification and solidifying identity is done in a proper manner, it brings feelings of high *self*-esteem, *self*-worth, acceptance of our identity, and feelings of comfort about being here. We have the strong feeling of acceptance of our *self*, of who we are, and feelings of being accepted by others.

The Developed Identity

The solid identity is a unique structure of the psyche where the fragments are aligned together in common goals and attitude. The psyche, which is presenting the consistency of responses, we are calling the developed individuality. The solidification of individual psyche is a conscious meeting of all the fragments with mutual understanding and sincere care. The solid identity of the individual is contradictory to the collective identity. In the collective, individuality is diminished to an insignificant level and assumed to be easily replaceable. Actually, the developed individuality in a collective structure is not needed, because it has strength to interfere with the ideology of the collective.

Many individuals want to be free from the collective, because they are not agreeing to be an insignificant part. Everyone who is part of the collective identity is suppressing his fragments and is not interested in the *self*-search. The collective mind does not tolerate individual fragments and often calls them by derogatory names. The government of the collective demands that the citizens be strong, insensitive, and obedient and that they avoid *self*-search, *self*-awareness, and *self*-analysis. Police used this psychology to help with interrogation and to manipulate ordinary members. The individual psyche was replaced by the collective mind in the workplace, in school, and even at home. The government suggested that the collective had a solution to all problems and had the power to provide affirmation for weak members. The collective made a lot of decisions for the masses and took over many functions from the individuals. The collective had a power bigger than each individual. With the collective came abuses of power, when members in high positions were easily manipulating ordinary members. The collective approach of solving members' problems is associated with a lot of injustice, rubber stamps, and brutality.

When we dream about fulfilling relationships and of relating to others on a higher level, we are thinking of developing a solid individual identity. The biggest pride of individuality is the conscious awareness that the psyche does not belong to a collective any more. The development of a solid identity becomes a goal for many, because of the opportunity to have unity and dialogs within their psyche. In individual thinking we are responsible only for taking care of our own and extended body. The extended body is our family and friends, for whom we are responsible and whom we need to protect from the harm of anger and fears.

We have various ways to relate to our fragments. Our relations are not easy. The way of the interrelation between our fragments resembles the way of interaction within our family in our childhood and depends on our perception of how functional our upbringing was. If we had a rough upbringing without love and support, then in times of stress and despair, we blame *self* for the wrong decisions. We do not believe in *self* and tend to call *self* by derogatory names and put *self* down. The interactions between our fragments repeat the dysfunctional interactions in our family. If our family members blamed others, the interactions between our fragments are on the accusative level. When we put *self* down and humiliate *self*, we copy from our childhood the dysfunctional ways of communication. We need to change our ways of relating. We cannot communicate inside our psyche the same way we communicate with others, because all our fragments share the same body. We promote a genuine dialog as the correct way of communication. This process involves the creation of the authentic way of connecting to our fragments. We are relating to the outside world from the solid base, where we know who we are and what we are presenting to others. We want to make our own decisions and do not want the one imposed by collective. When we make mistakes, we want the opportunity to learn and improve *self* instead of being put down by the collective and feeling dysfunctional. We want to have strength to face our problems, to have a real dialog with our fragments, and to save *self* from a fragmented identity.

The Congruence of Responses

The goal of our psyche is to achieve the congruence of our fragments. The fragment is the small characteristic of any psyche, and contains the packed-together responses. Because every fragment represents a part of our psyche, the congruence of the fragments is directly related to wisdom and reliability. The congruent responses of our fragments are characteristic of a solid identity. The main forces inside our psyche are splitting and unification. The ability of our domineering fragment to resist splitting and create the atmosphere of unification is the quality of a solid identity. The splitting and solidification of our fragments is the normal process of our development and is necessary to achieve congruence in our responses. We are always under pressure from the forces of splitting and unification, and by our audio responses, visual presentation, and the way we move our body, we are transmitting to the world the naked truth about who we are. The stages of our development may be represented by the correlation of the responses, which include the visual, audio, and kinesthetic.

We need to observe our reactions to various stimulations. We are presenting a contradictory identity when without a change in the environment our responses unexpectedly are changing, and we are suddenly presenting various audio, visual, and kinesthetic incongruent responses. It means that our psyche does not have a stable construction that has capacity, providing the stable response to the same stimulations. When our fragments, in the majority, are congruent, then our identity is whole and solid. We have challenge to function independently. Our identity is distinguished from others by difference in responses, including responses we have learned from relatives, friends, books, and life experiences. When those responses are incongruent, we see in front of us the fragmented identity, which may well be integrated to become part of the collective. We fall apart under little stress, feel miserable, and need protection from another, stronger structure, which may be ideology, cult, or crime. We need a roof to be a shield. We go through many humiliations to join the powerful group and obtain a protector.

The Development of The Fragments

In our psyche the process of solidification and splitting of the fragments is on the subconscious level. Our fragments became a part of our subconscious after interaction with other individuals and copying their responses. When we read books, we live the life of the book's heroes. When we go to a stage performance or see movies, we are surrounded by the many characters played by actors and feel the strong connection with those characters. For us, as spectators, the characters played by actors are alive, and the characters' imaginative responses became part of our psyche. The actor in a soap opera who plays a favorite character is like a real friend. We discuss the soap operas' characters as if those characters are real.

Our parents and grandparents may not be in proximity and might be deceased, but they are in our minds and we are unaware that we are copying their responses. Many of us feel a mother's disapproval or father's anger when they are not around. We are afraid of our boss even if the boss is not around. We are doing everything on a subconscious level. We are hardly aware that we are responding to the stimulations exactly the same as others whom we know. We also copy our responses from books and movies.

Because the fragmentation is on our subconscious level, we have difficulty to be consciously aware that our fragments are incongruent. At the same time on our conscious level we are not feeling happy, not satisfied with our life, and not sure about *self*. We want to find a congruent way of expressing *self*, and in our hearts we want to be sure that our responses are genuine and to feel happy with *self*. Those feelings are the motivation to start the process of having a quest for our solid identity. The restructuring is helping when our psyche experiences complications with congruency while trying to organize our fragments. To have successful restructuring we are identifying and bringing our fragments to our conscious awareness. We are meeting our fragments and engaging them in real dialog. We are in the process of building our solid identity.

The Diverse Ways of Responses

We are striving to get our responses in order, to bring them on the conscious level, and to have appropriate articulations. Our goal is to express *self* very clearly and congruently. Equilibrium within the psyche is a moment that is evident from the demonstrations when all fragments or groups of fragments are consciously aware of their feelings and are in a state of dialog. At this moment the divergent manners include audio, visual, and kinesthetic. Even if they are balanced, it is very important to be consciously aware not only of verbal representations, but of the diverse manners. The kinesthetic are the responses that relate to body movements. Kinesthetic responses are triggered by divergent stimulations. Anxiety responses, which are kinesthetic, may be generated by other stimulations, which include sounds, stressful news, or unpleasant observations. Visual and audio stimulations generate the fight-or-flight response, which is a kinesthetic response. Audio articulations are vocal and verbal responses. Besides audio stimulations many other stimulations that are not auditory trigger audio responses. For instance, yelling for help may be triggered by various stimulations.

Visual representations include drawing a picture, grimacing, talking with the eyes, and others. Visual words are partly learned responses and partly unexpected responses, such as suddenly blushing. To understand someone we check the styles of stimulations, because the choice of the responses exhibits the relationships between fragments. Even though the stimulations may be audio, visual, and kinesthetic, our responses are similar. It happens that our responses to dissimilar stimulations are in the same manner. When we produce the same responses to diverse stimulations, it means the responses are wrongly translated to the corresponding forms. The incongruent reactions to the diverse styles contribute to our blurred and fragmented behavior. We lose the originality of the responses.

The wise scientist appropriately answers all audio questions about science. When observing his visual responses, we see that they do not match the audio because the scientist is reacting to females with a smirk and sending sexual messages with his eyes. His kinesthetic responses are also strange, because he is waving his hands excessively but the rest of his body gets tight and cannot move. The scientist's audio responses are logical and sequential, but his visual responses show the impulsive part of him as well as his visual immaturity. The kinesthetic responses are inconsistent with his audio responses, because his body is tight and does not move, whereas his hands move in all directions and seem out of his control, showing the scientist's anxiety and fears. The responses all together present us with his disjointed identity. We saw the educated man with a high verbal ability, but his visual responses did not contribute anything to his image. In fact, it was the opposite: they were completely destroying his audio representation. The kinesthetic responses show us the shy and anxious nature of our scientist. In conclusion of our observation we understand that our professor has a blurred and fragmented identity.

The Fragmented Identity

The fragmented identity is a structure of the psyche where our fragments are not aligned together, do not have unity, and may be involved in fearful or hateful behavior toward others. We are calling a fragment the group of identical types of responses. In our fragmented identity our little fragments are building materials for our psyche, which has a chaotic configuration and an unstable construction. In our fragmented identity our fragments are not aligned and their responses do not contain any clarity and are confused about the needs of the other fragments. The splitting of our psyche, which is a subconscious process, creates lots of harm to happiness and *self*-esteem.

In our psyche the responses are more sophisticated than our simple reaction on the visual, audio, and kinesthetic stimulations. Our response formation includes our life experience, analytical complexity, ways of controlling impulsiveness, and many other characteristics. Depending on our brain structure, education, life experiences, and brain's abnormalities, our psyche has various amounts of fragments. Because of severe stress and other physiological problems the association between our fragments becomes loose and the construction falls apart. In this analogy, our psyche with the loosely connected fragments reveals the messy and abandoned construction site, which is ruined and deserted.

Our goal is to complete the construction or rebuild, and to build our solid identity. Our task is a challenging one. First, we need to recognize the pieces of our psyche consciously and to find a way to put them together. In our fragmented identity our fragments are loosely connected, but each fragment has a specific manner of response and might be identified by a specific name. The name of our fragment is usually pointed out to the character whose responses our psyche is copying. In our fragmented identity the discovery of our fragment's origin is a complex task but very important and allows our fragments to meet on the conscious level.

More of The Fragmented Identity

When parts of our psyche are rigid and negatively affecting areas of our functioning, we are experiencing a fragmented identity. Our psyche contains the fixated fragments that are having rigid manners of responses. To deal with these problems we bring our responses to the conscious level and become aware of the structure of our psyche. In the process of restructuring we are alerted to the rigidity of our fragments and analyze them. We are sensitive to the interaction between contradictory parts of our psyche, because in one instance those interactions are energizing but in another they may completely drain our energy.

The drain of energy happens when during the transfer of our responses to the conscious level, we get the emotional imbalance, transferences, contra-transferences, and catharses that are rigid responses based on our life experiences. We feel the lack of energy when we access our fixated fragments to deal with the significant one in our life. In our fixated responses we intuitively replicate the rigid perceptions of our parents. In other words, since childhood we have been copying our parents' responses and they are imprinted in our psyche, so the physical presence of our parents is not required anymore. Eventually, the suppression we are feeling from our parents is no longer coming from their physical presence, but from our own psyche.

The imprinted fragments affect us during our lives and in some instances entirely take over all our interactions. In childhood we fight the influence of our parents, and then in mature age we act exactly like them. The fragments of our parents are the rigid parts of our psyche. Actually, our identity is affected by hundreds of imprints because our whole identity is a combination of many fragments. The fragments, as building material of our psyche, sometimes represent a complete structure but also may well be a sign of ruins and an abandoned construction site. When we restructure our psyche, we realize we are running away from our identity and living someone else's life. To find our identity is to understand who we are and why we are here.

Harsh life stressors, lack of resistance to the pressure, and some genetic trends are reasons for a split of our identity into loosely connected segments. A fragmented identity is the cause of our unhappiness and a stressful lifestyle. The energy is generated when our fragments are connecting in a way that forms real dialog. When our fragments have plasticity, we learn new skills and reshape our ways of responding. Any amount of our flexible fragments is not preventing the establishment of a clear and solid identity. If the fragments are congruent and connected, our strength is our connectedness. It provides a congruent response and stable identity. When our fragments are not congruent and are loosely connected, our identity is not clear.

The Positive Characteristics of Splitting

When we are victims of violence and other victimizing forces, the splitting may well be one of the needed functions. The splitting is not a detaching but separating the compromised part of our psyche from the serviceable one. This process helps the functional part of our psyche get stronger to be able to nurture and protect our damaged part. Our future goal of the splitting from trauma is getting over the pain and finding a way to achieve genuine dialog between the functional parts of our psyche and the parts damaged by violence.

In the situation when trauma occurred, the fragmentation is needed as a component of healing. The two processes inside our psyche that are affecting our identity are the splitting and unification. In many instances, to save the psyche, the splitting force is as necessary as the unification. The splitting force helps us get together all the functional parts and become the nurturing force for parts that are weak, damaged, and underdeveloped. The ideologists were saying, "Forget about your internal feelings and focus on the big goal to build the future for your motherland." The government was telling the weak that by joining the collective they would become strong.

Neglecting the needs of the weakest and the crippled creates the opportunity for heartless and vicious dictators to take over. They use the disadvantaged to point out the failures of individuality. The forceful incorporation into the collective by a powerful group, who lure the cowed with attractive slogans, is not a solution to misery. The forceful incorporation of fragments is also wrong for a psyche. In the psyche organization we do not want to ignore the damaged fragments by incorporating them into the strong, because eventually, the strong fragments would blame the weak for all the mistakes and call them derogatory names. Our psyche uses splitting to localize and identify the damaged parts. The goal is not to put them down, but to provide nurturing and healing for trauma.

When we experience staggering, aphasia, or any other speech symptoms, it means that our responses to audio stimulations are severely damaged. Our damaged visual responses are exhibiting *self* in overreaction, fearfulness, and inappropriate facial demonstration. In many instances our kinesthetic responses are paralyzing and unpredictable. If the one style is damaged, we look for other forms that are not damaged. When damages occur in one manner, we use other ways to assist the damaged one. With splitting we identify the damaged fragment and the approach where the damage occurred, and provide support by using other styles of illustration. When several types of expression are not working properly, then by splitting we are letting the rest of the styles function correctly. We bring to our conscious awareness the little fragments that sustained the heavy damage. By temporarily splitting from the damaged fragments we have the opportunity to assess the damage and design the next step to unify our psyche.

The Intuition

Our intuition plays a big role in recognizing the internal process in our psyche.

In analyzing the structure of our psyche there are unpredictable processes. Our sense of right and wrong is indistinguishable. We instinctively follow the way of feeling good. We are feeling good when we are moving in the wrong way. After being a victim our vigilante's images of revenge help us become emotionally uplifted and in a better mood. Our vigilante's revolt starts after the process of declaring independence from the fears and incorporating into our psyche the fragments of aggression and violence. Our splitting becomes a pleasurable process, which may well be compared to sexual arousal and being under the influence of drugs. Our new goal as vigilante is violent behavior, which consists of inflicting on our assailant physical and emotional trauma. With the new fragment we act in a critical situation the same way our abuser does. We are no longer frail and weak but strong and aggressive. We are leveling *self* with our abusers in viciousness, and in our imagination we are becoming even more powerful. Our vigilante's feelings get reinforced by watching violent sports, movies, and so on. We are seeing our past in reverse and doing to the perpetrators what was done to us and even more.

We are splitting from one victim's role to the other, copied from the abuser's behavior. It meant we are having a new behavior. We are declaring defeat of our *self*. It is an attempt at preservation and survival. The view of the split is very confusing. One of the defeating views is that the split is similar to surgery, in that we are getting rid of damaged tissue that is not being salvaged later. Our most important goal is to preserve the functional part of our psyche. Our approach makes us feel better because we do not need to deal with our painful issues. We are entertaining *self* with vigilante thoughts and images of inflicting pain on the assailants. Our images give us the chance to freely express our emotions, which mix together our kinesthetic actions of beating and kicking the assailant with the audio, i.e., calling the assailants derogatory names. We are letting them know in internal conversations what we would do to them for revenge. The process, when as an abused one we are having vigilante feelings, is not a detachment, but a splitting from depressive and frightened fragments into brave, aggressive, courageous, and violent fragments, which are copied from the assailants. The split in our psyche involves the establishment of new fragments, which are copied from the imagined abuser's behavior. Our abusive fragments are becoming part of our psyche.

In another approach we keep assault as a deep secret. We feel that after a tragic experience we must not dwell on it but should forget and continue with our lives. We still have very confused feelings, and unification of the fragments is not helping us. As victims of violence, we have a tendency to detach from the trauma. We have an instinctive desire to hide from our problems. Hiding is not a very effective way to deal with our trauma and in the long run is not effective, because we are not progressing. The main feelings in our life are fear and despair. As a result of detachment, our psyche suffers from flashbacks and intrusive thoughts. Our feelings of fear of being tortured again mix with the desire for revenge. Sometimes we believe our trauma will not be repeated, and most likely we immediately decide that we need somehow to split from the painful experience.

The third view is oppositional to splitting and is more about preservation. It considers that our psyche has only one body to share; we do not abandon or leave alone any parts of our psyche, because if our injured psyche throws away our damaged fragments, then our dumped responses will take over our psyche in unexpected situations and become our defeating force. When we make an attempt to preserve and rebuild our psyche, only intuition is helping us choose the right path. We are always in conflict between doing something right and doing something to feel good. Our way to preserve good feelings is disassociation from our trauma and not dealing with it, but the right way is contrary. We are not cutting, killing, and getting rid of any parts of our psyche. Consciously, we are counting our probabilities and considering our future. We are preparing *self* to deal with the unexpected and with our pain and suffering. If our trauma repeats, then we are ready to meet an intruder.

The Nature of The Overreaction

When our responses are stronger than the stimulations, the responses and stimulations lack congruency. This is a sign of our fragmented identity and the splitting type of the psyche organization. Little stressors are triggering the splitting of our functional parts into fixated fragments, which are aggressive and fearful. The overreaction is our replay, which is far stronger than the situation requires and is often a defensive response. The overreaction is a form of violent tendencies in our life.

When we are suffering from overreaction, our psyche has a fragment that we are calling an agitator and a troublemaker. Our fragment is prompting the excessive responses. When we analyze our overreactions, we remember that in the process of overreaction, we had thoughts and images that were diminishing and threatening. In many instances our excessive reaction does not depend on the stimulations from outside but on our own reaction by the troublemaker fragment.

The process of overreaction is a result of the splitting. It easily takes over our psyche, because after the venting of our emotions, it creates pleasurable feelings of liberation. Sometime we get addicted to excessive responses of rage and then feel liberation. Our aggressive responses are internal, and bring the desire to fight our own troubled fragments. During a real crisis, when our life is in danger, aggression does not help us too much. In this situation a cool head is more helpful. Usually in a crisis, the best response is to cool down and avoid aggression, but sometimes aggression is the only way to resolve the crisis. If, with aggressive response, we scare away the attackers and prevent violence, then in this situation, aggression is a congruent response.

In a crisis we are always under pressure to negotiate between our responses, which are too strong or not strong enough. When we are in a crisis, the feeling of paralyzing fear prevents us from finding an appropriate response. If we are not able to resolve the crisis, then our inactivity may be a sign of splitting. In other circumstances, inactivity is the best way to avoid violence and to resolve the crisis. Then the inactivity is a congruent response and a sign of unification. When the level of congruency of responses to the stimulations is out of our conscious control, then it is on the subconscious level. When we are acting intuitively, we do not have any explanation for how we came up with the appropriate responses; we only know whether these responses are congruent or not. The most important characteristic of the response is a congruency with stimulation. The congruency of the responses is a sign of a solid identity. All our responses are a sign of splitting or unification. When we analyze the process in our psyche from the point of the alliance or the division, we have more pragmatic ways to understand our internal life. Overreaction occurs when our responses are not congruent with stimulation, and is a sign of a fragmented identity and divisions in our psyche.

The Clear Identity

Some would question the fairness of the initial design of our psyche, because some have an unmistakably clear identity, whereas others have a blurred one and spend many years clearing it. Our psyche has ways to get organized, and as a result, we have inherited the capacity to solidify our psyche when others are suffering from a fragmented identity.

Sometimes we have a clear and solid identity from an early age. Our pathologically splinted identity exhibits *self* in the early ages too. From an early age we are hooligan, thief, or egoist. In some instances our identity does not form until our later years and is affected by harsh upbringing and deeply hidden secrets. As a result of troubles in childhood, our psyche develops a fragment, which it uses for protection and as a secret keeper. This fragment takes the attention away from the secrets and painful history.

Professor Stepan Kryvoruchko's identity was not developed right away. He was using the stereotyped mask of collective identity, which was provided by the ideology to be a good son of workers' paradise. As a young man, he was just Stepan Kryvoruchko and lived in a collective, but in the later life cycle he was outside a collective. He experienced the unconscious drive to consolidate his identity. The most important task for him was to develop a solid identity and be proud of *self*. He was not afraid of the challenges and inconveniences on the way. He had a strong intuitive feeling of stagnation and that his identity was fragmented. Without his conscious awareness, he was making the tremendous effort to build a solid identity. He was unifying the congruent responses under the name Stepan Kryvoruchko. He solidified his domineering fragment and his other fragments, which represented his parents, grandparents, friends, acquaintances, and heroes of the books he read and movies he saw. The product of his effort was a solid identity with the name of Professor Stepan Kryvoruchko, who represents the hero of our time—the honest, honorable hero, who never would betray and deceive his own quest.

In the collective, the trend was that we should sacrifice our own happiness for the collective. In many situations, we are sacrificing many desires for others, but in reality we are pushed by the collective to give up our identity for a bigger cause. Stepan Kryvoruchko was risking everything for the liberation of his identity and to have his identity cleared from stereotypes of the collective. He was sure his identity was not a perfect one, but it was his own and he was proud of it. His goal was to have his identity liberated from the oppression of the collective and to be free. He feels content and proud, because he has the power to freely identify his *self*.

"We" can Unify with "Self."

We are a collection of our fragments, which are contained in solid *self*. Inside of our psyche, *we* are free, not suppressed and attacked. We do not push any of our fragments but want to unify them. The unification of fragments is easy because we do not have a detached part of us. All our fragments are informed and aware of everything about us. *We* have diverse ways of processing our stimulation. When *we* are unifying our fragments, we become congruent, and *we* get a solid *self*. *We* have a number of fragments inside of *self*, and *we* are a solid *self*. When our psyche is splitting, *we* do not have *self*.

The radical collectives wanted to bring all members to become analogues and to fit their particular stereotype. The difference between our psyches and radical collectives is the relationship with *self*. The radical collectives were asking us to forget about our individuality. They would not allow us to have solid *self*. *We* without *self* became the main point of their ideology. They wanted to unify us in *we*, *but* deprive us from *self*. They pushed us to unification by giving us an external stereotype and the fictitious goal, which is a Utopia, of creating a futuristic society of harmony and wealth. Opposite, inside of our psyche the unification is creating the realistic harmony between our fragments. The internal harmony is not a Utopia but a very important state of mind. The realistic goal for everyone is to have *we* together with *self* and live in harmony.

"We" might Unify with "Others."

The meaning of *we* and *others* is easier said than understood. If we do not have a strong harmony inside, it is complicated to create harmony with others. When we are building a solid *self*, then there are possibilities for unification. Otherwise, the split is healthier than pretentious unification.

The Real Meeting

A dialog between our fragments is the prerequisite of our meeting, when one part of our psyche is having the full understanding and compassion of the others. Only when we have the dialog are our fragments in the state of the meeting and together with dialog. Our internal dialog and meeting are associated with unification. Unification through negotiations does not create a meeting, but is unifying without a dialog. There are other forms of unification through force and without dialog. The forceful unification does not have a meeting and is as bad as splitting. Our internal splitting is associated with objectification, confrontation, and manipulation. These forces of splitting and unification are the main driving forces in our psyche. It is very demanding to follow the physiological processes in the brain and the brain's neurological passes, which are displayed in emotions during our interactions. When we are suffering from splitting, our fragments are dividing from the others. After splitting, our fragments become loosely associated. We feel confusion and our emotions are unpredictable. When we are unifying, our fragments are bound together and we feel in control of our emotions. In some instances we split to survive because of a threat to our life environment and a hope that later, in a better environment, we will have the power to achieve meeting and unity. A meeting is a state of unification through the dialog.

Because of secrets in his life, Professor Kryvoruchko's psyche had many fragments. To be real and to survive he needed to be someone else. His identity fell apart. When he identified many crucial parts of his psyche and took them under his conscious control, he was able to have meetings with his fragments. When his fragments got involved in dialogs and meetings, his psyche became solid. Professor Kryvoruchko discovered his identity and those around him accepted him. He dealt with the deep secret that had caused his psyche to fall apart and was able to unify all of his fragments. He enjoys solid self-identity and high self-esteem. His good feelings come after the meeting of his fragments and from his ability to enjoy meetings.

With our solid identity we are proud of our presented *self* and are always in a state of dialog. When we have a vague identity, we are deprived of feeling high *self*-esteem. We get confused when some fragments take over our psyche. On the subconscious level we want to unite our fragments and have our wholeness. Our unification is the driving force of our mind. Our main intuitive desire is to achieve our unification, but without a dialog the drive for unification only splits our psyche more and more. We live for dialogs and meetings, but dialogs and meetings are not happening too often. Many times we get lured by the agitators of the radical collective to unification. When we are having the pretension of meetings, the pretension is not creating real happiness. The pretension is more associated with drug abuse, detachment, gambling, sex pathology, unhappiness, and suicide. With a fragmented identity we are the easy quarry of the collective.

The Quest for A Solid Identity

Our behavior in the quest for a solid identity is not easy for others to understand. Our quest for solid identity is on a subconscious level. We may not verbalize the reason that we are not complete. We do not feel whole and are suffering. Professor Stepan Kryvoruchko's identity was emerging when he decided to leave the collective. When the masses of minorities departed from the collective, they created confusion. The brainwashed members may not have understood why the minorities were leaving the workers' paradise.

Professor Kryvoruchko, or at that time just Stepan, was an illustration of a typical repatriate. He was leaving the collective state, which had the beautiful sceneries of nature, the heartbreaking songs about military victories, and the pretentious workers' paradise. If he had stayed, he would have had the ability to have a happy life, but something was not right behind the cheerful words. Now we know that the repatriates were not leaving their country because they were poor, but because the dominant ethnic group was so jealous and did not have the generosity to share pleasure with others. For the privilege to stay as equals, the ideologists were asking a lot. They were encouraging the future repatriates to completely forget their identity and overlook who they really were.

Stepan Kryvoruchko loved many things in the workers' paradise, but he did not want to pretend he was someone he was not and spend the rest of his life between similar pretenders. He understood that the government would lavishly reward him if he decided to abandon his dream and stay put. He avoided this temptation to stay in familiar surroundings and decided to leave. Similarly, in the time of the Cold War, many citizens dealt with the same questions of how to stop being a mechanical device and identical to the others. They decided to leave. If they stayed, they became a product of the hungry machine, which would melt them into the collective. Now, the victims of the ideology who did not fit into the mechanical image, and resisted, vanished in the resistance; they are the heroes and revered.

The individuals who intuitively left the collective to look for a new identity do not feel like traitors anymore. If they found their clear identity, they feel good about *self*. They are the heroes of our time. They left the workers' paradise, served in the Israeli army or went to the jungles of the wild West, and eventually became free from the power of the collective. Stepan Kryvoruchko was open to new customs. He was flexible. He only wanted to search for his own identity and became a man free from the collective. For us who left a collective state, the quest for solid identity was our main motive to change our lives. From sailors we have many who did achieve their goals, but there are some who continue with their quest. Some sailors, to become complete, went back to their roots. They forgot that their psyche already had a distinctive structure. The Jewish people, who followed Moses' leadership, left slavery in Egypt and became free. If they go back to Egypt with an old mentality, they continue to be slaves. If they continue their quest and become free, they have the capacity to come back with a changed view of life and with a solid identity. The same thing happened with members of the collective who went back as reformed and enlightened. They were free, even when they went back.

The Solid Identity

Many would agree that a solid identity is important but is not a reason to recklessly change our lifestyle. As sailors, we drop everything and leave a comfortable place. We may not control our intuitive quest for our real identity because it is a combination of our genetic tendency and our life experiences. We want our real identity as soon as possible, but we do not stop to confront thoughts of surrender. We are sailors and have our genetic inclinations transferred from generations of honorable individuals. As sailors, our experiences were commendable because they included our noble intentions and our sacrifices. Outside of the collective we did not become crooks and misfits.

In the same way as many others, the young Stepan Kryvoruchko went to Israel. He worked in a kibbutz, served in the Israeli army, and married a Canadian woman, then went with his wife to study in Montreal and, eventually, became Professor Kryvoruchko. From his genetic past Stepan Kryvoruchko came from several generations of strong warriors and was not afraid of battles and duties. Both of his grandfathers were fighters in World War II. He had relatives who died in the Holocaust. His father was a survivor from the atrocities of war and is a director of a big military plant in workers' paradise. His mother is a medical doctor and a professor in medical school. His sister graduated from the prestigious Moscow University. His family has done very well. He recognizes that he has strength from having a very comfortable life back in the collective, but he also knows he was not willing to give up his identity. He would not fail his internal quest.

As a matter of fact, the millions who left the collective were thinking the same way. Only a few, despite the harsh stress of adaptation, returned to the workers' kingdom. With the reality that more travelers wanted to leave, the myth of a collective as the accomplished dream of the workers' paradise was shredded. The myth of the collective was shaken by harsh reality, which included the war, the frequent disagreements between the powerful, and doubts about what direction to follow. The members of the collective faced doubts and the confusion between the propaganda of the ruling elite and paralyzing uncertainty. They did not know how to make any decisions or what to do in a crisis. They could not decide if they needed to fight the differences or accept them. They were surrounded by spreading confusion and an absence of clear goals. The uncertainty contributed to the general disillusionment. The resentment was not exported from outside but boiled up within the collective. It seems that everyone who had thoughts of leaving was contributing to the breaking of the rules and stereotypes of the collective. Because of the mass desire to split from the collective, an enormous synchronization of energy was building up.

In that time the main desire of Stepan Kryvoruchko's psyche was to reinforce the area of goodness and to make the evil weaker. The collective identity was synonymous with evil for many. It became clear that the time had come to achieve their goal of rebirth and of getting identity, which was clear from the collective. Stepan Kryvoruchko felt the waves of freedom. He felt validated that for the sake of building a solid identity he risked many things and left his parents' home.

Consciously, Stepan Kryvoruchko and many others did not know the real reason for their departure and what they were looking for. Definitely, everyone who left the collective had their own reason. The question is still open about whether they found what they were looking for and understood what happened to their psyche on a subconscious level.

The Drive to Build a Solid Identity

Building a solid identity is a complicated process. Our parents are partially responsible for our identity, but unfortunately, they do not do much. They just clone their children's identity in their own image; even they are not sure that their children are happy. Stepan Kryvoruchko's parents wanted him to be a good member of the collective, but he had his mind focused on something else. He rejected the blueprint they designed for him and wanted to find his own way. No one else can possibly tell if his way was better or if he would have benefited more by staying with his parents. Only if he is happy with *self* and his life may he tell that the result is good.

Professor Kryvoruchko loves his wife, but he was also very glad that she was helping his child to be a Jew. She was chosen from both sides. Stepan Kryvoruchko had a father who was chosen, but his mother was ethnically not chosen. Because his mother was not chosen, in the Orthodox Jewish law he was not chosen either. If his mother practiced Christianity but had a Jewish ethnicity, he still would be 100 percent chosen. Historically, the Jewish race through hundreds of generations has passed ethnicity to children only through mothers.

Stepan Kryvoruchko got along with his wife. He allowed her the freedom to enjoy her friends and surroundings. His wife spoke English, French, and Hebrew, and she always had friends around her who spoke several languages. She was involved in charity organizations that were raising money for Israel. She also was a happy woman who expected her first child.

Stepan Kryvoruchko was enjoying his life in Montreal, where destiny brought him another challenge. He was meeting a sailor who decided to embrace the Western lifestyle and urgently needed help. For a sailor his actions were crucial. This meeting gave him a boost for the arising of his own identity. He was able to identify and unify his fragments, which were the saviors and protectors of the goodness. His identity was unifying a significant amount of his own fragments, which have the strength to function as a group and provide congruent responses.

Moses was taking his nation from Egypt and wanted his people to unify with the world as equal and free. They were splitting from slavery and from the collective mentality of slaves. In Egypt they were hiding their true identity behind the collective stereotypes. In the desert they searched for forty years for their own identity to be free. Similarly, Professor Kryvoruchko's identity emerged as a survivor from the brainwashing of the propaganda, which was luring him to be like everyone else. He was open to distinct experiences. He was answering the questions of who he is and why he exists. He was embracing the unification of his fragments to become solid and free.

World Leaders are Affected by Splitting and Unifying Forces

The contrasting subconscious forces inside their psyche are affecting world leaders in the same way they are affecting ordinary individuals. In the world leaders' psyche, as well as in every other psyche, the forces, which characterize identity, are splitting, and unifying. Our identity depends on significant amounts of united fragments and our relationship to the rest of our fragments. Part of our united fragments has the structure, which is striving to unify with the rest of the fragments through dialog. The other structure continues splitting our fragments with the same goal of unification, and the third one is functioning as the combination of splitting and unification.

As leaders, we are inspiring the followers whose structure of psyche is similar to ours. We may belong to any political affiliation. We are the products of our psychological structure, where ideology is only a tool. By energizing the followers with big causes we desire to expand our structure on others. Our subconscious goal is to spread out and motivate our followers to reorganize their psyche's structures. Abraham Lincoln was a leader who united his country over a very important cause. His cause was only a tool for unification. He pardoned the unbelievers who disagreed with his cause. With his leadership ability he was able to build a structure, which is still unifying the energy of the citizens.

Some leaders were imposing a completely alien psychological structure on the population. In the past history before the collective, the country had a clear desire for unification. It produced many leaders to lead the unification with the West as well as with the East. Unfortunately, this was a forceful type of unification. The trend was present through the centuries. Suddenly, the new trend was a creation of splitting structure. The splitting started a long time ago until it became apparent. The splitting brought out strong leaders, and they found many justifications for splitting.

Under rule of the radical collective our country had a big history of internal splitting. The leaders put a significant part of the population of the country in working camps. This trend continued and reached the absurd. Under the splitting leadership, half the country's population became informants for the secret police. Because the splitting type of leadership is more vulnerable to the storms and turbulence of the time, the splitting leaders pretended they were unifiers with the goal of building a big collective. They were preparing the followers to be strong in the moment of historical clashes. During the wars, the collective was pretending that it was preserving unification. In reality, the collective was only testing its ability to dominate.

Because of the fears of the tyranny of the collective, the citizens of the distinct countries are carefully choosing their leaders, who are winners and survivors together. They have the splitting and unifying tendencies. They lead and help their followers acquire a survivor's identity. They are exhibiting the ability to excite with a cause. They are providing attractive goals, and have the capacity to move forward. As leaders, our ability begins with the organization of our psyche, where we display our strong talent to organize our fragments into a clear identity. Our leadership contains skills that are inspiring our followers dealing with stimulations in a consistent manner. We are convincing our followers that presented structure is beneficial. We are uniting their psyches with the notion of the purpose and cause.

The structure of our psyche is affected by many forces, which include a genetic predisposition and our ability to be sharpened by environmental needs. Some leaders do not want a meeting but just want unification by all means and to build a big collective. Others, the opposite, want to split from the collective. Between the leaders with unification and splitting abilities are some who really want their followers to live in a better world, and also many villains and tyrants. The majority of the leaders are distinctive individuals. They have a special organization of their psyche that exhibits the ability to motivate followers. Throughout our history we have seen many leaders with the sincere desire to unify individuals through meeting. They are worshipped in history and their ideas are alive. Those leaders have many followers. The leadership with an organization that is striving for meeting has the force to be considered a stable one. The most cherished leaders are the ones who use meetings and dialogs to unite their country. Unfortunately, those leaders are not always appreciated by others who have different political views. Just like Abraham Lincoln, the leaders get assassinated. Only after their death do they get admiration and love from their country's population, and admiration is not affected by opposite political affiliations.

Leaders with a Splitting Type of Leadership

The contrasting forces in our psyche organizations create certain types of leaders who are the unifiers, the splitters, and a combination of unifiers and splitters. Our leadership structure, which has the splitting function, is completely opposite of the unifying type. As splitters we do not use meetings and dialogs. As splitters, sometime we appear as unifiers, because often we agitate one group against another with the goal of unifying everyone under our leadership. The splitters are a form of controlling leadership. We control by splitting and by agitating others. By making others feel incomplete and cheated we are easily installing the need for protection. Our leadership of splitting is not mature enough. We are not tolerant of the fact that the followers are free. We are not allowing unification with the dissimilar forces of the universe.

Our splitting structure represents us as leaders who doubt the stability of the presented surroundings and the sincerity of our followers. We are suspicious and unforgiving. We do not believe in meetings and dialogs. We need lots of reassurances to satisfy our feelings of insecurity. We predict the worst scenarios of disasters and prevent imaginable crises by creating destructive turmoil. Our fears are that a worse time is ahead. To cope with our fears we create many rules to screen nonbelievers.

Our splitting structure is unstable and requires a lot of excessive force from us as the leaders. When we are characterized by splitting leadership organization, we are putting the main emphasis on controlling, ruling, and enforcing a tyranny. We are not concerned about the feelings of our followers. We are monsters, but we are also very vulnerable to revolts and our flammable ideas do not survive for long. As leaders of the splitting organization, we are vulnerable to takeover of our psyche by the fragments of troublemakers and villains. We understand that something is wrong with us and are very sensitive to criticism. Our type of leadership is producing a lot of the villains and dictators. As leaders with splitting abilities we are feared and hated.

Some Leaders Represent The Mixed Structure of Splitting and Unification

Many successful world leaders have the mixed leadership structure, which allows appropriate time to endorse splitting, but in changed circumstances emphasizes unification. They have the psyche that tolerates split and encourages unification. The organization of the psyche with contradictory tendencies somehow shows more flexibility than other structures. This structure produces a lot of intermediate and also significant leaders, who are real survivors. By being flexible, the leadership structures of split and unification are presented more than other psyche organizations. The structure with unification and split tendencies is constantly overcoming many challenges, and is less susceptible to falling apart under stress. This leadership organization is represented by characters who would not give in to any pressure and whose main function is to survive. They often deliberately put *self* in a vulnerable situation, deriving pleasure from being survivors and of avoiding bad repercussions. These leaders are not breakable by crisis because their life is a continuous crisis. This leadership represents leaders who are not tyrants and are not villains. The splitting and unification tendencies help many leaders become significant players in human history and be remembered by followers and respected for their deeds.

Internal Strength is Characteristic of A Solid Identity

With a solid identity we feel good about *self*. We do good things for others. We are generous, have strength to resist selfishness, and express concern for other people's well-being. In Montreal, Canada, Stepan Kryvoruchko met a defector who jumped the ship that belonged to the collective. He was on break from his university classes and was sitting on the grass, reading a newspaper in his native language. The park was in front of the university, where a sailor was hiding in the bushes. The sailor saw the newspaper in Stepan's hand and figured Stepan knew his language. The sailor started talking to him.

He disclosed to Stepan that he was in danger and afraid the Canadian authorities would send him back to his ship. Within a couple of minutes Stepan brought the sailor to the students' legal aid office, which was inside the university. Right away the lawyer in the office made a call to the immigration office with information that the sailor did not want to go back to his ship. The legal aid lawyer also called the police and told them that he had a sailor from the collective next to him and that the sailor was afraid his life was in danger. Soon the Canadian immigration officer came and asked the sailor to fill out and sign some papers, and then police arrived and workers from the embassy of the collective.

Boris, the representative of the collective, quickly filed a "missing person" report with the police. "Our sailor was kidnapped by the Fascists," he claimed. "He wants to go with us," he said. Stepan had already called a few of his friends and they were around the sailor. The embassy's workers wanted to grab the sailor, but the students around him did not let them do it. The Canadian police officer and immigration officer were neutral. The workers from the embassy of the collective yelled to the students, "You do not know what a dangerous game you are playing."

Stepan Kryvoruchko knew the danger he was getting into, but did not realize yet how big the danger was. He was very vulnerable because he had parents in the collective and the secret police of the collective had the power to retaliate by hurting his parents, but despite the danger he was unshakably on the sailor's side. The desire to help another human being without any benefits for *self* and despite perceived danger to *self* is characteristic of a solid identity. In this moment Stepan did not care that his life was in danger. He felt good about *self,* and this feeling would not allow him to betray and deceive anyone.

Some Fragments in Our Psyche are Weaker than Others

When we are checking the responses of our psyche, we observe that some of them are strong and others are weak. The sailor, Andrusha, was impulsive and naïve. He was not strong and needed help. He was not looking for ways to leave the collective for good, but just wanted to see what freedom looked like. When Andrusha decided to sign up for an assignment to sail abroad with a tourist ship, he got his job with one condition—that he would secretly listen to passengers and report their conversations to an officer from the secret police. The desire to see the West was so strong that Andrusha agreed. Without this condition he would not be able to sail on any foreign cruises of the collective.

The passengers on the ship did not know that Andrusha was fluent in five languages. In his presence they talked free and carelessly. Andrusha hated his assignment. He hated all the structure of following, listening, and reporting. Because his father was a policeman, he lived from childhood with despising this kind of life. He did not want to be a spy. He also did not want to betray anyone. Most important, he was concerned about the well-being of the passengers on the cruise ship, who trusted him.

In his home he knew a lot about spying. Being the son of a high-ranking security officer and also a newlywed, he did not have any intention to defect. His wife, the daughter of a security bureaucrat, shared his desire to be free from the control of the collective. They understood others. From early childhood they were instructed to keep quiet and not talk much, because the wrong word would affect their fathers' jobs as security officers. Only families with connections to state security know how uncomfortable it is to be watched all the time. Just like Andrusha's grandfather, his father was working for state security. Andrusha and his wife compared their life to that of a squirrel in a cage. They always felt isolated.

They were jealous of the commoners, who were traveling abroad and talking to anyone they wanted.

Andrusha went to a good school, where children of bureaucrats were studying, but other children knew his father was a policeman and avoided him. It was the same situation in the sailor's school. He did not have the right to invite anyone home without getting clearance from his father. The life of the secret police operatives and their families showed incredible duality. They appeared to be the hunters, but at the same time they were the prey in their own homes. Andrusha was not a fighter. He was very honest and naive. He was good and sincere, but he did not have the strength to stand up for his beliefs. Andrusha was confused and possibly did not resist his impulses. To be stronger and to have dialog between his fragments he needed to identify them.

The Fragmentation Affecting Our Self-Esteem

The feeling of low and inadequate *self*-esteem is characterized by internal feelings. Some individuals feel good about *self* and some are always annoyed and dissatisfied with *self*. The feelings of satisfaction and dissatisfaction do not come from the outside. It is a big mistake when we think that the resentments we experience and other feelings come from outside of self. Resentments are always inside of us. The environment may well trigger those feelings to come out. Those feelings are previously formed responses, and they are in the form of fragments.

Fragmentation is the reason why our responses are dissimilar to those of others. Our responses are formed by our genetics and life experiences. If as children we learned how to fear, then when the fragments from childhood take over, we experience unreasonable fears. When we are facing a life-threatening situation and our paralyzing fears prevent us from making a sound decision, we are exhibiting a sign of fragmented identity. To overcome our fears and make a right decision we have a dialog with the fearful fragment, calming down and focusing on the problem.

Because of fragmentation, we easily give up hope in a crisis, and do not want to use any other responses besides submission. The notion of giving up in a crisis is another sign of our fragmented identity. The fragment, which responds with hopelessness and helplessness, takes over our entire psyche. When our response is incongruent with the real situation, we are producing a sign of fragmented identity. The quick change of our dominant fragments is a sign of the loose fragment's connections.

When we have fragmented identity, we usually are putting up with our low *self*-esteem and our low *self*-worth. We are not solving our problems and do not generate responses congruent with the situation. We are suffering from low *self*-confidence, are not making decisions for *self*, experiencing our inadequacy, hate, and lack of ambition. Our *self*-confidence is increased when we have the ability to reinforce our fragments, which do not have the strength to provide responses that are congruent with our situation, with the more functional fragments. Our *self*-respect is lifted only by responses that are congruent with the situation, our ability to deal with a crisis, and our capacity to confront anxiety and paralyzing fears. When our life becomes more thorny, the fragments that are more congruent with stimuli take over our psyche, handling situations in an appropriate manner and solving our problems. With solid identity we rely on *self* and make sound decisions and find solutions to various problems.

The Dialog With Members of The Collective

Stepan Kryvoruchko was raised in a collective state and had a few fragments, which represented a collective. Somehow he learned to deal with those fragments. As soon as he left the collective his psyche organization was changing. We know it is impossible to have genuine dialog with members of a radical collective, because the identity in the collective is built on pretension and primitive stereotypes. We may have dialog only with individuals who have the quality to embrace differences, but with the collective we can only negotiate. In dealing with Andrusha, the collective rejected the negotiations and wanted to use only manipulation and confrontation. Even the sailor did not present to the collective any risk of losing some valuable information, but nevertheless the secret police by all available means wanted to get the defector back on his ship. They did not want any precedent of an easy defection for other sailors. The representatives of the collective were guarding their subjects. The terrible secret police of the collective, the most feared organization in the world, were represented by the suppressing forces in Andrusha's psyche the same way as in every member of the collective.

For his part, in his mind, the sailor resisted the message from the collective, which spoke with his father's voice: "Remember, Andrusha! You are not an ordinary Jo-Shmack. You had a good life in the collective. You were in the best school in the city of St. Petersburg. You did not live in the slums but in front of the Hermitage. You enjoyed the best summer camps for elite children on the picturesque Black Sea. You attended prestigious Dzerjinskaya sailor school. You always had private tutoring and as a result you speak five languages fluently. You are just fresh from the sailor school, and you right away get the privilege to sail abroad." For Andrusha these words were blaming him for being ungrateful and selfish.

Meanwhile, Andrusha felt guilty that he had defected, but he also knew that he would not go back voluntarily. He did not see any possibility of having dialog or even negotiation with his father. His defection was his declaration that he had the right to be free. In his mind Andrusha answered to his father, "I do not want to go back to the ship. I am not spying anymore on the tourists, monitoring their conversations and reporting them to the secret police. Nobody kidnapped me. I am defecting from your beloved collective, to Canada." He declared a split from the collective to his independent *self.* Several times the embassy workers were grabbing the sailor but the police interfered and allowed the sailor, surrounded by students, to leave the legal aid office. He was free and had power to have dialogs between his fragments.

The identity may need to unify the fragments, but with some fragments dialog is impossible. We cannot use force. We are unifying the fragments, which want dialog. We may not push anyone to be involved in a dialog, and this is a needed precaution. We are looking only for fragments that are willing to have a dialog, because real unification includes meeting through dialog. Instead of dialog we still have weight to have negotiations. For example, we may not have negotiation with the fascist party, but we may negotiate with someone who has fascist-party membership but still has human feelings and perhaps has saved many lives. If many no fascists had saved many desperate lives, as did fascist Oskar Schindler, then probably we would not have seen so many dead in the gas chambers and concentration camps.

The same criteria apply to secret police of the collective when we are having a dialog with a human and honest part of the secret police. The ex-secret policeman ended up being a very popular president and prime minister of the new country, which is free from the radical collective. The president, who in the past reinforced the stereotypes of the collective, now is supporting the liberation. We are having a dialog with anyone who shows human feelings, compassion, and a desire to experience a dialog and have a meeting.

The Solid Identity is Manifesting Self

Despite the fact that his parents were in the collective and were vulnerable to retaliations from the secret police, the courageous Stepan Kryvoruchko was saving the sailor and manifesting a solid identity. Stepan's relatives were very comfortable in the collective after years of struggles and adjustments. Their decision to go along with the system paid off lavishly. They knew the ruling structure was restrictive, but for them it provided needed stability and order. Stepan's parents had lived through the war and anarchy of the war and were happy even with a minimum of stability. Solid identity is always tested on the resistance to split, because when identity is broken, it is not solid anymore. Often, we are pretending that we have a solid identity, but only the really solid identity has the strength to face the uncovered challenges.

Stepan, being a warrior and a son of a warrior, could not overlook the suffering of another soul and betray anyone because of his own fears. He, like a knight of previous centuries, was ready to save anyone who asked for his protection. To the end of the collective the secret police were vicious and unpredictable. At this time everyone was afraid of the secret police and their retaliatory practices. The meeting between Andrusha and Stepan Kryvoruchko was a real meeting of wandering souls. This kind of meeting had influence to build a strong identity. A meeting of souls may be everywhere. It does not matter if the meeting is in the outside world when we meet someone or inside of our psyche when we are writing an imagined story. It later became known that the sailor belonged to the upper class of privileged and did not have any materialistic reasons for defection. He was following his heart and his desire to be free.

In the workers' paradise the police operatives had always followed Andrusha because his father was a ranking secret police officer and knew many state secrets. On the ship the sailors were constantly watched too. When the ship docked in Montreal, the sailors were allowed to go ashore in groups of three. It was insulting to have to walk together everywhere, even to the bathroom, and to watch others. Andrusha was in charge of a group of three sailors. As soon as he saw the happy faces of vendors and buyers in shops, he spontaneously decided to defect. At the first opportunity when other sailors were busy buying some merchandise, he left the store undetected. He ran as fast as he could and looked for a place to hide. He was hiding in the park when he flagged a man reading a newspaper in his language.

Andrusha needed to initiate a real dialog quickly with anyone who might be his savior, because his life was in danger. He met the right one at the right time. Someone who is running to help if another is in despair. The question is, who needs whom more? The savior is discovering *self* as a strong human being with a solid identity. He is helping the one who is in despair despite the danger to *self*. The desire to save another soul is increasing the strength of identity and under duress is speeding up the process of unification in his psyche.

Dialog and Manipulation

The radical collective wants to unite members too, but without meeting and dialog. It is manipulating our psyches. Real unification requires that all sides be free and get unified without any manipulations and that the individuals get involved in the dialog only because they want the dialog to happen.

Stepan Kryvoruchko was helping the sailor get settled in Montreal and fight nostalgia. They became friends. The sailor told Stepan, "You are the only one in the whole universe I am trusting. My family is ashamed of me and my father probably disavowed me, but I do not care. I received letters from my parents. They are urging me to return. They promised me there would not be any reprimands for my defection. They are saying that I would be free and would be allowed to continue working in my field. Let's think that they are right and I would not be jailed, which I doubt. I know for sure that by paying for my defection I would need to spy on all of my friends and colleagues and to report all my conversations with them to the secret police. Thank you. I did enough dirty work for the secret police and I have had it up to my neck. Thank you again. I want to live here, like everybody else around me. I do not want to report on my friends and coworkers. I also want to be in Canada. I cannot understand, why is it a big crime to live in Canada?"

Very soon the sailor found a nice apartment and bought a car. The embassy sent him a barrage of letters from his parents and his wife. The sailor was questioned by the Royal Canadian Mounted Police (or Mounties) but did not tell them anything about the secret services. The Canadians were not very comfortable with the negative attention from the embassy of the collective, because the embassy was threatening. Canadian authorities did not want to be involved in the politics of the collective. They did not want any negativity that may possibly be brought to the city because of the sailor's defection. They were tired of the petitions from the embassy, which demanded that they send the sailor back home. The exchange of tourists and ships was in jeopardy.

The most vocal was Boris, an embassy man, who had a lot of connections in Montreal. He was talking to the Mounted Police, the mayor of Montreal, and members of the city council. He implied that the sailors in Canada were not protected enough from enemies and that fascists were kidnapping them. The forces of splitting were applying manipulation techniques by lying and deceiving the Canadian authorities. The lies and manipulations were not getting together with genuine dialog, but manipulators had the capacity to skillfully mislead people into thinking they wanted a dialog.

The embassy was projecting feelings of sincere caring for the sailor and manipulating Canadian authorities into believing they had legitimate concerns, which was a lie. Genuine dialog and manipulation do not exist together.

One Force Fools The Other by Pretending

The forces of splitting are fooling another side by pretending they are having interest in a dialog only because they did not have influence achieve unification. In the process of dialog two sides must be involved that are equally interested in the process. When the real dialog happens, the unification of the fragments is observed, and the forces of splitting weaken. When forces of splitting do not have the strength to succeed, they are using the new approach for retaliation and splitting.

One day Andrusha saw a middle-aged woman coming to the door of his home and recognized his mother. His mother was brought to Montreal to persuade Andrusha to come back to the collective. His mother stayed with him for one week. She begged her son not to be too stubborn, to not talk back and tease the angry embassy workers. She mentioned that one of the embassy workers, Boris, somehow appeared angrier than the others. Despite the fact that she was the wife of a high-ranking security officer who spent all his life fighting the enemies of the state, Boris was yelling at her. He was insinuating unbelievable lies, and eventually insulted her with accusations that she was an unfit parent. He acted in front of her as a model citizen who was angry because someone was breaking the rules. He yelled that her son was a disgrace to his beloved collective.

Andrusha's mother was not afraid of Boris. She answered him that she still loves her son. She knew Boris was exaggerating and that her son is an honest and very gentle young man. She only mentioned to Boris that her son would not talk in such an aggressive way to a woman. Nevertheless, she was surprised by the intensity of his anger. She even tried, but without any success, to calm him down. She felt that, for some unexplained reason, Boris took Andrusha's defection very strangely. When Boris talked, it sounded like Montreal was only his city and that Andrusha defected with a goal to somehow hurt him. It was strange that even when he sounded as if he was overreacting, he seemed sincere.

She also met many of Andrusha's friends who were recent immigrants. They had left the collective because they were Jews, the minorities, and had ways to leave legally. At that time it was impossible for members of the dominant ethnicity to emigrate. This was the main reason why her son jumped ship instead of legally leaving the collective. The new immigrants were very proud of what they had done, did not feel any shame, and were not afraid. She believed that soon everyone would be able to emigrate.

When Andrusha's mother left him and went back to the collective, she thought the commotion would calm down very soon. She hoped Andrusha would be happy in Canada and eventually, would be able to be reunited with his wife. Apparently, it was not to be. The commotion was not calming down. Andrusha's mother did not know this was the last time she would see her son alive. All the merits that her husband deserved did not work. When the techniques of patting the shoulders and appearing nice were not effective, the embassy's workers had many other methods. Despite their modern look and appearance of sincerity, when the desired goal was not achieved, they were using the old methods, which had proved effective. The forces of splitting were planning the physical association. She also did not know that Boris was the man who demanded the killing of her son. In his report he articulated that no one is above the law and that big bosses needed to watch their offspring or be punished.

The Killing of The Fragment

Killing someone is the process of complete elimination, but the fragment in our psyche is not possible to kill. The fragment lives as long as our psyche is functioning. In real life Andrusha was killed, but in Professor Kryvoruchko's psyche he is alive as long as the professor's psyche exists. The fragment, which represents the killed one, is alive in our psyche and appears in our responses. When we interact with the fragment, which represents the significant one, we feel strong emotions. We are not only grieving after his death, but are also putting together all the special memories of him. In other words, in our psyche we are automatically creating a fragment that will represent him.

One fragment of our hero's psyche is Andrusha, who is surrounded by very painful emotions. The tragedy happened when Andrusha had already lived in Canada for more than a year. He had a well-paid job as manager of a bowling club. Although he was not talking to anyone about his ties to the collective's secret police, the commotion inside and outside of him did not calm down. He continued to have disturbing telephone calls from Boris and other embassy workers. He was very sensitive and had a lot of premonitions of perceived danger. Before his death he did not feel safe, and he could not stop his worries. He felt that something ugly would happen to him. He disclosed to Stepan Kryvoruchko, "I do not feel safe. I feel that someone is watching me all the time. I know this feeling because back at home it was the same. As a child of a secret police officer I was always watched. I hate to be watched. I know that Canadians are not doing it. I know who is watching me. Why won't they leave me alone? Otherwise I am feeling happy here."

Several times the sailor said to Kryvoruchko, "I did not tell anything to the Canadian Mounties because I am afraid the collective may have a mole over there." He continued, "I love freedom and I hate to be scared. I know exactly what kind of torture the secret police is capable of inflicting on me, but I am ignoring them. I hated my father because he was one of them. He probably did not realize it, but he always scared me. He wanted me to be one of them and to spy on the passengers of the ship. He liked scaring and using others as robots. Now I realize that the main point of my defection was getting away from my father." Andrusha disclosed that he was happy in Canada but splitting forces perhaps did not tolerate his happiness and were planning to destroy him.

Dialog with Splitting Fragments

When restructuring our psyche, we are appreciating our fragments, which are ready for unification, and in the most efficient way, we are dealing with the splitting fragments. If the virus of radicalization was completely taking over our psyche, we would not have any possibilities of using a dialog. The dialog could be used with a fragment that is splitting from the radical collective. Splitting from something destructive does not prevent us from a dialog with our destiny. Because the splitting forces are part of our psyche, we perhaps have dialog with a splitting fragment.

Our sailor, Andrusha, was splitting from his father's beliefs because he wanted justice for everybody, but his father wanted justice only for the working class. His father was part of the splitting power in his psyche. His father, Ivan, was a cop and also the son of a security official. He was sniffing and snooping around. Andrusha was afraid of his father and of others like his father. When in his school an operative of the secret police approached him and asked him to be an informant, he refused. His father did not understand how Andrusha could possibly refuse the noble task of protecting his country. It took a while for Ivan to understand that nobility exhibits *self* in another way. Whereas Ivan thought that the meaning of nobility was to hold up to his oath, and to protect the working class by any means, his son's feeling of nobility was to be truthful to everyone and protect his and others' personal freedom by any means. The dialog between Andrusha and Ivan was impossible because they did not have any understanding between them.

Andrusha was an idealist and paid for his naiveté with his life. His father, Ivan, was always looking for clues to protect his beloved country. He honestly hated the foreigners who, he assumed, wanted to destroy the first in history, the workers' paradise. To be a boss in his country, he postulated, higher education, family ties, and extraordinary talents were irrelevant. He believed that the most important thing was having fidelity to the cause of liberating the working class. Ivan, as well as his late father, was very dedicated to protecting the existing structure. He did not mind doing any dirty job. He was completely committed to his cause. He also mistakenly believed that he never neglected his family and was a good father to his son. In his opinion he provided his son with everything that was possible in the collective.

From childhood, Andrusha was able to participate in various activities that only the privileged could afford. These activities included figure skating, fencing, swimming, boxing, music lessons, and language classes. All these activities were free in the workers' paradise. Andrusha always had his own room at a time when the collective did not accommodate other members with living space and several families lived in shared apartments with many inhabitants in one room.

If Ivan, in his mind, would be a king, his son was definitely a prince in his kingdom. Every year, in the summer, his wife took his son for a month to the prestigious sanatorium for government officials on the warm Black Sea. The sanatorium was free. The rest of the summer vacations his son spent at their dacha, the family's country house on the shore of the Baltic Sea. When Andrusha declined his father's recommendation to enter the secret police school and wanted to be a sailor, Ivan placed him in the best navy school. Andrusha attended the prestigious sailors' school, named by Dzerjinsky, a father of the secret police in the collective. The school was a military one, but Andrusha did not serve even one day in the navy and was commissioned to a civilian fleet. Ivan sensed that, by having so much comfort, his son got soft and was not dedicated to the cause of the working class. He felt that the comfort made Andrusha a mama's boy. He remembered that a few times his son was beaten up by thugs on the street. His son tried to run away from them but could not, and was crying.

All of his life Ivan never avoided a fight and never cried. When he found out that Andrusha was assaulted by thugs on the street, he told his son to stop crying and instead to use the buckle on his belt. He taught his son how to make a weapon from an ordinary belt with a heavy metal buckle. He trained the boy that by waving the belt around his head he had the power to hit his assailants indiscriminately. Ivan showed his son how to keep the belt far-reaching in his hand, how to swing and erratically hit with the buckle any parts of the offender's body. Only once did Andrusha do exactly what his father told him to do. He used this technique and the assailants ran away. As result a few of the attackers had big bruises on their heads and all the beatings stopped, but he did not feel victorious, because he was regretful that a few boys were injured.

Ivan did not understand how his son could possibly feel sorry for those boys with a few bruises on their heads. He wanted his son to be strong. Several times Andrusha witnessed his father beating thugs on the street because they offended him. Every time it was terrible. His father punched them with his fist, and when they were on the ground, he kicked them. Andrusha was confused about why his father used violence instead of arresting them. If they had insulted him, why was he not incarcerating them? He asked his father this question. Ivan answered that during his work time he arrested only enemies of the state, but that he was teaching other delinquents a lesson in his spare work time. Ivan was not a cruel father, but he was teaching his son to be strong like him. He was a proud man. He came from an honest and somehow naïve family and dedicated his life to serving justice. His father was a security officer and fought the enemies of the state. His father loved and died defending his country. During World War II he was in blockaded St. Petersburg and had an assignment protecting the bakeries against the mob. At that time, no food was left in the city surrounded by the army of the enemies. The citizens of the city received a little ration of nutrition every day. The ration pretended to be a piece of bread and was very small, less than a third the size of a hand. It was not real bread, and did not look real. Inside were very little grain, some grass, and a lot of melted wood, which was boiled and soft. A piece of this bread was enough to keep someone alive. This wooden bread was a ticket to live one more day. A lot of the inhabitants of the city were sick and hungry, and they also had loved ones who were sick and hungry and desperately waiting for a piece of bread. They badly needed this portion. In one area of the city a hungry mob attacked the individuals who were leaving the center and robbed them of their rations. Ivan's father died defending victims from the hungry mob. He was reluctant to use his firearm on the desperate and was killed by the mob.

In contrast, Ivan was not naïve and never hesitated to use his gun, because thugs needed to be taught how to behave. He did it for their benefit, because they did not know how to conduct *self*. All his life he obeyed orders from his superiors. The order implied that he needed to cut out an infection, in the form of betrayal of working class dreams, before it was too late. He did not have a second thought about the validity of this order and never questioned his assignments.

His love for his son, who was part of the unifying forces, helped him with the transformation. He was splitting from the virus of radicalization, but the direct dialog between father and son was not achieved until the son's death. The transformation was not easy, but during transformation Ivan became more flexible. He was learning to understand and appreciate the differences. In the meantime, he started genuine dialogs with his other fragments. Because of his grief, Ivan was thinking deeper and understanding more, and was engaging in a direct dialog with his son. Unfortunately it happened too late. The dialog between father and son became possible only when his son was already dead.

The Splitting Forces Using Killings

The virus of radicalization has a variety of methods to accomplish its goal, which is inflicting pain. Killing is one of the most extreme methods, but one of the most proven and popular in a radical collective. When the splitting forces of a radicalized collective are getting out of control, they are using killing. They cannot stop and are doing it again. Splitting forces are numb to other members' feelings and hurt them. It appears that splitting forces are deriving strength when they are destroying happiness.

Andrusha became a target of the splitting forces. They presented him as an enemy of the collective, because he did not prove to them the purity of his thoughts. Every citizen of the collective was a target. Even though Andrusha appeared to be happy and thought he had made the right decision by defecting, he had suspicions that he was a target. His happiness did not last long, and soon he was killed. It officially appeared that the sailor died in a car accident.

Stepan Kryvoruchko was shocked. He remembered Andrusha's premonitions and was not convinced that the cause of the sailor's death was a car accident. He believed his friend was killed, but not by a car. Something was not right. Before his death, the sailor had called him from the hospital and mentioned that physically he was feeling good but that he was afraid of secret police operatives. He did not feel safe. He had suspicions that operatives might kill him in the hospital. Now Stepan felt sorry that he had not believed his friend, who had been in danger. He did not see his friend's offenses against the collective as so severe that the operatives of the secret police would risk assassinating him. Somehow, he assumed that the ugly guys from the collective who were killing innocent people were only in scary movies. He thought his friend was exaggerating things.

After his friend's death Stepan concluded that his friend had not imagined danger and had been killed. He also knew it was possible that he would not prove it. He called the police to share his suspicions with them. He asked for a homicide investigation but no one took him seriously. Meanwhile, Stepan revealed his doubts to a few other acquaintances. Boris, through his channels, somehow found out that Stepan did not believe that Andrusha's death was caused by the car accident. Perhaps Andrusha was right and Boris had a rat inside the Canadian police who was selling information. After Andrusha became a victim of the splitting forces, the splitting machine was in need of more victims. Because of the perceived danger, Boris targeted Stepan Kryvoruchko to become the next victim. The splitting machine wanted more killings.

Ivan's Structure

Ivan was part of splitting forces, but his strong emotions moved him away from the radicalized collective and brought him closer to having real dialog with forces of unification. After the tragedy of losing his son, Ivan changed. His splitting forces used manipulation to achieve their goals, but did not have the strength to succeed. Ivan had a hard life, but he was able to establish his place in society. He had done everything to become important and he succeeded. He was a guardian of the workers' paradise. As a young man he helped his father, who was a role model for him. Andrusha may have easily continued in the same direction.

Ivan was in terrible shock, as if his own life had come to an end. His son did not leave him a grandchild. Ivan also did not believe that his son's death was just an accident. As an operative of the secret police, he knew that accidents did not spontaneously kill a defector; someone had ordered it. His son's death was a horrible dream from which there was no chance of awakening. He continued his struggle because he did not understand why Andrusha had defected. Ivan's anger was against those who had taken his son away from him. At that time, the only answer for him was that the enemy of the country had seduced his son to defect. In his grief Ivan did not accept that he may have played a big part in his son's defection and that he had not fulfilled his obligations to his son. Ivan was stuck with one question: what had gone wrong? He might not be able to figure it out. He did not blame *self*, because his son had everything that a young one might dream of.

His son had also had a very attractive wife who admired him. They were a very nice couple and had the ability to have beautiful kids. Now Andrusha's wife, a young woman, was a widow. Her face was a dark color after all the tears she had cried, and she looked like an old woman. How had Andrusha had the audacity to give up everything? What was the reason? Eventually Ivan concluded that, being new to the West, his son had acted immaturely, was carried away with his impulses, and was blinded by his emotions.

The Canadian authorities informed him of the accident. His son had been a passenger in the backseat of a four-door sedan together with two other passengers. In the front were the driver and another passenger. A disoriented driver had crossed from the other side of the road into the opposing traffic and hit the car in which Andrusha was a passenger. The hit was exactly at the place where Andrusha was sitting. An ambulance took Andrusha to a nearby hospital for observation. It seems he did not need to be admitted to intensive care and was admitted to regular care, but he suddenly died from respiratory problems. Ivan took the news skeptically that in Montreal, under strange circumstances, his son had died in a car accident. Reading all the information about the accident, he got the feeling that it was an assassination by covert secret agents.

Ivan was confused. As a secret-police officer, he understood that his son, by defecting from his country, had committed an offensive crime, but it was not so severe that it warranted this kind of punishment. He also was sure that his son did not know anything that would have been helpful to the Westerners. Because of strict police security, Ivan never kept at home any official information and did not talk about his business outside his office. Many defectors with more knowledge of state secrets than his son were left alone. He sensed that something was wrong, because considering the nature of the offense, his son definitely did not deserve to be assassinated. Ivan also felt that knowing that Andrusha was his son and knowing of his father's dedication to his country, the secret police must not have authorized an operation to terminate his son.

Ivan knew that something was not coming together in his son's death. If his son had been assassinated, he needed to know the truth about who had ordered it and why. He was sure none of his superiors would approve of assassinating their own children despite the fact that their children were spoiled and dishonest. Presently, their children were alive and well, but his only son, who was a real gentleman, was dead. His son was a sweet boy, and was killed apparently for no valid reason. Ivan vowed, with the memory of his father, that he would get to the bottom of this crime and that the monsters who were involved in Andrusha's wrongful death would be punished. Even in his despair Ivan was still a policeman who knew how to get to the bottom of any crime. As a cop, he was absolutely sure he was acting appropriately by questioning the validity of the accident report from Canada, because it looked fabricated.

For first time in his life Ivan was crying and doubting his superiors, but he knew that his informant, Sam Kaufman, was in Montreal and would get to the bottom of this crime. When Ivan had sent Sam to Canada, he had wanted Sam to be firm with Andrusha and help if he possibly could. After Andrusha's death Ivan ordered Sam to start an investigation into the involvement of foul play and his son's wrongful death. The transition from splitting forces to unification requires the meeting and the real dialog with at least one fragment that is transitional to the unifying forces. Ivan was in the process of understanding his son and of stopping the way he judged his son's decisions. He wanted justice.

The Change in Structure

The structure of our fragment changed when the rigidity gave up, and the plasticity became more visible. The rigidity of our fragment was an indicator of our splitting. Our unbending fragments, which were the slaves of the collective, were the trademark of our splitting forces and were the part of manipulation. The splitting forces around Ivan were engaging in exploitation of his naiveté with a goal of splitting him from the truth and tying him to the collective. The plasticity is opposite of the rigidity and is a part of the unifying forces. Ivan experienced a terrible tragedy. His son died. Only after the death of his son could Ivan have a real dialog with him. Ivan was showing the sign of plasticity when he reevaluated his feelings toward his son. The dialog in his psyche took place because the fragments were not dying. Andrusha is forever part of Ivan's psyche.

Any fragments are parts of our psyche while we are alive. In our psyche the relationships between fragments may change. Very drastic tragedy, such as the death of his son, was affecting Ivan's psyche. His misfortune made him feel miserable. He thought that by being a guard dog and carrying out without any questions the orders from his superiors he had wasted his life for nothing. He knew many of his superiors were heartless bureaucrats and profiteers from their position. Ivan hated to think, but did not have the strength to detach from his thoughts, that by organizing the assassination of his son, someone in his agency had received a promotion or other benefits. These kinds of thoughts were coming to his head. He was deeply hurt, because he had believed that the secret police would never attack their own.

He had already started his own investigation to get the truth out. He understood that whoever had assassinated his son was filled with anger and driven by hate. He did not believe that Andrusha had generated this kind of anger with his defection. Ivan also guessed that the assassins' anger was directed against him. It was possible that someone hated him and had killed his son instead of him. He felt guilty that he had not been able to protect his son. He promised *self* that punishment for the assailant would be severe. He would retaliate as strongly as he could for all the cruelty he was enduring.

Ivan did not blame the system that had created an injustice, because for him the collective was untouchable. He blamed the individuals, who were using bad judgment; in his mind, the collective had nothing to do with their viciousness. Ivan perhaps did not blame the system of the collective, which he had defended all his life, but he was admitting that the components of this system were rotten. Ivan was reevaluating his devotions. This was a sign of plasticity. When we are ready for a dialog, we show the plasticity of our responses. Plasticity is a sign of unification with truth and is essential for our genuine dialog.

Leaving The Splitting Forces

Stepan Luchko was part of splitting forces too but later became part of unification. The transition of the fragment from the splitting to unification is hard but possible. In Canada, Stepan Luchko miraculously met his grandson, Stepan Kryvoruchko, who was named after him. During World War II Stepan Luchko was a partisan, captured by enemies. He was sent to a concentration camp but didn't die. In the concentration camp was a neighbor from his village, who told him that enemies had surrounded the partisans and that his wife and daughter were captured and executed. He took this news very hard. He did not value his life, and wanted to die but take with him as many fascists as he could.

In the camp he did not forget his oath to the collective and was doing the most dangerous assignments. By the command from the center he joined the army of rebellious General Vlasov, who switched sides from one collective to another. General Vlasov surrendered his army to fascists, and in the combat was fighting on the German side. The soldiers in his volunteer army were of the dominant ethnicity and many were prisoners of war. Some of them hated the workers' paradise. A lot of them just did not want to die in prisoner-of-war camps, because their country did not join the Geneva Conventions to regulate humane conditions for prisoners. They were the soldiers who were captured to die in a concentration camp.

Luchko's assignment was documenting atrocities to civilians at the hands of Vlasov's soldiers. Vlasov's soldiers did not participate in punitive actions against civilians. Opposite were the Gestapo and the Village polizies, who had recruits of many ethnicities. They were mainly nationalists, criminals, marauders, and heartless killers. They had a variety of punitive assignments toward civilians. They were dressed in similar fascist clothes. Even Vlasov's army was wearing the same fascist uniform, but had military honor and ethics.

Stepan Luchko got another order to learn about the logistics of military operations of the enemies. With the help of other agents he entered Vlasov's command office by pretending he was working as an orderly. In reality, he was looking for military information. Out of pure luck, he found a map with planned military operations. He regularly checked the garbage and was able to pick up a throwaway copy of the map. When he was cleaning the offices, he collected the carbon papers from all incoming orders and transferred them to his handlers.

Some carbons had important information about planned operations and in many instances helped the antifascist forces to resist an offense.

After the war Luchko did not return to the collective. Following the command from his supervising officer he went to Belgium to work in a coal mine and report on the surviving Vlasov's soldiers. As a military man he did not want to spy on soldiers and felt that he might be more helpful to his motherland in another capacity. He asked for a transfer. He got an assignment to move to Canada and live in Montreal. Before coming to Canada Luchko changed his first and his last names. In Canada he remarried a Ukrainian woman with a daughter. He owned a store, where he sold jewelry and repaired watches. He made a good living and was financially independent. He never asked for any money for his work as a spy. He risked his life in the most dangerous assignments from the collective because he was an old believer and a patriotic man. His store was a meeting place for secret agents.

He loved helping newcomers, and many new immigrants from the collective were coming to his store. His wife always had pirogis, blintzes, and *warenikes,* which are boiled pieces of paste with curd or fruit, ready for his guests. Stepan Luchko was glad to offer Seagram whiskey and Moscow vodka. The unselfish dedication of his life and others like him helped prolong the agony of the collective. Being a spy, Luchko immediately found out that his grandson was in Canada and might be the next target of crazy assassination. The desire to protect his grandson pushed Stepan Luchko to change, by having a genuine dialog with his grandson and joining the forces of unification.

Choosing The Right Forces to Join

We are moving from one collective to another when our splitting forces are pushing us to switch. After adjusting to a new reality the structure of our psyche is not changing. We do not need to forgive the unfortunates, people who end up between the two splitting forces. Were they really enemies? How could we possibly understand them? Evidently, genuine dialog is not possible between two radical collectives. Nevertheless, there are some fragments that were part of splitting forces, and we might possibly negotiate. We are giving credit to our fragments that they were dynamic and looking for something better. To understand misfortune we compare our psyche with theirs.

The majority, which was attached to the fascist collective, is already dead, and perhaps now is the time to acknowledge a few of them. Understanding the opponent is the first rule of getting prepared for a negotiation and revision of our feelings. Often our feelings are too powerful and the pain is so strong that we are not even trying to get through our emotions. The world united against the fascists' collective, and this world unity was a glorious moment in human history. The fighters on the fascists' side became pariahs. The stigma attached to them was that they were the enemy's soldiers and traitors. Now, when only a few are left alive, we are trying to understand those misguided and simple foot soldiers.

Their commander, General Vlasov, was a traitor and collaborator, and his army was fighting on the fascist side. General Vlasov was a naïve and misguided man who made wrong choices. History is unpredictable, and others who make similar choices and become traitors are not always turncoats but sometimes are heroes too. The antifascists, who were splitting from the fascists' collective, had some who were collaborating with Stalin and also did not make the best choice. They chose to be together with the biggest tyranny of all time. Soldiers from Vlasov's army are living in various countries. They are called traitors. They switched from one collective to another. They were associated with the fascists' collective, and many of them were in misery and suffering from feelings of guilt and shame. Their choice was not the best, but our judgment was not very fair either.

Both collectives had an ideology to kill individuality. The structures were very similar and the adjustment did not require change. Several types of soldiers joined Vlasov's army. The first group consisted of the prisoners of war, who were dying in prison camps and did not have any other way to survive but to join Vlasov's army. The Stalinists' collective did not think about the foot soldier and did not sign the Geneva Conventions to protect prisoners of war. Many of the soldiers were abandoned by their own collective. They were forced to make the wrong decision and join another collective. The soldiers in the second group were counted by thousands and joined Vlasov's army because they were nationalists and hated their own torturing collective. They were oppressed and victimized by a vicious regime in their own country.

In their opinion Stalinists' collective was as bloody and as derisive as the fascists were. They joined the fascists as a protest against Stalin's collective. The soldiers in Vlasov's army did not know much about the fascist ideology. Deep in their hearts they did not accept the right of Aryans to rule the world, and did not participate in atrocities. With millions of oppressed in their own country Vlasov's soldiers were desensitized to the fact that the fascists were screening everyone, even their own, for subjugation and annihilation. The fascist ideology was genetically based and glorified the German spirit. Vlasov's soldiers did not have any part in this ideology. The Holocaust, which was directed against the genetically non-Germans, may eventually turn on them too. The main targets were Jews, Gypsies, antifascists, and everyone with a nontraditional sexual orientation.

Similar to Stalinist's collective, fascists had no mercy for anyone. The political opponents were oppressed. Some of the oppressed were Germans and fascists. The loyal and genetically appropriate Germans were called Aryans and were destined to rule the world. They gassed civilians and burned them in crematories. The shadow of the Holocaust and fascist ideology was transferred to Vlasov's army. It was not fair. They were just brainwashed simple foot soldiers who were splitting from one of the torturing collectives to another. Both collectives were built on slave labor, and everyone, indiscriminately, could well become their victim, including fellow comrades. Justifiably, many may argue that Stalinist's collective, as a killing machine, was worse than the fascists'.

Vlasov's army was a part of splitting forces that switched the bad for the worse. The foot soldiers of Vlasov's army paid for it with their future happiness. Some of them were hiding in exile. Many soldiers were killed. They were dying in the labor camps of the victorious collectives. After the war Vlasov was kidnapped by the secret police and killed by the triumphant collective. He was not a vicious man, but mainly a confused man. After many years have passed we may eventually understand the foot soldiers in Vlasov's army.

There are No Winners in The Confrontation Between Forces of Splitting and Unification

When our psyche experiences the confrontation between forces of unification and splitting, the confrontation is not bringing any winners, but only traumatizing and bringing horror to our psyche. As the winners, we are changed too, because from the enemy we copied the characteristics of splitting. During the confrontation our splitting fragments are pushing our psyche to feel hatred and anger. In the same way as the whole outside world, we are making internal choices. Our fragments are splitting, aligning, and grouping together. Inside, we are experiencing a replica of the outside world, including the notion of heaven and hell. The splitting creates turmoil in our psyche and pushes us to join the evil forces. When splitting forces are winning, we are producing evil responses.

There are many evil responses in our psyche. Those responses breed persistently because of our confrontation between splitting and unification. It is unending and the new wickedness is replacing the former. The place of our malice never gets empty and one bad character replaces the previous one. The fact that helped our world to survive is that the villains are not united and always fought each other. When evil feels strong, it is attacking. Evil does not want anyone else to fight his cause. He is paranoid and does not trust others. He is fighting dirty and using unclean methods. In front of evil we do not have the luxury to stay and watch. We need to get united and have our act together.

In the critical moment every choice that contributed to unification against the evil is very important. To survive, we are getting together with the lesser evil and getting help from it. Eventually, because we become united, the dreadful evil with all its rhetoric and incredible pathos gets defeated. We have survived as a result of the alliance of many forces, but the fight is continuing. Our evil lives in our mind. Very soon another evil will come and replace the previous one. In our psyche the evil never die. When we are fighting evil, we are actually fighting *self*. After the defeat of our evil he is still staying in our mind and pushing us to do evil things. The manners of presentation of our splitting responses are always the same. It does not matter if one evil does not look like the other. Its appearance is only a form, but his essence of splitting does not change. Our splitting forces are speaking unrelated words, but the meaning is the same. There are the same splitting forces and they are using the same weapons, such as fears, anger, and panic.

Many of our responses are a collaborative effort of several fragments. We need to remember that our responses are formatted according to the choices of our fragments. Because of our failure to unify our fragments by dialogs and meetings instead of confrontation, the splitting forces are getting reincarnated in diverse forms. Our choices perhaps make us more fragmented or help us to unify our fragments to become solid. Only by understanding our fragments are we taking them away from the splitting influence, having meetings and dialogs.

The Power to Weaken The Splitting Forces

To be a part of splitting forces we need to have a lot of hate and fears inside of us. What happens when we are experiencing love? Because we are not fighting love, our splitting forces are weakened by love and allow the unification with our contradictory fragments. Our love is the sign of unification. Luchko knew a lot of hate. He remembered the hate he had against the enemy for killing his family. The hate made him a spy. He was a soldier and hated the perceived enemy. The common logic is that as soon as hate stops, the soldier is not capable of fulfilling his duties. Soldiers might not kill without hate. In other words the soldier without hate is not a fighter. The soldier is protecting *self* by quickly killing the enemy; otherwise, he would be killed by the other side. In our psyche, simple logic was not working. By request from his superiors Luchko checked everyone who was surrounding our defector, the young sailor. Through his contacts Luchko was able to read the new immigrants' papers and found out that Stepan Kryvoruchko was his grandson.

He also understood that his wife and daughter were alive. He figured out that Stepan Kryvoruchko was the son of his daughter, which meant he was his blood relative. The old soldier was crying all night long. He felt very happy and uplifted. At his request, one of his informants befriended Stepan Kryvoruchko and brought him to his store. He had conversations with Stepan Kryvoruchko and felt very proud of him. He was also proud of his daughter, who had become a medical doctor and was teaching in medical school. He did not tell Stepan Kryvoruchko about their blood connection. Luchko found out that his grandson's wife was pregnant and that very soon he would be a great-grandfather. He also understood that Stepan Kryvoruchko had a sister, his granddaughter, with children. He asked Stepan Kryvoruchko to tell him more about his family, specifically about Stepan's grandmother. What he learned made him think. He needed time to sort out everything and put his thoughts in order. Everything that happened was unbelievable. The first news was that his wife and daughter were alive. His wife was married to his old buddy Alexander Kryvoruchko, who was now Stepan's grandfather. At the same time his daughter was married to Leonid Kryvoruchko, who was the son of his old friend Alexander and was Stepan's father.

Luchko remembered Leonid as a little boy and could not imagine that now the boy was the father of his grandson and granddaughter. He did not know what to feel.

He had dealt with the death of his wife and daughter a long time ago, and now they were alive. His life was so hectic and chaotic that he had completely forgotten his past. Now, when he knew that his wife and daughter were alive, he was envious. Instead of him, Alexander Kryvoruchko had been enjoying the company of his lovely wife, Galena, for a long time and was a father figure to his daughter. His friend had taken everything he loved. To him the whole thing seemed like a bizarre situation. Eventually, he decided not to hate Alexander. There was enough hate in his life. From his grandson he found out that his ex-wife and his daughter had a good life. His daughter, Marinka, had a very good marriage, two children, and a comfortable life. She was a successful doctor and lecturer at a medical school.

His heart was overwhelmed with love. Luchko understood that it was very easy to hate. When we are giving *self* permission to hate, we are shooting down our wisdom. He did not want any hate around him. Luchko knew how to bring *self* to the state of calmness and tranquility and how to stop all the destruction in his mind. Many years before he had learned how to meditate and reflect. He knew the best way to achieve the level of calmness and continued to repeat his mantra. The fact that his wife was married to his friend did not bother him anymore. He was just happy that his wife and daughter were alive. Stepan Luchko had been identified with splitting forces for a long time, but then he experienced love. The moment of transition from splitting to unification was the most important in his whole life.

Splitting Forces Taking Over The Psyche

Stepan Luchko obtained knowledge about immigrants—newcomers—through his new informer, Sam Kaufman, an immigrant who became part of the splitting forces because of his struggles, which brought hate and anger to his life. Sam's childhood was in the western part of the workers' paradise, in the city of Bobruisk, which was populated mainly by Jewish people. He was the younger of two children in the family of a store manager. His father sold merchandise, produced and delivered by illegal factories that were not registered with the government. The merchandise was of good quality, and shoppers thought it even better than merchandise from the government factories. His father made a good living by sharing illegal business, but someone in the chain of dealings implicated him.

Shortly after Sam's birth his father was arrested for embezzling money from the collective. The police confiscated the family's car and jewelry, and threatened them with eviction from their apartment. They were occupying twice the approved limit of personal space, nine square meters per person. In the end the family moved all their furniture into one of the rooms in their apartment and another family moved into the other room. The two families used the same kitchen and bathroom. They built a small hallway to separate their rooms. The two families hated each other. To understand the splitting force we need to put *self* into the opponent's shoes. With his life experiences Sam was not able to escape from hate and anger, which were trapping him in the splitting energy.

Inflicting a Child with Hate

Sam's mother physically abused him. The splitting force requires the presence of hate, and it does not matter where it comes from. Hate is like a disease and is capable of being spread by anyone, including our mothers. Yes, some mothers can be contagious and infect us with negativity and hate. Sam's mother was taking her own frustration and misery out on her child. She was always irritable and he was helpless, hopeless, and very confused. In a small room he did not have any place to hide. His sister occupied one corner of the room. She was always reading books and appeared very busy. She was separating *self* with books and high grades from the outside world. In the room also was his grandmother, his mother's mother. His mother was always arguing with his grandmother. The grandmother tried to defend Sam when his mother was beating him. His grandmother would put her hand over him, getting the first hitting and protecting him. He did not understand why he was punished, but felt guilty. His mother hit him without any explanation.

Sam remembers that he was about five years old when his mother was angry and without any reason pushed him out of the apartment into the backyard. Older and, probably, delinquent children were throwing stones and then all together threw the stones at him. Several of the stones hit his head. He got dizzy, felt sharp pain, and started to cry. It was unjustifiable cruelty, but the boys were laughing. Sam wanted some comfort and, perhaps, some justice. He entered his apartment crying and found his mother sitting in the dark. He ran to his mother and all of a sudden received a slap on his face. His mother continued to slap him and yelled, "Stop crying! Otherwise I will kill you!" He did not know how to defend himself from his mother and was always afraid. He was wetting his bed. His mother, who was supposed to care for him, inflicted pain and the feeling of helplessness from being betrayed by someone who was the most significant person in his life. Sam's mother initiated the process of splitting his psyche. As a result he did not hate his mother but he hated everything about *self*.

The Victim's Role

The victim's role causes the development of the fragmented identity. Some call the fragmented identity broken. Sam's identity could perhaps be compared to a broken mirror that had been hit with a hammer. His fragments were lying motionless, without any interaction between them. As pieces of the mirror were reflecting in all dissimilar directions without focusing on anything in particular, the remains of his psyche were broken into pieces and his responses were incongruent. Sam was very sensitive. He felt that his biological field was very weak and that everyone had the strength to bump in. The children at school touched and pushed him as often as they wanted. His mother, when she was in an angry mood, waved her hands in front of his face, and he was very scared. He did not have any good feelings about *self*. He felt that others had strength around them but that he did not have any of his own. Sometimes he tested his power. He would stare at other children's backs and repeat in a low voice, "Turn! Turn!" No one ever turned.

It seemed that all the children ignored him. Sam was responsive to children staring at his back and always turned when anyone looked at him from behind. It appeared that he did not have any protective shield and was defenseless. Why was he able to record energy when other children were not recording his? He did not want to explore another possibility about his sensitivity and lifting his spirit. If he wanted to feel better, he may perhaps be more removed from reality. He may attribute his sensitivity to a third eye on the back of his head, which is a form of the energy receiver. Unfortunately for him, he did not want to find any other ways to feel better. He was sad and negative. He also had an opinion that Jews were sad and miserable and it was bad luck that he was one of them. He felt that they also had spiteful humor. He was ashamed to be a Jew and was disappointed and gloomy that he did not belong to the dominant ethnic group. He loved them. He always felt that they were the real parts of the collective but that he was not. He wanted to be a part of the collective. He believed the dominant ethnic group was strong, generous, and romantic and would defend their own like in the movies. He loved movies where he could see many astonishing-looking boys and girls with pure Slavonic souls who were always smiling and happy. Usually, Sam was confused and unhappy. Movies were his only escape from sadness.

He daydreamed a lot. In his daydreams he pretended a lot. He entertained images that he had died in the service of the collective and everyone was crying, sorry that they had treated him so badly, and saying at his funeral that he was a boy of the dominant ethnic group. Sam's fragments did not interact. His psyche was pretending that, instead of disassembled fragments, he had a solid construction. To support the fictitious claims his psyche added fictitious parts, which were responses to fictitious beliefs. He believed he was not equal to the dominant members and needed to prove that he was good. His identity was fragmented and his victim's role was the cause of his unhappiness. He also was at a complete loss, because his psyche was producing confusing responses. He did not understand where those responses came from. He also had very low self-esteem. The trauma that Sam suffered in his childhood caused him to have a fragmented identity.

The Fragmented Identity is A Multigenerational Process

The split may be a multigenerational process. The breakdown of Sam's identity started many generations before. Just like her own mother, Sam's mother came from a big family. She was youngest of eleven children. Her father died in a work-related accident when she was three years old. The family was poor. They lived in Siberia, in the city of Votkinsk. The city was dull, despite the fact that it was the birthplace of the famous composer Peter Ilyich Tchaikovsky. Sam's mother was afraid of her older siblings, who were very abusive.

Her mother was illiterate and did not have any profession. She cleaned houses and did laundry for the neighbors. She could not buy shoes for every child. The weather in Siberia was very harsh and the little girl did not have the strength to go barefoot outside. The one pair of shoes was for three little girls, and they were always fighting for shoes to go out from their apartment. As a little girl, Sam's mother did not have a chance to get shoes for herself and to play outside the house. Her sisters beat her up and called her names. When her tired mother got home after a day of cleaning houses, she did not have the strength to deal with the various complaints from her children. She was always depressed. She cried from helplessness and to get bitterness out of her system. When we have a fragmented identity, we appear broken. We have our psyche broken into pieces that do not interact with others. We are producing similar children, who continue indulging in the destructive patterns of previous generations. From an early age Sam's mother understood that she did not have the power to get justice for *self*. Sam's mother's psyche was broken into pieces. She did not have any protection, and her responses were blind anger. She was not able to have congruent responses to life stresses. She was daydreaming about a safe, sheltered environment. She knew she did not have the power to take care of *self*, and she wanted a rich man to take care of her. She was ready to give up her independence and was searching for someone to lean on.

She was good-looking and decided to marry, without waiting long for a rich guy, whoever came first, and then live in luxury. She was introduced to a man who was perceived to be rich by the standards of the city of Votkinsk. He was a visitor who flashed his money in front of her. She married, despite the objections of her family, who knew that she did not love him. With her husband she moved to Bobruisk, Byelorussia, and had two children. She had a good life for five years. Her husband bought her furs and jewelry. She also had a live-in maid to help with the household.

After her husband's arrest, she could not accept the reality that her life of privilege had ended and she was poor again. When she had married a rich man, she had sincerely believed that her days in poverty were over. Some irrational beliefs were helping her create fictitious fragments and build an identity based on pretentiousness. The first storm was breaking the construction to pieces. In the same way as her mother, Sam's grandmother, who avoided dealing with stress and did not protect her daughter from older siblings, she dealt with stress in a dysfunctional way. She became helpless. She did not give Sam a chance to build a solid identity. The multigenerational trend may be a part of the splitting forces, which eventually leads to fragmented identity in the offspring.

Dealing with A Trauma

As victims we avoid touching places of the psyche that were traumatized and pretend those places do not exist. It becomes clear that our injuries were causing a lot of emotional pain, anger, and shame, but we are not dealing with those feelings. This is the reason we detach from painful experiences. To completely detach from terrible experiences, we get involved in the process of splitting. We have the impression that our psyche has a big hole in the middle, as though a big hammer had hit a mirror. To avoid the pain and to cover up the hole in the psyche, we fabricate fabulous and fictitious stories. It appears that we are trying to put a patch on our hole. It means that on the subconscious level we made a big effort to protect *self*.

We use lies for a better impression. Those lies are not for financial gains or any materialistic purposes but are only a way to escape the harsh truth. We fabricate our lies only to cover up the fragmented identity and make the impression of having a solid psyche. We need our life of pretension to protect our traumatized psyche. By pretension we avoid the truth of being a victim. We use the assailant's behavior to cover up the hole. We operate on the false beliefs that, by acting like the assailant did, we look tough and will be protected. Many abusers were previously abused, and many bullies cover their inadequacies with their behavior.

Bullies use violence and victimize for many diverse reasons. One of the reasons may be that they enjoy power that they lacked in their family of origin. Another reason is that they may fear appearing weak, because they were victims. Many of us, after being victimized, have transferred to becoming bullies. We were waiting for the justice to happen, but never got it. We are displaying the misplaced anger. We also have the subconscious desire to prove to the world that we do not deserve harsh treatment. We do not know how to achieve our goals and just act as if nothing unusual happened because the violence is universal. There are many other dysfunctional ways to cover up our trauma.

The Process Beyond The Anger and Irritability

With our fragmented identity we get easily irritated, fearful, and angry. The reason beyond the irritability and anger is the presumption that others are in the business of messing with our identity. We express our anger and irritation to keep others at a distance from us. When we are the victims of violence, we have shattered identity, and we quickly respond to the perceived danger with irritation and anger. We develop lies and pretensions to deal with trauma and often act out to protect our lies and pretensions. We are the guardian of what is left of our identity. If we are driven by our impulses, it does not do us any good if someone speaks to us from the point of common sense. Our process of pretension is on the subconscious level and is out of our conscious awareness. Our anger is directed toward *self* and toward others. We direct anger toward others to protect psyche from destruction. When anger is directed toward us and we do not have any *self*-protective capacity, we experience the urges to hurt *self*.

The *self*-hater and excessive feelings of guilt are the very strong splitting force. The splitting force of the anger is sometimes so strong that all construction of the psyche becomes unstable and breaks to pieces. We protect our construction from falling apart and misplace the anger. We explore the contradictory roots of anger, which include the inherited one, environmental, and psychological anger. When we are dealing with psychological and environmental anger, we understand that our environmental anger is external and the psychological anger is internal. The anger has the capacity to be expressed by someone who has a genetic predisposition toward anger. We may not find any signs of victimization, but without any valid reason we get angry. We call our anger a temper. We assume that we are born with diverse tempers because we have a distinctive intensity of anger in similar circumstances. When bullies are attacking us, we experience external anger.

When bullies victimize us, they trigger in us a contradictory type of hate, which is not against them, but against *self* for being in the position of the victim. The psychological anger is directed toward ourselves. Instead of being angry at bullies we get angry at *self*. In our opinion, the reason why we got victimized is that we acted stupidly and recklessly. When we have a solid identity and are confident that our responses are appropriate to the situation, we have the strength to appropriately analyze what happened. We understand that nothing in us made bullies be violent and assault us. Most important is that we are not sharing any responsibility for the bully's behavior. The shame, fears, guilt, and *self*-hate, when we get abused by bullies, are signs of splitting and are the biggest injustice we do to *self*. We are sure that we do not do anything to be ashamed of. As a result, we are dealing appropriately with our fragments. Instead of the anger irritability, as a reward, we have a genuine dialog between our fragments. We do not allow the bullies to push us into feelings of guilt and shame. We need to protect *self* from further abuse. We are also going to *self*-defense classes, reading books, and learning how to deal with bullies.

Only unification is a form of resistance and protection of *self*-respect, *self*-worth, and honor. We are not blaming *self* for the bullies' attacks. We deal with the misplaced anger by understanding that it is part of a splitting force. In situations when we are under assault, we focus on correct responses. When we meet a bully, our first reaction is to run away from the danger. To avoid guilt, which may destroy our life, if we have responsibility for someone, we are not running away. In the school taken over by terrorists, mothers did not leave their children to die alone. Even more, they went to the school where terrorists were holding their children. Instead of running away, they preferred sharing the horror together and to die together with their children. If somebody we care about is depending on us, then we may possibly share all the misery with him.

During the occupation of the Ukraine as a boy an old man was hiding with his sister. One day the polizies got his sister. He was around, but did not say anything. He was scared and did not have the strength to interfere and do something. Now, we do not know what would have happened if he had interfered. It might be that the polizies would have left the little girl alone. Or perhaps he would have died together with his sister. Instead he ran away to save *self*. Later he sneaked back to the same place and saw how polizies raped and killed his little sister, who was only thirteen years old. He lived a long life but perhaps no one could call it a life. He never got rid of his fears, guilt, *self*-hatred, and misery. He was always angry and irritable. He appeared alive, but he was not really alive. He was already dead and died emotionally together with his sister. He lived in misery because the forces of splitting, which displayed his anger and irritability, controlled him for the rest of his life.

One is Becoming a Victim

We are becoming victims not by our own choice, but because of circumstances beyond our control. For many of us the victim's role started in our parents' home. Sam Kaufman did not suffer from fascist atrocities. He did not feel any ethnic hatred. Sam Kaufman suffered from his mother's anger. The children in kindergarten and then in elementary school saw him as a frightened boy and everyone took advantage of him, because he did not know how to fight back. He was a victim and acted like a victim. The victim's role is not easy to carry. His victim's fragment was kinesthetically based. In stressful situations this fragment was a cause of the complete shutdown of all his functions. In moments of danger Sam froze and transferred to a catatonic-like state. It appeared that he was in a stupor, and even though he was hearing and seeing everything, he did not move at all.

Many times he was beaten up by his classmates and by children on the street. The children gave him the nickname of the stereotyped village idiot, Affonacy, and called him Fonia, copying the villagers' pronunciation. They laughed at him because he was not circumcised. Once they checked to see if he was circumcised. They pushed him onto the floor in the classroom and pulled his pants down. Sam was lying helplessly on the floor and crying. He did not know what to do. He was confused. He knew he could not complain to his mother about anything. He also knew that if he fought back, his mother would blame him anyway. His mother, to justify her abuses of him, was telling him he was the worst child and deserved punishments. Every time he complained to his mother, she would say, "It is probably your own fault. I somehow know that you provoked these children." Eventually, Sam decided to report what happened to his teacher. His teacher was a little old lady. She knew how to deal with the delinquents. As a punishment she confiscated the students' belongings. If students misbehaved, she would take their backpacks and briefcases and give them back only after several hours or the next day. In the meantime, the students needed somehow to carry their books.

To carry their books students would tighten their belts around them, but in the meantime, they needed to keep their pants from falling down. They also needed to explain to their parents what had happened and how they had ended up walking home without their briefcases. It was a very effective disciplinary measure, and children were respectful of their teacher. When the teacher heard about the assaults, she asked Sam if the boys did anything else to hurt him. Sam told her that nothing else had happened besides unbuttoning his pants, pulling them down, and checking his penis. She asked Sam, "Why are children calling you Fonia?"

Sam answered, "I do not know; they were just kidding."

The teacher said, "These children are not respecting our brothers in the collective. It is outrageous."

Sam knew that for disrespecting the dominant ethnic group, the children and their parents might have a lot of troubles. The next day early in the morning there was a knock on the door and all the children with their mothers were outside Sam's house. Sam's mother was confused and asked, "What is the matter?" The mothers together explained that the teacher had contacted them and that they had brought their children to apologize to Sam for their inappropriate behavior.

His mother played the generous woman. She said, "You might go. No need for apology, because the children were just playing." Sam went into the bathroom and cried. These children had violated his feelings of *self*-respect. They had humiliated him, forcefully pulled him to the floor, undressed him, and checked his private parts, and his mother had let them go without any apology. Sam also remembered how before his arrest his father entertained his guests by forcefully feeding Sam the homemade cream named googol-mogul, which was made from eggs, sugar, and sour cream. The rich in the collective were feeding their children googol-mogul. Sam did not want to swallow this creamy yellow substance. In front of his guests his father pushed Sam to the floor, holding his hand while Sam's mother fed the cream into Sam's mouth. Sam was spitting the creamy mass and was covered in the yellow cream. His father's guests were laughing and had a good time. This situation may well be very amusing and provide a lot of stimulation for pedophiles. What could a little boy possibly do to keep his parents from destroying his life? Nothing at all. To his friends his father denied doing anything harmful. He just mentioned that perhaps a boy should not be so sensitive.

He mentioned that he tried to be fair to his children but that he loved his daughter more because she reminded him of his dead sister. Sam's mother, to justify her abuse of her son, told her friends Sam was an impossible child and that the only way to control him was with corporal punishment. Abusers have nerves to find a thousand reasons to justify their abuses. The abused child was blamed for being victimized. In Sam's situation the abuser blamed her child and said her child was provoking the abuse.

Sexual Abuse Affects The Little Boy

Sexual abuse is as damaging to little boys as it is to little girls. Sam Kaufman was molested and his identity suffered a lot. When he was only ten years old he lost his naiveté and the capacity to love romantically. He was used as an object. The neighbor family, which was living in a communal setting with Sam's family, had only one child, a girl six years older than Sam. The girl liked to read and became a friend of Sam's sister. One day this girl decided to explore a male's sexual parts. When her parents were not home, she called Sam into her room and started to play with him, laughing and touching him. She said, "Show your dog and I will show you my cat." She unbuttoned Sam's pants and grabbed his penis. She did not wear any panties. She took Sam's penis and started to rub her clitoris. Sam was lying motionless. The penis became big, and when he instinctively wanted to move deeper inside, the girl told him to dress and to leave her room. She was afraid Sam might disturb her virginity. Sam obeyed but was completely confused. He was as red as a cooked lobster. In the hallway he heard his mother call him. Sam ran out of the house into the fresh air. He had a shortage of breath. He was hiding from everyone to understand what was happening to him and to get over the new sensations of his body. This incident was very shocking for all his functions.

As a future sexual human being he became frightened of girls and would run away from intimacy. Another incident made him even more confused. As part of his practice to work in the fields, he was sent to the countryside with other schoolchildren, and there were no toilets. When he went into the forest to urinate, he suddenly saw two older boys involved in a homosexual act. He got very scared and ran away. Sam was awakened to the sexual side of human life earlier than he was supposed to have been, and he was not ready. He was a little boy and got confused about feelings that he could not handle yet. As a result of being exposed to these experiences, which he did not have the strength to handle, his psyche was broken by splitting forces. As a boy, Sam got holes in his psyche. He was an easy target for the splitting forces, and his future life was full of pretension to cover up these holes.

The Ugliness of The World is Affecting Us

When we meet the ugliness of this world, we understand that life is not fair. Splitting forces take over our psyche and negativity becomes a way of life. Not too many, after observing the ugliness, have the strength to function as optimists. Usually after seeing this malice we become scared and disappointed in life.

When Sam was fifteen and drinking vodka for the first time, he observed the molestation of a drunk boy who seemed to pass out. The drunk boy was lying on the couch in the dark room where Sam was sitting unseen in the corner. Sam, in horror, saw another boy come into the room, unzip his pants, place his penis in the mouth of the drunk boy, and start to rub it. When he needed to ejaculate, he took his penis out of the mouth of the intoxicated boy, ejaculated next to the boy's face, and left the room. Sam from his place observed that the movements of the molester were so fast and so mechanical that it put Sam in a state of complete shock. It seemed that the molester, also a teenager, was very sure about what he was doing, and that when he saw his prey, he reacted immediately. When the boy molested in his sleep woke up, he felt the thick white liquid next to him. A terrible odor was coming from his mouth, but he was not aware of what had happened to him. The boy said loudly, "Perhaps I vomited in my sleep."

The boy will never know what happened to him, because he will always think that he vomited in sleep. He was seeing the face of Sam, who knew what happened and did not have the power to look into his eyes. Although the boy never realize what happened nonetheless he will suffer from the effects of molestation all his life. Sam felt pity for him, but he just shook his head and passed him. Sam never talked to this boy again, but the act of ugliness brought a lot of negativity to his own life. Because he witnessed the assault, it seemed that he was affected by it even more than the boy. He also felt guilty for not interfering, but he did not have the power to do so. He was frozen by his fears and was not able to move. In the meantime the predator did not feel any guilt at all and was acting like nothing had happened. Later Sam heard that he was forcing younger children to satisfy him orally.

In this situation, ugliness came to Sam's life from a teenager who was a monster. He was definitely not human. The perpetrator pushed everyone to split back into animalistic feelings, in an atmosphere of hate and fear. If, let's say, Sam had reported this incident to the police of the collective, they would have done nothing. The collective did not want to interfere. The police were somehow afraid to deal with the issue of molestation. In the collective, propaganda talked a lot about a new man, reformed by the new system. The existence of the ugliness of molestation was never, ever made public.

The Collective and Molestation of A Man

The deepest secret of man's psyche is about being a victim of molestation by man. According to macho logic, the situation of a female molesting a boy is perceived as a good thing and a good learning experience. As boys we told stories of being molested by older females. For us it was appropriate to tell stories of being molested by a female and of having a sexual experience at an early age. Of course, we were very proud when we were telling others a contradictory fictional story. We told each other about great females who were like a fire in the bed and taught us a lot of funky things. Being molested by a man triggers completely different feelings in us than being molested by a female. In the collective the molestation of male by male was a forbidden topic, and we did not talk about this crime. In the old law, the rape of a man by a man was not considered a rape but only sodomy. The collective did not feel compassion for the victim of molestation, who was deprived of his manhood. We were splitting from the horror of being used as an object, and dissociating from hideous memories. In many minds the molestation of a male was not as traumatic as the molestation of a female. When the ugliness happened and Sam saw the boy who was molested, he felt abhorrence, but in a few minutes everything was back to normal, as though nothing had happened. The predator actually was a skillful rapist, but the fact was that he did not look different from other boys.

Sam was traumatized by what he saw. He was very scared and confused, largely because the rape he witnessed looked ordinary and was very mechanical. He was afraid of the molester. He tried to detach from what he saw as though it had never happened. He was not able to force him*self* to forget. After this incident he never, ever drank any alcohol at gatherings. For many years Sam had nightmares of the penis in front of his face and was very sensitive to odors. In the collective, the main trend of thoughts about rape was based on the notion that only women could be raped by men. We did not talk about men as victims of rape. We felt that a molested boy somehow was asking for it because he had a homosexual orientation and was seductive. The collective was macho-man oriented, and we did not have sympathy for a boy who was a victim of molestation by a male. We blamed the victim because he did not have the strength to defend him*self*. Our ignorance was of benefit only to the rapists, who without any second thoughts or fears of punishment were raping males and bragging about their crime. Rape is a crime of dominance and force. Many ordinary males would not divulge that they were raped when they were intoxicated or were forced into submission. The experience was emasculating for boys, and to regain their manhood, they tried to forget it. Sam was severely traumatized by what he witnessed, a teenager being molested by a teenager. For him the cruelty of this offense was not dissimilar to the spitefulness of the other crime, when a female is molested by a male.

In The Soviet Collective were Many Thieves, Abusers, Bullies, and Molesters

The Soviet collective covered the extent of criminal activities. Only after the fall of the collective, on its ruins, were the huge amount of bandits and their wars perceived. Presently, the number of thieves, abusers, bullies, and molesters is not coming down.

Ways to Rehabilitate Them

Authorities are using diverse methods that include chemical castration, incarceration, and forceful counseling, but the results are not too great. In my opinion, the best way to reduce the number of offenders is to screen potential thieves, abusers, bullies, and molesters during their childhood. The young offender is more susceptible to rehabilitation than the adult. We need more screening done during the school years to identify potential thieves, abusers, bullies, and molesters. Citizens would benefit by having more screening and preventive treatment for violent tendencies when they are at school. This is better than doing it in a jail after the offense. Sam Kaufman did not deal with the issues of ethnic or social inequality in the collective society. He was a victim of violence in everyday life, which is an unfortunate part of the collective structure.

In the collective the issue of bullies, the children who were abusing the other children, was not a center of focus for educators. The sexual predators who were children were not dealt with seriously. As a result of child's play, children often beat up another child and raped a boy or a girl. In many situations the violence by boys toward girls was dealt with, but the instances when boys abused boys and girls bulled girls were not taken seriously. The violence when a girl was the predator was not dealt with. The teachers were hesitant to react when girls abused girls or girls abused boys. The predicament was that by fighting one of the ugliest forms of evil we completely forget the other evil. In general, the situations when the adults were abusing children did not justifiably overshadow the situation when children were abusing other children. In some instances we saw that the children who abused other children looked adorable and the abused children sometimes were nerds. It is also happened that if the victims were using drugs and alcohol, we were reluctant to defend them.

This fact that victims were not perfect children doesn't change anything, because we were supposed to protect every child. Children are not supposed to be abused if they are nerds or experimenting with drugs and alcohol, are thieves or have a physical disability. Abused children who did not use drugs and alcohol before are more susceptible to drugs and alcohol after the trauma and in future may become predators too. By replaying the evil done to them, abused children become the evil carriers. The evil may be fought in any shape to avoid contamination even when we see it in the deeds of an adorable child. The collective did not take seriously the children who were bullies and predators, because it believed that they would grow up and stop the behavior. The collective had lots of hope that youth organizations would help to change the delinquent behavior, but this approach was a fantasy. It was not complicated to predict that a child who is a bully and sexual predator will continue to behave in the same way when he grows up. In the meantime the young offender would damage the lives of many children.

We need to learn from the failures of the collective. We do not want to take the risk and wait until delinquent children become criminals. We need to make a reasonable attempt to rehabilitate them when they are children. For the little offenders, depending on the seriousness of the offenses, we need to have trials at school and in rehabilitation settings. It may sound absurd, but nevertheless, for offenders we might have military-type rehabilitation schools, summer boot camps, and settings that look like military detention facilities. Every offense must be dealt with appropriately, and perhaps only the military with their its experience has the strength to help us deal with these youngsters. For their offenses they might be isolated in military-type barracks.

Corporal punishment is not an effective modality; more effective punishment is taking away privileges and imposing isolation. In the collective the old teacher who punished small offenders by taking away their briefcases did more for the future of those children than all the other teachers in the school. The collective was insensible because it believed in peer influences. It was wrong. The children were abusing other children. We need to have specific modalities to deal with diverse offenses. If we use a general approach for all modalities, we will not achieve our goals and the offenses will continue. We may perhaps not be surprised that we are still dealing with an increased quantity of abusive adults and sexual predators. As it is going now, the job would never be finished, because although we stock our jails with adult offenders, on the streets youngsters are immediately replacing them. We need to learn from the mistakes of the collective and in the earliest ages in our schools screen children and increase our emphasis on rehabilitating those who are thieves, abusers, bullies, and molesters.

Children with Different Types of Offenses

The collective approach in rehabilitation is not effective, because it does not distinguish between distinct offenders. Adult offenders are all mainstreamed. The criminal structure in jails provides sorting by offenses and keeps similar types of offenders separated in groups. Young offenders must not be in rehabilitation together with bullies and sexual predators. As young offenders who are mainstreamed with others, they need to be protected from any type of predators. When they are arrested and incarcerated, they are kept together with thieves, bullies, and sex offenders. The justice system places together in prisons all types of offenders and is concerned with only one issue: how to guard them. They are kept in a regular setting, but they need a more secure setting. They need more protection from predators.

In schools the mainstream approach is very effective when children without disabilities are placed with those who have physical disabilities but not emotional problems. The children without disabilities learn how to relate to children with physical disabilities. Nevertheless, the children with emotional problems are separated from others. Their behavior is not predictable. The emotionally challenged can be violent. Because the wrong behavior is easy to copy, the children who have committed certain offenses are not in a mainstream setting. We need to rehabilitate children by using specific modalities. For example, the strictness of rehabilitation schools or boot camps is very effective for children who are not motivated, exhibit uncontrollable truancy, or problems with attention and concentration, impulse control, and compulsion. We use the boot camps only as a playing ground and do not get obsessed with power. Boot camps are not effective with children who are antisocial and mentally distorted. We are giving up on the rehabilitation of our children when we put the victims of the crime, who also have divergent delinquency problems, with bullies and sexual predators.

The bullies are educated about their offensive behavior using appropriate modalities. The children as sexual predators are educated by using diverse modalities getting to the roots of their disorder and learning how to deal with their urges. Our goals are to unify all the diverse fragments inside our psyche, but sometimes we require splitting until we find the right approach to unity. To rehabilitate the delinquent child we are protecting them from predators. Bullies and sexual predators are supposed to be protected too. Separating the child offenders makes our job more complicated, but the goal of protecting even those children with delinquency is more important than our discomfort. The first emphasis is on the safety of every child. Our rehabilitation system does not provide it yet.

We are operating on the cancerous growth until we learn how to deal with it in a distinctive way. The divergent delinquents are an infection that spreads around. Very often we impose quarantine, which includes a lot of disparate restrictions, to separate the infected areas. In the past we separated those sick with leprosy from others. We did not confine the tuberculosis and leprosy victims together. Unfortunately, young offenders are not separated by the type of offense. If we do not have in our modalities emphasis on a safe environment, then our rehabilitation is not effective. The strictness of the learning is not helping offenders or would help very little. We may not use reliable educational methods to deal with specific delinquency. Dissimilar child offenders must not be put together in the same rehabilitation setting. Mainstreaming child, who was an offender, is not effective and more restrictive environments work better. Our jails too are not efficient at rehabilitating offenders.

The Date Rape

In the collective, at one point, rape became a very serious offense after many complaints about abuse of women. It was a political issue. Date rape was a controversial type of rape. Date rape offenders were not considered serious criminals. They had a choice to marry their victim instead of going to jail. Many were married by the court system and stayed together for a long time. It was one of the ways for a girl from a village to marry a city boy from a good family. Nevertheless, rape in whatever setting is still rape. Many will argue that a young man who was physically abused, a victim of molestation, and a witness to rape was probably just misguided, and not a hard-core sex offender. Sam Kaufman completely fit the definition of a misguided adolescent. In his later life he never exhibited any sexually offensive behavior. His behavior was mainly influenced and shared by the rape he witnessed. Sam's experiences in his childhood mainly were abuses and violence. Sam was a befuddled adolescent. Despite the fact that he saw many ugly sides of life, he also was very naïve. He observed only ugly sexual episodes and did not know anything about love and sex. His father was in jail for many years and did not provide any fatherly advice. His mother was sexually frustrated and never talked about love and sex.

When Sam completed high school, his father got out of jail. The family moved east from Bobruisk to St. Petersburg, where his father had a few friends he had met in jail. His father's friends helped him get a permit to live in the big city. During the time of the collective, exchange was easy. Legally, it looked like his father exchanged his room in Bobruisk for a dwelling in St. Petersburg. Sam became a student there at the state university. His first experience with real sex was in the dormitory of the university and was terrible. Being inexperienced and scared, Sam was more forceful than necessary with his first girl. He did not talk to his date about his feelings and acted like a senseless robot. The paradox was that his girl wanted to be intimate with him, but he was rushing too much. For some reason, he was afraid she would change her mind. He sensed her odor and got completely dumb. He used force, which was absolutely not needed. Without any reason, he pushed the girl too strongly. The girl was justifiably offended and perceived Sam as a disrespecting, offending low-life. She pushed him back before the intercourse started and left. She also went to the police right away and filed a complaint.

Sam was arrested the same day and taken to the secret-police headquarters, named the Big House. By the next day the girl had cooled down and took her complaint back, but the arrest moved Sam in a distinct direction for the rest of his life. Before the arrest he was without any direction. His life was very boring, even when he was striving for adventure. He wanted to be a valuable member of the collective. The arrest brought some direction to his future life. Because of his arrest he felt needed by his beloved collective. He also found an adventure and the guidance of a male role model, which he had not had before.

The Sexual Offenses

In the workers' paradise were many disgruntled members with the desire to do something bizarre. The acting-out behavior and particularly the offense of date rape is an indication of fragmented psyche. Sam wanted an adventure and needed direction, which he did not have from any adults. Many fragments in his psyche were abused children or scared adolescents. Because he witnessed a rape, he had a fragment that he copied from a molester. Sam observed at a teenager's party the molestation of a teenager who was intoxicated, passed out, and in the complete power of a molester. Sam despised the molester and was afraid of him, but by being a witness he shared with the molester the fragment that copied the molester's behavior. This fragment was obsessed with complete power. During the date Sam's fragment eventually had a chance to present it*self*. Sam was accused in the attempt of the date rape. Despite the fact that he did not look for a victim in a dark alley but was invited by a girl to her room, he was perceived by the girl as an offender because he was rough and offensive. He knew the girl was attracted to him and did not ask for verbal consent.

He actually felt like a hunter who needs to get his prey down. He did not have any tenderness and gentleness. He acted as a callous machine and expected the girl to act in stereotypical way. He wanted her to surrender. He was a victim of violence and wanted to compensate for the past, when he was used as an object. His sufferings did not give him the right to inflict suffering on somebody else. Instead of a love story Sam participated in an ugly episode of attempted date rape. The girl left because she felt violated. She wanted tenderness and love but got roughness and mechanical force. Sam's psyche was taken over by a fragment that he shared with the molester. He detached from the fragments, which were victims, and became a violator. He separated from the fragments that represented powerlessness and insignificance to be with power and strength. The date rape attempt was a manifestation of his splintered psyche and a cry for help.

Sam was Splitting from His Past

Sam did not like his life and was splitting from his past. Unlike Stepan Kryvoruchko, who wanted to get away, Sam wanted to stay and be part of the collective. For him it was crucial to be part of something bigger and bring his own contribution to the collective, in his perception a good thing. He was ready to change his destiny and bond with a policeman, the first acceptable stereotype, which the collective would provide him. We see the difference between hero and antihero. For Stepan it was vitally necessary to unify all his fragments together in a solid identity, but Sam wanted to split from his past. For a long time Sam was chasing many of his dreams, but he was tired and dissatisfied with fantasy. He wanted something more tangible and real.

The collective provided him with concrete directives and desirable simplifications. Sam did not care about individuality, but he loved parades, decorations, and awards. He needed unification with something glorious to bring some meaning to his life. He did not have any desire to be a hero, but he wanted do heroic things. There was nothing in his previous life that resembled anything heroic, but he dreamed of climbing out from the pits, where his life took him, and doing something meaningful. He became an informer, the antihero who was admiring a collective. When he got hold of a stereotype, which the collective provided him, he never let it go, and was able to advance his goals. He felt that unrealistic ambitions and members' imperfections were the reason for their desire to pull away from a collective. He was splitting from the crap of individuality and was happy to be part of the collective. In his life he had gotten confused so many times that now he wanted only to split from everything complicated and to unify with simplicity. From now, it would take a long time for Sam to become able to accept the deepness of life. Eventually, it happened that Sam was feeling love for *self* and accepting *self* as an individual.

The Job of an Informant for The Police

Being a faithful servant of the collective brings significance into insignificant life for the fragmented psyche. In the collective were many voluntary servants who were secretly and sometimes openly without any rewards informing on fellow members. The fragmented psyche was getting attached to a construction, which appeared to be whole, and feeling very comfortable and powerful. It was ready to pretend that it knew all answers about unrelated things. Sam's life was miserable and lacked any ideas of *self*-growth, dreams of creating something meaningful but not taking risks and perhaps not having the power to achieve something important. He was a drifter in his life. His wings were burned by others with insensitivity, viciousness, and malicious intent. He did dream of doing important deeds in his life and becoming important. The date-rape incident changed his life. After that he got something bigger than anything he had had before. He was given a chance to achieve something significant.

After being arrested Sam was taken to the headquarters of the secret police, the Big House, at the request of Ivan. Ivan had already ordered that, instead of the local precinct bringing him an offender who was a student of the university and of Jewish ethnicity. In the Big House Sam was taken to Ivan's office. Ivan needed a Jewish snitch in the university to report on the repatriates to Israel. Sam was presented with an offer to become an informant or to be expelled from the university and go to jail. He also was told that he had a chance to clean up his life and help the collective in the fight against traitors. Sam knew that by marrying his accuser he would not go to jail and would not be expelled from the university. Nevertheless, he chose to become an informer because he was striving for adventure and wanted to be helpful to the collective. Sam signed all the necessary papers. The secret police also paid him a little salary. Sam had an assignment to inform on the Jewish political underground.

Sam did not feel any guilt about informing on Jews and becoming an informant for the secret police. Instead, he felt excited. Inside, he did not feel Jewish. Long before this, Sam had split from his Jewish background. He was ashamed of being unpopular and of being a Jew. He wanted to be a part of the dominant ethnic group. He wanted to join the collective as a proud man. He would do everything to achieve his goal. He also did not understand the Jews who wanted to leave the collective. He always thought they were traitors. Otherwise why were they so impatient to abandon the workers' paradise? Through his job as an informer, his fragmented psyche got unification with patriotic stereotypes of the collective. He did not feel any guilt and remorse at doing his new job; even more, his fragmented psyche became more functional and increased his ability to function in a noteworthy way. His choice was to be an antihero. Only inside of the psyche do hero and antihero have meeting and dialog. For the hero the role of an informant meant an end of his desire to be an individual, but for the antihero it was a needed light at the end of tunnel.

The Splitting Forces Take Over
The Entire Psyche

Sam's psyche was taken over by the splitting forces. He split from his ethnic roots and became antagonistic. He split from many things. He did not have any feeling of belonging and did not feel any blood calling. He accepted the collective's stereotype of Jewish people who are without gratitude and honor. He felt that by informing on them he was cleaning up *self*. He felt he was showing gratitude toward his homeland. He got closer to the dominant ethnic group and became one of them. He felt like he was granted an honor to protect the collective from traitors. In the meantime Ivan liked Sam's work and reported to his superiors that Sam was a real patriot and was more valuable than a dozen ethnically pure dominant members. Sam went to all *refuseniks* meetings. Refuseniks were denied permission to leave the collective.

The refuseniks who had been denied an exit visa from the collective, mainly to Israel, met in parks and sometimes in the apartments of the individuals who were leaving the collective. Lots of refuseniks were students at the university. At these meetings he met a lot of girls who wanted to leave the collective. They were naïve and trustful and saw in Sam a man who shared their dreams. Their dream was unification with their heredity. Sam went out with several of them. He lied to them that he wanted to be a real Jew. He was not circumcised, and he told girls about his desire to be circumcised. He pretended that he was angry at the government because he did not have a chance to be circumcised. He lied, but did not feel guilty. He felt nothing inside, but he was ashamed of his Jewish roots.

When he talked to one of the girls, he found out that she was not Jewish and was a daughter of the dean of the faculty of his university. She was dreaming about the Western lifestyle. The girl was not happy with life in the collective. She studied French and English and wanted to come across a good Jewish man and leave the collective. She was good-looking, a typical princess, and also smart. Sam felt that the girl was really attracted to him, but his heart was empty. He wanted to have sex with this girl, but he also knew that he needed to report her to the secret police. He did not want fall in love with her and decided he would not be intimate with her. Still, the girl was after him. She was in love and many times was waiting for him near his house. He was hiding from her, but she saw him anyway. She cried and asked only for a chance to love him. Sam had a hole in his psyche and the emptiness that was impossible to fill.

Sam did not know about the feeling of unification when two become one. He was numb to the feelings when we have a real meeting and sex is a part of dialog. He did not know that we share our bodies and want to give as much pleasure as possible to each other, and that we feel our partners' needs and know exactly what to do to please. Sam was treated as an object and treated others the same way. He understood that the girl had real feeling toward him, but he did not feel anything besides lust. Nevertheless, he decided he would not report the girl. Sam's contract with Ivan was to report only on Jews, and the girl was not Jewish. Sam felt better after he decided not to report this girl, knowing he was saving her from the files of the secret police. Sam realized that even if he did not betray this girl, he was not responding to her feeling of love. He was not responding to love, but he was aware that this girl was real and that he was a fake. He was very skeptical about what love he might possibly have for Jewish girls. He called them Jewish princesses. He believed that girl of the dominant ethnic group would love him more. By protecting his sweetheart, Sam was splitting from the forces of manipulation and pretension and coming closer to the feeling of individual love and caring.

Pretension is Causing Depression or Protecting from Depression

The collective encourages pretension. Pretension helped Sam avoid severe depression, and was his defensive shield. Pretension made him feel that everything was not real, and he was insensitive to his real feelings. He did not feel guilty that he was reporting on refuseniks. He did not feel depressed, but after a significant period of his honeymoon with pretension, Sam was disgusted and went through a period of *self*-hate. He did not have the patience anymore to pretend, and felt a big empty hole in his psyche. His pretension was completely swept away. He hated *self* for his emptiness. He did not have the ability to figure out what was wrong with him. He thought about death a lot. He was daydreaming a lot. He entertained *self* by visualizing *self* lying dead in a coffin. He saw in his daydreams that others were feeling sorry that he was dead and were speaking well of him. In contradictory daydreams he was pretending that he was the Count of Monte Cristo or another famous revolutionary and his vigilance did not have any limit.

In his daydreams he was returning to others what they had done to him. He was completely empty. In daydreams he saw *self* as a patriotic man who loves his country but no one has understood and valued him. He was proud that, eventually, he got a chance to do something for his country. He knew his father was doing tricks on the black market and never paid taxes. He often thought that he needed to report his father. He hated his parents. He did not report his father only because he was not asked to do it. His assignment was to report Jewish emigrants leaving the collective. In the meantime he continued to have daydreams about fighting the world and winning. He felt that others were his offenders and was proud to report them to police. He was sure that everyone deserved to be informed on. He also was certain that he had the right to do it. Ivan was a symbol of his revenge. All of a sudden, he got confused. He had not yet figured out why he had decided not to report the university girl.

Consciously, Sam did not know he was spending his life in pretension, but he already knew that he had encountered real love. He was not able to deny it anymore. He knew that after he found that someone loved him, he did not have reason to pretend that everyone hated him. The university girl displayed toward him her real feelings from the bottom of her innocent heart. Intuitively, he understood that he had a chance that might come along only once in a lifetime. He was loved innocently and unselfishly. It was a shock to him when for the first time in his life a girl told him she loved him. He was stunned, because he did not love anyone and did not believe anyone loved him. He did not have any real feeling from which to respond. He was completely amazed by the thought that this girl loved him when all others hated him. Suddenly a change happened and he realized he had been wrong. He lost the shield that had protected him. The thought that he was loved and did not need to hate all others was very uncomfortable. The structure of his psyche was falling apart. He was depressed, but the girl's love saved him and helped him join forces of unification.

The Criminal Psyche and A Business-Oriented Psyche

The business-oriented psyche is possibly criminal, but by nature the criminal and business psyches are poles apart. The collective had a structure closer to criminal than to business. Because criminal structures have their own way of doing business, they are experts in the illegal way. They are not acting in good taste in a legal business. They also have many inflexible rules and regulations known only to them that are not compatible with the legal ways of doing business. Even though business is all about flexibility, they are rigid business partners. The structure of the criminal psyche is very rigid and they must obey the criminal codes that were established long ago by criminal authorities. Contrary to criminals, as businessmen, we do not have a rigid structure and we have good intuition. As successful businessmen, we need to have a lot of flexibility, because business requires a lot of instant and unorthodox decisions.

Often by pressure our intuition fails and our business psyches are taken over by the criminal structure, becoming prey to the criminal structure. By nature Sam's father was business oriented. Unfortunately, the collective was projecting onto business its own faults. Under the collective every businessman was labeled as a black marketer and potential criminal. In the rigid collective structure there was not a valid system for collecting taxes. The black market included all the workers who besides the factory were working at home without paying any taxes. The small enterprises that were producing merchandise items, including raincoats, shoes, slippers, toys, and so on, under collective rules were all illegal. They were unlawful because they were pronounced dangerous to communal life. The collective did not want them to be legal because it was not easy to control them. The merchants were always afraid. The collective's rules were very rigid. They were written by the demagogues with party membership.

Sam did not know his father very well. His father wanted to do business legally, but it was impossible under the collective. The collective did not want the business-oriented individual to use his creativity. Sam's father was driven to the criminal world by forces of ignorance that seemed unifying but in reality was splitting. He did not have the base to live up to his potential. He had a drive for business and ambitions to achieve something in the business world. He was very careful and did not talk and brag when business was good. Nevertheless, he did spend some time in a jail. He had a usual roof, which means he had someone in the police who was protecting him. He was working as a manager of a home improvement store and made good money by using the market economy and selling deficit items for double and triple prices. He shared his profits with his roof, a ranking police officer. Unfortunately, the roof leaked because the officer was involved in other enterprises that failed and an investigator found his connections with Sam's father. After his release from prison Sam's father wanted to find legal ways to make money. He decided to move to the north and sell beef in places where there was not enough meat. He came to St. Petersburg, where because of the harsh winter, beef was in short supply. He had some money stashed and decided to use it to buy a house in the countryside outside the big city.

Sam's father already had a room in a communal apartment where he shared all the conveniences with several families. He bought a comfortable place in a village very close to the city. Instead of being in his communal apartment, which he was sharing, he spent time with his wife at the dacha, the country house, close to a beautiful lake. He built a big barn in his backyard and there raised small bovines. The place was secluded and he was able to raise little bulls for sale without being noticed. He was making a lot of money by selling the best veal at the public markets or bazaars. The market in St. Petersburg was very good for fresh beef, because the city did not have a stable supply system to feed so many customers. Sam's father's business was doing very well until the criminal structure became aware of him. The criminals were everywhere and were enmeshed with police and diverse food controllers. They had a lot of power. Very soon the police got wind of his business. The police, the infection controllers, health department, and other bureaucrats wanted a piece of his profits. Very soon his enterprise was not as profitable. Sam's father decided to leave the country and go abroad. Even though some of his friends went to Israel and did well, he wanted to go to some Western countries. He also wanted to be as far away as possible from his friends and do a clean business.

Sam's father told his wife and children that the family would go abroad. Sam was not surprised that his father decided to emigrate, because a lot of individuals were leaving the collective in search of freedom. Many business-oriented men dreamed about America, but the hard-core criminals went there too. Sam's father did not want to be around criminal structures. He felt that the best place was a distant Canada, where he had an opportunity to make legal money. In Canada business was less criminal and promised a lot of good opportunities. Sam's father became a businessman. He made the right decision. Now he is the biggest supplier of beef in Canada. In the collective, a wrong opinion was created, that business and criminal psyches are similar, but in reality business and criminal psyches are working in their own way. As we already know, business in some instances is overtaken by criminals who are not capable of doing business legally, and the stigma unjustifiably gets attached to all business.

Orientation to The Business is Staying in The Families Through Generations

Contrary to the radicalized collective, which causes splitting by manipulation, intimidation, and confrontation, the business-oriented psyche is striving for unification because trading is best when our mind is stable, contained, and focused. To unify fragments we are not always using dialog. To keep our psyche unified we, as businessmen, bring into play various forces that are negotiations to set contracts. When our psyches do not use dialogs, we are exposed to pressure from the splitting forces. Under the collective our business identity was under constant pressure and was very fragile. To protect *self* our business psyche needed to hide and was presenting *self* in contradictory ways and not respectable forms, including impertinence and effrontery. Sam's father was polite and willing to please, and had a good head for commerce. His family had a business-oriented structure that was using negotiation and contracting, and was basically individualistic.

Business-oriented people were the main resistance to the rules of the radical collective. For the collective was easier deal with the members of the criminal structure which in origin was closer to the collective, than to the business structure. The radical collectives did not like the business people and treated them badly. To break them to their rules and regulations, the collectives incarcerated them and stigmatized them as criminals. In jail, to survive, they were incorporated into the criminal structure. As business-oriented individuals, they suffered a lot, but they were not giving up their identity. Sam's father and grandfather were merchants buying and selling merchandise. They endured a lot, but did not stop their endeavors. They were two of many who pushed forward the biggest underground structure and the black market economy, which was free from the rules of the collective. Sam's grandfather was on the run from the police for the biggest part of his life. He was the richest man in the city of Bobruisk. The secret police, through informers, were aware that he was hiding gold and valuable jewelry but did not have the ability to find it.

The militias, the police of the collective, made five complete searches of his house but were unable to find anything. Eventually they took Sam's grandfather together with his family, including brothers and their children, to jail and kept about twenty of them in a little room. They were prevented from sitting and were standing up day and night. In the corner was a hole for excrement. The room had a terrible odor and was very hot. Sam's older uncle did not have the strength to take it anymore and confessed where the gold was hidden. The police found the hidden place and took the gold. Sam's grandparents were arrested. His grandmother had a heart attack and died. Sam's grandfather was taken to Siberia. After several years he escaped from the workers' camp and died as a free man.

Sam's father adjusted to life in the collective, but the memory of his time in jail and his father's terrible fate reinforced his decision to leave the workers' paradise. Sam did not know about his family history, but by blood he was destined to be a rich man. He had a harsh childhood and adolescence and was driven away from his family's identity. After emigration to the West he will discover *self* as a very capable businessman and will enjoy freedom and make a lot of good business decisions. The business mind is poles apart from the criminal and is programmed to produce instead of destroy. In many families under a collective the business identity was hidden but somehow transferred to the next generation.

Engagement in A Split and Unification as Soon as We Leave The Country of Origin

When we hate our identity and leave our country of origin, we do not want to remember our past. We want to start a completely new life in the new country, and to be assimilated into the new reality. Our move from our country of origin to another does not always present a split. We are going to countries that are unalike with the desire to see unrelated lifestyles. We also are traveling just to earn money, and for other business reasons. It is not an indication of splits because we do not hate our old identity. We do not split from our identity but are unifying with the unknown. Sam Kaufman left his country, but he will never give up his newly found dominant ethnicity, because he loves everything about it and will always be helpful to his motherland. Ivan completely trusted Sam. They developed a very close relationship. Many times Ivan thought it would be a blessing if Sam were his son. Sam also was very fond of Ivan and thought of him with high respect. He immediately reported to Ivan that his father had decided to leave. He was obligated to do it, because his assignment was to report on emigrants.

Surprisingly, Ivan liked the news and ordered Sam to prepare for the emigration. Ivan was thinking about the new opportunity. He wanted Sam checking and informing on some secret operatives who had been sent to Canada long ago. He needed to understand the connection between secret operatives and the Mafia, which had stolen our national treasure from museums of the collective and was selling it to the West. Sam would carry the icons in his luggage marked with chemicals to monitor them. Ivan told Sam he would help him get some antique items through customs, because the customs officers were working closely with his department. Sam would have a green light with his luggage. Ivan also was worrying for the safety of his son, who was in Canada. Because through the Directorate of Foreign Affairs he was not getting needed information, Sam could perhaps provide him with information about his son.

Ivan shared with Sam some secret intelligence information about some operatives abroad. He said he needed to find out everything about the stolen antiques, including which hands the money from the sale of icons eventually ends up in and where the money was kept now. He also ordered Sam to help his father in his goal to reach Canada. Sam did not need do anything more to encourage his papa to go to Canada, because his father had chosen long ago the country in which to emigrate. Later Sam informed his father that he knew Canada had a good market for icons and that he had a way to buy them and get them through customs. Sam took his assignment with feelings of excitement for having a new remarkable adventure.

In contrast to Sam, more than a few of the new immigrants had a split: a constant feeling of being unsatisfied with the culture and customs of their country of origin. The split probably existed a long time before those expatriates decided to move out of their country. The emigration for Sam was a way of unification with his patriotic feelings. He was leaving the collective on the special order from his superior. He had a special assignment to help his motherland. There were not any ethnic separations in the West, only language differences. All the immigrants from the workers' paradise who used the dominant language were called the dominant ethnic group. For Sam, it was a chance for unification with the rest of the world as a member of his beloved dominant ethnicity and an opportunity to discover *self* as a very successful businessman. Later, he provided a big financial contribution to the distinct institutions, which included the Orthodox Church and the Jewish Federation.

Unification with our Dreams Through Marriage

Marriage is an act of unification and may include unification with our desire. For Professor Kryvoruchko marriage was the unification with his roots and an opportunity for his child to be Jewish. He did not want to give up his identity when he left his country. He left the collective state with another goal to be a Jew, but in the West he was part of the dominant ethnic group. His first language and his religion were not problems. He did not want to forget his past, but his goal was to enrich his identity and to unify with his roots. He had a Gentile mother and was not raised with Jewish customs. He did not know much about being a Jew, but he wanted his children to have knowledge he did not have. He understood that for his future children a Jewish upbringing was possible only through marriage to a Jewish woman. Luckily, he fell in love with a Jewish woman.

For many, a marriage was unification with their dreams. They got married to receive an exit visa. Sam's sister married a man from the dominant ethnic group who wanted to leave the workers' paradise. Her husband joked that a Jewish wife was not a luxury but a way of transportation. For Sam Kaufman the unification with his dreams to be a real man was through marriage to a woman of the dominant ethnic group so that his children would have the proper upbringing. Eventually, Sam married a woman of the dominant ethnic group. He eventually found someone who from the deepness of her heart was expressing her love to him. She was also a daughter of the dean of a department at the University of St. Petersburg. The young woman, Lana, was fascinated by Jewish youngsters, who did not want anything from the workers' paradise but permission to exit. She was born into a family of bureaucrats. Her family would never think of breaking any rules. She was hearing something that did not make any sense.

In the collective the members of the dominant ethnic group were saying that Jews were staying in the collective only because they loved lard and wanted to take the whole lard of the collective for *self*, without sharing it with the dominant ethnic group. Their jokes didn't make very favorable references to Jews, who by religion are not supposed to eat lard. The meaning was that Jews are greedy, do not care about anything, and do not have anything sacred. They love lard so much that they do not care about their own identity. The antagonists of Jews insinuated that incurable immorality was a reason why Jews needed to be forcefully ejected from the collective. They always laughed and joked that Jews would not go to Palestine because they might not survive without lard, which is so tasty. Lana saw that it was a lie, because meanwhile, the government was refusing exit visas for Jews. Many who were not granted permission for the exit visa were called refuseniks. They created their own new world of danger, adventuresome actions, and world fame.

Lana was a romantic girl. She studied French literature as a university student. As any girl, Lana dreamed of her future husband, but in her dreams she was not strongly physically attracted to a built-up blond of the dominant ethnic group. She was attracted to a tiny redheaded, thick-spectacled Jew. Sam fit the stereotype. Lana was in love with him for a long time, the first time in his life Sam was close to someone who really wanted to be with him. When he was kissing Lana, he felt her passion and love. He also felt something incredible happening. Because of Lana's love, Sam the loser and underachiever became a real man. Sam needed someone like her close to him, because he knew their child would have a good upbringing and be a member of a dominant ethnic group. His son would be someone whom Sam was wishing to be. Sam and Lana married in the government district office, which issued marriage registrations.

They did not have a big wedding reception. They were agreed that it was no way to bring together the dean of the university, who wanted to keep his job, and Sam's parents, who wanted to exit from the collective. They had separate dinners with the parents from each side, and with a friend they had a little bash in a restaurant. The Kaufmans applied for an exit visa to Israel, knowing that they were going to Canada. The dean valued Sam, who was a good student. He was aware that his daughter was deeply in love with Sam. He told his daughter that he did not want her to emigrate, but that he did not have the strength to stop her, because she was an adult, and he and her mother would sign all requested papers. At this time both parents needed to sign the permission for their children to leave the collective, even though the children were already adults. Sam and Lana were happy. To succeed in marriage requires the consent of the parents. The road to unification is much wider when parents give their blessing to the marriage. Sam's and Lana's parents did not have any objections to their marriage. Meeting with Lana and marriage to her was the best thing that happened in Sam's life. The marriage helped him to join forces of unification with his dreams.

The Split from Feelings of Compassion

Luchko was in Canada by order of the collective and did not allow any feelings to interfere with his duties. He did split from all his feelings, including compassion. He also did not know who Ivan was and how he was related to Andrusha. He did not know that Andrusha had a powerful father, but even if he had known, Luchko would never have disobeyed any orders from his superiors. The partisan Luchko continued to fight in World War II as the unseeing soldier. His heart was cold and he never questioned the orders of his superiors. In the meantime, Luchko's jewelry store was popular among immigrants. He was always ready to help them from the goodness of his heart. He always had food and drinks available for newcomers. Many expatriates knew about Luchko's hospitality and his generosity, but they were not aware of his other side, which was far removed from them.

Sam's order was to become acquainted with Luchko without telling him that he had ties to the notorious secret police of the collective state. Sam did not tell anyone, even his wife, about his association with Ivan and about his special assignment. He came to Luchko's store with another new immigrant and got involved in long conversations with Luchko. He told Luchko he was a believer in a collective doctrine and that he had left the collective only because all his family had left and he did not want to be left alone. Luchko vaguely told him that, as a patriotic man, he might be helpful to his homeland here in Canada. After talking to Sam a few times, Luchko believed he was a true supporter of collective doctrine and took him under his wing. In the end they had a verbal agreement that Sam would help when Luchko needed information. Sam emphasized that he was agreeing to become an informant but did not want any monetary rewards.

In the collective Sam had worked as an informer for the secret police and received some money, but he did not do it because of the money. He had worked for the secret police because he was not happy with *self*. He wanted to do something important and be helpful to his beloved collective. He believed that others, like his father and grandfather, wanted to destroy the workers' paradise. Luchko too with all his heart was a true believer in collective ideas. He hated heartless capitalists and had the strength to give up all his life for the best future of the workers' class. Luchko had a duty to protect his homeland from the capitalists. He felt that he was a guard dog for his country, which he loved more than anything else in the entire world.

Manipulation is a Form of Splitting

The collective uses a lot of manipulation, which is a form of splitting. The manipulation is based on using an opponent as an object. It is implied that in treating someone as an object, we are suppressing our own feelings, which include guilt. When we treat someone as an object, we are splitting from sensitivity. Sam had an assignment from Ivan to get included in Luchko's group, and he was doing everything that needed to be done to achieve his goal. Decisions about whatever lies he told Luchko and whatever truth he did not say were not made because he wanted to mislead. There was nothing misleading in his actions. He was just doing his job. Sam's assignment was to investigate a smugglers ring. He did not feel any guilt about spying and reporting on Luchko. They actually had a similar approach to life.

Sam was impressed with Luchko's dedication to the collective. He shared the same feelings. He did not want to express his emotions, because he needed to complete his assignment. Sam was successful in entering the Canadian collective's agents' cell as a volunteer and an outsider. He was working hard, but in the bookkeeping information he was not viewed as a contractor, because he did not receive any money for his services. Every other day he sent mail to another city in Canada, where someone was collecting his letters and forwarding them to Ivan. The information was written in such language that only Ivan had keys to the cryptographic code to understand it. The main information was on Luchko and everyone surrounding him. He was an owner of a store that sold and repaired watches and jewelry, and he had the potential to make easy connections to the antiques market. This fact made him a main interest in the investigation of the art stolen from the museums in the collective. Sam had already reported to Ivan that he did not yet see in Luchko's store any activities that might lead to the Russian antiques and stolen art. He also mentioned that one of the customers, Boris, might be connected to the antiques.

From the secret files given him by Ivan to read, Sam knew that Boris worked as an attaché in the consulate of the collective and was a secret agent of the collective. Boris usually came to Luchko's store with several antique watches to repair or with a job to mount precious stones on beautiful frames. He never paid for the repairs, because he implied that he needed those jobs to justify his visits. Sam felt that it was not right that Luchko was spending so much time completing the jewelry work for Boris but was never paid. He told Luchko that he had a couple of icons to sell but did not know how to proceed. He asked Stepan Luchko to introduce him to someone who might be able to help him with selling his icons. Luchko introduced him to Boris. Even Sam was manipulating Luchko to get introduced to Boris and did not feel bad about it. He did not feel any shame in using Luchko as an object. He was sent to the West on an assignment and needed to discover the smugglers ring. Nevertheless, the fact was that he was using manipulation and did not feel guilty about it. He did not think about it not being nice to treat someone as an object. He did not know that manipulation is a form of splitting.

Estimation is The Tool of Manipulation

As manipulators we estimate how easily we can fool others, although for the real meeting and dialog we need the ultimate regard for each other. When we are manipulators, we lose humanity and treat others as objects. We want to scam our opponents into believing us and want to cheat them. Our goal is to check them to find their weaknesses and how dangerous they are. Sam had an assignment from the secret police to infiltrate a ring of art smugglers. He did not know any other way to deal with criminals except manipulating his way into their circle. Police methods are very different from using dialog and humanity. When the police deal with criminals, they often use the same methods criminals do. The police do not expect killers and smugglers to have real meetings and get involved in genuine dialog with law enforcement structures.

Criminals are not interested in having a dialog with anyone either. They only need to manipulate others to submissiveness. Sam needed information about a smugglers ring and needed an estimation of the players. Without raising any suspicions he needed to convince Boris that he was not a threat and that he only wanted to sell his own icons, whose market value was allegedly unknown to him. In reality, he knew the real value of his icons and was using their meeting to check if Boris was part of the ring. Sam brought his icons from his apartment, which was in the working-class area, to Boris's place in a high-rise building. A doorman, who called Boris through the intercom to ask permission to let Sam in, greeted him with a bow. For his part Boris wanted to use this meeting to check Sam out. If Sam was somehow aligned with Stepan Kryvoruchko, he was prepared to use the meeting to scare Sam into submission. Being obsessed with perfection, Boris wanted everything to go according to his plans. He was a good planner and counted all probabilities.

Boris already knew that Sam was Luchko's informer. He knew he could safely say anything. Boris had many other ways to play his games, but his biggest trump was his ability to inflict fear. Boris was planning his traps ahead of time. He invited Sam to his apartment to shoot down his resistance. He knew that when Sam saw the art collection, he would feel insignificant. Boris was a master at playing with others' brains and at brainwashing. He never did anything without a plan. His plan was to make Sam a slave. He met Sam wearing a golden gown. Sam was very impressed by Boris's apartment and his attire. The place had a lot of beautiful items of art but also reminded Sam of a storage area in a museum, where works of art were leaning against the walls. When Sam was sitting on the chair next to a table, Boris all of a sudden told him that Sam's friend Andrusha had sat in the same chair and was now dead. Boris was looking straight into Sam's eyes and asked him, "Do you want to die?" Sam shook his head. His heart was palpitating very fast and felt like it would jump out of his chest. His body was very heavy and he did not have the strength to move. He understood that he was in a very dangerous game, because Boris was a vicious opponent.

Sam became short of breath. He said rapidly, "I do not want to die! My wife is pregnant and I want to raise my child."

Sam's face was red and he realized that Boris was playing with his mind. He heard Boris say, "Good! You were in the car with Andrusha when he died and what did you see?"

Sam answered, "I have not seen anything. I was asleep." Sam understood that he needed to be very careful and reassured Boris again that even though he had been in the same car with Andrusha, he had not seen anything strange.

Boris continued, "It is a very good answer. Do you meet Stepan Kryvoruchko? How does he know what happened? Did you tell him anything?"

Sam answered again, "I know Stepan Kryvoruchko, but I did not tell him anything about the accident."

Boris told Sam, "Keep your eye on Stepan Kryvoruchko and you will be rich. He is putting his nose in someone else's business. Presently he is healthy, but he may not be so lucky for a long time, because someday he will end up in the hospital." When Boris needed a lens to check Sam's icon and left the room to look for it, Sam breathed more freely. He understood that Boris had planned this conversation, which was the main reason to invite him to the house. Boris was very smart, but he underestimated Sam. He had made a mistake this time, because Sam was not someone who would easily fall into his trap. Sam had been scared many times in his life, and eventually, he got tired of being scared. He was imagining a hero of the collective, Dr. Zorge, who was fighting the fascists and would not be scared. Dr. Zorge was Sam's role model, the man who was a patriot of the collective even though he lived in Japan. Dr. Zorge was a spy and until now his fate is unknown.

When Boris was not in the room, Sam made snapshots of the several items with his small camera, which he had received from Ivan. Boris came back with a lens and started to examine the icon's cover for names, inscriptions, and silver claims. Boris saw right away that the icon was from an unknown master and he would not be interested in buying it, but he said loudly, "I am very interested in this icon. This icon is from a good master, and if you will leave it for a couple of days, I will tell you the selling price, which is different from the buying price. If you will keep your eye on Stepan Kryvoruchko, I will give you my commissions too. Definitely, I can assure you that it would be good money. It will be my present for the birth of your child." If Sam left the icon, he would give Boris a chance for blackmail. Later Boris would not hesitate to tell Sam, "You want your icon back, do things for me." Boris was planning his next step by magnifying the value of the icon. He was pushing Sam to leave the icon for a couple of days until he found a buyer. He needed Sam to think that his icon was very valuable. If Sam would think the icon was worth a lot of money, Boris would use it as a manipulation tool to make Sam compliant and to do everything at his command. In gratitude for Sam's work, Boris would give him back his icon, which had not cost much in the first place. Sam thanked Boris for his effort to sell his icon. He promised that he would do whatever Boris asked him to do.

Boris was sure he had lured Sam into a trap, but his plan did not work. Sam knew the icon did not have any value, but still did not leave it, because the icon gave him a chance to have contact with Boris on a diverse level. This time Sam was a better manipulator than Boris was. Sam too had prepared for this meeting and listened to instruction from Ivan and from Luchko. Boris did not know much about Sam, and he played his cards too soon. Boris was playing intuitively and was relying on his skills. He did not want any dialog. He played a chess game. He used the meeting as a tool to estimate his opponent and used pretension, which resembled a real meeting.

Splitting Forces Lead to Paranoia and Then to Killings

The radicalized collective uses splitting as a main tool of operating. The splitting psyche organization is very sensitive to paranoia. It perceives danger from everywhere. Sometimes splitting does not have any limits and goes to extremes. When someone is with splitting structure, he becomes homicidal, because he may not have partial satisfaction and wants the ultimate splitting by completely destroying his opponents. When splitting forces are out of control and take him on the road of killing, he may not turn back. He needs to do more killings until he gets stopped by someone stronger. Boris knew that Andrusha was the son of a ranking official in state security, but he did not care. Boris considered himself untouchable. He had connections in high places and even in presidential circles. In that time the family members of powerful bureaucrats who belonged to the collective elite were selling antiques to Western collectors. They needed the money in foreign exchange to buy Western appliances and clothes.

Boris had good contacts in the collective and was a middleman to sell native art. He was a secret police officer within the famous Directorate of Foreign Affairs. He spoke several languages and had the best grades in school. His weakness was that he did not have any connections by blood to powerful members of the collective, but he had some blood connection to the Mafia, which was stealing the antiques and jewelry from museums and private collectors in the collective and selling them abroad. He was working his way through both the diplomacy and Mafia world by deceiving, blackmailing, and flattering. Boris was involved in smuggling and selling native art to Montreal. He felt very good there and sometimes thought the whole city belonged to him. Here, he met distinct art collectors in a beautiful restaurant called Troika, where the waiters wore ethnic clothes. The restaurant was beautifully decorated, and many good singers performed there. Andrusha's defection woke up the sleeping atmosphere in this Canadian town.

By defecting, Andrusha brought attention to the space where Boris was operating. Boris represented the highest elitist families in the collective, and they did not need attention from the Canadian security police. Boris needed somehow to protect his enterprise. He was under big stress, and his intuition deceived him and he overreacted. He was afraid of massive defections. He came out with a plan to stop defection of the sailors by sending a strong message to future defectors. He was planning to get rid of Andrusha. He decided to use his agents and also his contractors, who were the paid executioners. He presented his plan to the Directorate of Foreign Affairs as an emergency measure to stop the defection of sailors because of the importance of Montreal as a friendly city. He justified his extreme measure by emphasizing the importance of Montreal as a seaport, where many ships from the collective were coming. He implied that massive defection might constrain the collective's relationship with Canada.

Boris wanted to take away the attention of future defectors from Montreal. Meanwhile, his plan to resolve the critical situation in Montreal was accepted in the highest quarters in Moscow. His bosses were pressed by members of their families to normalize the tensions. At the time of Andrusha's defection Montreal was a heaven in which to sell smuggled art. Through the beautiful antiques shops of this city went many gorgeous pieces of native art that later ended up in the best collections in the world. In Boris's mind, for purposes of security, the life of an insignificant sailor did not have any substantial weight; even the sailor's father was a heartless bureaucrat who was doing an impossible task of repairing the severely damaged system of the collective.

When Boris found out who the sailor's father was, he wanted to get rid of him even more. He also was scared that the security officer's son, who was fluent in English and French, might somehow interfere with his business. Later Boris understood that he overreacted and needed to avoid the young sailor. Boris made a big mistake by underestimating Andrusha's father. He did not know that Ivan was one of the respected members of his organization. Ivan was not corrupt, and really believed in the doctrine of the collective. At this time Boris felt overconfident and perhaps did not foresee any possible consequences of his actions. At some point his splitting forces were reaching their extreme and manifested *self* in paranoia. They exaggerated the danger and minimized the consequences. Boris was a slave of the splitting forces and did not see any other way to get out of his predicament except killing. He was driven by splitting forces and was also paranoid.

The Splitting from Shame and Guilt

The main symptom of being infected by a virus of radicalization is desensitization to feelings of shame and guilt. Criminals learn from early childhood to split from those feelings. When someone is splitting from shame and guilt, he is experiencing traits in his character that are poles apart. He possibly is narcissistic, antisocial, and very fearful that he is detaching from reality and disregarding his own feelings. He also does not have much resistance to the influences of very powerful ideologies or attractive lifestyles. Criminals do not have feelings of shame and guilt, and feel very proud when they have the power to play tricks on the innocent. Boris was a troublemaker who was preventing various fragments from having meetings and dialogs. The troublemaker fragment is responsible for the splitting and turmoil in the psyche. From his childhood Boris learned how to suppress feelings of shame and guilt and never had those feelings. His narcissism kept him grandiose and caused him to lack empathy for others. His antisocial parts allowed him to violate the rights of others.

He was an agent of the secret police, but he never cared about the security of his country. He used his position to create a smuggling enterprise. He always saw the weaknesses of others and used their imperfections to justify his own worst deeds. Without any second thoughts Boris took articles and money and did not return them. He did not feel regrets about it. He had two sets of ethical rules, one for himself and one for others. In his ethical rules he would justify and approve any of his own dishonesty and theft. When he borrowed from others, he already knew he was not planning to repay them. He justified his behavior by telling *self* that it was nothing shameful, but was just the nature of any business. He was reassuring *self* that businessmen are supposed to be tough and that in business everyone is for *self*. In contrast, when someone was dishonest with him, he felt betrayed and complained that he should probably not trust anyone. He complained for a long time about others' indecency. He had an excellent memory even though he forgot to pay back his debts. He just didn't want to pay. When he wanted to be, he was good at remembering birthdays and anniversaries.

He always had a hundred dollars as a gift. Besides this one good mark, he was a man without any morals and was selling stolen and smuggled native pieces of art that were country treasures without any guilt or shame. He paid very little to the suppliers compared with his profit from the sale. He got it for almost nothing. At this time in the collective the value of the dollar was very high and he made the owners beg and cry for their money. He made them wait until their items were sold and sometimes did not pay them at all. He never hesitated to use wives of his suppliers to satisfy his needs and to satisfy his sexual fantasies. He did not care about women. He used marbles. He would put them in the woman's vagina to increase his satisfaction. He was proud of *self*, because he had, in his opinion, a good life and made a lot of money. He was protecting his enterprise from unwanted attention. He kept his money in cash in safe deposit boxes in diverse banks. The fees for the boxes were automatically withdrawn from his accounts, which all contained modest amounts and did not bring any attention to him.

Boris was an undocumented partner in the antiques shops because he was the biggest supplier of the art. Being a secret agent who had a lot of money, and having connection to the cream of the collective's elite and Mafia, he was able to smuggle any items through customs. He had an exceptional memory. He had the ability to learn and remember things, but he used it only to deceive others and to enrich *self*. He was a troublemaker. We need to identify in our psyche the negative effects of the troublemakers and their role in sabotaging our desire to have real meeting.

Troublemakers use fear, greed, and other disparate tricks to prevent meetings. The split from feelings of guilt and shame helps them to use the radicalized collective to their benefit.

The Splitting from the Moral

Splitting from the moral may occur through generations. Our parents, who split from morality and choose the immoral lifestyle, have infected us with the virus of radicalism. When we split from moral to amorality, we are never again unified with moral values. How deeply we stick in radicalism depends on the level of splitting in which we are residing. Boris grew up in an atmosphere of stolen goods, lies, tricks, and putting everyone down for their honesty. Starting from Boris's early childhood the idea was planted in his head that to be intelligent means to outsmart others, by tricking them and then laughing at them. Boris was a complete splitter from any moral values. He was educated, and definitely knew the rules of morals and ethics, but by his own choice he completely ignored them. In his understanding only fools followed those norms. For him the deceived were the same as the ram from whom the shepherds cut the wool. The sheep does not have a soul and we need not have any regrets about wearing the sheep's coat or eating a lamb. The sheep is mainly an object to be used for the consumer's needs. In the same way, Boris thought someone trustful needed to be manipulated because all the world is a food chain. In the animal world the strong eat the weak. The relationships between humans are the same as in the animal world: the smart rule the less fortunate. He thought that although everyone wanted to take advantage of others, only the smartest had the power do it. He thought he was the smart one.

Boris is an example of one without any morals and he used others as objects. In his psyche was a fragment of his father, which told him not to be shy and go get from everyone as much as he could. The fragment declared that he punished only the dumbest, who are not careful enough. This fragment was very rude. Boris's father was a Lithuanian named Donatus. He worked in a pawn shop and bought items from anyone who needed money. He bragged to Boris that he swapped diamonds in front of his customers. He had quick hands and had mastered show tricks with games and cards. When he was buying items from patrons, he had the ability to make any item look so insignificant that customers would feel lucky that he took their merchandise. For him the honest way equaled stupidity. In his opinion everyone was around for only one reason, which was to be tricked by guys like him.

Donatus had good connections in the underworld of crime, because he was good at the card tables. He had the ability to shuffle cards in both ways and he always won. In the criminal world Donatus was always imperceptible and was respected for his skill, because if he was ever caught cheating, he would die for sure. He was married to Boris's mother, a woman from a dominant ethnic group. Very often to annoy his wife he called all members of the dominant ethnic group stupid. He often bragged that he outsmarted everyone. He was actually making fun of any ethnicity, including his own. Donatus was a fragment of Boris's psyche and split him from moral values and from humanity. The immoral treat others as objects. The splitting from morality in some families might continue for many generations.

Some Manipulations are Appropriate

When we are dealing with someone who is stigmatizing us and treating us as an object, then negotiations are not possible. Only in this situation, and only as a response, is manipulation appropriate. In our heart we do not want to manipulate and we always want negotiation, but in reality everything is far removed. In negotiation we need to have two sides that agree to have a negotiation. In negotiation we want to change the opponent's view by justifying the need for change. We provide the reasons to explain why the change is beneficial. Conversely, in manipulation we want to trick the other. We are looking for negotiation, because dialog is happening very rarely. When we want a negotiation and another side is not responding, then negotiations become just an internal talk. We have an internal talk when our psyche has interaction between several of our fragments. We may split or consent to have a dialog. Dialog between our fragments is very desirable. To have a solid identity our goal is to identify our fragments and to engage them in a dialog. In many instances our monologue in reality is a dialog between fragments. When we are talking to others, often we mistake the dialog between our fragments for a dialog with others.

We are aware of dialog and negotiation, but we are not ignoring manipulation and recognize it too. Manipulation is a process of splitting. Every time someone is treated as an object, we are manipulated. We are not negotiating when our life is in danger. We may not even engage in monologues. We must plan how to protect *self*. We are using all available means, because the very skillful manipulator would drag us toward despair without any hesitation. If we are too open and do not protect *self*, we become easy prey. The only antidote for manipulation is manipulation, because we may not have any way of negotiating with someone who does not respect contracts. As long as the world has villains who take advantage of us, we need to use manipulation and confrontation to resist them.

Sam was engaged in a game of manipulation with Boris and did very well. Luchko had cautioned him not to give anyone his icon without an invoice. Sam knew that icons do not have any market value, and he decided to respond to Boris's game by using manipulation, despite the fact that after the scene of threats and intimidation, he was scared of Boris. He decided not to leave his icon with Boris. He pretended to believe in the high value of the icons and asked for an official receipt. He figured out that Boris would not give him any receipt, because as a diplomat he would not compromise *self* with selling icons. Instead of writing a receipt, Boris gave Sam cards from antiques stores that might give him a desired receipt. Sam saw that Boris was not very happy. The plan that Boris designed and often used did not work. Sam did not leave his icon with him without a receipt, so Boris started plan number two. He congratulated Sam on his wife being pregnant and as a present gave Sam a banknote of a hundred dollars. Boris said, "I may make you a very wealthy man, but I need some help from you. I want you to help me deal with Stepan Kryvoruchko."

Sam left Boris's place with relief. He recognized that Boris was playing with him as with a stereotyped Jew, who is not really a fool but is very scared and greedy. Sam was absolutely clear about how Boris's mind was operating. If Boris was not able to scare him into submission, he would buy him. What Sam hated most was to be identified as a greedy Jew. Sam loved his native language, culture, and glorious history. He would do anything to be identified as a member of the dominant ethnic group. He was working with Ivan not because he was scared. He knew that by law in the collective he had the option of marrying the girl who accused him of rape, and then the case would be closed. He did not get scared by accusations. He did his work with Ivan to prove that he could be helpful to the collective. In his heart he was a patriot of the collective. Today Boris did not deal with him as an equal but as a greedy Jew. Sam, as an informant for the secret police under Ivan's supervision, was trained to think as a real secret agent. In his analysis, Boris made a big mistake and would pay for it, because he did not know that in front of him was a born manipulator.

The act of manipulation involves severe confrontation but also uses tricks to masquerade the confrontation. We are not justifying any war, hot or cold, because war is brutal confrontation. Unfortunately, in the middle of conflict we need to manipulate and split, because any unifications are not possible. The reason for unification is to build a solid identity, but in the unification with a troublemaker we completely lose our identity and transform *self* into something ugly. We may not be able to afford such a big loss. In a situation when we are dealing with a troublemaker and the interaction is threatening our safety, the unification is not needed, and the manipulation seems appropriate.

Business Relations

The world of business, including selling art, is not built on a dialog and is based on manipulations. When we talk about a dialog, we are right away thinking about fragments of our psyche that are aware of others' feelings and want to unite in solid identity. Conversely, big conglomerates do not use dialog, do not know, and do not care about others' feelings because they worry only about profits. They use manipulations to take over and suppress as many small businesses as possible in their sphere of influence. When Sam went to the antiques stores, he understood that Boris was known there and was a powerful associate in those stores, at least. Both the antiques dealers and Boris, who was a main supplier, dominated the antiques market in Montreal. The owners wanted to retain the sliding buying prices and were united to keep them down. Boris, who brought a huge amount of antiques to their enterprise, was able to dictate his own prices. He was a serious supplier of many priceless pieces.

The dealers did not know anything about where the items came from and whether the antiques were stolen or contraband. They were far from being naïve, and, if they wanted, they had ways to find out. They did not care about the sources and became Boris's partners. Nevertheless, they did not know how little Boris paid for those items. He was cheating them by quoting higher prices than he had really paid and pocketing the difference. The owners of the antiques stores badly needed money and did not have high standards of morality. One owner, a short man, spoke the language of the collective and mentioned that his father had dealt with the aristocracies of the czar and that he loved native antiques. He needed a lot of money to maintain the lavish lifestyle that he presumed a aristocrat would have.

Another owner, a tall man, had many illegitimate children and needed a lot of money to support them. Neither dealer cared where the art came from. Sam went to a store that was close to Boris's place. He was greeted with a fireworks of distinct reflections from icons, silver, jewelry, gold, and paintings. There was the little man, who was a relative of the owner. Sam told him he was from Boris and wanted to leave his icons for appraisal and needed a receipt. The little man took the icons to his office to write a receipt. In this time Sam made a few snapshots of the store's inventory. When the short man returned with the receipt, Sam said he had changed his mind and wanted to bring his icons next time. The short man returned his icons. Sam went to another store, which was within walking distance. When Sam went inside, he was shocked by the sight of icons with silver and enamel, items from the collective, including old silver, Faberge eggs, painting, tapestries, and amber. When Sam asked to see the owner, he was told that the owner had already retired for the day but that if he waited ten minutes, one of his sons might help. But he had already found what he needed. It took only a couple minutes for Sam to make snapshots of the icons and other antiques with his little camera. He observed that everyone in this store was tall and had similar facial features. He checked how they were talking to the clients and understood that all the tall young men were the owner's sons.

Sam told the security guard in the store that he wanted to walk for couple minutes and left the store. He felt very sad that behind the beautiful art were so many dirty things. He was disappointed that the art business was built on manipulation. He was distressed that the hands of thieves were manipulating the art market. Unfortunately, the numerous collectors were engaged in skillful manipulation to obtain priceless items. The manipulation in the art business was getting too hectic and included breaking the law. When we see the world of art, we do not want to think about manipulations and want only to enjoy what we see. We want to detach from the world of manipulations and to be in the world of lyrics. When Sam went to the antiques stores, he was uplifted by the magnificence of the art but kept his head cool. He was in the business of investigation of theft, and his actions were pure manipulation to find the truth. He negotiated with *self* that he was detached from the excitement of being close to such incredible art. Sam was splitting from the world of lyrics to the world of manipulation.

Manipulators and Criminals

Not all manipulators are criminals, but all criminals are manipulators. Some of us in the business world are manipulators, but only a few of us are members of the Mafia. First off all, the Mafia endorses the rigid criminal structure. This criminal structure assumes honesty with partners in the criminal enterprises, but many criminals are not honest with their partners and use them with manipulation and confrontation too. If manipulation does not work, they use confrontation. They are known for fastidious squeamish interactions, which end up in violence. Montreal was a very profitable place for Boris. He was proud about *self* that in this city he brought to life the market of antiques. It was his territory and he did not want any unforeseen problems. This was one of the reasons why he was in such a hurry to stabilize the situation with the defecting sailor. He did it in a way that only he knew, and he did it, as he understood, in a quick and efficient way that had always worked. This time he was wrong. It is always a mistake to underestimate others. Because of his sophistication in swings and manipulative tricks, Boris felt above everyone. He was alone, fighting each one who was in his way.

Boris was suffering from grandiosity and thought he was higher than any structure and any law. He had been buying and selling antiques for a long time. He was not endorsing the traditional criminal structure, because he was not honest with his partners. Boris was not a regular criminal. He was a criminal who felt that he was above the criminal structure. He felt that he was special and that he had the power to do whatever he wanted and that no one had the audacity to disturb his business. He committed brutality and did not feel any shame or guilt. He was breaking the limits of manipulation. For many, manipulation was limited to business, but Boris used manipulation in all parts of his life. He did not have anything else in his life beside manipulation. To his selling partners he always lied about the real value of items. He did not tell them where he got the items. To the owners of antique items he quoted prices that no one could verify. He understood pretty well how much everything cost, but for them he made the selling price very small. Sometimes he found excuses to not pay suppliers at all and pocketed their money. He never depended on anyone and did not have real partners. Boris kept his partners in antiques stores in the dark about his connections.

He applied good marketing techniques. When he talked to others, he always promoted *self* as an example of honesty and how he was suffering by helping others. He insinuated that many were stupid, greedy, suspicious, and did not understand him even though he was helping them. His scam was working and many trusted him. He was taking precious art from them without any written receipt or promissory note. He was getting many beautiful things from many who believed in him. For him it was very important to get his hands on as many antique items as possible because the market was hungry for old native art. The antiques sold for good money. Western art dealers also knew that rich families had a very strong interest in our native antique treasury and were providing it. Boris, who was a supplier of the antiques, found out that Stepan Kryvoruchko was sticking his nose into his territory. He would not allow anyone, including Andrusha or Stepan Kryvoruchko, to destroy his business. As before, he would deal with any threats to his enterprise. He was completely consumed by forces of manipulation. He was more than a criminal—he was a dangerous maniac.

The Criminal Fragment

When we have a criminal fragment in our psyche, we look for other fragments that are capable of dealing with the troublemaker. In Professor Kryvoruchko's psyche we have a fragment that was an honest policeman. We were enlisting the old and shrewd Ivan to deal with a criminal troublemaker fragment. Ivan was using all traps to get a mad criminal who assassinated his son. He was the best man to neutralize Boris. He was unbreakable and immune to Boris's tricks. An old policeman who was not corrupt is a good match to deal with a criminal. In the first place the policeman is supposed to guard against criminals, and in our psyche our relationships copy the outside world. Boris has a mental condition, a combination of narcissistic, antisocial, and paranoid traits. This condition is tricky to treat. Boris and Ivan are antagonists, but they are similar in many aspects. They both had a cause for which they fought hard. Each one had a goal.

They put a lot of thought into designing steps to achieve their goals. Ivan is a workaholic and dedicated to protecting the workers' paradise. He was putting all his energy toward care for his country. He gave his pledge and spent all his life protecting. The uncompromising Ivan did not do anything for *self*. Because of his honesty and dedication to the truth, he was capable of joining forces of unification. When Boris got into his custody, the interactions with a troublemaker were limited. A dialog with a troublemaker is not possible, but we may have dialog with the guard who is responsible for watching Boris and preventing him from doing any harm. Through genuine meeting and dialog with a guard we may understand *self*, to build desirable identity and also better manage the fragment who is a troublemaker. The fragments of Ivan and Boris are very rigid and inflexible. If those two fragments are clashing, they are releasing a significant amount of energy. They have the strength to damage others and produce a big emotional turbulence and split. We need to shield our psyche because the dramatic internal split may incapacitate our body and create a breakdown. The big question is how to protect our psyche from an antisocial, sick, homicidal, or suicidal fragment. We are reinforcing a guardian fragment with the other intermediate fragments to have a dialog.

Because of Ivan's uncompromising skills, he is the right one to guard Boris and to understand all his tricks. Sam is an intermediate fragment to have dialog with him. In the outside world we are not sure yet how to deal successfully with troublemakers. We do not know how to deal with the terror structure either. By studying the troublemakers inside us, we may learn something. We do know for sure what we must not do in our psyche. It is clear that we must not have any dialog with troublemakers and that they do not want to have any dialog with us. Unfortunately, in the outside world we are sharing the same Mother Earth and all existing life may be destroyed if confrontation goes too far. We do not have the power to say that if dialog is not always possible, let the scalpel cut the tumor before it is too late. We may look for a solution inside of us, but the structure of our psyche is not an exact copy of the real world. In our psyche we do not have the power to destroy any fragments and death penalties do not exist for any of the fragments. We continue to live with all our fragments and need special guards to stop troublemakers like Boris from affecting our identity and causing split.

Unfortunately, split would not protect our psyche from being taken over by a troublemaker. When we do not have the strength to have dialog with all our fragments, then before splitting we try negotiations. Also it is not possible to have negotiations with Boris, because he does not want any honest negotiations. Negotiations are impossible, because instead of negotiation the troublemaker will use tricks and lies to mislead and to confuse, but we are not completely splitting from a criminal. The criminal fragment may be isolated and watched. We are giving a criminal the benefit of the doubt, and we are checking if the criminal is willing to change. In the real world criminals rarely change their attitude, but in our psyche every fragment has the opportunity to grow and mature.

The fragment that represents Boris was putting all his energy toward protecting his own enterprise and feeding his grandiosity. As individuals, we have a responsibility to the world and must not allow the troublemaker fragment to take over our psyche. We deal with a criminal fragment by isolating and delegating responsibility to a fragment of guarding and starting an alarm if the criminal wants to take over our psyche. We need to keep a troublemaker in detention and the guard helps us. When the guard sounds the alarm, it means the defender is bringing the fact of the planned takeover to our conscious awareness. When we are consciously aware of what is coming next, we are preparing *self* for a planned invasion. We are ready to resist. If everyone in this world would guard against his troublemakers, we would not have so many troublemakers in the outside world.

The Split Between Love and Hate

To understand our identity we need to remember that our psyche resembles the external world. The same organization that we have in the external world, we see in our psyche. When we became part of a radical collective, we have our psyche to resemble the outside collective. The radical collective teaches us to hurt and hate because of the love of an idea. In our psyche we have two contradictory kingdoms, one aligned with hate and the other with love. Those kingdoms may have unlike shapes, but they are both replicas of the outside world's duality. Unfortunately, our psyche may not have love without hate. Most important, each of the kingdoms strived for expansion because of the need for followers. The kingdom of hate is always more powerful because we have many reasons to hate and we do not need to learn how. The knowledge of how to hate comes from the animalistic part of us and is always there. Hate is inheritably smart and very mobile. Love comes from more sophisticated feelings, and is less mobile and more sensitive. Hate has the power to replace love. Sometime we justify hate in God's name; we hate in the name of love. Both hate and love are internal feelings. Hate brings splitting, but love brings unification. Love is not a reason for hate, but nevertheless, hate has the strength to be everywhere, even around love. Experience helps us to fight hate, but only wisdom helps grow real love, because we strive for unification with a strong desire that comes only from inside of us. We have unification only with someone who, if he does not love, at least understands us.

Our hate may hide behind diverse feelings. We feel hate if we lack something important to be a success. When we do not have important, out-of-the-ordinary skills, we hate others who have them. The jealousy is mainly possessiveness. When we are jealous, we are capable of destroying a more successful pretender. When we feel cheated by someone who broke a promise, we feel hate. When we are helpless and believe that life is not fair to us, we feel hate. When we lack some skills to achieve the object of our desire, we hate. Jealousy is the situational feeling that has the power of hate. Sometimes we feel hate because we have a need for justice that comes from negotiation with the outside world. The lack of negotiating skills gets replaced by hate. Some feelings are not hate but only triggers for hate. It doesn't seem like a big difference, but it is still an important conceptual distinction.

Stepan Luchko was an example of mixture of hate and love. He loved his country and hated the enemies of his homeland. His psyche resembled the organization of the radical collective. His hate came from his beliefs that there are simple answers for everything. As result, he lacked the inspiration for negotiation. He did not let *self* have any second thoughts. He did not even have evidence that Boris, who was illegally selling a huge quantity of our native art, was working with our native Mafia. Even Luchko who was a bright man and experienced agent, failed to see that the secret agent was involved in contraband art, and that the art items that he sold were stolen from native art museums.

The forces of hate were suppressing Luchko's love for humanity. He got involved in the crime of assassination of a very good young man. He was mixed up in the unjustifiable slaughter of a defector from the ship of the collective. He had not done anything to stop it, and worse, he continued to obey Boris's orders. He also knew and did not report to the Directorate of Foreign Affairs that Boris was recruiting his contractors from those who had been convicted of numerous crimes. He knew that the guy who was driving the sailor's car was a thief. He also realized that the other driver, who collided with the sailor's car, was a criminal too. Luchko was acquainted with the man's father, who often complained about his son's criminal nature. Stepan Luchko knew that both the drivers received money, because he transferred the envelopes with money to them. Boris borrowed money from Luchko. He also left a parcel in Luchko's store, and Luchko passed it to the nurse at the hospital. Luchko later figured out that he was handling over to the nurse an untraceable lethal injection. To his surprise, he found out that the nurse, who participated in an assassination, was a friend of his stepdaughter. He did not have any idea how Boris was able to recruit her, because she was not paid. He also understood that he did not have the luxury to trust anyone and did not have any place to relax, because Boris's contractors were everywhere, even between his stepdaughter's friends. Officially, Boris was an attaché in the embassy of the collective. His diplomatic work was a cover for his real work as a secret agent. To recruit his contractors, he was mingling with a lot of scumbags in a variety of bars and pubs. Boris was a criminal with diplomatic immunity.

Antithetical to Boris, Luchko was an honest, dignified man who wanted more than anything else to have justice for the working class becomes a reality, but unknowingly, he was helping a heartless criminal who loved only money. Luchko knew that in the past the secret agents and their contractors were deeply involved in the ideology of the collective. He understood that it was very unusual for a secret agent to use criminals as contractors, because the collective cared about public opinion. His first mistake was that he did not report to the center that Boris was using criminals as contractors. He did not know that later, his mistake would come back to hurt him badly. Hate consumed his feeling of love and made him a co-conspirator in a crime. Hate brought him too far, to the point that he was hurting an innocent one. He got in a dangerous predicament because his love was too abstract and too far away, whereas hate was very close, concrete, and mobile. Unfortunately, hate has the strength to quickly sneak in and consume love. How to avoid the partnership with hate? What to do with terrorism and other evils of the world? Hate is a big and complicated issue, and we do not have a simple answer. Definitely, we must stop hate with any available means. Most important, we need to defend love. We may not use love for justifying hate. Terrorists' hate is based on their love for God or on their radical ideas. For our part, we hate them in the same way, because of our love for democracy and humanity. As a result, they hate us more and more. We need to stop feeling love and hate at the same time. The feeling of hate mixed with love gets us nowhere. It is time to focus on love. We cherish our love as something very precious that happens to us.

We need to protect our love from hate, but no order exists that was issued to protect love. We must voluntarily and consciously resist mixing hate and love together. We are capable of protecting our love and perhaps may not shame it with hate. We may do it only by our choice. We will succeed if everyone will not allow *self* to love and hate at the same time. We love for love and hate for hate. Let's separate love and hate forever. We do not hate because of love. We do not need any lies. We are not helping anyone by using love as an excuse to hurt.

Playing Games with Our Mind

Usually manipulating forces are playing very sophisticated games with our mind. The radical collective, which claimed to be the workers' paradise, gave a lot of opportunities to many manipulators. Skillful manipulators have a lot of power to do a lot of damage and to destroy lives. Their game resembles chess, which is about controlling the board and pushing the opponent out of the way. Manipulators use everyone as if they were inanimate figures. Many in the collective were playing a chess game. Boris, who was an expert of the manipulation game, designed a sophisticated plan of assassination. It was not a primitive hit-and-run plan, but one that was misleading. His plan resembled a pyramid with numerous layers. The deadly blow was delivered on the higher layer of the pyramid when everyone thought the game was over and no one expected anything else to happen. Without any guilt or other distractions, he calculated all the moves in a presented masquerade. He was an expert of manipulation. Sam Kaufman, who was a quick learner, was no match for Boris. His assignment from Ivan was to stay close and to become Andrusha's friend. He was watching Andrusha but did not become

Andrusha's confidant because that place was already taken. Andrusha was very close only to Stepan Kryvoruchko.

Sam observed that Andrusha spent a lot of time with Stepan Kryvoruchko. Nevertheless, Sam was near Andrusha and reported to Ivan that he had completed the first part of his assignment and was keeping his eye on Andrusha. Sam rented an apartment in the same high-rise where Andrusha lived. Once in the elevator when Andrusha was in the company of the new immigrants, Sam introduced *self* as a newcomer and they talked in native language. Sam invited Andrusha to a housewarming. Later, Andrusha became a usual face at Sam's family dinner table. Sam knew very well the city of St. Petersburg, where Andrusha and Sam's wife, Lina, were born. Andrusha and Lina found few mutual friends. They talked about the city where they both were born and also shared diverse stresses of everyday life. They had many things to talk about. Eventually, Sam, who spent a lot of time with Andrusha, was also introduced to Stepan Kryvoruchko. After talking to Kryvoruchko, Sam was sure that Andrusha was safe in his company. To complete the second part of his assignment Sam became a common face in the jewelry-repair store owned by Stepan Luchko.

In this place he saw the man who was at the picnic on that terrible day and had driven Andrusha's car, the driver of the car that later hit Andrusha's car, and then the nurse. At this time Sam did not have any idea about any assassination plot against Andrusha. It was by accident that he was in Andrusha's car when everything happened. The tragedy happened on one of the weekends when Stepan Kryvoruchko was visiting his Israeli friends and was not in the city. Andrusha's acquaintance called and invited him to go out from the city and have a picnic with him and his girlfriend. He asked if he could possibly drive Andrusha's car, because his was in the garage for repair. At the same time Sam was in Andrusha's apartment and heard this conversation. He right away expressed an interest to go with Andrusha and asked if his wife too might join them. Andrusha talked to his acquaintance, who was not opposed. During the picnic everyone was very friendly. The acquaintance and his girlfriend brought food.

Andrusha brought sodas and dessert for everyone. Sam and his wife brought wine, a Frisbee, volleyball, and badminton. Everyone had fun. Andrusha became sleepy during the picnic. Sam later figured out that the acquaintance had put some sleeping drugs in Andrusha's drink. When they drove back, the minor accident happened. A car from the other side made a wrong turn and hit Andrusha's car. Police came. Because Andrusha was drowsy, they called paramedics and he was taken to the nearest hospital. Sam went to the hospital too. Andrusha appeared normal but stayed overnight for observation. He asked Sam to park his car at a usual place. No one had any suspicions that something bad would happen. Only later did Sam realize how viciously and skillfully Boris had played his game. He understood that Boris used him as a figure in his game. First of all, he brought wine, so he might be a suspect if experts found any drugs in Andrusha's blood. Second, the driver expected him and his wife to be witnesses that no one had done anything wrong. Like most manipulators who knew the game of the collective, Boris was very smart. Sam felt very bad that he had overlooked important evidence, but he had not yet realized that he too had a high IQ and would figure out all the hidden layers of Boris's game.

In his past he always was in crisis, and he used his intelligence only to survive. From now on he would use his IQ to fight evil and help others. Boris, who was an expert of manipulation, was sure no one would be able to discover the facts. Like a spider he created a big net of cobwebs to cover his tracks. He manipulated minds to disguise the truth. He was a master of masquerade, but a new sheriff was already in town. Sam would discover all the facts of Boris's cruelty and would make everything right.

We are with Goodness if We are Not with Evil

The splitting forces of evil pollute our minds because they prevent us from questioning the viciousness of the evil. The radical collective would not allow any questions or even curiosity. The collective knew that by questioning the roots of evil we unify with goodness. For them it was very important that we not reject evil because then we would not accept goodness. Evil is able to manipulate our minds by fabricating many unusual excuses for hate. Evil's reason for a mixture of hate and love is covered with deceptive smoke and appears to have a valid basis. We need to have good judgment to recognize the real reasons behind the smoke. Boris justified assassination by his love and care of the image of the collective, but the real reason he got rid of the sailor was his fear that the sailor had connections to the secret police. He was protecting his operation. Even before the tragedy Luchko suspected that Boris was doing something bad, but as a soldier he did not question his superior officer. When he started thinking about the validity of Boris's orders and using his insights, he refused to be a robotic participant.

In the past it was absolutely impossible for Luchko to think that he had enough strength to disobey his superior, but after Andrusha's assassination he started to doubt his superior. He did not know the reason for Andrusha's terrible fate, but deep in his heart he questioned the wisdom of the harsh actions against the sailor. He may not have understood why in Montreal, where several sailors jumped from various ships, only Andrusha was punished. He knew Andrusha and remembered the bright and honest young man. Andrusha seemed to be very impulsive, but he would risk his life to help anyone, even one he did not know. He was very well mannered and delicate. Luchko remembered the little things about the sailor that showed his generous and gentle parts. Luchko had offered drinks and food to newcomers and everyone had used his hospitality, but only Andrusha had brought flowers to his store. In the meantime Boris found out through his channels that the Canadians were barraged with complaints from Kryvoruchko about the sailor's death. He wanted to get rid of Kryvoruchko, and somehow he was able to get approval from his superiors. He emphasized in his request to his superior that Kryvoruchko had close contact with the sailor and that he knew too much and needed to be removed.

Very soon Luchko had another order from Boris, that he must organize a killing of Stepan Kryvoruchko, his grandson, who carried his first name. Luchko, who already had bad feelings, was proven correct in his suspicions about Boris's next step. He was an honest and honorable man. In his past he had been used by forces of evil because he had not questioned the evil's orders. Present circumstances were pressing him to resist the evil by using all his knowledge. He realized that he was not aligned with evil anymore and was looking for unification with goodness.

To be A Patriot

Patriotic feelings are feelings of unification. Normally, these feelings do not demand that patriots split from their families, but the radical collective pits brother against brother and son against father. The collective teaches that family is not important and that collective needs are more important. The extreme in anything, including patriotic feelings, is an indication of a desire to cover up some emptiness and evil intent. For many that have emptiness in their psyches, it was very handy to use the patriotic feeling as a patch. They may cover up the hole in their psyche. Actually, if we have a solid psyche, patriotic feeling is a big joy, because we unify our children with our country's customs, our language, and teaching. Normally, being a patriot means loving our country and enjoying it together with our family and friends. As patriots, we take pleasure in serving our country and making it more beautiful.

As a patriot Stepan Luchko was glad that his country was doing well. Even though he lived outside of his country, he enjoyed his Ukrainian ethnicity. He also liked his cultural proficiency in the dominant language. He was never disrespectful of other ethnicities. He spoke many languages, including English, German, and French. He learned French when he was working in the coal mine in Belgium. Every day he was speaking French and English and living in a bilingual city. Stepan Luchko was a patriot and he also was a soldier. When he heard that his family had been killed, he dedicated his life to the cause of liberating the working class. He gave to his country everything he had and even more, but his homeland always wanted him to do the dirty job. During collectivization as a young man he, together with other commissars of collective, was pushing farmers out of their land and collectivizing it. His orders from the collective were clear.

He was imprisoning farmers, whom he hated as enemies, making them vacate their land and deporting them to Siberia. He was risking his life and might be killed by angry farmers. The farmers did not have anything to lose because they were robbed by the collective of their land and possessions and sent to starve and freeze to death. In the meantime he was studying at night to become a teacher and help children to understand the beauty of their land. He was always giving his time and energy to his country, and the collective taught him to hate and love at the same time. During the war he was ready to give up his life but miraculously survived. He did not know that his wife and daughter were alive. He thought he was the only survivor from all his family, and after the war he continued to be a soldier and never refused any orders from superiors. He thought that he was helping his homeland to fight its enemies. He felt he had paid his debt to his country in full, but suddenly, he had an order to kill his grandchild. He would not do it. The emptiness of his psyche was filled up, and he did not need feelings of grandiosity. He did not need to pretend that he was extremely dedicated to his cause. He was able to listen to common sense.

In the past Luchko was just brain dead because he was listening to the slogans. The scumbags were using his honesty for their own gains. He realized that as a patriot, he was far from being a member of a cult, where the membership required him to give up his entire life and all ambitions. He was a patriot with all his thoughts. Also he was sure that to be a patriot he did not need to give up his private life. He also understood that in his circumstances the extreme demand was not valid. He definitely did not find any reason to sacrifice someone of his family. He loved and served his country well, but he would not comply with an insane demand from a sick and shoddy supervisor.

The Real Meeting is Affecting Lives

The real meeting brings meaning to our life. It possibly is a goal of our life. Without real meeting our life is incomplete. Without genuine dialog our meetings are impossible, and without the meetings our life is not complete. We want a genuine dialog together with a real meeting. We need them to create a solid identity. The meeting is the biggest joy in our life. Luchko was very lonely. Suddenly, he was meeting his past. He had dialog with his grandson, which opened the road to the meeting. He had meeting with *self* as a family man who got reconnected to his lost family. Before meeting with his grandson he was a man with emptiness in his psyche. Now, his emptiness was filled up with joy, excitement, and a sense of fulfillment. He was a lucky one and had a real meeting. The real meeting gave meaning to his entire life. His meeting with his grandson also brought the internal dialog with the missing parts of his life. Through dialog he was meeting *self* as the father of an accomplished daughter who is a medical doctor and medical school lecturer. He was meeting *self* as a grandfather of two grandchildren. He also was meeting *self* as an ex-husband, whose presumably dead wife was alive and married to his best friend.

He asked Sam to help him to organize a meeting with Stepan Kryvoruchko. When they both met, Luchko asked, even though he knew it, if Stepan's mother's name is Marinka and if his father is Leonya. Stepan nodded to clarify that those names are correct. Luchko asked if Marinka's father had the first name Stepan and if her maiden name was Luchko. Stepan Kryvoruchko nodded again. He thought the man in front of him was a friend of his grandfather. He added, "My grandfather died during the war."

Luchko answered, "Not exactly! Yes, I almost died at the hands of the Gestapo, but good luck helped me. I am alive and I am your grandfather, and I know that you have the same first name."

Stepan Kryvoruchko was speechless and did not know what to say. He asked, "If you are Stepan Luchko, how did it happen that you are here with another name?"

Luchko did not want to make up any stories. He said, "It is a long story, but I was in the army of General Vlasov and need to change my name in order to immigrate to Canada. Listen, I do not believe that our meeting is just a random occurrence. It is more than this. I know for sure from the contacts of former Vlasov soldiers that the same forces that ordered the assassination of Andrusha are now against you. It is very serious."

Stepan Kryvoruchko said, "Let's go to the Canadian police. They will help us."

The meeting was gratifying for Luchko and for Stepan Kryvoruchko too. The grandson met his grandfather, but he was not yet ready for a genuine dialog. For both of them everything was very sudden. Stepan Kryvoruchko had not seen his grandfather before, who was presumed dead for long time, and all of a sudden, his grandfather has flesh and is alive. Everything was surreal. He was meeting the grandfather who was a hero of his dreams and a legend. He needed time to understand consciously with whom he was meeting, but later he would understand. He did not know yet that this meeting with his grandfather would save his life. He did meet a grandfather who was ready to protect him with his own life.

The Dialog in Our Life

In our life the most important dialog is about surviving and how to protect our life. Without surviving we do not have a future and do not exist. The dialog is the tool for unification and to build a solid identity. The life of grandfather and grandson were split by forces beyond their control. Now, their lives had a chance for unification, which is saving lives and requires complete trust. Even though everything came at Stepan Kryvoruchko very suddenly and he felt like he was on a roller coaster, he knew that he trusted his grandfather with his life. His parents worshipped his grandfather. He eventually recognized his grandfather from the family's photos. He remembered that in the living room of his parents' house there was a large portrait of his grandfather that was painted by an artist, and that decorations of a hero were attached to his grandfather's chest. He realized that he needed help, and he was overwhelmed that his grandfather had showed up in his life at the right time, when he had just lost his best friend. He understood that he was facing very strong forces.

Stepan Kryvoruchko was not able to get any justice for Andrusha, and now, his own life was in real danger. Stepan Luchko told his grandson that he had a suspicion that inside the Canadian police was Boris's mole. He also explained to his grandson that he must not tell Canadian authorities his real name, because he might be deported. He did not tell anyone at the time of immigration that he was in Vlasov's army. He told his grandson that joining the Vlasov army was the only way he could survive, and that he did not kill anyone. He did not want to scare his grandson by disclosing that he had enlisted in the Vlasov army and then immigrated to Canada by the order of the collective. He asked his grandson to keep their conversation a secret for the time being. He also mentioned that he needed to protect his own source, because he was afraid that otherwise his source would get executed too. He emphasized again that he would not allow anything bad to happen to his grandson. He asked his grandson to leave the city for a couple of days and, for the time being, did not tell anyone what was going on in his life.

Stepan also mentioned to Luchko that he still held an Israeli citizenship and was acquainted with one Israeli attaché. He proposed to call this man, whom he had known since their time together in the Israeli army. Luchko told his grandson to be careful and to be sure that someone new would not make this situation worse. He said it would be better if he would check out this attaché. Stepan Kryvoruchko was very happy that his grandfather was alive and helping him. He also was overwhelmed and astonished at how his grandfather found out about the killings. He trusted his grandfather. He lived his life as a hero of our time and suddenly, he met his grandfather, a hero of World War II. Eventually, the two heroes had a dialog that was based on mutual trust and admiration. This dialog was the most important event in both of their lives. This dialog helped them to join forces of unification and saved them from hate and split.

The Love for Family

Normally, family love is stronger than any ambitions and ideological convictions. In many instances we hold up fanatically for our ideology; we protect our own flesh and blood, even if they do not share the same convictions. We also see the other side, when one is unresponsive to his family.

The radical collective was justifying that as members, because of our ideological convictions, we had the right to kill our brothers and to inform on our fathers. By providing many historical facts the radical collective showed that we may not care about family ties. If we were having other ideas, we were enemies of the state. The ideologists of the collective were demanding more love from us for the collective than for our families. They encouraged the publication of stories about the aristocrats, who were torturing and killing other members of their families. Those stories included killings in royal families. The French kings killed and kept many members of their family imprisoned. The English royals also had their share of killing family members. The czars Ivan the Terrible and Peter the Great killed their sons, and ideologists hinted that Alexander I of Russia somehow participated in the killing of his father. The soviet ideologists implied that many historical figures did not want to sacrifice their own ambitions for their family.

Stepan Luchko was a man who did not have any career ambition, and he thought he had lost his family a long time ago. He dedicated his life to his beloved country. He believed that the world is not a fair place and wanted justice for the working class. He fought for his ideas, but he would not sacrifice his love for his family for evil, which was covering up all his malicious deeds with lies. He would never betray his family. He loved his family with all his heart and would defend them to his last breath. The emptiness in his psyche was filled with love, and he did not want to serve the forces of evil anymore. During his many years in service of the collective, he was proud to be a soldier. He did not allow his feelings to show, but in his heart he always felt bitterness and emptiness. He was remembering his past life as a family man with a beautiful wife and little daughter.

The new reality was suddenly open to him and took away all his bitterness. He was a father and grandfather with his daughter and wife alive. He felt only love. He opened up to his grandson and let him know how dangerous his situation was. He was letting his grandson see the truth. He knew well the system of secret police and how dangerous this situation was. He was sure there was no way to avoid the coming disaster except to get to the Canadians and tell them everything. He also knew that in the police was Boris's mole, and that he would be killed for sure. He did not think about *self*, because if he did not act very fast, his grandson may be killed. He would not allow an execution of his grandson, who was the continuation of his bloodline. When he told his grandson everything, he did not have any fear of death.

Luchko was a foot soldier who was serving his homeland, and now, as a soldier, without any second thoughts, he would die to let his grandson to live. Even if Boris would be a god, Luchko would not sacrifice his grandson for ideology. He was not doing any more work for Boris, who did not serve his country but was making his pocket bigger. He also understood that Boris was just abusing his position and using others to do his dirty work, which had nothing to do with ideology. Boris was one of many evils of the collective who were using ideology to cover up their grimy business. But, when love for the family was unifying someone's life, luck was with him.

Luckily, Sam Kaufman was in the store during Luchko's disclosure and overheard the partial conversation with his grandson. From the conversation Sam understood that Luchko was the grandfather of Stepan Kryvoruchko. The appearance of Sam was good luck for Luchko, because Sam was helping him defeat Boris.

The Meeting and Dialog

Meetings and dialog may happen at any time when we are involved in interaction. They also happen with the fragments inside of our psyche when they are interacting. When we realize that they are having dialog, then we also know that we have a meeting. We do not know about our capacity for being engaged in a dialog, and we do not have the knowledge to recognize right away what is happening to us. The meeting of allied minds is possible only through dialog, which is based on our mutual respect and concern for the well-being of both sides. During the dialog we find out that we have lots of feelings to share and then meeting happens. Unfortunately, genuine dialog does not happen too often, but when it prevails, we feel stronger. When inside of our psyche our fragments have dialog, the unification forces fuse together the fragments, and after the dialog our identity becomes more solid.

By unifying we win a chance to have a solid identity. The psyche subconsciously strives for unification, but we do not have too many conscious tools to achieve this goal. Unification by love is our very strong intuitive unification. With love we are unifying with our spouses, children, family, and friends. Love is the most used subconscious tool of unification. Hate and fear also have the power to unify us for particular moment, but it is the weakest form of unification. The radical collective does not recognize our dialogs and meetings and declares them a waste of time, because we are supposed to spend our life so that our biggest joy is worshipping the collective. The ideologists of the collective speak about our equality, but allow equality only in submission. We also have dialogs and meetings with divinity. The radical collective does not want any dialogs, because it is not able to control our subconscious mind. It does not accept that our psyche gets unified on the intuitive level. Our intuitive dialog is a form of unification that comes from our desire to have a meeting and to feel equal. When we are experiencing a genuine meeting, we are having a dialog. In many instances we start a dialog with the hope of meeting a kindred soul.

After meeting with his grandson, Luchko also had a get-together with Sam Kaufman. They too opened up. Luchko explained what had happened. He said he would not allow Boris to organize the killing of his grandchild and would use any means to stop him. He trusted Sam and wanted to caution him about a risk. He mentioned that Sam might be in danger because of their association. Luchko had entered the country with another name. He also disclosed that if he asked Canada for protection, he might be in trouble with the police. He added that he had been indirectly mixed up in Andrusha's death. He also revealed that, despite the overall complexity, he might be forced to ask the police for protection of his grandson. He mentioned that if he broke his cover, he would also be in danger of being punished by the collective. The foreseen split of his identity had been triggered by the need for survival of his own blood, which he had discovered not long ago. He needed to lose the biggest part of his life by choosing splitting; otherwise, his grandson's existence was in danger.

Sam was very flattered by Luchko's honest revelation, because he wanted to be helpful. This was a real adventure. For the first time in his life someone had a desire to caution and protect him. He decided to tell Luchko about his mission and that he was working for Ivan, Andrusha's father. He revealed that he was in Montreal on special assignment to find a connection with thieves and smugglers of our precious antiques. He explained to Luchko that he had found a connection between Andrusha's death and the smuggling of antiques. He added that the killing of Andrusha was organized to protect Boris's operation. He also mentioned that in his report he had sent evidence that implicated Boris in the contraband and in selling stolen goods.

The dialog between Luchko and Sam consolidated their unification against evil forces. When we have a genuine meeting, we also have a dialog. The dialog and meeting may be right away or after some period of time, when we eventually acknowledge what happened to us. We meet others through the dialog as like-minded individuals. Our meeting is not based on fear and anger when we are driven to others by the necessity to have more strength on our side. The dialog between Luchko and Sam revealed friendship and admiration. Their meeting was a real meeting of the minds through a genuine dialog.

The Real Meeting and Intermediate Fragments

We have the ability to meet and have dialog through intermediation. If the unification of the fragments is complicated, we have intermediate fragments to be catalysts of unification. When we are in a direction of unification, we have many fragments that are experiencing a dialog and meeting. The fragments, which are having comparable feelings, would intermediate in arranging a dialog. When identity becomes more solid, the psyche is using internal logic to support a dominant fragment. The requirement of opening a dialog inside our psyche is that the fragments may have the similarity in taking action and in responding. Stepan Kryvoruchko did not know anything about Ivan, but they had similar feelings and responses and they did have a meeting. Their meeting did happen through Sam Kaufman. The meeting was very important because the life of Stepan Kryvoruchko was in danger. The most important dialog about his survival was done without his presence and through intermediates.

The responses of Stepan Luchko and Ivan were to save lives. Sam and Luchko had dialog and meeting. They were united to save Stepan Kryvoruchko. For them saving Stepan Kryvoruchko became the most important task. They were united against forces of evil. The meeting showed that Luchko and Sam had the same feelings and the same convictions. Sam told Luchko that Boris ordered the killing of Andrusha as an act of protection of his smuggling operation, and Luchko confirmed the validity of Sam's discoveries. Sam's opinion was that the secret police would not keep an officer in their organization who was connected to Mafia criminals as a contractor and was him*self* a smuggler. Sam told Luchko, "I know Boris ordered the killing of Andrusha, and he needs to be stopped. I believe that Ivan, even if he has limited power in the Directorate of Foreigner Affairs, may stop the killer of his innocent son from killing again. I have proof that Boris is an American connection for the thieves, who stole from museums priceless national treasure." He asked Luchko to wait a couple of days and not to go to the Canadian authorities until he had an answer from Ivan.

Sam sent to Ivan all the evidence and testimony from Luchko that Andrusha's death was not an accident but a planned professional killing. He also added that he had been in Boris's house and seen the items that resembled the stolen ones in pictures he saw in Ivan's office. He included in the report the photo snaps of Boris's collections and of items in the antiques stores. He also reported to Ivan that the next target of Boris's killing was Stepan Kryvoruchko, who was Andrusha's friend and a grandson of the undercover agent. In this situation Luchko and Ivan did not meet face-to-face, but through Sam Kaufman fate brought out-of-the-ordinary opportunities. Ivan was a man dedicated to his cause who wanted to crush the alliance of smugglers of our native art. He also suspected that his son's death was not an accident, but now he had evidence that Boris had had his son killed in order to protect the smuggling operation. Ivan understood that he was not able to bring his son back, but at least he might be able to save the life of his son's best friend and fight for postmortem justice for his son. Ivan, through Sam Kaufman as intermediary, was getting a meeting with Stepan Kryvoruchko and Luchko.

The Split or Dialog with Someone Whom We Have Never Seen

It is possible that we do not have to see someone with whom we are having dialog or split. For a dialog we need to know something good about someone to have a positive experience. For split we may well have a valid reason too. In many instances, we let an individual or a book enter our psyche as an imprint and become a fragment in our psyche. Later, we have the internal conversations with the imprint. We keep in our psyche the numerous imprints of significant ones and imprints of our own responses that we had on the diverse stages of our life. We form an opinion, based on the feelings gathered from imprints. We are sensitive to their influences. We choose the direction where the new information is leading. We may have dialogs or we need to protect *self* and to split.

Splitting and dialog may be possible in the diverse manners. When we are having negative response, we are splitting. It is easier to split. Sometimes we split because we do not like something about the other. It may be the look, the voice, the way he moves, or how he touches things. The split can happen when we are receiving information through intermediate sources. We are splitting because we are receiving negative information from someone whose opinion we trust and with whom we are having congruent thoughts. When we split, we do not have a meeting. The meeting is happening when we are seeing, listening to, or reading something that is creating a meaningful interaction and a feeling of acceptance. This is the first step toward meeting. Dialog becomes possible when we receive positive feelings from a letter, book, stage play, movie, or someone we know, or something we do not know and have not seen before. We may well have a dialog in diverse sensory forms. By comparing the interactions when we have visual contact with others and when we do not have the opportunity to see them, we understand that visual contacts bring more information.

When we are seeing, hearing, and observing the body's movement, we are getting in our memory brighter imprints that are a creation of our sensory assessments. When we are sharing positive visual, audio, kinesthetic, olfactory, or tactile information internally or externally, we are having a meeting. During a meeting we recognize that the new information belongs to the forces of unification.

The feelings of being understood and accepted are a precondition for a dialog. The capacity to have dialog and to have meetings is the most important in establishing a solid identity. The information that creates an atmosphere of a dialog may arrive from letters and feelings that were transmitted through the others. When Ivan received mail from Sam, he ordered him to develop the negatives. He compared the photos of icons and paintings from Boris's home and antiques stores and found that they were exact matches with pictures of items stolen from museums. He also read Sam's report and realized that Boris had ordered the killing of his son and was preparing an assassination of his son's best friend.

Ivan was reliving the tragic death of his son and was not able to hold back his tears. Ivan definitely did not want anything bad to happen to the friend of his late son. He also understands that his son's friend is a grandson of a secret agent, who also is a hero of the collective. Ivan had already lost his son and understood the emotions of his comrade, who is working undercover in Canada. He could not allow his fellow agent, who sacrificed all his life in the service of his motherland, to be victimized by a smuggler and thief. Ivan understood the complicity of his mission, because in the Directorate of Foreigner Affairs everything was classified and had a lot of red tape. Ivan decided that he was not taking any risks going through official channels but he would see a chairman through his own contacts. He was aware that, normally, it is impossible without going through red tape to have an appointment with the head of the most powerful secret police. He would need to explain to many low-level officers and then submit a written report. The whole procedure may take forever. He also understood that every second of delay might bring back the same tragedy that happened to his son, and he needed to move fast.

Ivan decided to use the connections of his in-law, the father of Andrusha's wife, who knew many of the very important bureaucrats in Moscow. His in-law called one of his friends in the headquarters of the secret police, who made contact with another close friend from the Directorate of Foreign Affairs and was very close to the chairman. In the phone conversation with his contact, Ivan first apologized that the investigation was informal and that he had moved to the foreign territory without authorization; then he told his contact about Sam's discoveries. He asked for permission to come immediately to Moscow and to deliver the evidence. The permission was granted. Ivan took a flight in a military airplane that delivered top-secret mail. In one hour Ivan was presenting evidence to his contact. He asked him for permission to talk to the head of the secret police about a very confidential incident that happened overseas and was about treason and the death of an innocent one.

Ivan told his contact he was concerned about Boris's cronies in the chairman's surroundings. In one hour his contact was able to organize a secret meeting in his office. The chairman him*self* listened to Ivan and looked at all the evidence. Stepan Kryvoruchko and Luchko were unbelievably lucky and were saved. It took Ivan only a few hours to arrange a meeting with the chairman, which normally takes months when others are going through regular channels. The chairman vaguely remembered Andrusha's case, but for a long time he continued to feel uneasy about being dragged into a murky Canadian case. Now he understood that Boris had duped him and he apologized to Ivan. The chairman did not like to look like a fool and be manipulated by his subordinates. He remembered that Boris did not have any blood relationship to any of his bosses. This fact made Boris insignificant and very easy to replace. The chairman immediately wrote the order to permanently recall Boris from Canada. He also recommended opening an investigation into Andrusha's death, and after the investigation, punishing Boris and his contractors, including the nurse, who was Boris's mistress. She was the one who administered the deadly injection that killed Andrusha. The chairman recommended that Boris's contractors be investigated for being accomplices in smuggling stolen art.

Later, it was discovered that Boris used government funds to pay carriers for delivering stolen art. He was falsifying the payrolls. In the conversation, when the chairman asked what agent was able to do this investigation, Ivan mentioned that he got all the evidence from his informer, who was not even an agent. He said he trusted Sam Kaufman with his life and considered Sam his adopted son. He made a recommendation to send Sam a letter of gratitude, which for Sam was more valuable than any promotion. By the right of one who had uncovered treason, Ivan asked that Luchko's grandson not be hurt by the secret police. In case Kryvoruchko did something wrong the secret police of the collective might overlook it because of Luchko's sacrifices. The chairman definitely understood a hint and his face got a reddish color. Ivan implied that he was not appreciated enough for his work by the high command and that this was why they did not grant mercy to his son.

During the meeting, Ivan's contact, who knew about Luchko's work, recommended raising Luchko's morale by sending him his decoration for being a hero of the collective, and a letter of promotion assuring Luchko that the homeland is remembering and valuing him. The dialog happened even though Ivan was not able to have a meeting with Luchko face-to-face and despite the fact that Ivan never saw him in his life and had never heard about him before. He accomplished the task of saving a grandson's life and the grandfather's honor. They were mainly a product of his imagination, and now he had a meeting with them. The dialog was not visual, not audible, but he was able to meet those individuals because of the invaluable information he got from his informer. By acting fast and being smart he was creating a huge field of unification with his tremendous effort of saving the life of his son's friend. By speedy and precise moves he was able to prevent future killings.

Boris was urgently called to Moscow for investigation. By splitting from Boris Ivan was splitting from the evil forces. He did know that Boris was even splitting through the intermediaries. The split was necessary to save lives in memory of his son. Ivan also had meeting and a dialog without any audio and visual contact, but most important was that the dialog occurred and lives were saved.

A Burst of Joyful Emotions Occurs After Thoughts of Inflicting Torture and Pain on Perpetrators

Thoughts of inflicting torture and pain on perpetrators make us, as victims, feel better. We are having a burst of joyful emotions, because in our thoughts we are doing to the perpetrators the torture that was done to us. As victims, we perhaps may identify *self* with perpetrator. Yes, our psyche is looking for justice by inflicting pain on the perpetrator, but we also are copying exactly what was done to us. In the radical collective the ideologists talked a lot about martyrdom and sufferings. They used our sentiments to justify their own atrocities. They were very good at manipulating. It's the same process we see in our psyche. By inflicting pain on the perpetrator in our thoughts, we are in reality somehow pleasing the fragment that contains the victim's characteristic. Ivan lost his son and was traumatized and looking for revenge. When Boris came to Moscow, right away he was taken from the airport to the secret-police headquarters and interrogated by members of Internal Security. Boris was prickly and obnoxious with them, but this approach did not work.

The investigators from the Directorate of Internal Affairs were not as polite and nice as the officers from Foreign Affairs, and he did not know any of them. The allegations were that with his illegal operations, he was misleading the Directorate of Foreign Affairs. He had associated with all kinds of criminals, which created the potential to jeopardize all other operations in the Western Hemisphere. He was involved in smuggling and selling art stolen from museums. He requested unneeded financing for his illegal schemes. Many times he requested additional financing and tightened up the resources needed for something else. He also butchered the operation to return the sailor by pressuring him with threats. He did not consult anyone to find sundry solutions. He was deeply obsessed with the necessity of getting quick results. The interrogators mentioned that his bullying only scared the sailor from returning. He was confronted by the sailor's mother that he had ignored her tears and begging even though she guaranteed that without any pressure and only by using a nicer approach, she would bring her son back. She said she had proposed a plan that was rejected by Boris that with the influence of the sailor's wife and friends, she would be able to persuade the sailor to leave Canada and go back home.

Boris had not used the sailor's wife and friends as a motivation to return the sailor and hastily requested assassination. He also was confronted by Ivan, who said he had disregarded the fact that the sailor was the son of a secret-police officer. Ivan said he had alienated the sailor by using threats and did not use enough diplomacy and professionalism to resolve the situation. Toward the end of the interrogation Boris signed all the papers that were requested by the officers and admitted all his misdeeds. The Directorate of Internal Affairs employed very tough officers who in their job of interrogation were not limited by any restrictions. For them Boris was a common criminal and they were not worried about his connection to high places. The chairman of all the secret police gave them the green light. They were at liberty to use any interrogating techniques they thought were appropriate. They were rude, and Boris understood that this was not a place to play games and that his connections would not help. He had a few cards that he planned to use later. It was very important for him to show remorse and to buy time by any means, which included the complete disclosure and admission of all his misdeeds.

Very soon the interrogating officers had a list of Boris's bank accounts around the globe where Boris had his deposits. He also signed a letter of attorney and proxy to any bearer who would be assigned to manage his accounts and receive money from antiques dealers. Sam Kaufman received the list of all Boris's bank accounts, a letter that said he is the present holder of Boris's estate, the list of Boris's safe deposit boxes, and a letter of gratitude. He also had a letter of promotion for Luchko, and a copy of the certification from the Ministry of Defense that Luchko is a hero of World War II. This information was needed to please a part of his psyche that is dreaming about various ways to restore fairness. To have closure Ivan and his wife needed to see their son's killer apprehended. The vigilantes are only dreaming of the revenge and retaliation. They are having vigilant thoughts by inflicting on the perpetrator physical pain and humiliation. In many movies the admired actors beat the offenders and make them suffer. The moviegoers love them, because this is one way to get even with evil.

Very often in our mind we are very vigilant and imagine that we are harming and torturing the perpetrator. Another way of getting revenge is making someone look ridiculous and laughing at him. The situation becomes more complicated when we are dealing with troublemaking fragments that are part of our psyche. We are not able to damage them because we are sharing the same body with them. Thoughts and images of the punishment of our enemies generate some commotion inside our psyche and give us some relief, but we forget that the perpetrator is one of our own fragments and we are torturing *self*. Being part of the collective, we never learned to forgive. It is easier said than done to forgive *self* that we got victimized. We bring to an end the enjoyment of violent thoughts inflicting pain. By refusing to follow the messages of the collective we are dealing with our troublemaking fragments in a nonviolent way. When we resist the violence inside of us, we decrease the violence in the world around us.

Intangible Objects as Products of A Dialog

The receiving of an intangible object, which we cannot touch, may be one of the fruits of dialog. Intangible objects have a lot of symbolic meanings and are the catalysts of a continued state of dialog within our psyche. The most valuable benefit of dialog is a genuine meeting, which creates good feelings about *self*. Those feelings include increased *self*-esteem, *self*-worth, acceptance of *self* by others, and having a solid identity. When fragments are having dialog, they are participating in a very important experience of building and maintaining a solid identity. The intangible objects that were created as a result of dialog are the links to a deeper level of unification. Intangible objects are the keys to fragment connections that are not visible. The radical collective did not recognize the existence of the subconscious mind, because it was not under control of the ideologists. The ideologists were denying that we transfer the subconscious feelings to consciousness and then have the ability to understand them.

The ideologists of the radical collective were always putting enemies in front of members and mobilizing a collective to fight them. The ideologists were not allowing us, the members, to look inside our psyches. They were forbidding us to print information about our psyche and preventing us from figuring out a structure of our psyche. They did not want us to have knowledge of how to organize and solidify our psyche. The radical collective was in fear of members, and was treating them as intangible objects and uniting them like robots. The ideas of the radical collective pushed all members to be identical and to rely only on the superficial gains of the conscious mind. We do not need this kind of shallow equality. If we knew something about our subconscious mind, we would not want a big collective with iron discipline. Our only wish would be to unify our psyche by having dialogs and meetings. We understand that each of our psyches has a distinctive subconscious organization. Many of our fragments have sub-fragments that are attached to one of the dominant fragments. It's like parts of the construction that were assembled together in a unique design. The intangible object may be an invisible connector between the parts of the psyche that have an imaginative design.

We have a dialog with all fragments based on trust and understanding. When Sam received the mail with the news of Luchko's promotion, confirmation of Luchko's hero status, and, addressed to him, a letter of gratitude, he was very happy. He felt that he deserved to be called a hero of the workers' paradise and that his homeland recognized him. He also satisfied his hunger for adventure and was proving to *self* that he is a real man. As the result of dialogs he had intangible connections that reconstructed his psyche. He became *self*-confident and ready for future adventures. He told Luchko that his grandson was not in any danger anymore. He also delivered the letters and the information that Boris was recalled to the collective and detained.

Luchko immediately called his grandson and reassured him that Boris, who had ordered the assassination of Andrusha and the other accomplices, was not a threat anymore. Stepan Kryvoruchko, who was hiding in New York, was safe from Boris, and it was clear for him to come back to Canada. Very soon Stepan Kryvoruchko and Sam Kaufman became fathers and everyone had a boy. Stepan Kryvoruchko had his son circumcised in the Jewish tradition, and Sam Kaufman had his son christened in an Orthodox faith. Both men and Luchko attended the services for the babies. Soon, Luchko was petitioning the Canadian authorities to change his last name to his original one. He disclosed that he was a soldier who was fighting fascists and that by order of the High Command he had infiltrated Vlasov's army under an assumed name. He attached letters to his petition from Alexander Kryvoruchko, his old friend, and from Ivan, who confirmed Luchko's story. His petition was granted, and Stepan Luchko was able to restore his name and to join the immigrants' association of veterans of World War II in America, which united his countrymen. His meetings were helping him have dialog between obligation to his country and to his family. He also was getting dialog with his fragments of being a hero of the war and being appreciated by his country. Before his genuine meetings his fragments were mainly transmitting the horror of the past. They created a lot of distortion in his psyche and the splitting was only one way of surviving.

Luchko was lucky to have meetings and dialogs. He was able to resolve positively a conflict between love of his country and love of his family. He did not betray his country and was recognized as a hero. His meetings with his grandson and Sam opened up internal dialog with his fragments, which were hiding deeply in his psyche. The dialog created the intangible associations that were inspiring the unification of his fragments.

The Dialog is Continuing Through Life

When the dialog starts in our psyche, it continues through all of our life. The power of meetings and dialogs is very strong, and empowers us to be more flexible and have a solid identity. When our identity has an opportunity for solidification by using an internal dialog, the process became permanent and our internal dialog does not stop. For external interactions we use a lot of intuitive assumptions based on our own responses. This is a reason why external dialogs are so rare. Very often we try to have dialog with others, but unfortunately, it happens very rarely and we get frustrated. If we do not have the strength to resist the wild fragments, we depend on the individuals with solid identity, but it does not mean they are having meetings. The meetings would not happen when we are not prepared and are not tuned in to meetings, because it is not easy to have a meeting outside of *self*. When we have internal interactions with others, we are dealing with the imaginative imprints of them in our psyche. We perhaps are learning some information about someone, including his temper, educational level, and job skills, but we do not have the knowledge to predict which of his fragments is taking over and in what time. We do not know all the circumstances of how his fragments were acquired. When we interact with somebody, we are taking lots of chances by guessing his responses. It is very complicated to have a dialog with someone, because we do not know how his subconscious mind is organized. We are putting *self* in a ridiculous position when we are using our own imagination to fill up the dark spots in someone's psyche.

The solid identity is very attractive to others, but attraction is not enough for having a dialog. Regrettably, the internal dialog is not always transferred to the external one. If we do not have the ability to engage in external dialog with somebody, we may have a dialog with the imprint of the same individual in our psyche. The solid identity is in a state of continuous internal dialog with the congruent fragments. The external dialogs are happening very rarely, and instead of external dialogs, we have the strength to hold negotiations. The negotiations usually are complicated and do not bring feelings of fulfillment, which may even be comparable to the feelings generated by dialog. If in the whole of our life we meet only a few or even only one individual with whom we are having a dialog, then our life already has meaning. Unfortunately, until everyone develops a solid identity, we desire to have dialogs with others but are not involved in negotiations.

In our internal interaction it is harder to have negotiations than dialogs. Even most successful negotiators have complications while negotiating the congruence of their own fragments. During negotiation between fragments we always have situations when one of the fragments has the better deal. As a rule the less successful fragments experience resentment that they did not have an attractive take. Their feud stresses our body. We always need to remember that all our fragments are sharing the same body and this is why we cannot afford any animosity between them. When we experience thoughts of inadequacy, the unsatisfied fragment is taking over our psyche. Our body suffers, because we are experiencing tensions and emotional pain. The unsatisfied fragment feels violated and threatens other fragments as animated objects, insults them, and calls them by derogatory names. We know it happens when we call *self* insulting names.

In our internal relations it is easier to have dialog than negotiation, because only in the internal exchanges are we familiar with all fragments inside our psyche. We know what effect they are having on our life and what kind of responses they represent. Our internal meetings may well be based on the honesty and connectedness of our thoughts and feelings. The internal meetings and dialogs between our fragments solidify our feelings about *self*. The psyche of Professor Kryvoruchko was continuing to maintain a state of dialog. His psyche has fragments, some of which come from real experiences and others from imaginative ones. His distinctive experiences made him a unique individual.

The troublemaker fragment, Boris, was not pacified, and the struggle was continuing. When the collective was breaking to pieces, new confrontations affected life in the post-collective space. Leonid Kryvoruchko, Stepan's father, who was a co-owner and director of the factory, found his life was in danger. He experienced friction with Boris and other former operatives of the secret police who were connected to the Mafia. They wanted to take over the factory. Time was precious and it was not possible to negotiate any settlements. The many fragments together, which included Stepan Luchko, Ivan, Alexander Kryvoruchko, Stepan Kryvoruchko, and Sam Kaufman, were united in Moscow to save Leonid's life. They were splitting from the extortionists, but between *self* they were enjoying a state of dialog. They needed to respond to the confrontation from the foe. They understood that between fragments a feeling of dialog existed, but with others they needed to negotiate.

Luchko and Ivan used their connections and the threats and pressure had stopped. Live were saved. Splitting from the bandits did not affect their unification, but only facilitated better dialog. To have meeting we must achieve genuine mutual understanding, caring, and positive regard. In many instances it is not possible to have it right away. For internal dialog we need fragments that are prepared to meet. It takes time to get them all set. Once we have an experience of real meeting, we understand that we are living for dialogs and meetings, and we look forward with a desire to find more and do not miss them. When we start having dialogs and meetings between our fragments, we do not need to worry anymore about going back. We move to another level of being and just enjoy the benefits of having a more solid identity. Stepan Kryvoruchko eventually became Professor Kryvoruchko. He lives in a state of continuous dialogs. He opened the road to having genuine dialogs, and he is continuing to have meetings and dialogs for the rest of his life.

The Internal Conflicts are Mirroring The External

The external life around us is getting mirrored and copied to our psyche in the form of imprints, which affect the internal processes of our psyche. Everyone around us creates a projection inside our psyche. The clarity of projection depends on our visual and emotional capacities. The imprints act according to our own standard and never become independent. In the radical collective the internal interpretations depend on the general way of perceiving any situation, which is very predictable. In the collective the members do not have free will and act according to brainwashing from ideologists. The mirror of the collective does not give an opportunity to figure out any absurdity of our existence, and we never realize how to deal with the outside world. In the collective our conscious awareness is affected by rules and slogans.

Our internal process acts according to common sense and instruction from the collective. The imprints do not have their own judgmental capacity and rely on our experiences for processing information. It is very sad that this process is subconscious and done without our conscious awareness. Most of our feelings were triggered by the external familiarity, but our responses are a result of the interaction of the fragments inside our psyche. In interactions with imprints our psyche reacts on a level of comfort and discomfort. We experience comfort in the state of the usual. Our psyche has the flexibility to adapt to any stable conditions and perceive them as comfortable.

There are many diverse stimulations, including images, odors, sounds, bodies, or movements, and most important, thoughts that trigger the troubling response. Disturbing fragments are the result of our psychological trauma. They take over when a situation has even the slightest resemblance to an experienced trauma. By using the knowledge of how the external affects our internal feelings we create a model that organizes our adjustment in a surrounding. The goal is our survival. In many instances our internal and external feelings are not congruent. When identity is fragmented, we experience complications taking the subconscious conflicts to our conscious awareness and resolving our internal conflicts. Another way of seeing our internal processes is by using our imagination.

The imprints of external life inside our psyche interact through chemical balances and imbalances together with discharges of biological energy. The fragmented identity is opposite to the solid *self*, and has been punctuated with a lot of imaginative holes. The conflict is represented by a range of bioelectrical disturbances that affect our responses. The disturbing energy is getting out through the imaginary holes in our psyche. The strong disturbances are affecting our responses to the point that they become uncontrollable. The electromagnetic disturbances represent the chemical imbalances. When we are always experiencing fears, it is an indication that our identity is fragmented and punctured by holes, and that fearful disturbances are taking over our psyche.

The radical collective is affecting our way of responding because of a strong correlation between external and internal conflicts. The external crisis is affecting us internally. It is splitting us because we are not having the internal dialogs but are acting on the orders from outside. In contrast, the whole magnetic field around our psyche, which does not have any disturbances, represents the stability and balance of chemicals in our brain. When the field around our psyche is not penetrated by any disturbances, we feel comfort and at peace. We have the power to control our life and to build a solid identity. We are achieving congruency between external and internal conflicts. Our identity is solid when we bring all our conflicts to our conscious awareness and are capable of resolving them.

Initially, the outside world was copied inside to our psyche. When we have conscious awareness of the disturbances in our psyche, we patch the imaginative holes in the electromagnetic field around us. We use a dialog to unify fragments and change the disturbing influences. The interactions of our fragments come out to the external world as our responses. We become free because our responses are the result of dialog between our fragments but are not a result of an order from a collective.

We are Analyzing Our Identity

In analyses of our identity we are analyzing our responses, which are attributed to diverse interactions in the past. The radical collective denies a member the opportunity to learn from his past and encourages him to make sacrifices for a Utopian future. It arrogantly declares that by looking to our past, we become weak. It declares that the wavering makes the collective feeble, because only the collective is building a courageous man who is offering his life for a bright future that he definitely would not see. The collective does not care about any processes in the individual brain. It implies that our interactions with others and the media provide us with atypical subjective conclusions, which in critical situations negatively influence our responses. Only outside of the radical collective do we learn something about our own identity. On the basic level our identity is represented by our brain chemistry and the strength of our bio-electric field. It is the way we interact with others on the bio-energy level. It is similar to the software and hardware of computer products. The psyche is software, where our identity was generated.

Our brain reaction is like hardware, but we are not dealing with our primary brain reactions, which are in the form of our brain chemistry and our electromagnetic characteristics. In our analysis we are dealing directly only with the secondary effects of brain functioning, which is our psyche. Nevertheless, we want to have the reverse connections from the secondary to primary reactions. Through our psyche we want to control our chaotic brain disturbances and uncover a way to stabilize them. To achieve our objective we focus on the fragments in our psyche instead of the very complicated chemical-electrical processes.

We identify the psyche's disturbances in the form of images, sounds, movements, thoughts, and feelings. To find our identity is also to understand the bright and dark sides of our psyche. We find our discontents of limitations, horror of captivity, hell, Shangri-la, and, eventually, God. We also understand that all the little bits of our identity are not recovered right away. Many great minds are understood only after their death. Sometimes it takes years after the death of an individual to find out who he really was. In many instances we may not understand *self* until the last day of our life. Unfortunately, we spend a big part of our life attempting to meet and pleasing others and we forget that the most important task is to meet *self*. To understand various parts of *self* is to understand our desires, how we move, hear, see, think, and most important, how we respond to the world. To analyze *self* we need to identify the several groups of fragments. One group includes the fragments that are responsible for meeting our basic needs and, most important, for having a safe environment around us.

It happens that our psyche has a fragment that is neglecting its responsibility of meeting our basic needs. The other groups include the fragments that satisfy our needs for intellectual stimulation, emotional well-being, the ability to be entertained, and so on. Each group relies on fragments with sundry responsibilities, which include the fragments for anger, impulse control, time and stress management, and others. Sometimes the lack of responsibility of fragments on the basic level is compensated for by fragments from the higher level. Some psyches deal only with the basic needs and completely neglect the other groups, but the best situation is when the psyche has a balance between diverse groups. The starving artist is driven by the fragments from the other group and creativity compensates for the basic needs. The imbalance between the dissimilar groups causes a fragmented identity. When we are analyzing *self*, we need to be aware of our psyche structure, how it is affecting our internal interactions, and if it is contributing things to the goal of having a solid identity.

We Identify The Conflict Between Fragments

The main goal of our analysis is identifying the conflict between our own fragments, bringing the conflict to our conscious awareness, and then somehow resolving it. Our psyche is always moving toward unification and split. The radical collective wants to stop any process in our psyche and transfer it to the masses, which are chunks of embryonic thoughts and emotions. It stops our further development and discourages us from being individuals. It forbids us to look and search for the truth inside our psyche. As members of the collective, we give up our identity for external slogans and stereotypes. We are feeling good when we resemble and look like stereotypes. The ideologists ridicule any search for our individuality. We are separated from internal congruency. Our feelings were disrespected. We were not allowed to have a solid and balanced identity. We were persecuted for our desire to know our subconscious feelings and to be involved in *self*-analysis. The ideologists understood that in *self*-analysis we were bringing to our conscious minds awareness of our limitations, and becoming aware of our own feelings. They knew that they were not able to pollute our subconscious with their slogans anymore.

When we choose individuality, we move away from stereotypes and practice *self*-analysis. We are in the process of identifying the troubled fragments, and we are relying on our knowledge of how our psyche operates. We have many groups and subgroups with out-of-the-ordinary abilities to interact with others. When we do not feel good about *self*, it is an indication that a troublemaking fragment exists in our psyche and does not allow us to feel content and successfully interact with others. This troublemaking fragment was a conflicting one. It was always spoiling our good feelings about *self* and bringing negativity, derogative feelings, and disrespect to our internal world. In our psyche when one of our fragments is a troublemaker, we feel turmoil. To effectively remedy our problem we need to find what fragment is causing the conflict and what type of psyche organization we have. We can compare the identification of our diverse fragments to the recognition of numerous ships in the ocean.

We see military ships with military discipline and military order, and it reminds us of the part of our psyche that is strict, organized, and follows orders. When we see a lot of cruisers in the ocean with travelers lying in their chairs on the decks and doing nothing around the swimming pools, they remind us of the relaxing part of our psyche. When in one of the ships we see the combination of a fishing boat, cruise and cargo ship, the crew of this ship is baffled, confused, and in turmoil like the fragments in our psyche. These are models of the fragmented identity, and some of the fragments are acting as if they were completely lost. Because of the convolution with identification of our feelings, we were producing the unpredictability of our responses. We may preserve the solid identity only in cooperation with all our fragments and the psyche organization, where the fragments respond appropriately to particular stimulations. When we see the usual merchants' ships, tankers, and fishing boats, where sailors know their responsibilities and are busy keeping the merchandise in good condition, they remind us of solid identity.

Self-analysis helps us find an obstruction to our quest for a solid identity. The understanding of our subconscious is giving us a chance at *self*-growth. In some instances, our inability to have a solid identity becomes evident when we identify our fragment, which is putting on *self* a lot of diverse responsibilities but not performing them. By using a dialog we help our fragment delegate some of the responsibilities to our other fragments that are more capable of performing those tasks. When we have responsibility that we have the strength to carry on, and we become appropriate in our responses, then our fragments are in agreement. We respond appropriately to the stress and feel content.

The conflict between fragments is the main cause of our feelings of discontent. The radical collective pushes us to look outside of *self*, and we are losing *self*. To find our identity we need to look inside. The feuding of our fragments is on a subconscious level and the task of finding the conflicting fragment is very challenging. It requires lots of guessing, assumptions, and *self*-analysis. It requires the knowledge of the structure of our psyche and approximate understanding of what groups and subgroups the fragments belong to. It makes the task of analysis less complicated. It spares us from wrong assumptions. Our internal conflict was identified and we understand what fragments were affected. We know how to restore the state of balance in our psyche. When we were content and our identity was solid, we looked forward without any fears of losing our identity.

Fragmented Identity and Our Self-Esteem

A fragmented identity does not allow us to feel good about *self*. The disturbing fragments with the goal of splitting bring a feeling of misery to our existence.

The radical collective masks the internal obscurity by encouraging us to focus on the external, and gives us an easy explanation for our problems. Usually, the radical collective proclaims that we are victims of an unfair distribution of goods and suppression of some social, religious, and genetically dissimilar groups. In the radical collective we want to achieve and to bring fairness into our lives, but we are pushed to have easy solutions, which never bring us closer to our goals. We do not need to sacrifice our lives for fictitious ideas and unreachable goals forever.

When we reach a moment of being astute, we understand that it does not matter how far we sail, because we do not have the strength to get away from *self*. We have the possibility to go everywhere and be happy when we feel good about *self* and our environment. We need to make order in our own house; otherwise we may be in the richest country in the world and feel like orphans. To illustrate the importance of balanced identity we can analyze the responses of one scientist who is also a new immigrant. The scientist came to America from Eastern Europe. He is fluent in several languages but speaks heavily accented English. His identity as someone of wisdom was not appreciated in his new homeland and inside he felt downgraded.

When the scientist was interacting with the outside world, he expected to share his knowledge, but because of his accented presentation listeners ignored his scientific brilliance. The scientist feels frustrated. He could not understand how other scientists could make such grave mistakes by not accepting his ideas only because of his accent, which has nothing to do with science. He decided to prove to everyone that they were wrong about him. He worked harder on his new discovery in science. His ideas are ingenious, but natives still do not accept them because of his language impairments. The troublemaker fragment does not allow him to enjoy what he can achieve, and this creates discontent inside. The professor scientist has many talents to be proud of and has capacities that others who rejected him did not have any clues about. Part of his upbringing involved reading great books, including some written by philosophers, scientists, and novelists. His identity incorporated the information mainly from the books, then the life experiences, emotional losses, traumas, relationships, and life stories that embellished his life and became part of his identity.

The natives who rejected him were ignorant and uneducated, and had very narrow experience in science. Perhaps they should not get in the scientist's psyche and affect his *self*-esteem, but somehow they did. This situation illustrates the ignorance of a few but also shows that the scientist has problems with his identity. The scientist needs to be proud of his background and his knowledge, and the opinion of ignorance may well be irrelevant for him. The lack of knowledge from locals about a scientist's contribution to science is not a reason for him to be discontent. Many scientists who speak the language of the country perfectly will be in the same situation, because the problem is not in the language but in the ignorance of the locals who do not understand anything about science. Many scientists were marked as insane by locals and died in poverty because they were a hundred years more advanced in their thoughts than locals who rejected their science.

The terrible fate of many scientists was in being rejected and living in poverty, and after their death, being worshipped as geniuses. The scientist was perfectly aware of this injustice, but his *self*-esteem still suffered because of the opinions of the less knowledgeable locals. He had a troublemaker fragment that was poisoning his mind with negativity. The conflict that the professor was facing was an internal one. If his identity was solid, the external stimulations would not affect his psyche by lowering his *self*-esteem. Because the process of fragmentation is on a subconscious level, we are always looking to justify our weaknesses by blaming something or someone else.

The fragmented psyche sometimes acts similar to the psyche of the mentally ill. The difference is that the fragmented psyche acts like a mental illness only in some instances. By contrast, this behavior is a constant in mental illness. We have an opportunity to learn a lot from schizophrenics about how the psyche operates. Schizophrenia is the clinical pathology of the fragmented psyche and is affected by audio, visual, kinesthetic, and olfactory stimulations. They do have a persecutory delusion and may identify some objects as fear generators. When we have a fragmented psyche, we are afraid to identify our sick fragments because we are afraid to be labeled mentally ill.

The best quality of a solid identity is a capacity to learn from everyone. We are learning a lot from the mind of the mentally ill. The main difference between mental illness and our merely fragmented psyche is in resistance to the troublemaker fragment. The troublemaker fragment in the psyche of the mentally ill creates a devastating effect. Our fragmented psyche without a mental illness experiences less severity from the troublemaker fragment. This is a reason why the fragmented identity fails to identify the troublemaker. Our fragmented psyche attributes any discomfort to external causes and suffers from low *self*-esteem.

Old and Newly Developed Fragments

The unification of the old and newly built-up, recently developed fragments in our psyche is a very delicate process. Our relationship between new and old fragments is splitting and unifying. The radical collective proclaims that it has the power to create new character. It does it by suppressing our individuality. The process of our suppression is a splitting from our original fragments into a stereotype. Antithetical to the radical collective, the individual psyche empowers all existing fragments and is unifying with the new. Sometimes the new fragments do not want anything to do with the old ones and ignore them. It also happens that the old fragments split from the newly developed, or resist recognizing them. In our psyche it is not possible to get rid of the fragments if they already developed and the confrontation has begun. The unwanted fragments take over our psyche and retaliate when we least expect it. We are talking about morals, *self*-dedication, and being honest, but as soon as temptation comes up and other fragments take over, we act greedy, without morals, and deceive loved ones. In this example our psyche is developing two parallel sets of fragments with opposite responses.

We act contrary to everything we were preaching. In many instances we are not consciously aware that we have two sets of opposing fragments. The scientist is an immigrant who sacrificed a lot in his life to come to America. He is ready to make his new home proud of him. He believes that he may contribute a lot to the well-being of his new homeland. His interaction with the outside world is to learn about his new country, and he expects that natives will welcome him. When he does not receive a warm welcome, and inhabitants of his new homeland do not want to identify with him, he gets frustrated and angry. He decides to do everything to prove to his new countrymen that he will be a very valuable citizen. His old identity does not serve him well, so he decides to split and to develop a new one. This process is painful because he perceives *self* as a traitor when he decides to give up his old identity. He is devaluating his prior knowledge and his prior life experience. His *self*-esteem is low.

He feels guilty, but if a scientist got a welcome reception in a new country, he would not have any need to desert his old *self*. When someone is forcefully abandoning his old fragments to develop new ones, as a result, we see the split that caused the birth of an ugly hybrid. The newly developed fragments are the result of pretension that the old fragments are not needed anymore and possibly will be deleted. The outcome of the abandonment is the arrival of a new identity that has secrets. One secret is presenting the kinesthetic part of the scientist's mind. The scientist is a sex addict. He uses erotic magazines to get excited while masturbating. The scientist, when he was a teenager, masturbated a few times by looking at his naked mother from the hole in a bathroom door.

Later, he understood that he had done something inappropriate by looking at his mother. He substituted adult publications. The scientist was manifesting internal conflicts that include attachment to the good breast, unresolved object relations, and many more. He did stop using his mother as stimulation for having orgasm by masturbation. He responded to his strict moral code and fears of castration, but he also substituted the old breast for the atypical one. His psychological addiction is a sign of fragmented identity. In his search the scientist did not find the perfect breast. After arriving in a new country the scientist is splitting from the old fragments without resolving a conflict. He is living with the pretension that he was able to find a new way of living. He disagrees that the only good thing in his life was nurturing from his mother when he was a baby. He denies it.

His psyche has many fragments that are splitting, and his identity is fragmented. It may happen that the scientist will never find the better breast and continues his addiction. Only by unification of his fragments through dialog and meetings will the scientist have the strength to stop his sex addiction. In a dialog he may find the missed good breast. We have the strength to stop addictions only by unification through the dialog. Many addicts use pretension to cover one of their addictions with another. In many instances addicts use drugs and alcohol as a cover for something that is hiding deeper. When we are achieving meetings and unifications, we also are stopping all our addictions. We are leaving the splitting forces to joint unification and transferring from them all our energy. The goal is to unify our fragments, because the solid identity is not susceptible to any addictions. When we do have time for *self*-analysis, we are using dialog to keep our psyche together.

Sometime, when we are short on time and do not have the opportunity for self-analysis, unification forces use the negotiations to balance our internal processes. The unification of fragments through negotiation is not a very stable method, but for the time being it keeps our psyche unified. The negotiating method completely depends on the skills of the negotiator. The goal of negotiation is to achieve mutual understanding. By using negotiation we do not have a goal for fragments to have a meeting. The negotiations do not keep fragments united for a long time, because the best way to unify fragments is by achieving meeting. Our psyche has the desire for a dialog and for the harmonious relationships between the fragments. It is developing the coalition of the fragments. The relief from the psychological addiction is based on the motivation of the addicts to have a dialog. Intuitively, in our psyche many new fragments avoid splitting and unifying with the old one and build an alliance. Our psyche is in agreement only when the unification was achieved through the meeting and dialog.

Plasticity in The Responses

When in our psyche some fragments have plasticity in their responses, they have the power to function appropriately even when they are surrounded by the energy of splitting and with the rigid fragments. The goal is to pacify the internal demons, the troublemaker fragments that are disturbing others. In the radical collective the internal demons are a sign of weakness. To fight internal demons the members of the collective must repeat the citation of the leaders. The leaders provided all discreet recommendations for their followers that are supposed to show the strength of their character. They provide distinct ways for dealing with weaknesses that includes focusing on common goals. The radical collective was against any analysis, because in analyzing our psyche we do not listen to any slogans and just identify our troublemakers and the inflexible fragments. The fragments with plasticity are not affected by troublemaker fragments and are the strengths of our character. Plasticity and flexibility are qualities of the fragments, which accept the fact that the forces of splitting and unification are normal occurrences of our psyche.

Our recognition of the constant existence of those forces and acceptance of the fact that nothing can be done to get rid of them is the first step toward achieving plasticity in our responses. The fragments with plasticity are joining the unification forces. The opposite of plasticity is rigidity. The rigid fragments are splitting until their psychological drive allows it, without any consideration for consequences. The rigid fragments, by splitting, are releasing the enormous energy discharge and the splitting continues until the energy is exhausted. By the end it is not a winning situation. The splitting is bringing on just more splitting. The extreme form of rigidity of our fragments is the attempt at eradicating their opponent.

As soon as one splitting was demanding an excessive response, right away the other splitting is requesting extreme measures. Without any capacity to be flexible, the rigid fragments do not have the strength to stop splitting and their confrontation becomes excessive. It is an unending process, because is not possible to purge the fragments from our psyche. The abolished wreckage is not disappearing. Some fragments that are involved in the confrontation with the troublemaker's fragments do not have the energy charges and suffer a lot. In the mentally ill psyche the troublemaking fragments that cause splitting are extremely strong. The difference between a schizophrenic psyche and a functional one is the difference in the strength of the troublemaking fragments. The adventure movies display notions of extremes similar to the ill mind. In those movies we see parallel worlds, when numerous fragments float between two polarities.

The movies are entertaining with the assassination of leaders and sundry conspiracy theories. They are filled with very dangerous characters that are pushing their cause and driven by the desire to split. The leader is perceived as an obstacle carrying the splitting energy. The authorities are devils, and unification with those forces is impossible. Sometimes the two opposite parts in the movies are not necessarily clearly evil and good. They function in the same ways and have similar frames of reference. Many are based only on splitting forces. To be entertaining the movies are modeling the schizophrenic mind. The troublemaker's fragments in the schizophrenic mind are not opposite of the feuding characters in the movies, where we see the feuding opponents. In the movies we rarely see energy forces that are unifying. It may appear that some fragments are splitting because of the goal of unification. We are entertained even when they are not sincere. In contrast to the movies, the conflicts in our psyche are not entertaining at all. When the fragments are splitting, we are in turmoil and feel bad.

The fights inside our psyche are the confrontations between feuding parts. Both sides are transporters of powerful splitting energy. The rigid fragments are the carriers of incendiary ideas. Some of them seem to split in order to unify, but they are not frank. The splitters are using the goal of unification as a destructor, because they really do not want any unification and only want to split. We need to remember that in any confrontation inside of our psyche there are not any winners and all of our fragments are losing. For safety reasons and in the instances when our lives are in danger is splitting a helpful thing to do. We justify splitting when it is a threat to our safety or the safety of our loved ones, our way of living, and our health. We are splitting when the flexible fragments represent our peaceful and secure position. Plasticity is also the desired quality of the fragments, because when we split for safety, we rely on plasticity to preserve at least part of our identity.

The Unification of Psyche is Interrupted by The Splitting Forces

In the process of unification our psyche is easily distracted by splitting. When the splitting forces in our psyche wanted to prevent unification, they relied on our lack of motivation for unification and our lack of strength to resist splitting. The *self*-identity raises many issues, which had roots in our own experience. Professor Kryvoruchko is a naturalized U.S. citizen and has an Eastern European background. He was interested in issues that were affecting the various parts of the world and treasuring his relationship with the world. He has not yet discovered some splitting parts of his identity. Because he highly valued his heritage, he also wanted to understand the relationship between himself and new countrymen, and wanted to know their philosophy of life. He did not want any splitting and was looking forward to unification. He saw that they love their legendary worriers, whom we are seeing as their defenders, as examples of courage and bravery.

He saw that everywhere we are fighting others who have the same type of heroes. We look the same way but we see the opposition as a bunch of cowards and traitors. We are striving for unification, but we do not have the power to resist the splitting. The agents of splitting are weakening our motivation to unify. When the dialog and meeting became our most important goal, then forces of splitting are not forceful enough to prevent our unification. With a solid psyche we have an awareness of self-identity and the desire to build a solid identity. When we have a solid psyche, we have congruence between our approaches. We select our heroes to be visual representations of our land. It is hard to find them because only a few fit the picture. We also are sensitive to audio stimulations because we have uncommon accents and dissimilar ways of saying words. We do not feel like heroes.

Our kinesthetic responses are not perfect. We are not expressing *self* through movement. But mainly we are not heroes because we treat others as objects. We hate our neighbors because they are expressing *self* in their own way. We have perceived them as not equal and stigmatized them as stupid. Perhaps we do it when our psyches struggle to unify fragments, which in the audio, visual, kinesthetic manners are functioning in dissimilar ways. Only the translation has power to change our perception. We need to translate our audio response to kinesthetic, our visual to kinesthetic, and vice versa.

If we are stingy, after translation we appear generous. Now, the stingy is not a grandfather who saved money and paid for the grandchildren to go to school and to have higher education. When we are accused of being liars, after translation we become dreamers who live in visual fantasies and do not benefit from our lies. We just want to make reality more presentable. If we are dishonest, we may be weak and may not have the strength to achieve the goal of unification. Because we are smarter rather than just powerful, we create the funds, which we distribute to the disadvantaged. We need to be sure that the splitting force does not sabotage the process of unification.

We are always punishing suspected collaborators. Because they do not hate our enemies enough, they are despised and persecuted. We hate the collaborators even more than the enemies. In this situation the splitting forces celebrate a big victory and the losers are the force of unification. We need to know that our psyche organization is susceptible to splitting and having barriers with unification. Our motivation for unification may be on diverse levels of visual, audio, and kinesthetic approaches. The influence of assorted styles of demonstration is increasing if it is a dominant one. The process of unification is sabotaged by negativity, which is a sign of splitting. To succeed, we must prevent the splitting forces from sabotaging the process of unification.

Splitting and Unification are The Basic Qualities of Our Psyche

Splitting and unification are the basic function of our psyche and are running on the intuitive level. By bringing this process to a conscious level we have the ability to understand the basic process in our psyche and to build a solid identity. When our psyche is unifying, it appoints one of the fragments to be a spokesman and to be responsible for our identity. Just as restaurant chains have a logo that identifies them, the leading fragment is a logo for our fragments. When our main fragment is in a state of unification with the majority of our other fragments, it has the opportunity to serve as the representative of our identity. When we have a solid identity, we acknowledge that we have many aspects in our psyche. We have appointed one of our fragments to be a spokesman for our other fragments. We make a significant effort to prove that this fragment, which has the duty of being the spokesman for our psyche, deserves this appointment. We have many fragments, including a soldier and an emigrant who lived in a separate country, that we identified only to carry a logo for our identity.

We acknowledge that splitting and unification forces are the universal law and that they are constantly present inside our psyche. When we transfer these forces to the conscious level, we become responsible for the splitting and also for the ways of unification. We are not unifying by all available means, which include brutality and treachery, and are very careful of unification by splitting. It is problematic to find anything that may not possibly split in this world. The world is dualistic, and even the smallest parts of the substances are continuing to split. In the universe the little particles are unified in the bigger substance until they form the cosmically large figures and then our world. The unification and the split are the main function of any psyche.

When we deal with any radical collective, we explore the thoughts of what behavior we are representing, which may be the heroic, the cowardly, of the follower, or antagonistic one. Any new generation has numerous interpretations of those basic behaviors. We get easily confused. Are we heroes or are we cowards? We perhaps can be little bits of everything. In our psyche we find the fragments that represent evil, and our discoveries may bring us to terrible conclusions. In some instances the evil fragment has the ability to take over our psyche. It twists and tarnishes the meanings of heroism, friendship, and love. Sometime we break the rules and negotiate with terrorists when our loved ones are in danger. We may deviate from the usual trend of courtesy and become hostile and resistant. The splitting and unifications are always continuing in our psyche. They are the basic forces behind every emotion and thought.

Unification by Splitting

Unification by splitting is the most common intuitive way of unifying without having a dialog. Our experience in the area of negotiation shows that, when together we hated someone or something, we were able to communicate better.

The collective uses these phenomena and finds an enemy. The radical collective is built on unification by split. We perceive something as very valuable when we are united together to protect it. We are splitting because we do not experience the good feelings toward others, and we resist complying with an unwritten contract that we are suppressing hate toward our confederates. It is complicated to find love, but it is very easy to find partners in hate. The collectives created a culture of hating and splitting. We are splitting from religion, from the noble and wealthy. As members of the terror structures we are hating and splitting from all infidels and wicked. In our perception everyone who is not a follower of the great teaching is just an object and easily replaceable. As ordinary members we do not have the right to have our own opinion. The goal is to split us from infidels by unifying in hate and violence.

Hate is not able to replace love completely, but it puts limits on love. The members of a terror structure probably are very kind to others with similar beliefs and to their supreme leaders. They do not respond to negotiations with opposition. The negotiation with them is only on a confrontational basis. We learn to hate in response. We had changed when we were the objects of hate. We love our country, our motherland, but then we are not sure what meaning the word *love* has. We also do not know if we love the other's countrymen. We assume that love and respect may be the basis of our relations, but as often happens, if we are from the northern part, we are prejudiced and hostile toward citizens from the south and vice versa. If we are from the West, we do not like citizens from the East. We know from our birth how to hate others, and may easily find a reason to do it. We do it without any hesitation.

In many instances we try sweetening hate with love. We have the audacity to declare that we hate others because we love our land and need to protect our race, ethnicity, and God. It is so easy to hate. With sadness we admit that hate actually unites us more than love. As neighbors we hate others. We do it despite the fact that we are close to others and have many emotional ties. We have the ability to hate very passionately and bring more emotions to others' hate. In a hate process, we constantly think about the opponent. It is amazing how we convey hate to others. Hate generates lots of energy in us. In contrast to love, we have the capacity to express our hate freely without appearing weak or corrupt. Our fragments have the power to achieve unification in hate, where they express our negativity. We often use shrewdness in our hate. Contrary to real dialog, which comes from real love and requires wisdom, the message of hate is an indication that we are handicapped and are in pain because we do not know how to love, or might not find loving partners, and do not have satisfaction in love. Some may understand our grievances, but it is not possible to find wisdom in replacing love with hate.

The hate and splitting is an animalistic feeling and one of the basic instincts of survival. We hate and split from others to protect our way of living. We hate the things we do not understand or are not used to. For a limited time we appear in agreement when we are united in hate and splitting. To unify by love, we need to make an extra effort and stop hating, which is not easy.

Refrain from Unity with Individuals but Unify with Fragments

Professor Kruvoruchko's relationships were very susceptible to splitting. We get together because of common need, and our conscious negotiation is a tool to keep us together and to avoid splitting. Internally, our psyche is looking for unification to reach peace of mind. Our psyche keeps the collection of the imprint of significant individuals and needs to have some structure to unify those imprints. The disarray between our fragments creates emotional disturbance. Our psyche wants to avoid emotional outburst by unifying our fragments, but it may not succeed and splits. The real unification of our fragments is possible only through real dialog. On the intuitive level our psyche often is not successful and failing in the unification of our fragments. Then instead of dialog, it tries to unify our fragments on a conscious level by using negotiation, which is not the best way to unify fragments. Negotiation would not produce a strong unity. As a result of negotiation our fragments feel they are being cheated. To have a strong unity our psyche needs to have genuine dialog between fragments.

For Professor Kryvoruchko, building a dialog for unification of his psyche was not easy. His first reaction was a split. Fortunately, he avoided unifying his psyche by hate. He has many diverse and valid issues to get split, but even he was torn by his multiethnic heritage. He wanted to understand each part and to build consent and mutual respect between his fragments. It was easy to split by using just common sense, logic, emotions, and prejudice. By using dialog and meeting between fragments we avoid splitting. If we do not intervene, the splitting stays through several generations. We inherit it from our ancestors, who were the subject of persecution, oppression, and fear. We do not feel good about those who make us feel inferior and fearful. The children of Holocaust and genocide survivors inherit the hate, anger, guilt, and shame, which cause the psyche to fall apart. The destruction of our whole psyche by the feelings of anger, shame, and guilt creates a rigid semi-independent fragment that takes over as a representative of our psyche and creates turmoil. Our previously cheerful, playful, and lovable fragments get replaced by the hunted fragments of the trauma, which are fearful, hateful, and unpredictable.

Professor Kryvoruchko said we need split to survive and when the time is right we unify our fragments by having a genuine dialog. If we do not have the power to reach a dialog, we negotiate. We split as the last resort, which includes, if needed, a physical altercation. Because confrontation is part of splitting, we cannot be ashamed that we do not have the ability to resolve our conflicts peacefully. If others are treating us as objects, we cannot use dialog and negotiation.

Professor Kryvoruchko believes that we all will have genuine dialog, and not only within our psyche. If we are able to have a dialog and meeting with others, our life is not wasted.

BIBLIOGRAPHY

Bandler, Richard, and John Grinder. *The Structure of Magic I: A Book About Language and Therapy.* Palo Alto, CA: Science & Behavior Books, 1975.

Buber, Martin. *I and Thou.* 2nd ed. Translated by Ronald Gregor Smith. Edinburgh: T. and T. Clark, 1937.

Friedman, Maurice, *Martin Buber's life and work: the early years, 1878-1923*, New York: Dutton, 1981.

Klein, Melanie. *Envy and Gratitude: A Study of Unconscious Forces.* New York: Basic Books, 1957.

Kohut, Heinz. *The Restoration of the Self.* New York: International Universities Press, 1977.

THEORY OF FRAGMENTATION

From Author
Search for holographic mind
Theory of fragmentation

Psyche continued to fascinate everyone. Voyagers, sailors, are traveling inside of their psyche in search of new sacraments of mind. One of the secrets of our mind is ability to create the images, similar to holograms. The hologram is a physical structure that uses light diffraction to make an image. The image can appear to be three-dimensional. Our psyche can do the same. It does not need any hologram's projector or laser light. Everything is already built in our brain. We see the images of our past, our relatives and our friends. We take all of those for granted. Dreams are the examples of holographic movies. We want to discover our capacities. Our psyche is our property and we make use of it in the many ways. We are the rulers of our psyche and we want to investigate our abilities. We want to explore what are our inherited capacities. In our holographic mind we can achieve the place described by futuristic philosophers as the eudemonia, (Greek: □□□□□μ□□□□ [eudemonia□]). Eudemonia is a Greek word commonly translated as happiness, welfare, human flourishing, prosperity and blessedness. It seems that this word can describe a notion of unification of our fragments in the holographic collectivism that is place of truth and happiness.

Our psyche has variety of fragments that are the storages of holograms. Each fragment contains his owns holograms. In my book I use concept of the Sailor, the traveler, who wanted to explore his psyche to find the holographic collectivism where is not place for false dogma and cheating. His goal is to discovery the treasures of the self-grow. Sailor is identifying the purposed fragments in his psyche and unites them in solid entity (identity). Sailor does not accept concept of the pseudo collectivism that killing individuality. Inside of his psyche he is creating individual holographic collectivism.

Fragment contains subconscious and conscious imagery. Those effigies can be involuntary, like the flashbacks, and also voluntary one, when created by our will. With more effort those representations can be three-dimensional and can appear real. Psyche is capable to accumulate many metaphors in form of dreams.

Holographic mind is a place to amass and recreate our impression as holograms. It is appeared that, somewhere in our brain, can exist a holographic projector. The physiology of this process needs more research. I am only guessing where place of holographic projector can be and share my thoughts with my readers.

The mind work is enchanting. The psyche creates variety of fragments with many holograms that are forming notions of particular situation or time of life. The psyche that contains the unidentified fragments looked like a library without catalog. We need to identify to what theme the holograms belong. When we ascertain our fragments we bring our subconscious dreams to conscious awareness. When we understood our fragments we better understand our self. With some training the psyche can activate images that are nicely formed and have some degree of the opacity, density and can appear as the paintings and photos. Our goal is to recovery holograms in united system. We always can use mysterious holographic projector built in our brain to unite our fragments. Sailor can find holographic collectivism in his psyche and build the solid psyche to make life more pleasant and more relaxed.

With respect,
Chester Litvin, PhD
Psychologist

CONTENTS

In memory of my late mother, Polina Gimelfarb,
and my father, Max Litvinov.

INTRODUCTION

WHO WE ARE

In my practice as a psychologist, I observed the pattern of miraculous transformation in people who were able to solidify their identity. I was enthused to write a book about the people's spirit. I see people as sailors on the voyage to find the self. Sailor travels inside of his psyche. My hero is a fictitious character, a sailor with a solid identity. His psyche is a collection of fragments that represent the different experiences. The sailor discovers and identifies his fragments; he is on the journey to unify his fragments.

Many famous psychologists with different views on human nature, including Heinz Kohut, Murray Bowen, Carl Rogers, and many others, recognized that the main goal of psychological development is building a solid identity. We as sailors do not need to pretend that we are somebody else; we must know who we are and accept all our fragments. As emigrants from radicalized collectives, we were deprived of the discovery of who we are. The radical collectives use brutal force to impose their point of view on us. They split us from our internal feelings and focus us on exaggerated externals, which are characterized by grandiosity and pomposity.

It is not a true that the poor get radicalized more easily. The radicals can be part of any society, poor or rich, peasants or aristocrats. The wishes dictator, Joseph Stalin, did not have any noble blood. Catherine de Medici, mother of French king Charles IX, orchestrated the St. Bartholomew's Day Massacre to kill Huguenots (French Calvinist Protestants). All radicals want us to be their servants and follow them, while they impose on us distinctive mannerisms and pretentions. They split us from congruent audio, visual, and kinesthetic stimuli and feed us pervasive stimuli. They distort our vision with a model of zealot, without any love of self, like a robotic device serving the radical causes. They put in front of us enormous paintings, monuments, and constructions glorifying collectives. They do not want us to hear any messages of our uniqueness and want us to be indistinguishable fighters for their radical cause. They encourage us to attend parades and marches, just being part of a crowd. They are conditioning our brains to provide the pervasive responses. All our fragments become rigid and inflexible, and we are left with few—or even none—of the neutral fragments that can provide impartial responses.

Radicals change our brain chemistry by supplying our brain with pervasive stimuli. Instead of keeping our individuality, our domineering fragment leads us to be a servant of distorted doctrines and unproven theories. Our brain chemistry changes, and we become deficient in the objective responses. In the big proclivity with a lack of neutral fragments, we do not have the opportunity to reject any pervasive stimuli. Our brain structure becomes similar to the brains of addicted, impulsive, and psychologically distorted individuals. In the same manner as mental illness, the radicalized collectives create distortion in the brain's function, ingeniously using the incongruent stimuli to control masses. The pervasive phraseology freezes our logic, and we get confused and powerless. It causes incongruence in the release of our brain chemistry. Instead of being individuals, we become a crowd with identical responses. By incongruity of stimuli, people can easily split us into throngs, mobs, and packs.

Only by restructuring our brain chemistry with congruent, realistic stimuli, which emphasize our individuality, can we reject the pervasive phraseology. When we query the exaggerations and question distorted doctrines, and do not embrace the unproven theories, we can sail inside our psyche. Without any misleading mannerisms and pretentions, we can achieve the internal unification of our fragments. First we learn how to respect our fragments. We can guide the self to value our experiences as individuals and be proud to be individuals; we embrace our uniqueness. The tools of restructuring are the internal dialogues with our fragments and negotiations with others around us. As sailors, by going on voyages inside of our psyche, we create connections between our fragments; instead of rigidity, we bring flexibility in processing the stimuli and bring congruency in our responses. Our mission in life is to unify our fragments and to resist external splitting. Our goal is to keep our individuality. We unify our psyche in the solid identity, and we do not need to pretend. We accept the self and are happy. We become sailors, and our voyages through our experiences are pleasant.

The mind travelers are sailors. To understand our mind and create a comfortable self, we get on the voyage that is in many instances pleasant but sometimes can result in trauma, particularly in a radical collective where everything directs us to be analogues. We are discouraged to explore our psyche. We can be hurt if we do not obey the draconian rules of radical collectivism. The radical collective does not want us to know who we are.

For us mind travelers who want to reach our destination, the question of who we are is important to answer. When we answer this question, we are sure of the self and know that we are unique and special. We fit the environment around us. We are well adjusted and happy with all our endeavors. The fewer unanswered questions we have about our selves, the easier our interpersonal interactions. We see others as unique and special. However, when we do not know who we are, we are confused misfits. We are a mess and can hardly function, if at all. The vagueness about the self is a barrier in our interpersonal interactions. The mystery and secrets of our past drain our energy and our creative juices. When we do not know who we are, we feel tied up, as if we are paralyzed.

Some of us do not want to know who we are; we are afraid of self-analysis because we can discover the can of worms. The damaged mind fragments, which have deep secrets, are split by resentments. They are afraid that secrets can get out, and they do not believe that they can deal with the resentments. These minds are endorsing splits and detachments. By splitting our mind we created the chance for future splits and detachments. The piles of unresolved splits do not bring relief and only accumulate misery. We get healed when we unify and resolve splits. The split is only helpful when our lives are in danger because it helps us to survive. Otherwise we need to resist splits. The battle between split and unification continues for our entire life.

The desire to be an individual is an inherited quality of our psyche. Everyone who is pushed to be homogeneous feels resentment. Part of our personal freedom is to have identity. Nevertheless, some want to be like others, and when it is done voluntarily, it is accepted. These people choose someone's role to follow. Few do it of their own free will, but many are victims of brainwashing and are tricked into becoming a copy. Even some who enjoy the originality of psychology do not know how to achieve peace between their fragments.

The real meeting with the self is a moment of recognition of our uniqueness. Through genuine dialogue and real meetings, we can have the unification of our fragments and also achieve balance in our psyche. We call it utopia, but inside our mind we have a place for utopia and fantasy. We have a strong desire to unify our fragments, to balance our modes of expression, and to see our dreams come true. The modes of expression are visual, audio, kinesthetic, and olfactory. When we have balanced the mind, we can easily translate different responses to different modes of expression. Our facial expressions, voices, and body movements are congruent. The balanced mind provides the self with peace and tranquility, keeping our psyche unified.

Our mind can provide us with feelings that all our wishes achieve, and we reach our deepest desires. Only inside of our psyche can we create utopian relationships. Our mind is a place where we can achieve infinite glory and many personal aspirations. We can create the individual heaven inside our psyche. Even radical collectives cannot impose limitations on our thinking, if we really resist. To achieve our wishes and see our desires in real life are commendable, though it gets more complicated when we impose our powers on others. We cannot hurt others, but as a result of our actions, which are based on irrational thoughts, others get hurt. We are pushing others to take defensive responses; they cannot allow the carrier of the irrational self to hurt them. We have an obligation to stop our abusive behavior. The main point is to limit the irrational self and to prevent hurting, exploiting, and humiliating.

Our mind plays tricks with our perception. When loose fragments affect us, we cannot correctly analyze the pervasive data. As negligent parents, we see the self as adequate. If we are very thin, we see the self as fat. If we are fat, we do not believe that we are grossly overweight. Those discrepancies between individual perception and others are not easily to resolve. Sometimes we do not consciously understand that we treat others as objects. In many instances our mind does not care about others and wants to change others to our liking. We have a responsibility to contend those irrational urges and restrain our antisocial fragments. In those complicated structures, we trust the objective experts' opinions to see discrepancies between our perceptions and others'.

When a kinesthetic mode of expression is out of balance, the main symptoms are anger, anxiety, and tension. With visual darkness comes fears, negativity, and depression. The audio misbalances bring schizophrenia and paranoia. When the olfactory mode of expression is out of balance, the imbalance signifies the organic problems. The imbalanced psyche has a lot of splits and as result suffers from the feelings of the misery and despair. It cannot build resistance to danger and is vulnerable to split and radicalization. The carriers of radical structures push their ideas on imbalanced psyches.

The manipulating of others and using them as an object does not make our goals nice. In analysis we have to identify which fragment is responsible for our antisocial attitude. In our mind we could enjoy many of our goals, but we could not allow the release of antisocial responses. If we have conscious awareness of our antisocial tendencies, then we can modify some of our behavior. By balancing our responses on audio, visual, kinesthetic, and olfactory modes of expressions, we can get control of our responses.

Every mind can get a self built on its likeness. Many have thoughts of infinitive glory and desire to send the self on a special mission to save their ethnicity, their religion, or the world. As soon as the self gets out of our mind and pushes others to get violent and attack, the self is radicalized. It seems that radicalization affects our self the same way parasites affect our bodies. The radical ideas are always there, but for some reason in different locations they are more powerful and quickly spread. The infected self has a different perception of all our basic values. The radicals reject the Ten Commandments, and the most common harm is that radicals do not value the gift of life.

The radical ideas randomly affect the world's population, like viruses. Too many of us get sick with radicalism and spread infection at an epidemic level; those infected become the puppets and recruits. Nevertheless, some are immune to the viruses and may become leaders of resistance—or victims. The few antisocial people exploit the epidemics to increase their power, using weaknesses of ailing mentality to their own advantage. They promise protection, remedies, and justices, and they appear to be givers but are vicious takers.

The good thing is that viruses do not stay forever; otherwise, we all would be dead. In time people build resistances to viruses and the epidemic passes, but a big margin of the population is already damaged by the disease. The radical ideas pass as well, but the damages are tremendous. The individuals with a solid identity have an antidote to manipulation by radicals and keep their mind immune; they are unaffected by deadly viruses that are polluting our brain with unproven radical theories. By building a solid identity, we get stronger and build resistance to radical ideas. In my book a fictitious character has a solid identity and is immune to viruses of radicalization.

Like my hero, the mind travelers are sailors, building a solid identity as individuals. They are not the puppets of untested doctrines and have a goal of unification with harmony of universe. The emigrants from the collective are sailors and resist split. The split changes the psychological structure and imbalances our brain chemicals, and we produce pervasive responses. The split from harmony leave us helpless in front of invasive, untested assumptions. We see around us many people who split and radicalized, and they stopped being individuals. They radicalize in groups and also in imperial collectives, and as radicals they are always afraid of something. They split in groups with the desire to clean up their surrounding from blacks, Jews, heretics, and other perceived issues. They also split into collectives to clean up the Arian spirit or to get rid of exploiters, the wealthy, infidels, aristocrats, and more. In reality the split to small and big is always the desire to achieve hegemony. Splitting is very difficult to recognize because the architects of the split declare that all the atrocities of split are necessities for survival.

Our psyche is based on the summary of our responses and is built from our impression of audio, visual, and kinesthetic stimulations. The redundant responses are rigid fragments in our psyche, whose main functions are unification and splitting. The splitting creates a lot of pathology; if fragments conflict and are loosely associated, our psyche cannot serve us adequately. We split when we are not happy with the self or others, and when others are not happy with us.

To be an individual, the sailor unifies his psyche. It happens that several of his fragments split from the rest of his psyche and are rigid. By encouraging dialogue, the sailor is able transfer his rigid fragments to flexible. He uses a dialogue as a tool to unify the psyche, and he enjoys meeting of his fragments. His psyche becomes whole and successfully deals with psychological pathologies. By using dialogue to unify fragments, people who suffer from mental problems can reduce the intake of psychotropic medications, or in some instances even stop using them. The unified psyche is well adjusted in life. People with a whole psyche enjoy the interactions with others and others feel good about them. The sailor has a solid identity and is immune to splits.

The duality between moment and eternity can be understood through dialogue. Subconsciously our desire drives us to have dialogue. We want others to understand us, but the others want us to understand them, and we do not know how connect. To bring our point across, we use confrontation and manipulation. Nevertheless, the desire for dialogue and meeting is as strong as sexual drive. The drive for dialogue starts in the mind but brings physical pleasure. It can make us part of universal forces and can make us whole. Our desire for unification works in many different ways. We can have the meeting with the universe through a deity. We can encompass the unification with the universe by meeting others. Our mind is a part of the universe, and meeting with the self is unification. Through dialogue we can have an understanding of unity and connectedness. In our self we create harmony; to prepare others to connect, we negotiate. Successful dialogue and negotiations create unity.

On the other side of the coin, the unsuccessful dialogue gives us physical discomfort and separates us from the universe. After the split we get fixated in a little space, and our responses lack congruency. Because we are in restricted space, we build our psychological structure with what is available. Our fixated responses and inability to change our rigidity are the result of unsuccessful dialogue.

Many times we feel that we are failing in our dialogue and feel frustrated, angry, and confused. We do not know that we may have an internal dialogue. We wrongly attribute the successful internal dialogue to unsuccessful dialogue with others. When we do not recognize the internal dialogue, we trigger splits in our psyche. We are not able to understand that we have successful dialogue with our self. We perceive failure in our interaction instead of good feelings.

We are sailors, travelers inside our minds, and through our perceptions we explore the deepest oceans of life. We need to understand our internal world. Instead of conflicts and violence, we strive to enjoy peace of mind. The goal of the mind travelers is to make their internal world a better place. We can change our perception through our brain power. As emigrants, we are mind travelers with the goal of arriving at a desired place; in the new destination, because everything is different, we go through a cultural shock. Things that were negative in our home country became positive in the new one. We need to change our perceptions. As real sailors and mind travelers, after a strong resistance we switch to the new mentality and to the new perceptions.

People move to faraway places to find happiness. Because they are sick and tired from internal struggles, they change the old scenery to more comfortable one. In the beautiful new place they have many positive feelings. A few never settle down and constantly travel the world. In the self-analysis, sailors can travel inside their psyche and meet their fragments. Their analysis starts with identification of fragments, and they do not want to ignore any of them. In supportive surroundings, sailors deal successfully with their splits and achieve a balanced psyche. Instead of traveling to different countries and distant mountains and oceans, sailors achieve more by having a mesmerizing voyage in the interior of their psyche.

Sailors knew that confrontation and manipulation result in a split of psyche, and they do not use them. They understand that people use confrontation as a way to impose their perception by force. Some people need manipulation to achieve their goals, with tricks and lies. Sailors feel resentment toward bullies and con artists, and they never use manipulation or confrontation to bring their point across. They are aware that only antisocial people feel good by achieving goals with those negative methods. By traveling inside their psyche, sailors achieve a balanced life, hold many dialogues with various fragments, and have many negotiations with others. They never get disillusioned with dialogues and do not use confrontation and manipulation.

With a deity we always have dialogue and meeting. The deity knows everything about us, and the relationship is easier than with others or the self. The deity is always whole and is everywhere, inside and outside our psyche. In a dialogue with the deity, we cannot fail; we always can talk to divinity. The deity has knowledge of our thoughts and secrets. The dialogue with divinity is completely different from a dialogue with others. The deity is much stronger and is wiser than we are; it does not have parts or pieces. It does not matter whether the deity is inside or outside of us; everything around us is connected with it, including fragments, the self, and others. Through a deity we have strong ties to religion and scriptures. The dialogue is internal and also external, and it comes without any conditions.

As immigrants, sailors do not know the language and lifestyle of the host country, but they adapt. In the meantime, they intuitively have dialogues and meetings with their fragments, adjusting their ways of expression to the life in the new country. They build a connection with others based on their subjective translations. Eventually they display the transformation and multiplicity of self. Emigrants are mind travelers and show very clear signs of unifications and splits. It happened that in countries of origin, the emigrants were placed in various collectives. Some collectives had flexibility and allowed the citizens to keep their own perception; others applied a uniform identity to everyone and restricted individuality. These restrictive collectives were easily radicalized: they had draconian rules that prevented citizens from having their own perception. The radical collectives were against any members who wished to explore their internal world and wanted a single, easily controlled identity for everyone.

Now sailors want to have their own perception and to travel away from the land of standardized robots. Sailors, as mind travelers, are not taking a trip on the water by big or small ships; some do not even have the physical strength to overcome the commotions of being on the open sea. Still, if sailors have inquisitive minds, they can start a fascinating voyage. They do not explore real rivers, seas, and oceans, but they survey the interior of their psyche. They accept as their individual reality whatever they can see in the deep sea of life. They want others to allow them to have their own perceptions. When their individuality is restricted, the sailors revolt.

Upon arriving at a new homeland, sailors' psyches get locked, and they get confused and disoriented. Their responses are not congruent with new stimulations and are exaggerated or inadequate. Unfortunately the traveling routes do not bring them to their desired destination; it is like they have gone for a very long ride in a car that turns only one way. It is impossible to turn their vehicles in another direction even though much better routes are available. The maps are useless because sailors cannot change their roads. Those rigid responses are called fixated fragments, and they cannot use flexible brain passes. As a result, sailors' responses are not congruent with stimuli. Sailors named the fixated responses by the names of familiar personalities who display similar traits when responding to stimuli. Their goal is to unlock the psyche and to have the responses be congruent with the stimuli.

The fixated fragments in people's psyche are produced by the repetitive and similar responses to variety of stimuli. It's like a broken record producing the same tune for different songs. People do not have a conscious awareness of their repetitive behavior, when they display obsessions, impulsiveness, overreactions, or underreactions. In order to identify responses, they need to bring them from their subconscious to the conscious awareness. People can manage their responses when they are identifying their fixated fragments. Only through meetings with their fragments can people achieve the transformation of fixated fragments to flexible. Without conscious awareness with what fragments they are interacting, people cannot change any responses. The goal of self-analysis is to transform the fixated fragments to flexible ones, which allow sailors to have flexible routes—the best way to respond to stimuli, which are the shortest paths to sailors' destinations. The sailors' desire is to have responses that are congruent to stimuli.

The sailors engaged in a self-dialogue expect to find congruent responses. The split fragments have access to sailors' memory. The loose and somehow detached fragments do not have anything to do with multiple personalities; they are part of one personality and can be united in the whole identity to help sailors with congruent responses. Good feelings about their responses bring self-dialogues and meetings.

Our psyche has a variety of ways to process stimuli and provide responses, and we have fragments on different modes of expression. We translate the stimuli and responses between different modes by using the universal translator in verbal form. The different modalities hold different types of information. Our capacities to relate to the self and others vary because of the various ways of accepting and responding to the information. We do not have all modes developed equally; a few of our modes can be less developed, and we cannot quickly analyze and respond to stimuli. We compensate our weakness with more adequate modes of expression. When we cannot have balanced replies, we exhibit overreaction and underreaction. We deal with these modes of expression by having balanced responses. When stimuli and responses are translated, we initiate a dialogue and a meeting between fragments.

Sailors know their internal world and understand the self. The internal world colors their perception of the external world. To understand the external world, sailors use the measurements and quantifications through their senses; they see the beauty and ugliness of the world through their perception. Their inner world can be changed with the power of their mind. Our external world is very hard to measure and quantify objectively, but sailors' inner worlds filled up with projective data. When sailors gather more data, they can change their perception of the external world and change their fearful and angry responses.

The dialogue with others is an external dialogue. This dialogue happens very rarely because we mistake our internal dialogues for external. When we come to different countries, we have many splits and disappointments and settle in the new reality to have many dialogues and negotiations. Often we are failing; over and over again our feelings represent only one loose fragment that takes control over our psyche. We cannot repeat the dialogue with others and get frustrated and confused. We fail because we do not know what fragment represents our psyche and which fragments represent the others. In times of confusion, the self-dialogue is very desirable and rebuilds our strength. If we do not have internal dialogue with our fragments, we are not consciously clear about what it means to be whole. Self-dialogue and meeting are possible because our fragments know everything about the self. As a result of the dialogue our fragments get united. Contrary to intuitive dialogue with others, we as sailors consciously have the dialogue with the self. To achieve self-dialogue we identify and meet the fragments.

Contrary to self-dialogue, in the dialogues with others we do not have the same easiness. Dialogue with others happens rarely, and the difficulty in dialogue and meeting with others is rooted in our incomplete perception of others. Our successful interaction depends on inner strength and the wholeness of the self. Our identity is a subjective perception of the world and depends on our ability to explore and interpret external objects, although it does not mean that we manipulate others as objects and allow others to treat us as objects. We need to admit that, unfortunately, we do not know too much about others, and they do not know much about us. We are limited in our experiences. No matter how hard we try, we cannot see what is going on behind us. When we turn back, we lose sight of what is in front. We also cannot read the minds of others, however we are far from being ignorant. We have some idea about what is going on in the minds of others, but it does not mean that we are connected enough to have a dialogue and meeting. In internal dialogues we correct our perception of others.

The minimization of the complexity of having dialogue with others can be damaging to our psyche. In the worse scenario, the failing dialogue with others can trigger confusion and our desire to push our perceptions on others. By being confused we can use confrontation and manipulation; we can display splitting when loose fragments take over the psyche. As a result, we cannot function without bullying and cheating others. As sailors we will never act on those urges; we engage in self-dialogue.

Our psyche is the place where our mind and consciousness are located. The self is inside of our psyche and is built on our individual perception. Our self is multifaceted, as our identity and our psyche's structure. The significant characteristics of self are individuality and uniqueness. By unifying our fragments, we get a whole identity and a whole self. With splitting fragments, we have a fragmented identity and a rift in the self. The reason we do not have a self-dialogue is because the lack of our knowledge about our self. We want to have a dialogue with others without meeting our real self. We can unintentionally have intuitive feelings about the self and have dialogue with others, but it does not happen very often. In general the failure to know the self results in splitting and distress. The split causes severe disturbances in our normal functioning, such as mental and physical illnesses and general unhappiness. To counteract the split, we meet with our fragments and unify within our self, which is the way to bring us to a balanced life. We enjoy our own perception and feel whole. From others we cannot expect the same reaction as we have from our own fragments. As sailors we respect different perceptions and do not impose our perception on anyone. To lessen the gap with others, sailors use the art of negotiation, which does not require a similar perception. With few exceptions sailors can negotiate everything with others.

The desire to have dialogue with the others is very strong, and we feel miserable when we fail. When we're so focused on external dialogue, we often fail to seize the opportunity to have internal dialogue with our fragments. Note that we can copy the other as a fragment in our psyche—actually, we can have in our psyche a fragment of anyone and still have an internal dialogue. The dialogue with a fragment does not give such strong satisfaction as dialogue with a real person, but by having dialogue with a fragment, we avoid the split from an unsuccessful dialogue with others. By using internal dialogue, we keep our psyche whole. As sailors, to avoid splits from the interactions with others, we negotiate with others our non-matching perceptions; this way we narrow our perceptual differences.

The split in our psyche can possibly be a result of psychological trauma, which is caused by external mistreatment or heredity. A split weakens our desire to have a dialogue. When we are treated as objects and become manipulated and confronted, we do not want any dialogue and meetings. Others feel discomfort in dealing with us because of a split in our psyche. When we split, others say that our psyche "fell apart." When we get unified, others perceive us as being together. To have a balanced life, we need to unify our fragments. To be happy with the self and feel that others are happy with us, we use self-dialogue.

Sailors' psyche has many fragments. Their fragments have a common goal: to look for their well-being and to have unrestricted access to their memory data. The domineering fragments take over sailors' entire psyche, but the dialogue between their fragments is still possible. By opening self-dialogue, sailors remedy the splits and promote unification; the internal dialogue stops rigidity and creates plasticity. When sailors have a difficult time creating dialogue with others, they are not frustrated. Instead of external dialogue, they can always have internal dialogue.

Internally, sailors have achieved utopian harmony, and they unify all fragments in a balanced identity. They consciously identify their fragments and have internal dialogues. Through identification of fragments, they have more understanding of the self as a complex entity, and they know it is a collection of many fragments that together are their identity. Instead of having external dialogue, they copy images of others as fragments into their psyche and have internal dialogues on familiar territory. To solidify their identity, sailors have external negotiations with others and internal self-dialogue with their fragments. The others cannot easily accept sailors' perception; because they are unique, sailors do not easily accept someone else's perceptions. To bring their perceptions closer to others, sailors have a lot of negotiations.

Before sailors have successful external dialogue with others, they have a successful dialogue within their own fragments and self. Only when the sailors have a solid structure and the responses are flexible will external dialogue happen. Sailors' solid identity can meet others' identity. The similar perceptions cannot be the result of brainwash, manipulation, or forceful imposition of alien ideas. After many negotiations, when two sailors with solid identities have a dialogue, they have a meeting.

When we travel to the magic place where we can unify our fragments and be a whole people, we are sailors. During our voyage our mood changes and we become dissimilar. It happens because our mood is taken over by diverse fragments, the small parts of our psyche. We need to know our fragments to know who we are. Our goal is to find the self, resist splitting, and unify our fragments. As sailors we get through many storms, which split us from our way to reach the internal Shangri-La. Nevertheless, we are searching for a place where we can enjoy our life, and we want to be whole, to unify with the universe.

We are analyzing the forces inside our psyche. From early childhood, we continue to discover who we are. The first discoveries are that we are human and our gender; then it takes our whole life to discover the rest of our complex psyche and our unique self. We want to unify the self to be whole, because the psyche becomes more fragmented when our self splits. Note that after each split, our fragments become more rigid and create rigid responses. When we split, we become more detached from universe.

Sailors make the rigid fragments flexible. This dynamic continues all their lives. Unification and splitting are the main forces inside sailors' psyche, and their experiences depend on their understanding of how to interpret their feelings. The interpretation should get them closer to reach their goal, which is building a solid self and becoming unified with universe. When fragments are unifying, sailors feel whole and content; when their fragments split, they feel discomfort and misery. As a result of their own experiences of unification and splitting, they get their individuality. Our mind is unpredictable, and apparently the sailors need to mobilize all their knowledge to go through the volatile areas. When they eventually unify their self, they feel like they can relax in a very comfortable pond.

Every mind traveler is an emigrant and sailor. His mind goes through immense turbulence, and he needs a military ship to survive the large waves. Knowledge about the self helps him to find his appearance and form his behavior. A sailor's mind is like a crew united under an experienced skipper: The fragments are the part of command, and every fragment knows his duty. The domineering fragment is a central commander who unifies other fragments. The unified mind can successfully overcome severe crises with minimum losses. Sailors' minds work the same way as a military ship with sophisticated technology keeps our internal Shangri-La protected from any intruders. The emigrants were urged in the past to rely for protection on collective; now they are far away from the uniform setting, and they are responsible for the self. To be safe, they keep the sailor's spirit.

The loose fragments create disarray in our psyche, and we appear hopeless and confused, responding in inappropriate ways to different crises. It is a signal that our identity is a fragmented and self split. We lost the touch with knowledge of who we are. To regain the sailor's spirit, we need to unify our fragments and regain our solid self.

As sailors we need to know our inner self on the conscious level. We have a responsibility to preserve our identity and to project the public image. The famous artist probably can dress as a homeless person, because the creativity of the artist's spirit is higher than the judgment of others, but often an artist wears a very elegant jabot shirt with the red tie. In many major corporations, employee do not deceive others, and everyone dresses according to status. The managers do not necessarily wear a tie and three-piece suits, but they dress nice enough to distinguish themselves from regular colleagues. The manual worker does not use dress shirts with ties; he prefers jeans and flannel shirts. Our mind is a complex entity and can have many sides; we chose one domineering fragment to represent us. Our appearance and our behavior are congruent with our identity. When we have a solid psyche, we immediately know how to provide the effective response to a variety of stressful situations.

Sometimes it is hard for us to identify which fragments are splitting and which are unifying; it gets very confusing when we have external split from something powerful. Let us assume that we are members of organization that is very respectable and solid. Nevertheless, as insiders we bring to light the misdeeds in those structures. On the surface we separate from powerful structures and appear to be split, but it is not a correct observation. We unify with internal feelings of honor and responsibility. For us as sailors, the process of the internal unification is more important than an external split. The internal unification is one of the ways to build a solid identity. On the other hand, for criminal psyches the unification with antisocial tendencies is more important; their external unity causes the split from the internal feelings of decency and humanity. When sailors are dealing with the abnormal, violent, antisocial, and criminal psyches, in order to achieve future unification, they can split from their belief.

The fragments or responses can be on visual, audio, kinesthetic, and olfactory modes of expressions. The different abnormality in sailors' psyche can be explained by loose and dissociative fragments, and they are incongruent to different modes of expressions. Severe trauma, strong sensitivity, explosiveness, and many other abnormalities can be easily explained by interactions between fragments that are in a state of splitting or unification. Many personality disorders and affective disorders are easily explained by rigidity and incongruence of fragments on different modes of expressions.

The processes of unification and splitting inside our psyche result in our feelings of well-being or misery. The process of unification starts with identifying different fragments. We assemble our fragments in groups, which pull together splitters or unifiers. We also need to identify to what mode of expression the fragment belongs. Our internal analysis also includes the identification of the level of the fragment's rigidity and flexibility. The process of healing transfers the rigidity to flexibility.

Underneath the flexible and rigid fragments, we have the tracks of neurons and synopses. All our responses have physiological bases, but we are checking the psychological effect. The rigid fragments have the same response to many different stimuli. In our life the rigid, fearful responses form on many non-fearful stimuli. The rigid responses have a high intensity that causes overreaction. The flexible fragments have the capacity to choose from many responses. We can distinguish stimuli by the severity and form appropriate responses. It means that as sailors, we do not overreact. Sailors do not get in fights or get numb if stimuli need a verbal response; they also translate stimuli and responses into different modes of expression. The feeling of fear and anger can be processed in many different ways, which creates a flexible approach to their responses.

Superficial knowledge of who we are is responsible for the luck of intricacy. Because of our lack of internal connections, we do not get what we deserve and satisfy ourselves with much less than we are worth. We bring our internal feelings to a conscious level, and then the connections start with an identification of who we are. To have the ability to connect, we need to do some work to unify our fragments in the whole self. Our fragments can be rigid or flexible. The flexible fragments associate with unification, and the rigid fragments have splitting tendencies. To get an easy connection, we unite our fragments and have a solid psyche, using dialogues and meetings to transform the rigid fragments into a flexible one and then unify them.

Sailors found the ways of relating because they know who they are. They know to whom, when, and how to talk. In the crucial moments the appropriate, flexible fragment takes over their psyche, and the successful connection is guaranteed.

CHAPTER I

Splitting from The Self

Professor Kryvoruchko is a sailor

Professor Kryvoruchko is fictional and a composite character. He has many fragments, and every character in this book corresponds to one of his fragments. Professor Kryvoruchko represents an individual who is immune to split and who is able to unify his fragments. He is a whole person, an individual with solid psyche who shows us how to respond to the forces inside and outside of his psyche. He represents flexibility, tolerance, and unification. To be a child of love, he wants to unify with the genetic heritage. Because his ancestors were massacred by Nazis, he has a lot of fears, but he understands his problems and deals with them on the conscious level.

Professor Kryvoruchko is descended from the unfortunates who were physically annihilated for the sake of a murky theory about genetic hegemony. He affirmed, "We were selected for annihilation on a genetic basis and were declared to be unfit to support the biggest pretentiousness of our time. We were killed by a mob that was thirsty for blood. The throngs were the fools of pomposity and used shovels to kill helpless children, women, and the elderly. They killed children in front of the mothers. If the fools had children and grandchildren that had a genetic defect, even if they were on the side of the villains, their offspring was annihilated too. Nevertheless, the villains did not cover their nature, and nothing may shake their belief in their cause, because they know that we are not them and we are not driven by hate. They were sometimes forced to change their cause, but underneath the same hate always was. The splitting, which was inflicted on our world, continues to affect many psyches. To deal with hate, we need to understand the social eradication, genetic abolition, religious obliteration, and the many divergent types of revulsion."

Professor Kryvoruchko is intended to be an individual with a solid identity, and his comments are important. He believes that our solid identity can take diverse forms. "We have potency to be part of any distinct religion, ideology, and ethnicity, but most important is that it has a foundation of love. We make a subconscious effort to achieve unification and to defeat the forces of hate. The splitting forces are very strong, but we also have a strong resistance to the hate. We need to find a future direction where our lives will go."

The splitting about religion

Professor Kryvoruchko's psyche is a combination of dissimilar fragments. He has a Gentile mother, but he also has the strong feeling of being Jewish. In every religion the members display distinct levels of devotion, and this reality may be a cause of splitting. The religious splitting is usually very antagonistic. The widely divergent groups of parishes are hateful to surroundings and take on the responsibility of estimating the acceptable level of devotion and setting up the norms and requirements.

Professor Kryvoruchko has strong feelings about this issue. "We are disturbed by the fact that even between the chosen, some frictions exist, including the Jewish Orthodox and the Reform movements. For the Orthodox believers, I am probably not a Jew at all; my relatives hid their identity and didn't eat kosher food, and my father married a Gentile woman. Nevertheless, I am proud of my cultural and ethnical background. For the Orthodox believer, those who do not have a Jewish mother are not Jews at all, and I need to go through a complex process to become a Jew."

Because Professor Kryvoruchko did not have a Jewish mother, he did not have knowledge about how to relate to his friends when they joked about Jewish mothers. His father was deprived from his Jewish heritage and hid his identity. His family lived in a harsh world, and they always needed to fight for survival; they were victims of oppressive social structures and inhuman ideologies. They were emotionally broken and very scared. Many families were in the same situation, and this was one reason why he went to Israel: he wanted to regain his pride and feel good to be a Jew. He had his circumcision, studied the Hebrew language and scriptures, and had a bar mitzvah at twenty-one. He was one of many who did not have a Jewish mother. He was a soldier in the Israeli army, and some of his friends were killed.

In the soldier's cemetery the dead ones that for some reason were not considered Jewish were not allowed to be interred next to their fallen comrades; they were buried behind the cemetery wall. Kryvoruchko felt that this was wrong. He was against this kind of distinction between dead soldiers, because they all fought and died for Israel. He believed if soldiers were accepted to fight and to die for Israel, then they were all children of Israel. Emotionally he felt apart, but nevertheless he did not give up his quest for self-identity. He needed to resist the splitting forces in his psyche and find the strength to have a genuine dialogue.

Professor Kryvoruchko believed that the solid self-identity is a representation of real love inside everyone, whoever they might be. To have love, we do not need any reason. We also want to identify with the smart and powerful. Professor Kryvoruchko understood that some groups were more precise in interpreting the Bible. They do not want to give up their restrictive attitude or be more flexible, because they do not want to be around anyone who does not belong. He wanted to understand both sides and did not know what was better for religion, to have a limited membership or an open enrollment.

Eventually he understood that both were needed but at different times. Nowadays we have a genetic test and do not need to guess about who is the father of the child. In the past the mother was chosen as the carrier of ethnicity, because genetic tests were not available, and it was not certain if the father was Jewish. The mother was chosen in identifying the Jewish ethnicity; everyone who had a Jewish mother was ethnically a Jew.

Professor's Kryvoruchko wife is a Jewish woman, and regardless of his own ethnicity, his son has a Jewish mother and has important clout to satisfy all requirements. His son also will have the facts to relate to the all jokes about Jewish mothers. Professor Kryvoruchko has very warm feelings about his wife. He mentions that he met and fell in love with his wife in kibbutz, where he was on vacation from his duties as a soldier. He is not ashamed that he was looking for a Jewish woman to love and to have a life together. Intuitively he believed in God, but being a member of the Soviet collective, he did not know much about religion. He wanted to do the right thing and went to a Jewish state.

Professor Kryvoruchko made a choice for the self: "I wanted to do the right thing, because for the terror groups it did not matter what kind of devotion to

God I have. It did not make any difference to fascists to what group of Judaism, Christianity, or Islam I belonged. We were slaughtered not for our religion but as an ethnic group. This massacre was based on our genetic characteristics. We were selected for annihilation, to be a target of hate and violence. We still suffer from very deep persecutory trauma. The big, poisonous cloud stayed over us for generations. It is impossible for anyone to comprehend the extent of our tragedy. It was also hard to imagine that we had power to recuperate and continue to function. In one family, where many members were killed, a little boy was able to survive—and he is my father. The offspring of this boy are searching for their identity, because we still suffer from very deep, persecutory trauma. The immense, venomous swirl took over our mind. Even we who have not been targets of hate have a big split in our psyche, because in this world everything is interconnected.

"The Holocaust was not only the tragedy of Jewish people but also of the whole world. The whole psyche of the world felt apart under attack of the hate and viciousness. We are still under the attack and do not have any guarantee of survival, only a hope. It is very sad that the children of survivors have a feeling of discomfort if they are affiliated with crowds, which the group perceives to be less devoted. Regrettably, religious groups are setting the standard of devotion to God and want the separation from the faction, which they labeled as less devoted. They feel like they are the protectors of traditions, and instead of unifying in spirituality around God, they are splitting. To unify, they must appreciate divergences, and we have to respect their beliefs."

The benefit of splitting through generations

Splitting through the generations in some instances is important for survival and for preserving the future opportunity to build a solid identity. The quest for the original identity perhaps may take many generations, and it is important that unification is central in building a solid identity, but splitting is also important for survival.

Professor Kryvoruchko had a goal to unify with his life, which was splitting from the horror and threatened his existence. He avowed, "The victims of the cruelty and violence are splitting from the damaged fragments in their psyche. The hope is that we will be able to rebuild our life. When it is not safe to maintain the original identity, our splitting continues through generations. Splitting through generations continues until life is more secure, and we have the strength to get back our original identity. When the events are out of our control, our split perhaps might be a necessity of life".

The split through generations

Professor's Kryvoruchko's fragments, his grandfather and father, were survivors of the Holocaust, and they were able to survive the tragedy because of the split. Professor Kryvoruchko is also part of a massacred family, which includes his grandmother, Rivka; his aunt, Lizochka, who was a baby at that time of carnage; and his great-grandfather, Hershel. They were the victims of fascist slaughter. The fragment of his great-grandfather Hershel is the one who made an attempt to avoid splitting by relying on past experiences. The grandmother, Rivka, felt that the split was necessary to survive, so if she had listened to her father, then Professor's Kryvoruchko would not be around to tell their story. The inhuman facts of history about the Holocaust and genocide are the worst examples of hate, which leave only one solution for survival: splitting and fragmentation. The fragmentation helps to protect a part of the psyche from complete destruction. After fascist occupation of part of Ukraine, the invading forces began the annihilation of Jews.

Professor Kryvoruchko acknowledges that sometimes for survival, one pays a terrible price. The two young adolescents, brother and sister, ran away from the Babiy Yar, the place of the slaughtering of Jews. When they traveled on the road, the group of young polizies, the local collaborators groups associated with fascists that traveled in the back of a truck, spotted them. They jumped from the truck, grabbed the girl by the hand, and lifted her up on the truck. Her brother was very scared and did not do anything to pull her back or defend her. He ran after the truck and saw how the polizies raped his little sister and then killed her. She was twelve years old, and he was sixteen. Hate generated their splitting and killing. They split from humanity to nurture their feelings of grandiosity and power. They anesthetized the self from feelings of compassion.

Professor Kryvoruchko declared, "They were killing and using us as inanimate objects. They did not worry about guilt, because we were not human and did not have feelings. When they were treating us as objects, they were detaching the self from our suffering; they were vicious, cruel, violent, and inhuman. The brother of the killed girl survived. He lived a long life, but he did not enjoy any of his days and was miserable. He suffered from nightmares and impotence, and he was afraid of everything and everyone. Everyone around him was miserable, including his wife and children. The misery was a price for survival. He lives, but his life is worse than death. He has a deadly mark, which he transfers to his family, and his split from happiness was generational. The hope is that after several generations, his future offspring, if they have a chance, will be able to unify with the joy of life.

By splitting, we protect loved ones

Professor Kryvoruchko states, "In some instances we need to split from the loved ones to protect them. Despite the danger we are facing, we do not want to split. We are not able to split and leave behind the beloved who need us, because we are dedicated to love. Contrary to self-sacrificing individuals, the selfish have the capacity to kill, betray, and be completely insensitive to suffering around them. They will do anything to stay alive and do not have any moral limits for self-preservation."

Professor Kryvoruchko's grandmother chose to be together and not to split with her baby daughter and her father. She was with them until the last breath and died with them. She wanted her son to survive, but even the split for survival would demand a heavy price from her boy. The split was needed as a hope for the future and to avoid the complete destruction of the family. Her son, Lyonya, will never again see his mother, grandfather, and sister. When Rivka decided to split from her son, she did not know that she was saving his life. Her son suffered a lot but was able to overcome all barriers and stay alive. In many instances, in moments of danger the psyche is resistant to splitting, and the split from the loved one sometimes is impossible. The mother does not have the strength to leave her sick baby daughter and her old father, who are completely helpless. The mother is choosing to share the horrors of death with her loved ones, and they were unified in death. The unification in death is the most awful way of unification, but the horror of splitting from the sick baby is worse than dying. During a terrorist attack of a school in the Caucasus Mountains, some mothers were allowed by the terrorists to get out with one little child and leave behind an older child. The mothers went out to bring a little child to safety, and they left their older child, but very soon they returned to be with second child until their death. The mothers chose unifying and dying with their children. The worst thing for a mother is abandoning her child.

Professor Kryvoruchko disclosed that his father, Leonid Alexandrovich Kryvoruchko, well remembered the year of 1942 in the capital of Ukraine, occupied by fascists. For Lyonya and, in later years, as Leonid Alexandrovich, his mind did always clear the memories of the day when there had appeared papers on the fences of Kiev, the capital of Ukraine, showing an order addressed to the Jews of that city. He remembers his mother's question: "What now? To what Palestine are they sending us?"

Grandfather Hershel kept repeating, "In 1916, during the First World War, a German officer was billeted in my house. He loved children and always used to give them candies. Rivka, the children of such a German, cannot possibly hurt us. If you are afraid, please do not follow this order. I will go by myself."

"I would like to believe you, Papa," Mother replied, "but you know neighbors are not saying things for nothing. If it weren't for Lizochka's fever, I would run away from Kiev with the neighbors. But look at her—how we can leave now? I will go with you."

Professor Kryvoruchko aid, "The resistance to the split was rooted in our sincere belief that humanity would be restored and that the scary stories were just the result of confusion. We want to believe that life is harmonious and fair. We have the complication to accept unfairness in our existence. By relying on past experiences and common sense, we were not prepared to deal with the tragedy caused by the fascists. Nothing in our past was closer to that magnitude of this hate. Despite common sense, the fears were causing the split. When we are completely destroyed, we do not have a hope that we may function again; we need to save part of our psyche. With fragmentation we are losing our identity and are acting on the mercy of the small fragments, which are taking over our psyche, but as a reward they give us a small chance for continuation. Only fragmentation gives a chance of surviving. If an individual has a way to survive, then it is a hope that the little fragments may be united in future."

We might be taken over by grandiosity

When our psyche is affected by pomposity and grandiosity, it requires more splitting and will eventually become a machine of splitting. Our fragments split from our own feelings to serve the radical ideas. The pompous and posturing people want everyone to be their servants. For the radicals everyone unlike them is an object, and they will slay him without any human feelings. Radicals believe that they have a mission, which is a foundation of the feeling of grandiosity. It allows them to split from humanity and to see others as objects. The split of radicalization is particularly vicious.

Professor Kryvoruchko's father, as a young boy, did not know this tendency of pomposity that graded those who were dissimilar as subhuman, but he understood that something very horrible was going on, and he was scared. For a young child who had been split from loved ones and from his mother, it was a very traumatic experience that haunted him for the rest of his life. He split and ran; otherwise he would be fed to the machine of pretentiousness of being superhuman, which strived to become bigger. To save Lyonya's life, his mother initiated Lyonya's separation from family. Rivka instinctively felt that the apparatus of pretension and mannerism was going to consume all of them. She did understand that the only way to save her son from being murdered by fascists was to split. She was aware that her child would be estranged from her, his little sister, and his grandfather and never see them again. This was a crucial point in Professor Kryvoruchko's life. Behind this split was his future life; otherwise the pomposity and grandiosity would consume him.

Lyonya did not know that he was spared from death and would have a long life. He would also meet a beautiful woman, marry her, and raise a family. At the time of splitting, he did not know anything about his future and was just a scared boy who missed his family. He did not know to whom he should listen. His mother made the decision, which was impossible for him to comprehend. Only later in life did Lyonya understand that to survive, sometimes we need to break away. The mannerism can always find justification for killing by presenting the self as a victim of somebody else's conspiracy. The pomposity implied that the Jews were guilty because they somehow damaged the pride of grandiosity. The fascists declared that the conspiracy of the Jews was very daunting and damaging, and they needed to suffer. In societies associated with pomposity, Jews were always the scapegoats and were already selected by the slaughter machine; the gaudiness did not need any new scapegoats.

By aggrandizing the self and downgrading everyone who was unlike as subhuman, the grandiosity was represented by huge projects in art, architecture, and parades. In the meantime, the little boy was a victim of the heartless apparatus and needed to survive by any means.

Grandfather Hershel believed in humanity. He had lived through pogroms and civil war, and he knew that men had the capability to be worse than a beast—but still he defended humankind and the stability of common sense. "You are doing the right thing by not running away," Grandfather told Rivka. "I am sure that the Germans will send us to Palestine. They won't let us take our belongings because of the war and a shortage of transportation." Grandfather chanted his prayers. He believed in God and humanity, and he thought that goodness would always overcome and that evil would lose. For him it was incomprehensible to think that someone may hurt him without any reason and any remorse. He was using common sense, which does not work with psyches infected by the virus of pretentiousness.

Lyonya, who was then twelve years old, helped Mother gather up some clothing and fed his three-year-old sister her medicine. The following morning the street was full of neighbors. His mother pushed a baby carriage with two suitcases. Grandfather held Lizochka in his arms. Lyonya carried a large bag and looked at the neighbors leaving their homes; they, too, carried some belongings. Suddenly Mother said, "Lyonya, don't come with us, son. I am worried. If all goes well, you will come back. Meanwhile, don't sleep at home during the next few days. If things are bad with us, find your way to the town where Auntie Polina is living." Aunt Polina, Mother's school friend, was a Ukrainian woman, and last summer the whole family had visited her.

Mother was crying as she kissed Lyonya, and then he kissed Lizochka. To this day Leonid can feel his sister's warm cheek on his lips. He embraced his grandfather. "Everything will be all right, Lyonitchka. Your mother panics easily; we shall only become separated because of her, but on the other hand, God takes care of the careful." Grandfather gave him some money, and Mother put some food in his bag and wept as she kissed him again. He was leaving them without knowing that he was escaping death. His mother stood still, and when he turned his head, he saw her standing near Grandfather, holding Lizochka in her arms. For Lyonya the only one way to deal with the deadly mechanism of pretension was forcing the self to disregard the desire to be with his family, and to resist the natural drive for unification. He did not know yet that the machine of pretentiousness of being superhuman had exterminated his family.

Professor Kryvoruchko mentioned, "My great-grandfather had displayed a lot of common sense, which may be expected from the old and wise man. His common sense applied to the Germans, but not to radicals. The radicalized would not listen to any common sense, because common sense contradicted their needs. When we are facing the splitting machine, then in order to survive we need to split. The interaction with radicals results only in two forms: confrontation or hiding. The radical ideology will twist all common sense, will not worry about humanity and the rules of decency, and will not leave space even for negotiations."

The killing machine employs as operators only special individuals

Professor Kryvoruchko acknowledges that the killing machine is one of the many modifiers of the apparatus of pretentiousness, which operated because of a high cause. It enrolled, as the operators, the individuals who had split from feelings of guilt. The splitting from feelings of guilt was influenced by the desire to be more active devices of mannerisms. The grandiosity aggrandized the quality of a low life by using the mannerism of being superhuman, pretending to have purity of blood or thoughts and, as result, feelings of being special. It made one believe that the superhuman has the right to label a disparate group as subhuman—and to exterminate the inferior group. The splitting machine effectively pushed a man to hate his neighbor. Many neighbors were massacred by neighbors.

The graves of those who were unified in death are everywhere. The splitting machine was programmed as a killing machine, to do the job without feelings of guilt. When a group was marked by the machine as subhuman, the machine denied them any human feelings and, most important, a soul. It was easier considering them animals and dispensing them as unneeded garbage.

We know that objects do not have human feelings. By destroying the object, we do not feel guilt or remorse. In the hierarchy of the butchery devices, we were marked lower than animals. It was similar to getting rid of a parasite. The slaughtering of us became the pride of the apparatus of pretentiousness. The splitting forces were able to convert many to be servants. The servants, responsible for exterminating, mainly consisted of the scared or brainwashed, which allowed the self to become a mechanical device. They were operated by the skillful manipulator, who actually might not even imagine the extent of his actions. Their leaders can be fanatics, tyrants, criminals, cult members, and many others who were miserable and looking for a cause to escape from misery and vanity. The assassination machine was always in motion, looking for the next prey and was blood thirsty. It did not matter that many servants of the assassination machine were not of a similar ethnicity as the superhuman, and their background was far removed from the extraordinary. They were marked to be the next group for extermination. The massacre engine is still working in our time, but by changed names and in diverse regions. The killing machine is reproducing the self by creating many varieties of killing machines.

Professor Kryvoruchko came from a country filled with mass graves of helpless women, children, and elderly. Many victims were buried alive, and a few were shot, but many were killed with crowbars and metal shovels, or asphyxiated in gas chambers. Many radicals ignored the suffering of the victims. Monuments for the dead were not built for a long time.

Meanwhile, Lyonya was able to escape the massacre. He walked all day in the outskirts of the city. At night he slept on the grass, using his bag as a pillow. On the following day, while walking through the market place, he overheard the market women talking tearfully in whispers among themselves. "The Germans shot everyone at Babiy Yar, more than the eye has strength to see. No one was spared—old, young, even infants."

One of the women was shouting loudly, "They were not Germans who did the killing. There were our Ukrainian boys. They have helped rid the Ukraine of an evil—it should have been done long ago!" Lyonya ran away, curled up on the grass, and cried. He tried not to believe that someone had killed his mother, his sister, and his grandfather, but he understood that it was true. He felt terrified and lonely. His thoughts also were of his father, who was fighting at the front as an officer and would take revenge.

The slaughtered were the victims of the killing machine, but we as survivors, we are the victims too, because we are forced to think about revenge and killings. We were able to survive but were splitting from our feelings of guilt. We executed the members of the apparatus of pretentiousness and mannerism, and we did it blindly without any feeling of guilt and remorse. We are also examples of the killing machines. Any fanatics are part of the carnage, which is operating by the feeling of grandiosity; they want to rise above the feelings of guilt and remorse. The killing machines are very damaging to whatever causes they defend, and they eventually kill their own, which are not pure enough. The grandiosity devices by killing and splitting take away the feelings of guilt and start the rampages, which they cannot stop.

CHAPTER 11

Splitting in The Child

Many victims are small and insignificant

Professor Kryvoruchko's father, Leonid Alexandrovich, was in the middle of carnage as a child, and he did not have anything left beside the hope that the new, stronger force would help him to survive. He was only twelve years old and was cut out from the family because of an inhumane doctrine created by the criminally minded. The feeling of being small and insignificant inside the killing machine is devastating, and it is hard to imagine being contained by the slaughter device to be consumed at any minute. The immoral minds are rigidly fragmented; they appoint a vicious and heartless fragment, proclaimed subhuman, as a representative to deal with the dissimilar. The heartless fragment has a rigid structure, is kinesthetic, and is not sensitive to audio and visual stimulations. It does not care about sounds of crying and visual pictures of victims slaughtered and covered with dirt in mass graves. The kinesthetic fragment is involved in marches and feels good by exterminating the undesired; it does not have any ethics or morals. This immoral fragment has a goal of emptying lots of space for more marching. It does whatever it desires and moves wherever it wants.

Because of the criminal intent of the apparatus of pretentiousness, Lyonya was left without a mother's care and depended on strangers who had mercy on him and could nurture him. He did not have any means to protect the self, and he needed to survive somehow. No one cared what happened to him. When we have an individual who is willing to burn or kill the self, we are dealing with someone who is expecting somehow to benefit from his actions. Perhaps one is in the trap of grandiosity and dreams of being the hero and having the admiration of many. If

Lyonya, in protest to this treatment, would have committed suicide, no one would have even blinked.

When we do not receive enough understanding, we victims think about retaliation—we want someone else to feel sorry for us. We feel that the world is cold and inconsiderate. As the real heroes, we kill the self to avoid the humiliation of being executed and to escape perceived misery. By the brave act of giving up our lives, we are pushing the world to express human feelings. If Lyonya killed the self, he would not get any feelings of remorse from anyone. He only was relying on the new killing machine to defend him and to get revenge for the slaughtered. To survive he may rely only on a miracle. In a time when his surroundings were a part of the killing machine, the marvel was finding the one part out of many that was not frozen; had a warm, human heart; and was listening.

Lyonya set out for the city of Hope, asking passersby for directions and begging for food. When passing through a town, he would find his way to the marketplace, and the bazaar women who asked many questions (to which he had answers prepared well in advance) would give him bread and sometimes a cucumber. When walking through a village, he would knock on doors. "Some bread, some bread," He'd plead.

"Where are you going? Where are your relatives?"

"Mother died of a pain in her stomach, Father is at the front, and I am on my way to Hope, where I have an aunt." Sometimes he would even get a bowl of hot Ukrainian borscht. He was not afraid of the Germans, because they paid no attention to him; there were many children roaming the countryside at that time.

Finally he reached Hope and found Soviet Collective Street. He stood outside hoping that Aunt Polina or one of her children would come out, but no one appeared. Suddenly he recognized a woman who was carrying a pail full of milk. It was the woman who would bring milk to Aunt Polina, and he recalled that she was friendly. "Auntie, don't you remember me? I visited this house last summer." The little boy was looking for a help because he was a small leftover of humanity. Lyonya was completely devastated. He was still alive, but for how long? He may well be consumed anytime by the killing machine. He was completely insignificant; a dog or a cat had more power than he had. He was marked to be killed, and anyone had a right to do it, without any reprisal. Even more, many would applaud the killer. For the boy, the chance to survive inside the killing machine was very slim.

The boy who lost his mother was looking for a replacement

The worst tragedy for a boy is to lose his caring and loving mother. The presence of a mother is crucial in the development of a child. Being without parents or any caretaker in the middle of a war made Lyonya chances for survival very slim. The brutality machine shredded any hope he had. He was jumping to embrace the first face who possibly would care for him. This moment could be a meeting between child and surrogate mother. Actually, it was possible to have an immediate bonding. Many children were saved by complete strangers, who on an impulse became adoptive parents and helped a child.

The bonding of the stranger and the child is a genuine meeting. It is an act of complete selflessness for a surrogate parent to forget about the dangers and prioritize the safety of a child. This is an example of dialogue between motherhood and the self; an episode of unification of the most beautiful fragments, which enlighten the further life of the adopting mother and the adoptive child. Lyonya was looking for a replacement for his mother, who had nurtured him well for twelve years. The woman was selling milk, which is the most nurturing substance. The milk woman, who hardly remembered him but had a selfless heart, helped him. She had a very symbolic occupation for nurturing and for supplying the nutrients the child needed. She also was the supplier of the needed emotions, a good attitude, and compassion.

Professor Kryvoruchko mentioned that as a fragment, the milk woman had a kinesthetic base because she generated some comforting movements to support the child or at least provide temporarily relief. The bonding between mother and child is an example of dialogue even when words were not spoken. The bonding is similar to the kinesthetic feeling of belonging. After the loss of his mother, Lyonya was looking for the feeling of belonging, the feeling of safety, protection, and trust. The boy was desperate to feel again a closeness to his mother, even though she was dead. He needed someone as a replacement for his mother in a bid to forget the horror of the last several days.

The unification with sensitivity and the split from fears might occur at the same time

Our unification with sensitivity and our split from fears may be a simultaneous process. When we are unifying with something, we are also splitting from something else. When we are splitting from our fears, we are having a dialogue with and meeting our courage. A stranger may possibly become a savior. We do not know in what form the savior is coming to rescue us from a killing machine, but this represents a dialogue with our courage. During the darkness of pretentiousness, our world was terribly insensitive; only a few had the courage to allow the self to be sensitive.

The milk woman became Lyonya's savior; her heart felt that the child was in despair. Lyonya approached her and introduced himself. She remembered him, but still he was a stranger, and she was not under any obligation to help him. She also knew one secret about Lyonya and clearly understood that by helping Lyonya, she may be in danger. Despite any frightening thoughts, she decided to take this risk. It was a mother's heart that could not allow her to leave a child without any help. The stranger was unified with her feeling of sensitivity, and she split from her fears. The unification with sensitivity is very risky. She was helping someone who was hunted and marked for eradication. During the time of occupation, the sensitivity was a luxury, which not everyone had the courage to afford.

By helping Lyonya, she was putting at risk her own family. We know many instances when some unselfish people helped victims of persecution, but there were more situations when no one bothered to help. The split from feeling of fears may be a lifelong process, or it may be immediate. The milk woman did not need much time to dwell on her limitations—the presence of a helpless child mobilized her courage. Usually we are driven by our sensitivity to help, but fears paralyze our effort. When the life of a child is at stake, however, then instinct takes over our common sense, and miracles may happen. The rainy day was changed by the shining sun, and the stranger became a savior. "Yes, boy, I remember you. You lived at Polina's with your mother and little sister. Everyone here left as soon as the war started. And where are your parents? Are you here all alone? What trouble, what misery!" She poured him a cup of milk, and after he gulped it down, she gave him another one. "Come with me; I have a place for you. But tell others as little as possible about yourself. Do you understand me?" Lyonya nodded his head.

The milk woman took him to a building that bore a small sign: "Home for Children." She entered the house and came out with an elderly man, the director. "You stay here, and I shall be visiting you; be well," she said to Lyonya. She quietly left the house, and before she left she gave Lyonya another cup of milk. Only later did Lyonya understood that she saved his life. The dialogue between sensitivity and courage may possibly bring a great satisfaction when we realize what was done.

In the many years after the war, the milk woman met a middle-aged man, who introduced himself as a boy whose live she'd saved. She cried because she realized that her existence was not wasted, and she did have reason to been proud of her life. She had a feeling of satisfaction, that despite her fears and common sense limitations, she was able to help a child. That moment, which did not continue for more than half an hour, enlightened all her life. In that short time she unified with excellence and split from mediocrity; she experience a real meeting with her sensitivity and courage.

Coming to terms with safety

Personal safety is important for survival. Lyonya did not have a safe place and may have even lost hope that this place even existed. He did have the strength to continue his search and to not give up, because we all have a dream. Our dream is a place where we are able to come when we need to be safe. Lyonya split from his family, from his identity, from his home with clean bedding and hot meals, and from many other things that we enjoy without second thoughts. After being hunted as a savage animal, he was fearful of everyone. The safe haven gave him a chance to have a meeting with safety, which is a complimentary process. When we get more feelings of being safe, then we have less feelings of fear. The safety comes together with feelings of trusting the surrounding environment. Lyonya eventually got to the safer place.

Safety as well as danger may be on separate levels. When someone moves from a very dangerous place to a less dangerous one, he feels that the new place is a safe haven and that he will never leave. Even a hero needs a safe place for a short time; only a few individuals have the strength to leave protection. If they have strength to leave the security, they are heroes. Sometime the hero leaves a shelter, and his reason for leaving is to strengthen the self, fight evil, be alert, and keep his identity from being compromised by the comfort of the sanctuary. Sometimes we have the safe haven only for a short time, but even if it was for a brief moment, the most important goal is to recapture the feeling of being safe. If the feeling of safety, as a cocoon, surrounds us for just a minute, we receive the strength to go out and face reality again. It is very important for the quest of survival to have a motivation of looking forward and believing that somewhere in the universe, we may have the luck to find a safe haven.

When we involuntarily leave a safe place, then it is a special situation. We are getting thrown out of a place of comfort to a world of injustice and danger. The rejection is more painful when we are kicked out by someone whom we trust and who appeared to be our savior. Lyonya liked everything about the children's house: the food, his bed, the kindhearted director. He remained there for over a month and may have lived there longer if not for the other children, who felt that he was frightened and started to tease him, calling him a coward. Then someone shouted, "Abbham," and the name stuck. The director heard about it and called him to the office; he had a serious look on his face. "Lyonya, why do the children call you names? Are you a Jew?"

Lyonya shook his head. "They are just teasing me." In this very hard time of his life, the secret identity followed Lyonya and destroyed his effort for surviving. Lyonya's unknown identity scared the director, who appeared to be a kind man. He became fearful and threw a helpless child out to a place of menace.

Perhaps one who appeared to be so nice reveals a lot of viciousness to expose another to certain death. An instinct for protecting a child did not work for this man, who pretended to be an educator. Lyonya never met the director again, but sometimes in his dreams he wanted to understand and meet him—but he also understood that he would not be able having a dialogue with this man. Despite our desire to have a meeting with everyone, we only have the opportunity to experience an encounter when another human soul wants to meet. The man, who called himself a mentor, did not contribute to unification with the feelings of safety and trust. He split from humanity and was driven by feelings of fear and by conformity to evil. He rejected the opportunity to become a part of unification. He crossed the border and left his own humanity somewhere else, becoming a part of splitting forces. The director denied the boy a chance of survival, but nevertheless, for a short while the boy felt safe and was able to have a meeting with safety.

Splitting from feelings of trust

An encounter with victimization also splits us from the fundamental feeling of trust. The injured, by abhorrence, do not trust their surroundings anymore. The victims of hate crimes are usually society's minority who are persecuted by haters and are not protected enough from predators. We do not know if our destiny is written in advance and why things happened the way they do. Someone who became a victim carries the label of being a victim throughout his life. Many victims are paying the heavy price for survival; they become mentally broken and do not have the strength to recuperate. Only a few may get over the trauma of being victimized.

Just as Lyonya during the traumatic event, we often detach from reality. We have many things beyond our conscious awareness. Lyonya did not have any place to go and did not have any means to get food, clothes, and a place to sleep. In the moment when the director told him to leave, his world felt apart. Surprisingly, in the most tragic moment of his life, Lyonya did not feel any animosity toward the director or blame him. He did not feel that a director was duty-bound to protect a child. He also did not feel that the director betrayed his feeling of trust. On the contrary, he felt guilty that he did not protect the director and made him feel uncomfortable. Only in later life did he realize that all his feelings of losing trust were on a subconscious level; he felt as a boy who did something wrong. Consciously he did not recognize a fact that the director deceived a child. Lyonya did not have knowledge of his own future; at the time, he did not know what would be better, if he stayed in the orphanage or ended up back on the streets. He did not know that he was only one of the few luckiest who was saved. He was not aware that leaving the orphanage was a way to get back his identity and recuperate some bits from his previous life.

Lyonya did not know that providence wanted him to be a victorious survivor. His fate was not to be scared and hide, but to become a partisan decorated with medals and a veteran of the war. His destiny was to have a family, to be a professional man, and to prosper as the manager of an atomic energy plant. Lyonya, who was a victim and was marked for extermination, survived despite many odds. In the meantime, he did not know about his future. In our life many paradoxical things happen. Sometimes leaving the sanctuary is better than staying in, but it is always a struggle to leave. Sometimes the one way to leave safety is to be thrown out from it. In times of danger the feeling of safety is very corrupting and may change our destiny. If Lyonya had stayed in sanctuary, who knows what kind of man he would have become. Sometimes to get over the victim's role and preserve our identity, we need to leave despite the comfort of the safe place.

Because we do not know our destiny, it is always a struggle to preserve identity. Even we were not victimized by radicals, we have a long journey to become a winner and to have an identity. No one is successful without the struggle of unification. The workers without qualification are just some of many on the employment market. Because we want to be important, we are not proud of our identity. It takes a long time and many struggles to become a needed specialist and to carry an identity as a professional, but we do not want to wait. As victims, we get confused and for a long period of time; we are avoiding truth, and we are not clear who we are. Some of us are constructing the false identity. Some will deny everything that happened to us or make it sound funny.

As a young boy, Professor Kryvoruchko rarely related to his father, Lyonya. He understood that Lyonya, was much younger than he when he was a victim of a killing machine. Lyonya had mentioned that in those circumstances, his life depended on his level of recuperation from the victimization. Lyonya was the victimized part of his father. Many children narcissistically assume that their parents were always strong in an old-fashioned way and did not express their feelings. For children of the survivors of hate crimes, the reality is distinctive; they know that their parents were victimized. The children of survivors live with the big guilt because they did not suffer as much as their parents. Because of the parents' misery, their children are always expecting a catastrophe. Their children also split from feelings of trust, and they suspect that their surroundings have ill feelings toward them. Sometimes it takes many generations to get over the victim's role. The splitting from the fundamental trust drives children of the victims closer to their parents and to their parents' experience of being victims of hate.

Splitting from life to death

The split from the human race has many forms, but the most primitive is the one to check someone's foreskin to condemn him. The selection process is to be marked for death because of circumcision, the lack of the skin on the penis. The cut of the foreskin was justification for denying any human rights and proclaiming that the man was less than a savage animal or less than someone infected with leprosy. In France on the Night of Saint Bartholomew, when many Huguenots were killed, the houses were marked by chalk to identify the presence of the French Protestants. In the Holocaust massacre, the observed cut of the skin was a mark for extermination. The adult man, an educator, was shaking with fear because he was sitting next to a boy who had not enough foreskins on his penis. The men lost his educator's honor and gave in to panicking. He gave up his resistance and became consumed by the killing machine.

The director's spirit was gone, and he was a part of the apparatus of pretentiousness. He lost the right to be called a human, because without the uniqueness of the soul, he was a part of the machinery. It was not Lyonya, but the director of the orphanage who felt the test of humanity. It started when he called the boy in his office. "Lyonya, forgive me, but please unbutton your pants." Noticing the boy's deep fright, the director understood everything. "I cannot keep you here any longer. You must realize what would happen to all of us if the polizies were to find out. Also, I have a family. Here is money; and I'll give you some food, but you should leave our city. You cannot remain here." The director was very afraid of polizies, the bunch often drunk and unruly boys, who were terrorizing the population in occupied territories. He felt that the lack of a foreskin on his student would have a bad reflection on him and his family. He was not acting as a director but more as a little rabbit. Opposite him was the director of another orphanage, a real human who accompanied his little students to the gas chamber. He was telling them beautiful fairytales to spare them from the horror of dying. This director was unified with his students in their deaths; he did not push his little students out from the orphanage to hand them to the predators. When he became a teacher, he took upon himself the responsibilities for his students.

The simple and uneducated, milk woman had more humanity than the educated, frightened director. His fearful reaction to make a boy feel guilty, and his mentioning of his family to justify his cruelty, was completely unacceptable for an educator. Without any second thought he sent out one of his students from the orphanage to certain death. He, probably was good at something, otherwise he would not be a director, but he was not a good educator. We do not have many chances to prove to ourselves that we are part of humanity. When we fail the rare chance of proving who we are, then we probably will not have another one. When we do not pass the test, we perhaps do not have right to call ourselves a human. This chance of proving who we are comes in an uncommon form. The test of humanity for Lyonya's director was in ignoring a lack of foreskin on his student's penis. The director, by failing this test, was not able to call himself a human.

Unification with hope

Lyonya had anticipation that something good and positive would happen. The unification of a positive belief may spare us from despair, because it is splitting us from misery. We are not trained in disaster and stress management; we are completely lost if our psyche does not believe in miracles. If we do not believe, then in the face of destruction we give up, and our preservation force is paralyzed. When the reality is very grave and does not support our spirit, the staunch belief in miracles helps us to survive. It is not true that belief in fairytales is only the privilege of children. It is true that as children, we have a psyche designed to protect us from depression, we have a positive belief in adults as our strong defenders, and in the external forces that are on our side and will come to our rescue. We are splitting from misery and detaching from reality to unrealistic expectations and wishful thinking, because the reality is so harsh that it does not support any of our good thoughts. As children, we have the ability to detach from reality to a dream world. The shock of a horrible experience has the power to easily destroy us, but the fantasy may save us. When nothing is possible anymore, it is better to dream about something good and pleasurable than to be driven by extreme fears and anxiety. The most famous teacher, Yanush Korchak, who did not abandon two hundred of his tiny students and went with them to the gas chamber, did not want his charges to suffer in the last moments of their lives, and he told his little students a fairytale.

Lyonya, who was thrown from the safe haven, was looking for another one. Unfortunately, safe havens were not so numerous, but children wanted to believe in the impossible. When a boy loses one safe haven, he hopes to find another one. When we are convincing the self in the possibility of a miracle, we are lying to the self. This situation is special because usually by lying we make false statements to mislead others. The lie is a fabrication, but when we disregard a harsh reality by indulging in a fantasy, we do it to survive. This is an attempt to preserve our sanity and to continue moving forward under extreme duress. Someone who makes up stories to survive is not a liar and coward—he is the opposite, a courageous person. The stereotype of a hero does not depend on fairytales and looking cool in the face of danger. He is the one who is experienced and knowledgeable in the handling of stress and disaster, and he is confident in his ability to act in an appropriate manner.

When a loved one is terminally sick, we believe in miracles; it is not an act of cowardice when we do not want to give up hope. Even the hope that is built on wishful thinking is still a hope. Our responses depend on beliefs. Some beliefs are very depressing. The reality was that Lyonya, a boy who lost his family and his self, did not have the strength to keep going for a long time; the end was near. Other beliefs were fantasy. Lyonya believed that another safe haven was close by, and he could not give up. His understanding was that the safe havens did not show up without a struggle; it was a reward for the endured sufferings, otherwise it would not be so fantastic. Lyonya had a strong belief in miracles, and his staunch resolve was not to give up hope. It spared him from despair, and he split with misery and unified himself with hope.

Unification with a miracle

The unification with a miracle has a very strong effect on us that changes all our chemistry and even the lighting around us. It takes us by complete surprise when a miracle happens: we are shocked and do not accept it right away. All of us somehow are longing for a miracle, but when it happens, it is completely unbelievable. We tell the self that the phenomenon we are observing is not a real miracle. We accept the miracle only after struggles and doubts. Professor Kryvoruchko says that to understand the effect of a miracle, we need to reach the bottom of our endurance, when our life does not cost anything and our existence is on the brink of disappearance. When we are experiencing a miracle, everything around us becomes distinctive.

The miracle brings the feeling of meaning to our life, and then comes hope and aspiration, together with a sense of relief. Even if nothing changes in our surroundings, when we are waiting for a miracle to happen, we see the bright light that comes from within. It is like our life was grey and dull, without other colors around and without any sensations and hopes, and then right away it becomes brighter. The phenomena bring ecstasy to our life and many dissimilar colors and shades.

No one could predict the miracle that changed Lyonya's life. He spent a week looking for the dairy woman but could not find her anywhere. He slept in a woodshed, but the nights were getting colder, and he would awaken in the morning half-frozen. All day he roamed the streets without food. The market women had changed completely. In the past they would always give him something to eat, but now their answer was, "God will help you; our own children are hungry."

One morning he saw a group of peasants near a wagon full of potatoes; they were eating bread, cucumbers, and onions. Lyonya suddenly recognized his father among them. He carefully looked at the man to make sure, and there was no mistake. The moment that his father stepped out of the group, Lyonya ran over to him and said quietly, "Papa." Kryvoruchko Sr. turned around, and Lyonya saw that he looked petrified. "Son, how did you get here? Where is Mother?" On seeing that Lyonya was about to burst into tears, he said quickly, "My son, you must not speak to me here—leave right now for the village of Pokotylovka. Take the main road, and I will be waiting for you in front of the first hut. We are leaving soon." Father went over to the wagon and returned with bread, a cucumber, and an onion. This moment of miracle changed everything in Lyonya's life. The day was still rainy and the peasants were nasty, but everything changed in a moment. This moment unified Lyonya with a miracle, and this unification gave him a chance to have a future. He became an important man and had many pleasant days in his life. In a moment of unification with a miracle, he split from death and all atrocities. He became a boy who found his father, and his father took responsibility for his safety and well-being. For the first time, Lyonya felt safe, warm, happy, and full of energy. The unification with a miracle changed his chemistry.

The unification of father and son

The fragments of the son and father are signs of stability and symbolize the natural passage of all wisdom through generations. The unification of the son with his father is very important for the two of them and also for their future generations. Professor Kryvoruchko declared that he is representing a new generation that did not experience the atrocity of war; nevertheless, his psyche has the fragments of his father, Lyonya, and his grandfather, Kryvoruchko, Sr. Those fragments are very important to show the organization of his psyche. His psyche has a very stable structure, with its concept of unification of the son and father. Lyonya was a survivor, and Grandfather was the rescuer of his son.

We see the suffering son who found his father, and the father the son under his protection. The tragedy of the survivors is tremendously big, and the victim is the whole family. The victims are the dead, as well as the others who are still alive, including the children of survivors. It is impossible to calculate how many generations of survivors would carry a trauma. By observing the survivors of atrocities, we may see already four generations of Armenians who carry the trauma of genocide. The psyche of the survivors is structured around the trauma. The important aspect is the future relationship of children of survivors with the children of the ones who were the carriers of the atrocities. Usually as the young children of a distinctive ethnicity, we have an ability to relate to others who are of a similar age. The children of survivors are an exception. Lyonya remembered that in the marketplace he saw the young native woman of domineering ethnicity buying vegetables in the company of the enemy's officer.

The fascist officer probably saw the hungry look in Lyonya's eyes. He searched in his pockets and found a candy which was still in its wrap. Shaking the candy in front of him, he called to Lyonya. "Do not be scared and come here!" Lyonya obeyed, and the officer gives him a candy. Lyonya was holding this candy as something most precious; he would remember this candy all his life, though he was puzzled by the unexplainable insanity of this time.

The enemy officer had shown a fatherly attitude to nurture the starving boy. If the officer knew that Lyonya was undesirable, then his attitude was arbitrary. The same officer who showed kindness to prolong the life of the starving child without any second thought would have pushed him into the gas chamber to die. Lyonya witnessed the duality of the role of the enemies during the war. He observed that the side that characterized the nature of the man to protect a helpless child was combined with the monster that was preying on little children. For many generations it would be tough to reconcile the monster who eats children with a loving father. The combination does not make any sense and makes everything very confusing; it's the question still not answered: how do we get captured by hatred and viciousness? The psyche is split and is in turmoil when the fragments of son and father are conflicting. As children we see the father in every adult. Fortunately, Lyonya met his real father, who would do everything to save him from harm. His father, by saving him, would establish the continuation of his lifeline. This moment was very symbolic because the wisdom of this unity comes from our dreams. The meeting of son and father is a confirmation of stability and a unification of our psyche.

It is impossible to have many parallel processes of the unification and the split

In the meantime Lyonya started walking. About three hours later, the wagon with his father passed him. It started to rain, and Lyonya hastened his pace toward Pokotylovka. It was dark when he reached the village, but Lyonya's father was there. His conviction that his wife and children were evacuated had vanished. He continued to keep hope alive, because if his son had saved himself, perhaps his wife and younger child were also alive. On seeing Lyonya, he threw himself at him. His son's clothes were wet, so he put his quilted coat over the boy and took him to the cookhouse. There he prepared the best he was able to find: hot potatoes, cucumbers, and a piece of lard. He watched his son eat.

It is true that a healthy mind does not have the ability to be involved in many parallel processes at the same time. We cannot produce separately unification and splitting at the same; we need to put one of two processes on hold until we are ready to continue. We process our feelings sequentially: first we need to weep for the passing of our dearest before we may enjoy survivors. Lyonya was united with his father, but he also brought to his father an announcement of death. For Kryvoruchko Sr., in one moment his son provided only one rationale to be alive, but also despair was very strong and was splitting him from joy.

Perhaps only the complementary responses might be processed. Contrary to the complementary, the two completely opposite processes did not run independently. It is impossible to have the opposite responses at the same time. Kryvoruchko Sr. was not able to express the terrible pain of misery and the joy at the same moment. Even though he was unified with his son, he was broken by news of his family's demise. He could not express joy that his son survived until he could grieve for the loved ones that were dead. He was not able to express pleasure and sadness in the same time. It is easy to say that we need to celebrate life when someone has died; even if it is a complementary process, but in many instances celebration is not possible. When our loved ones are butchered and put in graves alive, we cannot celebrate life—we are in sorrow about the torture and barbarism they experienced. The truth about massacre is unreal and horrible.

Kryvoruchko Sr. lost his wife, who gave birth to his children. He also lost his daughter and his old father. His father was an elderly man, but for children their parents do not have an age. His family did not deserve their fate. He could not understand why everything in his life was destroyed. He was not able to have an explanation for all the madness surrounding him. He was a soldier and knew how to fight another soldier, but he did not understand how someone had the viciousness to kill helpless children, women, and the elderly. He was not able to celebrate life and felt miserable because of the death of his family.

For Lyonya the meeting with his father was an end of his suffering, but for his father the meeting with his son brought torturing grief. The message of his wife's, daughter's, and father's deaths came together with his son's survival. He felt guilty that he did not show happiness because he did not have power to do anything with the self. The tears came from his eyes, and he looked at his son but saw his wife, his daughter, and his father, making the tears run faster. Very soon the son and father were crying together. They did not talk about the losses, but they were grieving together for their loved ones. They were unified in grief. First they needed to say farewell to loved ones, and then they could enjoy their meeting.

The split between being alive and humanity

In some instances we are split between survival and humanity. In times of atrocities and criminality, the meeting between father and son has significance. They are alive, and they did not do anything inhuman to survive. The unification of father with son plus a dialogue between them is a trinity, because enormous luck is present and is a very important moment in their salvation. The meeting between them reminded the faultless soul wandering in the butcher shop, who eventually found all others, that they had not lost their humanity. We often pay with our life to be human. Many of us would not leave our relatives behind to die alone; many prefer to die as human beings rather than live as monsters.

The unanswered questions are about how the world was able to tolerate this massacre. How was the world presenting aspiration to be civilized, when at the same time it allowed the defenseless to be butchered? Where was the world population after all? How could we look in the eyes of survivors whom we failed to protect?

How would the world react if one of the survivors was a cannibal? We may feel that it is despicable. If everything in the world has its purpose, we are learning something from our experiences, but how may we find any edifying message in this mess? Maybe in the future, when we become more sophisticated, we will be capable of understanding what happened, but for now nothing makes sense and we are confused. The victims need survival skills, but there is a limit to their vigor. If they are losing their humanity, then what is the reason of survival? The question is, what is more important than life?

Professor Kryvoruchko's grandmother, Rivka, decided that she would rather die than leave her sick daughter and her old father. Professor Kryvoruchko also confirmed that he is strictly kosher, but in that time, despite all the rules of the kosher, which include not eating the any pork products, his grandfather was feeding his son with salted lard, which was pork fat. When we are in danger of death from starvation, may we disregard dietary laws? Our relationship with God is based on the notion that he will always forgive, if we ask for forgiveness. By eating lard, Lyonya broke a biblical law. Would be he punished for it?

Lyonya did not know much about religion, because in the Soviet collective the religious ethic was not respected. He was a victim of atrocities and viciousness and needed to survive. Nevertheless, when faced with a dilemma to eat the pork product, many soldiers of Muslim background preferred to commit suicide than eat any pork products. It is always the line between good and evil, and sometimes it's hard to see the difference. In the city of Leningrad, which was blockaded from food supplies by enemies, one million died from starvation. Few who did survive this ordeal remembered that in the marketplaces there was always fresh meat to buy, and the vendors called it "rabbit". Was it human flesh? Everyone has a good idea from where this meat came. The desperate did not want to look deeper for the truth, and as a last hope for survival, they did buy this meat. It is not easy to judge them. We do not need to speculate how those who have bought the meat in the blockaded city feel about surviving. The line between life and death is very murky. It is against any belief to eat human flesh, but what about when we are near the end? Do we have the strength to resist? How many bought the questionable meat on the market of the blockaded city? We do not judge them. We also do not know how we would respond when we have a choice: to be alive or to be human. How do we deal with cannibalism?

Somewhere there exists a turning point: keep our humanity or die. We have many excuses for killing in a fight as a last resort to survive, but do we have any excuse to eat human flesh and to become cannibals? How do we deal with someone who consumed another human to stay alive? We have a choice, which is to lose our humanity and to be cannibals. We also have another choice: to give up our life and to die in order to remain a human being. Most important, we do not have the luxury to be concerned with issues that others may call stupid.

The kinesthetic dialogue

Our kinesthetic dialogue may possibly be triggered by our visual and audio communication. It is always a hope when we did not see the tragedy with our own eyes. We hope until the scary words are said. When we grieve together, we have a meeting and dialogue too, which is not necessarily only the verbal dialogue but may also be a kinesthetic one, when our energy is combined through our bodies movements. The kinesthetic dialogue as well as audio and visual may be of grief or love and has a very strong unifying effect. Our unification in grief is more in the kinesthetic than audio or visual forms of demonstration. In grief we have similar grieving postures. Our kinesthetic responses in grief are congruent with the responses of others, which are stroked by sorrow. Until the last word is said, somewhere deep inside we continue begging that a miracle happen.

The hope vanished in the moment when everything was said and there was not any place left for hope. Lyonya told his father everything. His father wanted to cry but could not, and he was unable to force the self to express joy at his son's survival. He felt as if he was turning into stone. When he recovered, he saw his son sleeping at the table. This small, wet bundle, his child, had been doomed to perish, but he had survived despite all the evil beasts. The father carefully lifted his son, carried him into the sleeping quarters, and put him in his own bunk. He did not sleep that night at all.

Kryvoruchko Sr. had too much to figure out, starting with the meeting of his son, then the horrible news, and eventually the grieving together. It is impossible to overcome the loss of a wife, daughter, and father brutally murdered by evil forces. The injustice was so strong that the organization of the psyche broke and never recovered in future generations. Professor Kryvoruchko has distinct ways to get involved in dialogues. He mentions that his grandfather and father had strong verbal abilities, but their dialogue was not verbal. Their dialogue was kinesthetic and prevented the generational break of their psyches. Despite heavy losses, their psyches did not stop functioning; the reason was in the miraculous unification of father with his son and their surviving. The tragedy for a father of losing his loved ones may have been the end of his family, but the meeting with his son was a promise of continuation. He needed to have a purpose, which would give him strength of existing, functioning, and moving forward to the unknown, even though he did not have any idea with what kind of fate he would be faced.

Everything was disparate when he was grieving with his son after their losses. Suddenly he knew that he needed to get over his grief and start taking care of his son. Lyonya needed to be around somebody who would motivate him to be active in this world, continue his kinesthetic functioning, and keep his hopes alive. The words he said to his father about the death of his mother, his sister, and his grandfather triggered the crying and other kinesthetic responses about the loss of the loved ones. When he woke up he was able to properly express his sorrow, together with his father. After months of running away from his feelings, Lyonya was safe to show his feelings without any fears. After what the son had said about the last day of seeing his mother, Kryvoruchko Sr. and Lyonya did not talk, but they cried, hugged, and were very close to others in a deep sorrow.

The ordinary issues unified with the dramatic

The ordinary may perhaps be easily unified with the dramatic, and it may even become unbelievable when we are talking and visualizing. The survival of Kryvoruchko Sr. in light of the enormous danger to his life and his coolness may sound very dramatic, but for him it was very ordinary. He was a trained soldier and officer, and he did not get scared in the face of danger. He did not talk about his survival, but in his life he used every opportunity to stay alive. He was not a hero, but he was a survivor. He was able somehow to function in places where many could not. Now his mission was to provide shelter for his son, and he would do it in an ordinary way without dramatic rhetoric. He did not express the self well in words, but he did well kinesthetically. He knew that he would always act as was required to keep his son safe. In his fortitude he did not see any exceptional episodes to talk about, but nevertheless many dramatic episodes happened. The war had found Kryvoruchko Sr. as an instructor of draftees in an army training camp. One day before the outbreak of hostilities, there came an order: "All vehicles are to be lined up on a platform and all fuel tanks emptied." He did not participate in a single battle. The entire unit was cut off and surrounded.

Everything was very ordinary: Captivity and inspections. Columns of prisoners stripped down passed in front of a medical officer, whose only assignment was to determine who among them was circumcised. The Jewish were separated from the others. When Kryvoruchko Sr.'s turn came to pass in front of the medical officer, the field telephone rang, and the doctor answered it. He was busy talking, Kryvoruchko Sr. joined the group of non-circumcised soldiers unnoticed, and his life was saved. The Jewish soldiers were later executed.

For Professor Kryvoruchko, the heroic is mainly ordinary actions and deeds that are verbalized or visualized as heroic by attaching to them some significance. In moments of dramatic actions, many did not think that they had done something dramatic. His grandfather did not see anything amazing in his escape from death; he also did not think about how breathtaking it was for him to meet his son in the market place. As a trained soldier, he did not think twice about following an order to empty all fuel tanks from the vehicles and tanks. He did not question any command, even if it was very strange for the high officers to employ such bizarre tactics. As a result of this strange order, he and his fellow soldiers were left to be helpless prey for the fascist collective. He did not feel that it was unusual for the Soviet collective to not join the Geneva Convention regarding the treatment of prisoners of war. He did not feel it was extraordinary that the government of his country, by not joining the Geneva Convention, was enabling the hands of the killers. He also did not feel bewildered that for the several weeks he was working on the farm with the other prisoners of war, they were in groups of ten. Their work consisted of digging up potatoes and taking turns at going to the marketplace with the peasants as loaders.

In the morning, the other nine prisoners were nonchalant and took it to be very mundane that Kryvoruchko, Sr. had adopted a homeless boy. They said, "There is enough bread and potatoes for everyone. Let the kid remain." Kryvoruchko Sr. mourned for his family and did not see everything as dramatic and heroic as it was. For him, ordinary and dramatic were the same, so he did not talk about it. He did not realize that everything in his life was very dramatic; at that time it appeared very ordinary.

The meeting between survivor and rescuer

In our psyche, is it possible to have a meeting of fragments who are representing survivor and rescuer? The survivor and the savior of his son are together in the psyche of Kryvoruchko Sr., and it is a very strong unity. He saved the self by his unimaginable luck and courage, and he was able to save his son, too. He was not a hero who gave up his life for a cause; he just used the opportunity to survive and save his son.

Professor Kryvoruchko stated that there are many survivors and rescuers who would do it with a heroic flair, but his grandfather was unique and did not want to express any drama or pathos. The best purpose of being safe was to do something to justify his survival. Some of the saved did nothing with their lives. They did not save anyone and did not look after their families. They did not care about their obligation, which was providing a base for prolonging the family line.

Others were able to continue their family line and save it from extinction. All the members in Kryvoruchko's family had a fragment with an assignment to save lives and to prolong the family line. Kryvoruchko Sr. was lucky that he was able to survive and also secure the continuation of his bloodline. The meeting between survivor and rescuer is the most significant one and includes a dialogue, which may be on a kinesthetic level. This dialogue is one of the most important in our lives.

The fragment of the bully splitting from compassion

The childhood fragment of the bully has the capacity to take over our psyche and split us from the feeling of compassion. The bully is a very punitive fragment and is associated with the behavior of disorderly children. We do not have conscious awareness that the bully takes us over. The problems of being a bully start in our childhood, when we suffered from bullies. Because our behavior reflects on our children, we secure the arrival of a new pack of bullies because the children depend on us. We are not fulfilling our important obligation of standing up to bullies and protecting a child, and by not protecting a child, we are damaging his psyche so that he grows up a weakling. He is not courageous enough to confront his own fragment of a bully. It becomes very nasty when we do not feel that we are responsible for a child. When we do not have unification with the badly treated child in our psyche, then the fragment of the bully takes over. It is easy to abuse a child, because the child does not understand how we may be so vicious and blame the self for our craziness; this is also a reason why the children copy us without understanding the cause behind the observed behavior.

As children we copy the bully's behavior, and when we grow up, our psyche retains two fragments: a bully and a victim. When a fragment of an abused child in our psyche meets with a real child, then our fragment of the abused child wants to protect the child, but because of weakness he does not. The fragment of a bully takes over our psyche, and then the bully is pushing both our own fragment and a helpless child to be a victims. The adult who has the fragments of a bully and an abused child is confused and does not understand why he wants to hurt children. The reason why he does not want to offer assistance to any kids is because he is splitting from his own fragment of an abused child.

In many instances the fragment of an abused child is a secret of our psyche, and it is hidden in a closet and guarded. When our psyche hides a fragment of a mistreated kid, our psyche is splitting from feelings of compassion. We always find justification for splitting, and as bullies, we are very egocentric and jealous of the attention children receive. Because we are scared of humiliation, only a few of us get the hidden fragment out of our closets. We are always pretending because we do not have the stomach for meeting the abusive past and experiencing a dialogue. The truth is that as the bully, we are hurting children because we are getting even with the world, which we feel in their past was unjust to us. The bully carefully chooses his victim and skillfully tortures the weak and the scared.

Lyonya was a perfect target. He was innocent and weak. Evil forces were attacking him, because he was small and not ready to deal with the imperfections of the world. He could easily be sacrificed and exterminated. The bully does not miss any opportunity to hurt a child, because the bully is afraid of unification with the abused child in his psyche. Professor Kryvoruchko affirmed that paradoxically, but the bully mainly wants to hurt the abused fragment of a child in his own psyche. Only the adult, who may unify with the abused child in his own psyche, is able to protect the other children.

The anger toward others is also anger toward the self

When we feel angry with someone else, in reality we are mainly angry with the self. It is not always true that we get angry if somebody bothers us. Often we are blaming the self for being weak, slow, and ineffective. The anger helps to refocus the feelings of guilt and shame. When anger takes control of our psyche, our actions became very nasty, because anger anesthetizes our psyche from the feelings of shame and disgrace. Underneath, the anger is displeased with the self because we are vulnerable allow ourselves to be bothered. Often we do not have conscious awareness of the roots of the anger and what is really triggering it.

Professor Kryvoruchko mentioned that he needed his anger to prove to himself that he was still capable of facing the danger and defending the self. When we are in distress, we are looking for a reason to exhibit protective skills and express anger. The anger also helps us to hold on to the little bits of self-control. When we are stressed, we get angry too often and too easily; in many instances the prompts for anger is very insignificant. We are consciously misattributing anger to unrelated irritants. By properly managing our anger, we look only for the correct irritant and do not jump on the closest one. We have many dissimilar triggers of anger. Together with audio, visual, and kinesthetic irritants, the trigger of anger also includes olfactory discomfort. The anger is based on emotion, which is both splitting and unifying. The anger perhaps may have a place in the unification, because our need of hating sometimes keeps the whole psyche together.

As a unifier, the anger may be an effective force against an intruder that is causing a discomfort, but anger can also be a splitter. If we are consciously aware of an unhealthy split, we need to prevent it by any means, because if uncontrolled it can cause damage to our psyche. Under the splitting command, the fragments that regularly would not think twice to attack a helpless child suddenly become heartless executors. The split probably was unnoticed, and when it is progressing, it is very dangerous because anger is a quick learner.

If a fragment with angry responses was humiliating, because the person was confronting a stronger target and perhaps may not win, then he would choose the next target more carefully, because he'd want to be sure that he was able to win.

Lyonya was weak and helpless in front of adults; he already knew that some people may be worse than animals, and he tried to be invisible. He slept under war prisoners' bunks. When asked questions, he gave the same replies that he used to give to the peasants when he begged for food, with the addition that his aunt had now been evacuated and he had no place to go. If it had not been for one unforeseen event, father and son may easily have spent the entire winter in the village.

Unfortunately Lyonya caught a cold and began to wet his bed while sleeping. The smell did not go unnoticed by the soldiers; at first they joked about it, but later on they began to grumble. "Who is Kryvoruchko hiding under the bunk? Who is that dark kid? Is he a gypsy or a Jew? He's smelling up the place and should be gotten rid of. If the Germans find out, we'll all be in trouble." The anger of the soldiers and prisoners of war was triggered by the olfactory irritant, but the real reason was anger with the self. They were defeated warriors and spent their days picking potatoes and living in a barn. They were angry with themselves. To protect their honor, they needed to find a target to express their anger and to anesthetize their feeling of shame and disgrace. By attacking the weak and helpless child, the anger shaped the minds of others, including their offspring, to be like them. The child was confused and depended on the adults to clear up his confusion, but because the adults were not helping, he continued to be confused. Confused children eventually become miserable adults, who also hurt the weak and helpless.

By saving someone, we usually are splitting from a comfort zone

When we save someone, we are using extra effort and are splitting from a comfort zone. The life saver usually goes through unneeded danger and overwhelming emotions. In many instances, the one who has been threatened to be thrown out from a safe place tries to change the stalemate by making an extra effort. We are uncertain what to do and how to avoid rejection; despite the additional attempt of the rejected part to keep dialogue going, the other side is not answering. We eventually become broadminded regarding many things, and we accept the fact that we are not able to force anyone to have a positive response. This detail is very hard to admit. We are objective to the information that animals cannot talk, but we do not accept the fact that we do not have the power to hold dialogue with others. We need the willingness of both sides to get unified in dialogue. When dialogue happens, we learn how to understand and to relate to others, because the dialogue is a fusion. Real dialogue also requires human wisdom.

Beside dialogue, the split is the most important process of our psyche. The split may possibly be the reaction of the pain and suffering that require isolation to heal the wounds. Some splits are based on real pain and suffering, but mostly splits come from altered perception that has nothing to do with real pain and suffering. In many instances we reject the reality for unproved ideas and unrealistic adventures. In time, when fantasy and reality overlap, everyone is in danger of having an altered perception. The notion of splitting carries important, independent validity, and it is not always a failed unification attempt. Meanwhile, we are not looking for any dialogues with a side that, for minor discomfort, rejects us and sentences us to die. The psyche of rejecters mirror the world around them. The evil part of our psyche is looking for excuses to deny others a chance to be saved. We are very quick to reject, just by providing the complementary rigid justifications. The most important rationale for denial is that by rejecting, we are saving our comfort.

The threats to be thrown again on the streets of the occupied city were very frightening for young Lyonya. The rejecters needed to split from their own fragments, which loved the comfort of the safe place. The split needed to be done immediately, because the delay probably would bring an end to their lives. The split from the comfort was an attempt at getting rid of oppression and the threat of annihilation, and to get to a place that had the opportunity for future dialogues. For Professor Kryvoruchko, who was a descendant of this family, it was important to provide a safe existence for others. The savior first of all needs to have a desire to save lives. Later, the father and his son were eventually surrounded by love. They would feel safe and would not bring any discomfort to their saviors.

Dialogue is only possible with trust

Dialogue is possible only in the atmosphere of the trust, when we have complete confidence in others. We need to feel safe with others before we open up. Usually, we are not ready to open up and need special surroundings; the setting of the place does not make a difference, but the atmosphere inside is very important. Even when the place of the setting is dangerous, we still distinguish this spot as a place of dialogue. This is why the meetings and dialogues do not come right away, and we need to exceed the ordinary levels of preparedness to be ready for them.

For Professor Kryvoruchko, the need to have a dialogue was a strong motivator for looking around and searching his surroundings. Sometimes we do not know that we are in the place that is very close to the one we are looking for, and we pass without stopping at the place of our desire. Then we spend a lifetime dreaming about the place of the meeting. What hurts very badly is that many times we look over the significant place, and because of our limitations, we do not have the vision to recognize it, so we move away. We keep looking for it, and only later in our life do we realize that a long time ago, we had already found the place, that we had missed an opportunity to embrace a meeting. We are completely unaware of our destiny and where we have a chance to hold real dialogue. Many live in peace and wealth but may not dream about meetings.

Perhaps it's because we are in a dangerous place, and suddenly we have a meeting between the ordinary and the exceptional. The ordinary had the extraordinary luck to be blessed with exceptional happiness. The dialogue and meeting was the unification of our spirits and destiny. Through this meeting, the ordinary became enlightened with the qualities of the exceptional, and the exceptional got something from the ordinary one. After the meeting our life was not wasted and had a meaning. It did not matter if we have meeting through the dialogue, or the dialogue came after the meeting—the most important thing was that we had something that only a few have through their entire lives. In the meantime we do not know about our future; we just want to run away from a dangerous place, and we need to find safe surroundings.

Kryvoruchko Sr. decided to leave the village as soon as possible, because these mutterings about the need for his son to leave would only lead to disaster. He had heard by then that there were partisans in the woods, and he tried to learn how they could be found. They finally got to the partisans—a small group of local inhabitants and some escaped prisoners of war who were camping in middle of the bog.

Discipline was weak, but everyone knew his duties. The commander was not an army man but a former school principal. The peasants would join the unit with their entire families, bringing their belongings and livestock, and they lived in mud huts. The Kryvoruchkos were told to share a hut with Stepan Luchko's family. Stepan was a former geography teacher. He was a Ukrainian, and his wife was part of the domineering ethnicity. He had brought his wife from far away when he was a young student, and she was a woman of the village. She was not a beauty queen but was very pleasant, good-hearted, clean, and organized. An icon hung in a corner of the hut.

The Luchkos treated the newcomers well and helped them to settle down. Stepan Luchko and his wife, Galena, were generous and tactful, and they never asked silly questions. After supper at the open fire, they usually had a discussion. Stepan Luchko had enough knowledge to speak on any subject; he was well informed and interesting.

Kryvoruchko Sr. often contributed to the discussion, especially regarding economic questions; before the war, he had studied accounting. Other partisans would join them around the fire. Lyonya and Stepan Luchko's daughter, Marinka, were especially fond of these gatherings. Marinka was slightly younger than Lyonya and was a well-mannered, clever girl. Although the children did not understand what was being said, they listened to every word. Stepan often expressed his horror at the news of atrocities committed against the Jews, and then Kryvoruchko Sr. decided to reveal everything to him. He told him about his own tragedy, which was part of the Jewish tragedy. For partisans who lived in mud huts, he was not unique. Kryvoruchko Sr. and his son fell very safe and were able to open up and have a dialogue. All of the sudden, in the most volatile place in the world and in a mud hut, they could have a meeting.

The meeting of Kryvoruchko Sr. and Luchko was very important because their lives were fused together forever due to the meeting and dialogue, which might be a part of the cosmic design. The hero, Stepan Luchko—who always knew what was right and what was the most important for him—was meeting the pragmatic man who had never done more than was required. Kryvoruchko Sr. never had any ambitions to be a leader or a distinguished figure; he always wanted to be like everyone else. He loved his family and never loved any ideas or ideologies. He was an ordinary man, and compared to him, Luchko was exceptionally bright and enthusiastic.

God gave Kryvoruchko Sr. a very important present, which was in the form of extraordinary luck. The meaning of the meeting of those two was that in the most dangerous place in the world, the miserable soul was able find one who understood it, created a safe haven, and initiated dialogue.

We need to find a villain inside our psyche

When we are dealing with a villain, we need to find one inside our psyche. First we need to deal with the **self**. When we meet our own villain fragment, we may well be strong. Only the fragment that experienced the meeting and dialogue may represent our psyche in dealing with the villain inside of us. Professor Kryvoruchko explains that the faces of evil are deceptive and sometimes appear as a loving one. They speak softly, but in general the wickedness is presented by violence and hatred. These are killers, bullies, criminals, rapists, kidnappers, and anyone who has an evil mind. If our psyche is carrying only faces of hate and nothing of love, we are hateful. In war time the ordinary mind is preoccupied with the desire to have justice and what to do with victory. The ordinary man is struggling with questions about how the world can deal with the villains and how to stop them in future.

Kryvoruchko Sr. knew that the cause of tragedy in his life were the carriers of the radical ideas. He understood that he did not have the right to forgive, because the victims did not give him this right—but he also did not need to kill in retaliation. He felt that if he ended up to be a part of victorious forces occupying the village of his enemies, it was not justifiable for him to kill several villagers as revenge for his family's death. Often he saw that partisans were killing the surrendered enemy soldiers. He rejected the thoughts of retaliation and knew that he would never do it. He understood that he would not hurt a helpless one who happened to be an enemy soldier; otherwise he was not better than the villains that did not show any mercy to his family. He recognized that he could find an easy justification for killing, but he already discovered and dealt with a villain inside the self. He knew that to kill was easier than having mercy and not killing. By refusing to kill he appeared weak, but he would never hurt a helpless one in front of him.

This discovery happened because of the meeting with Luchko's family. In his interaction with them, Kryvoruchko Sr. found that the base for a dialogue was the willingness to move beyond his own pain and understand others. The dialogue required a particular ground, and the special soil would possibly nurture the seeds of the dialogue. Dialogue was also nurtured by surrendering to compassion.

Trust had many faces, too. We carry those faces everywhere and for all our life. Those faces are the base of our strength. To grow and mature, we need the faces of love, which have to be mothers, fathers, grandparents, neighbors, favorite teachers, spiritual teachers, or friends. They are inside our psyche, and we will not lose them. The ordinary man, Kryvoruchko Sr., did not join the villains who without any remorse killed and beheaded the suspects. The victims did not wear any uniform and did not carry any weapons. For villains the massacre of the defenseless was not an obstacle, because the villains always found justification for their hatred. It often happened that they justified killing because the victim belonged to an ethnicity or religion that the killers did not like. The villains could be in the same uniforms as the victims. In many instances the killers were very predictable.

What can we do when we catch the killers? This question sounds naive because for a long time, the villains killed without any remorse or guilt. But really, what would we possibly do with the terrorists, and could we kill them? The quick answer is that we need to kill as many villains as we can.

The other answer is that before we kill, we need to recognize that the problem is within us and to acknowledge the fact that a terrorist might be living inside of us. Sometimes our moral victory is more glorious than a tactical one. To have a moral victory and to deal with surrounding villains, we need to learn how to deal with one who is hiding inside of us. Only by dealing with our own villain will we learn how to deal with the villains surrounding us.

It is almost impossible to hurt without emotions

Is it impossible to hurt someone without emotions and to replace hate with indifference? During our life we hurt many people, some whom we hate and some whom we love, but really it is not easy to hurt someone without expressing any emotion. The feeling of detestation is more natural than other feelings because it anesthetizes us to the sufferings of others. If we express repugnance, it means that something fundamental was taken from us and our main response is hate. Typically, extreme distrust goes together with doubts and destruction.

By justifying the hurting of others, we are hurting the self more. When we decide to hurt others, we feel confined, agitated, and miserable, and we give up the good feelings of being contained and serene. With hate we are always splitting. Many feelings may be replaced by hate. The feeling of love is fragile, easily lost to hate, and very hard to put it back. Because we are not satisfied with hate, we feel that something prevents us from being complete, though we do not know what it is. The answer is very simple. We are missing love. When we look inside the self, often we see revulsion.

In the depths of our hearts, instead of hate we are looking for love. We feel complete when we are in love or meet someone nice, and then we have the sensation that life gives us something precious. With love we engage in the process of unification. It is a very delicate task, because love is delicate and may be replaced by hate in a moment.

With time Stepan Luchko and his wife, Galena, became even friendlier toward the Kryvoruchkos. As for Lyonya's cold, it went away after Galena gave him some home remedies. Kryvoruchko Sr. was thankful to Luchko's family.

Kryvoruchko Sr. was thinking about his friends. "They are so beautiful, and they live with love. It is very hard to find anyone else like them. It is sad that nowadays we have hate inside of us. Probably the hate makes us energized and powerful. What is the result of this power? Is the biggest achievement of hate a lot of distraction and ruin? Where do I get the strength to stop it? Apparently I do hate my enemies with all my heart. I have the power to bring a lot of harm to them, but that is one thing I do not want.

"I do not want that because by hating them, I become their partner in hate. My enemies are winning when I hate them. I would not be distinct from them. I make them very important, and they are rewarded by becoming a part of my life.

"How do I resist hate? It is very easy to hate my enemies; I do not need to make an effort because it is a natural process. So what am I supposed to do? It is impossible to imagine that I just ignore them after what they did to my family. No, I cannot ignore them. I also do not want spend the rest of my life just hating them, and eventually becoming like them. It is a catch twenty-two. One thing I know is that they ought to be stopped.

"I also somehow need to protect myself and my closest one from the hate. I acknowledge that I do not know how to stop hate in any other way than by using force. I wish we knew special techniques to stop cancer or other illnesses without surgery. Doctors are cutting the cancers. Do the doctors hate the cancer? No, they just do what it is necessary; they are just keeping their patient alive.

"I do not know if the brutal force is an effective method of healing, though I think that the force is probably a needed solution until we become more advanced and find something else. I only know that I may well get rid of the cancer with any available means, but I also need to have a limit to my hate."

Professor Kryvoruchko says that when doctors cut the cancer, their patients are under anesthesia and do not feel much. Nevertheless, the doctors in an operating room still become machines, and the patients are the objects. When we retaliate against enemies, we want them to feel pain; we are hurting the invader because we are forced to protect the self. We do it with all our strength, and we want the person to suffer a lot.

How is it possible that we get anesthetized, stop our emotions, and become unresponsive to the feelings of pain? We may only do it by becoming a heartless machine and by treating others as objects. If our survival is at stake, and we do not have any other choice, are we allowed to split from our feelings and become a machine of hurting?

When we intentionally hurt others, it is not easy to do it without any emotion, but sometimes we need to hurt them in order to stop them from hurting us. Might we hurt someone without any feelings of guilt? When we hate someone and hurt him, we do not feel guilt.

When we hurt someone without hate, then we become a piece of equipment. It is hard to hurt without feelings, and not too many can do it. We are not monsters and were not built for it; we are not a device without feelings. The answer is that it is better to deal with our emotions than to hurt without feeling.

We do not know what future effect our actions will have. We may learn how to hurt without any emotion and, as a result, suffer even more.

Establishing a solid identity usually aligns us with love and care

The establishment of a stable psyche with a solid identity usually results in an alignment with love and care. The love and care are the unifying forces that create a new configuration for the psyche. The vigilante's psyche mirrors the external world, which has polarities but is inclined in one direction. The vigilante wants to reverse the poles replay the past in clashing directions. The past and future become significant only if they are connected to the trauma and activities related to trauma, which are the acts of retaliation to stop the possible reoccurrence and to have closure. In the vigilante's psyche, all brain organization is around the trauma.

During the process of reconstruction, the psyche gets more split. The new organization contains some good but also many evil fragments, which are not reconcilable. Those fragments are willing to punish the world for perceived sufferings and oppression. Without any second thought, they are ready to kill anyone who does not share their ideas. The first leader of the Soviet collective was a vigilante who retaliated against the ruling clan for the unjustifiable death of his brother. His mother, also a vigilante, financed any intentions to destroy the monarchy and agitate the power holders. She succeeded by starting an uprising. Her son actually destroyed the pre-Soviet ruling family together with the ruling class by making false promises and creating many mass graves. The fascist collective was also a vigilante, fighting for something unreal via illusory promises and leaving behind dead bodies and gas chambers.

Our world is on the fire because of the hate by many groups that are not able to resolve their grievances, and as a result we continue to hate. We do it because we want the acknowledgment of the atrocities from others, but others refuse to take responsibility and do not admit to what happened in the past. Many powerful leaders, driven by their vigilante fragments, are not interested in ending the conflict and want to find salvation in hate. They use the reverse, mirroring the evil and doing the same that was done to them. Vigilantes are obsessed and do not care about the rules and regulations; they have their own ideas about how to take revenge. Some of the vigilantes imagine the suffering of others and do not want any compromises, even if the suffering of others was only in their own imagination. Many societies will not accept the lynch law; nevertheless, there are still many various vigilantes, because the villain inside of us will never stop.

Some of us imagine others' misery or transfer our own guilt onto others. In some Eastern countries the victims who have powerful protectors may be forgiven for the acts of punishment. In Western society the punishment by the victim is against the law. We still have many unresolved conflicts that are very dramatic and cannot ever be resolved, but we are trying to deal with them in a civilized manner.

Nevertheless, we are not forgiving the self for being a victim. We are not willing to recognize that instead of the enemies, we are punishing the self because somehow the perpetrator gets inside us and calls for more blood. We do not know yet that punishing does not relieve hate. We, as self-appointed vigilantes, want not only the violators to suffer but also all their relatives, associates, and even some who were never involved in the violations. As self-appointed vigilantes we have very unsophisticated logic; we feel that even the victims are often sick and weak, the law enforcers do nothing, and we have a responsibility to be the doer. We take seriously our responsibility as defenders, and we are ready to hurt anyone, but in reality we are not hurting the guilty. It is very important to punish the guilty but not to dispense guilt. The guards in the concentration camps were the antisocial, and their sycophants were from many diverse ethnic groups. They were executors of innocent civilians. In the vigilante's judgment, everyone who belongs to the perpetrator's ethnic group is a candidate for castigation. It is the logic of blame and collective punishment that spreads across the whole ethnicity, and we need to have a stable psyche to understand it. In a solid identity and a stable psyche, the majority of the fragments are reconciled. We want to build the grounds of love and care after the tragic loss of our significant others. It is most important that we have the strength to withstand the distractions.

Professor Kryvoruchko mentions that hate creates the villain's configuration. His grandfather made a tremendous effort to keep his psyche aligned with love and care. When we have a stable psyche, we are putting a lot of effort in keeping our psyche in order, because under the storm of hate, our psyche falls apart. Hate has very destructive tendencies. When hate took over our world, it was falling apart and ended up being ruined. The intolerable psyches are repulsive in the form of the separated fragments lying everywhere. The displaced fragments in the rigid psyche are comparable to the ruins of a destroyed construction, which is the sign of mental destruction. We need to find a way to prevent the world from the distribution of hate. Our identity is becoming more fragmented, when the psyche is going through the process of severe splitting and is falling apart under horrible events. Only the fragments, which are crucial to survival, are keeping our psyche together. The function of our psyche is similar to the process in our bodies when we are starving: then the porky fatness goes away, and only a carcass that holds the construction is visible. After the trauma only the most useful fragments in our psyche are together and functioning. For our survival we need only a few fragments that contain the basic skills, and then in the future we are able to rebuild a solid identity.

CHAPTER III

Looking for Meeting

The unification with kindness

Unifying with kindness prevents the development of the vigilante fragment. Kryvoruchko Sr.'s psyche did not develop a fragment of the vigilante only because of his unification with kindness. As a soldier, he did his duty and later participated in battles. He faced the enemy and was part of the collective, but he was not radicalized. His external bonds with the collective wanted him to be vigilant and become a part of the killing machine, but he was unusual. During his service he never had any vigilante thoughts of revenge by killing or torturing in return for what was done to his family.

The soul of Kryvoruchko Sr. was saved by the good-heartedness of his new friends. After the devastating effect of splitting by hate and coarse treatment, the Kryvoruchkos found hospitality from complete strangers. Suddenly, to his total disbelief, he encountered unification with kindness. He had a real meeting that made a difference in his life and his soul, and eventually he found an exit from the butcher's shop. Unfortunately, during this time only a few were able to find this peace. When we have big losses, we have our own reactions. Even when we meet kindness, we have contradictory responses of pain and suffering. Some of us are overwhelmed with our pain and become completely insensitive. Many of us in similar situations have opposite responses, and we actually become more understanding and compassionate.

Only after facing hardship do we eventually understand the value of kindness and generosity: we were taking those qualities for granted, because in our life we never faced the indifference and rudeness. The friendship with Luchko's family restored Kryvoruchko's and Lyonya's trust in kindness and prevented their psyches from splitting more. They did not develop hate and aversion as the main driving force in their lives. They did not become incapable of showing kindness and friendship.

In the meantime Kryvoruchko Sr., as a new member of the unit, did guard duty, chopped wood, and took part in attacks on convoys carrying supplies for the enemies. Stepan Luchko had more responsible jobs: he went from village to village collecting information and encouraging the inhabitants to resist. In one of the villages he was betrayed and arrested by the polizies, who were corrupt wretches. The partisans attacked the village, but Luchko had already been taken to the regional headquarters. The partisans burned down the informer's house.

Galena and her daughter could not stop weeping. They constantly knelt in front of the icon, praying for Stepan Luchko's life to be spared. It was the Kryvoruchkos' turn to show concern for their friends, and they were ready to do everything for Galena and Marinka. "Because we lost our family, we understand others in the same situation. We are very grateful for all support." The Kryvoruchkos did not have any doubt in their mind that Luchko's family needed to be repaid for their hospitality. They would do everything to help this family, even if they needed to give up their lives. Now they were generating compassion and caring.

Galena and Marinka had a unification with kindness. Their spiritual power enabled them to keep hope and believe that goodness would prevail. The kindness of their friends also prevented their psyches from splitting and developing vigilante fragments.

The plasticity of the fragment

Plasticity is the ability of the fragment to provide several discrete responses— in other words, it can be flexible in responses. The plasticity is a sign of preparedness for unification. Contrarily, the responses with hate as a base are rigid and do not deviate; the rigid responses are always about destroying. The splitting fragments are rigid and do not have the luxury of flexibility. The role of the villain or vigilante is to prevent a rigid fragment from having responses other than hate and anger. The distinctive roles that are by each of the fragments are the signs of flexibility of responses. The flexible responses are about meetings and unification. Kryvoruchko Sr.'s friend and fellow fighter, Stepan Luchko, was betrayed by wretches. The first thoughts of Kryvoruchko Sr. at this stressful time were not about punishment of the traitors but about the most efficient way to liberate Stepan Luchko. The feelings of hate and vigilance did not overpower his feelings of compassion and friendship. His thoughts were also about providing maximum comfort to his friend's family.

Kryvoruchko Sr.'s psyche had a flexible and stable construction. He did not have any goals of destruction; his psyche was built on love. Contrarily, the psyche that is built on hate has a very rigid construction and creates the monster of destruction. The psyche that is assembled on the foundation of hate is very fragile and suffers from the lack of plasticity. Professor Kryvoruchko states that the fragments that have a base of love are able to generate several dissimilar responses. He consciously identifies the presence of those fragments in his psyche. Those fragments are Kryvoruchko Sr., Lyonya, and Stepan Luchko. They represent his father and two of his grandfathers, and they interact by using plasticity in their responses. They are a big dominance in his psyche. Because of their positive influence, he has a stable and solid identity. From the structures of Kryvoruchko Sr.'s and Lyonya's fragments, we see that they are the combinations of the victim, the warrior, and the savior.

Stepan Luchko's fragment was aligned with others. Primarily he was a warrior and savior, but recently he had added a victim side by being betrayed by wretches. The three fragments of Professor Kryvoruchko's psyche hold a construction that reflects the same belief system. Because they are represented by diverse manners of appearance, it's possible they may not be replaced by one fragment, even though they believe in the same moral values. Each of them is operating on distinctive approaches and sensory responses, which are visual, audio, and kinesthetic. The fragment that represents Kryvoruchko Sr. is a military man, and he has significant visual assertion. Stepan Luchko is a teacher and represents audio articulation. Lyonya is a boy who answers to his kinesthetic affirmation. Despite separate manners, those fragments have complete reciprocity in Professor Kryvoruchko's psyche, because the audio stimulations are accurately translated to visual and kinesthetic response, and vice versa. The congruency of translation, which is done on the conscious level, contains a big advantage in building his identity.

If the translation of the stimulations is wrong, then the responses become incongruent. The fragments would not have dialogues and meetings, and as a result we'd find it inconvenient to be unified. If our responses are incongruent, they lose their flexibility and we produce misleading responses. Our flexibility goes together with congruence, and our flexible fragments have a better possibility of translation to other forms of expression. When our fragments are unified in groups, where each of our fragments has an ability to provide several discrete responses, then we see the signs of plasticity.

The female's fragments

The female's fragments are important in the construction of the self, because they provide for us distinctive gender responses. Our mothers, grandmothers, and sisters are very important partners in dialogue; their responses help us to be more human. Whereas the male fragments represent warriors, the female fragments signify smoothness and homely life, and an abundance of the feelings of warmth and contentment. Every male has at least one fragment in his psyche, which represents his mother or another female and brings up positive feelings. The fragment of the mother as a unifying force carries a lot of good emotions. However, some of us definitely do not feel good about our mothers; we feel that our mother did not raise us right and split us away from love.

In Lyonya's life, his mother and sister were brutally murdered by heartless zombies, and therefore his psyche was almost consumed by hate and feelings of vengeance. His mother, who shared her last moment of breath with her daughter and her father, pushed him away from death to life. His father also constantly saw the horrifying nightmares, where his wife shared her last breath of air with his little daughter. The tragic death of his wife and daughter caused a separation from his love and his dreams; he was split in the horror of misery from the tenderness of his daughter's love and the warmness of his wife's hugs. The ugly concept of genetic purification was skillfully planted in the skulls of the many empty-headed followers. Because of the world's indifference, the loved ones were thrown in the coldness of unmarked graves and were accompanied only by the smear of injustice. The split created a hole in Kryvoruchko Sr.'s psyche, which was probably filled up with hate and resentment. Hate creates more hate and more split. Hate's opposite, compassion, creates the need for unification.

Galena and Marinka are fragments of survivors and saviors; they are very positive and reinforce an unstable structure. They represent compassion, care, and comfort, and their purpose is to be loved and love. They are far away from hate and aggravation. The one way to deal with hate is to strengthen the area of love in our psyche. The area of love gets bigger and enhanced, and in turn the area of hate gets smaller. The female fragments in the male psyche are usually associated with compassion and understanding. Our mothers are the unifying force and help to build a solid identity. In Professor Kryvoruchko's psyche, Galena and Marinka represent the unifying forces of the universe, bringing responses of love and compassion.

The fragment of the survivor

Our fragment of the survivor triggers splitting until a danger exists. But eventually, when our life is less dangerous, our fragments stop splitting, and when we feel safe, we join the forces of unification. After the danger is gone, many of us are not ready to stop fighting and therefore become vigilantes because we do not know how to rebuild our lives. When we are destined to survive, we have a choice to keep hate and vigilance, or to look for love and compassion. Some of us will always be part of hate and death and will not rest until we have closure. We may be sure that those responsible for the biggest injustice get their punishment.

During the occupation, the enemy burned Galena and Marinka's village. Many partisans were captured, tortured, and executed by the fascist servants. It was learned that Stepan Luchko had been sent to a concentration camp in Poland, but details about his fate were unknown. He was reported to be lost without any news, probably exterminated. Galena, Marinka, Kryvoruchko Sr., and Lyonya survived and at last were liberated. While Lyonya remained with Galena and Marinka, Kryvoruchko Sr. resumed his military service as a soldier in the Soviet army. He had no surviving relatives except his son; his wife and daughter were killed in Babiy Yar and interred in the mass grave. At the place of their death, for a long time there was no monument or memorial sign, which made him very sad.

After the war, he served a short term as part of an occupying force and was later demobilized because of his age. reunited with Lyonya, Galena, and Marinka. In his loneliness he became even more attached to Galena; she called him Alexander or Sasha. He did not want to live in the village, having lived in a big city all his life. He suggested to Galena that they move to the city, and she agreed. Alexander left first. In the city where he grew up, he found only strangers—all the Jewish neighbors had been killed. Strangers lived in his father's house and had many children. During the fascist occupation, they took Kryvoruchko's house, did not want to leave, and were very hostile. It was probably reasonable to evict them, but on the other hand Alexander did not want to fight with them. He understood that he would not be able to live in the house where everything reminded him of his losses. The war had finished, but the hate lingered and forced him to split more. When there is danger around us, we will continue to split.

The attitude of love can turn to hate

Love as a way of thinking can be reversed to hate. The feeling of love is easily translated to hate, but feelings of hate are very seldom transferred to love. We experience love and hate as complimentary feelings to the same individuals; our psyche uses some translator, interpreting love and hate to the dissimilar sensors. We express feelings of love and hate through sounds, visual perception, kinesthetic expressions, and smell. Our fragments are less rigid when our internal translator correctly interprets the stimulations. Our psyche also has an automatic verbal translator that verbally describes our visual, audio, kinesthetic, and olfactory experiences. We may verbalize the complementary feelings of love and hate; the internal translator contains an independent capacity to pick up material for conversion. When the translator is stoked by feelings of hate, it interprets only the experiences related to hate and brings up to our consciousness the images, sound, and movements associated with hate. In that time, we are sure that we have had closure on abhorrence, our feelings of revulsion are decreased, and we are dealing with them in an appropriate manner. When the translator changes the output of conversion from hate to love, we display the experiences of love with completely altered references. It translates only experiences attributed to love. The images of love might not be mixed with images of hate. To be sure that the psyche is avoiding mistakes, we identify the new experiences by a separate name. We have problems with conversion and severe disturbance when we mix together images of love and hate.

Kryvoruchko Sr. got to relatively safe surroundings and at last was in the process of accumulating love and altering his references. Because of the audio, visual, and kinesthetic changes that required significant alteration, for now he was identified by another name, Alexander. He would not love with references of the massacre and pain. He needed atypical references, because he was translating his experiences from hate, depression, aggravation, and despair to love and tenderness. It was very grueling to grow something on the ashes, and a new perception needed new surroundings. He was getting farther ahead from just being a survivor. Alexander wanted new experiences in life, to give love and to support others. He was ready to build a new family and to have a new nest.

Professor Kryvoruchko declared that because of those transformations, which had happened to his grandfather, Professor Kryvoruchko, who was not born yet, had so many opportunities. As the child of the survivors, Professor Kryvoruchko arrived as the messenger of the love. The process of transforming hate to love was not an easy one; when the main goal was to survive, love was a burden. Only when the new generation arrived could we understand that love was still alive. After the miracles of surviving, and after they gave respect to the dead, the transition from hate to love became possible. They dealt with very important issues of safety, which included establishing a safe nest. They were concerned about their ability to provide safety for future generations.

Professor Kryvoruchko's thoughts were, "We ought to be consciously aware of how we express our feelings, because the feelings probably are easy reversed. We need to be sure that love will not possibly become hate again. We need to be aware of what is going on in our surroundings. Many times by venting anger, we are just reinforcing it. To be ready for love, we may not only vent but must deal with anger. Only when we reach an agreement on a conscious level with the fragments of hate can we may perhaps process the fragments that are associated with love. We have diverse goals and want to encounter love. By experiencing love, we learn how properly to express our love; we translate the feelings of love from the kinesthetic to the audio and to the visual expression. If we do not deal with hate in a proper way, the translator automatically picks up our feelings and may also pick up previous feelings of hate. It is also very essential for us to understand that before we love, we need to know how we are handling the hate inside of us. We must identify and process the fragments that are aligned with anger. It is important to know our inventory before we start something new. We as the survivors are required find out what kind of underlining processes are below the surface.

"When we vent anger by hitting a pillow, we release the kinesthetic anger and then feel better and become contained. The problem is that we do not know for how long we will keep it contained; in some instances the ventilation does not help us at all. To deal with dissimilar experiences of anger, we have to inspect our visual, audio, and olfactory styles. If they did not vent anger and did not provide desirable relief, then we continue to be affected by brain chemistry associated with hate and anger. Because we do not want any shortcut solutions, we need to deal with anger on a deeper level. We should take as much time as we need to build a conscious awareness of the subconscious processes. We know that the experience of loving kindness is very fragile, and we cannot mix it together with the ventilation of anger. We need to be careful when we translate love to distinguishing senses, because we use the same translator to interpret our other feelings, including the feelings of hate."

Unification with love avoids love-hate responses

Professor Kryvoruchko also acknowledges we need to be sure that before we unify with love, we split from hate. He says, "By unifying with love, it is essential to avoid love-hate responses, because we do not want to add more uncertainty to our life. When we just hate, we have more clarity and understanding of our feelings; we just know that we hate with all our strength. The identity that is in transition from hate to love goes through the adaptation to the new way of being. Our overall responses are changing and, during the transition, might mix love and hate responses. It happens because hate is very strong and does not want to leave us; it takes us into another trap and hides behind love. To avoid love-hate responses, which cause only confusion, first we need to identify all the hate responses and properly process them."

Eventually the transformation from Kryvoruchko Sr. to Alexander was completed, but he dealt with hate and love for a long time. In his thoughts he was dealing with many questions: "If the opposite of hate is love, how come love does not resist hate? Love loses power and becomes weak when hate monsters use love to intensify hate, sneaking behind love and doing their dirty job. To achieve their goal, they use high love rhetoric, like patriotic love to country, love to God, love to their race, and love to family. The resistance to hate is in meditation and in reflection, and by understanding that we cannot stop hate with hate. I know that somewhere deep inside we have a knowledge about real love. I'm afraid that we lost the notion of real love because of life's hardships and ignorance. It is interesting that we never forget hate."

Alexander continued with his thoughts. "As little children we are aware of hate; we can imagine nasty things that we might do to one we hate. We can be very vicious and show no mercy. We do not need to learn how to hate. Our imagination is very intense, because hate brings a lot of energy to our lives.

"After venting hateful feelings, we probably feel good. We feel relieved as though we got rid of hate. We punch pillows and punching bags, imagining that we are punching someone who is the cause of our stress, the violator of our happiness. Feelings of hate are present during the venting. We get rid of hate by using anger and hate. Even though we feel relief, nevertheless we may not rely on hate as a healing tool—this is not a real healing. Real healing builds a resistance to hate and to learning about real love. The master of the universe is the one who can be immune to hate. He knows the secret of how to be cool, and how to fight hate without the overwhelming intensity of his emotions. We do not need to fight hate with hate.

"We need to use wisdom. Our future endeavor is to stop hate with wisdom. To do it, we might need to recognize that hate is inside of us. We might not be able to control the hate of others, but we can control our own hate. Wisdom is also knowledge of love, desire of learning more about love, and opening up our hearts to the experience of love.

"Wisdom helps us know our limits. Sometimes hate is so overwhelming that everything around contributes to it. We also know the power of hate. By its influence we get in a state where all fears diminish, including the fear of death; hate may be a painkiller or a narcotic. We need to know how much hate we can handle before we become addicted to it."

Our hateful identity is so miserable that eventually we are willing to split with hate and to unify with love. Love gives us dignity and pleasure, but we must be careful not to get ambushed again. During the transition from hate to love, we may get trapped in a mixed love-hate responses.

The experience of hate

We have dissimilar ways to display our feelings, and hate might be present in the diverse channels of emotions and expressions. Hateful grinding is a visual response of hate. When we hear hate in the timbre of the voice, it is an audio response. A response is kinesthetic when aggressive posture represents nonverbal expressions of hate. When we convey our feelings of hate, we are not concerned with what approach we use.

Professor Kryvoruchko mentions that we have inherited abilities to interpret our feelings from dissimilar types of expression. Our psyche has the translator, and we use universal frames of reference that are described by common expressions. We do interpret our experiences on verbal and nonverbal levels, and sometimes hate is expressed only by facial expressions. We receive many recognizable responses from distinctive modalities, and only after interpretation do we understand that we are observing hate. If the responses are not clear, that means there is not enough information regarding the feelings we are observing.

A most confusing situation arises when the kinesthetic expression is absent, because agitation produced by hate usually goes together with our tightness and aggressive postures. When we are relaxing, we are not tight and do not make any aggressive gestures; we assume we do not experience hate. That perhaps is a wrong conclusion. Our audio and visual responses are not free of hate. Some of us are masters of instigating hate, and we would not take a gun and shoot or push the helpless, but we have the foolishness to say or write a lot of hateful things, to influence others to hate, and to express hate by a brutal kinesthetic style.

Only in our fantasy may we feel that we are completely free of hate. If we do not hate anyone, then probably we are hated by someone. We need to accept the fact that hate will always be around. We cannot eradicate hate, but we need to find a way to limit the damages from it. Alexander wanted to understand how to deal with hate and discover its roots. He knew that hate and love were opposites and complementary, and for him it was very important to achieve the decrease of hate and the increase of love. It has not yet happened that love is bigger than hate, but the opposite has happened many times. Hate is easy to learn and to copy. In many instances, hate has a wider range of emotion than love. If more hate gets around, that means love is decreased. Unfortunately, real love is hard to recognize.

Alexander had the strength to function because he had a son who needed him. If his son had not been close, there would not be a reason for him to continue with his search for love. The father saved his son, but the son was a savior too. Lyonya did not understand that with his love, he saved his father's soul. He was an addition to the area of goodness, where fragments had roles of being victims to be saved, and being saviors.

Alexander's thoughts of hate included thoughts that hate had dissimilar manners. He declared, "I express hate in visual form and also feel it. I hate the enemy's radical collective. When I saw their marches, then I felt that I had completely given in to hate. A vicious enemy killed my family—I am not unresponsive and I hate. I am also part of a collective, but I believe that my collective is less vicious. When two collectives fight, they are driven by revulsion.

They hate in order to suppress guilt, increase aggression, and grab without any remorse. As an individual, I have an audio experience of hate when someone insults and degrades me. When somebody does terrible things to me, I lose my head and answer back."

The kinesthetic experience of hate is the desire to stop the assumed generator of hate by killing, damaging, and inflicting pain. The olfactory stimulations associated with trauma create hateful feelings, too. A particular odor may trigger a range of hateful emotions. To resist hate is to check our responses on diverse styles. Alexander continued. "I do not want to ignore the fact that I hate and that perhaps someone may hate me too. I feel that hate gets bigger and blows up in my face. We should not ignore hate until is too late to intervene. When someone is not attacking us physically but with his attitude, the tone of his voice, and of his facial grimaces, he helps us recognize hate. We need to detect hate and be prepared to intercept it by all available diverse approaches."

The protection of love requires planning ahead

The protection of love from hate requires planning ahead and making a lot of changes in life. Keeping love alive is a full-time job and needs a lot of deep thought and wise actions. Even small outbursts of hate have the strength to spoil love. Everything involved with hate remains with us as losses. When we want to have a second chance at living, perhaps it is wiser to go away from that place. When we miraculously survive but lose a significant one, safety becomes very important. When we decide to be together with someone, we need to be sure that hate will not damage our new beginning. We may well prepare the self to function on an uncommon level of awareness. Love includes unification on the visual, audio, kinesthetic, and olfactory level. In love we express our feelings verbally and by many beautiful words. We take care of our appearance, using fantasy and creativity to express our love. We want to make visual expressions, use vivid movements, and wear pleasant fragrances. Our expression of love needs a special atmosphere, well protected and not spoiled by hate. When we as adults are in love, the love includes intimacy. The atmosphere of the intimacy is very fragile and may be easily destroyed by hate. Because of hate, our intimacy can easily become a mechanical process without any feelings, and that can lead to the end of love.

Professor Kryvoruchko adds that the hateful feeling is not easy to control. It produces split and aggression in the form of special sensory expressions. It uses the hateful verbalization, which is consistent with a hateful look; completely avoids any fun; and is indifferent to the fragrances. It limits movement and pollutes our responses by hateful gestures. The split by hate separates us from many human feelings and as a result exhibits complete numbness to the suffering of others. When we want to protect love, the best decision is to move away from the place where hate exists.

The killing machine done its job well. The pomposity, pretension, and grandiosity split Alexander from his birthplace, where people were polluted with radical ideas. He decided to leave Ukraine forever and move to the east. He wanted to live in Moscow but settled for St. Petersburg. As a veteran of the war, he easily obtained a working permit; he applied and was accepted as an accountant in a military factory. He found a dwelling and later was joined by Galena and the children. When they received identification documents, Alexander and his son remembered their past and registered in the Soviet collective as part of a domineering ethnicity.

Lyonya did not want to go to regular school, where he was a little older than his classmates. He found work as an apprentice to a machinist in the same factory where his father worked. In the evenings he attended general education classes, while Marinka continued her studies at a regular school. Galena also found work in Alexander's office. In time, Alexander and Galena came to the conclusion that they could be happy together. In the beginning they were embarrassed at the mere thought of their feelings, but time heals all wounds. When wounded souls get together, they hope for good future. It is important to provide security to the new nest, and to succeed in life we need to make a lot of smart decisions, plans, and wise moves.

Hate is very adaptive

Professor Kryvoruchko acknowledges that hate may easily infect peaceful doctrines and concepts with rage and splitting force. Hate is very adaptive and takes atypical forms. By winning subsequent ideology battles, hate gets even for the defeat. Hate is very adaptive to diverse environments and changes its appearance according to circumstances. To forget the power of hate is to leave the self defenseless to new splits. Nevertheless, time is the important factor in dealing with hate, because time has an anesthetic power. It seems that when more time passes from the traumatic experience, we feel less pain, but the past is a lesson which we cannot forget.

A part of Alexander's psyche was designated to be a savior and protector. If a change in identification documents would protect his family, he was going to alter his ID, even it was illegal. He struggled with the question: "Is it important to be a Jew in front of others?" He did not appreciate any public displays and wanted very much to be a Jew, but only in his heart. He had learned his lesson—he did not have to prove anything to the hateful. He decided to be a Jew in his heart and did not betray the memory of anyone in his family, who were dead in the Baby Yar. His identity would not change, even though on his ID card, instead of Jew there would be printed the domineering ethnicity of the Soviet collective.

The Jews in the Soviet collective were considered an ethnic group, and this matter was reflected on an ID card. In the Soviet collective, on job applications, membership in a library or an athletic club, and any other application was a fifth important question. After the family name, address, and marital status, ethnicity was always questioned. Alexander felt that he did not need to be asked about his ethnicity—he was not able to learn from his history. In the Soviet collective Jewish schools were not available and religion was forbidden. It was wrong to assume that a member of the worker's paradise, even with his proficiency in the language of the domineering ethnicity, may be accepted as a member of this ethnicity. He was deprived from learning his own language. He actually knew little Yiddish, the language of the European Jews, but he did not know how to read and write in this language. He also wondered who the Jews in the worker's paradise were and what made them scapegoats.

Alexander also knew that the Soviet collective was very shrouded. It officially obeyed the existing law and went along with declaring Jews an ethnic group. The Soviet collective allocated to the Jews a piece of land in Siberia on the border with China. In reality this piece of land on the Far East, called the Birobijan, was only symbolic. It was mainly inhibited by Chinese and mosquitoes. The promotion of the Jews in the collective to the nation's status brought a lot of suffering to Jews; it was the same as giving them the status of scapegoats. In all of the republics of the collective and their satellites states, the Jews were easily identified and persecuted at work and sport, and during the distribution of goods. In many instances they were denied resettlement in big cities, which required special permission from authorities.

The Jews were blamed for everything bad that happened. In the collective rule, all the nations were supposed to be equal, but in reality only the domineering ethnicity was promoted as a hero by the government-controlled media. The other ethnicities were demoted to a mediocre level. During the war the strong nationalistic approach of the media helped to energize members to defend the Soviet collective. For the propaganda machine, the right way was to call all ethnicities in the Soviet collective "Kommi." Then they all would feel equal—but the name sound very much like "Nazi." The nationalistic tendencies continued after the war.

The glory in the Soviet collective was not equally shared by everyone. The radio played the very sentimental songs of only the domineering ethnicity. It appeared that the victims and heroes came solely from the domineering ethnicity. Because of the question of ethnicity in any applications, the benefits of winning the war were projected only on the members of the domineering ethnicity. The possession of the identification card made them proud because they belonged.

In the collective the other ethnicities did not have the luxury to be recognized, and it appeared that they did not suffer during the war and did not produce any heroes. Despite the fact that the Jewish soldiers and partisans contributed a lot to the victory of the Soviet collective, they receive recognition for their heroic fights and were not appreciated by the collective. They were the designated scapegoats and were put down by everyone with hatred in his heart. The biggest shame was that one of the greatest cities, where many Jews died from hunger and from defending it, exhibited the strongest xenophobic feeling. It was challenging to understand why this nonsense had a place in the wounded city. There were distinctive explanations, which could be relevant to the local situation, about many significant contributors to the hate in collective. But one of the simplest is that the hater came from members of the Soviet collective dislocated from the occupied territories. They moved to the city after the war, were angry, and kept hatred as justification of their crimes—and their children inherited their hate. When the collective fell apart, the hate came out in extreme displays.

The migrants were mainly women, impregnated by enemy soldiers. They were from the occupied territories and were connected with the fascist ideology. They moved to the city with their children and took the living space of dead defenders. They kept the hatred alive. The newcomers and their offspring carried the hate of the fascists, and the victory of the Soviet collective was not complete because the ideology of hate survived. Without any remorse the newcomers occupied the houses of the victims, which were starved to death. Because of a shortage of available space, the newcomers were finger pointing, calling the Jewish survivors insulting names and intimidating them. The hate easily adapted to the special place and to the dissimilar ideology.

We do not want to disclose information of our ethnicity

We must not be forced to disclose our private information, the information about our ethnicity and religion. When we are not comfortable to release it, this information must be protected and remain confidential. The government's request for the mandatory disclosure of this information is an act of discrimination. In the worker's paradise, the government asked the people to disclose our private information. The reason was not for their protection, but an intention to discriminate them by inventing the quotas. There were quotas to get employment, education, and justice. By any common sense in those particular circumstances, one should not reveal private information and did not need to answer trustfully. Alexander and Lyonya's history already taught them the painful lesson about answering a question trustfully. After the war, the power holders of the collective adapted the segregation rules for the ethnicity. They created for each minority the quotas for employment, housing, and praise. They did not want cultural adaptation—they wanted to screen minority out. The minority was marked because genetically they were not part of the domineering ethnicity. It did not matter that they perfectly knew the domineering language and history—they would never be equal. The genetic view of minorities came from the ideology of racism.

As minorities we were born and resided in regions of domineering ethnicity, but by regulations of collectives we are always minorities and never can have the domineering ethnicity. The fact that we have perfect command in domineering language and do not know any other languages did not matter. If we'd been members of the domineering ethnicity and lived somewhere else as minority, then we'd cling tight to our region. When we move back to our ethnic region, and even if we'd never lived there before and do not know the domineering language, on our ID cards we are identified as a domineering ethnicity. Without knowledge of language and history, we are closer to minorities who are perfectly speaking the language and know the history.

There was genetic screening in the Soviet collective. Minorities in every region of the collective were subject to undisclosed but very specific quotas and limits. Those limits were a reason to deny the minorities benefits to which they were entitled. The official propaganda glorified the members of the domineering ethnicity and attributed to them exceptional and far-fetched qualities, which were exaggerated. It looked like minorities did not participate in any heroic actions. This attitude continued after the war, the same way as the fascist ideology to screen the genetically inferior, and the working paradise wanting the domineering ethnicity to be more protected. The Soviet collective declared through their policies that the domineering ethnicity had a government that provided them with very valuable benefits and safeguarded them against minorities.

The propaganda fabricated evidence to justify the entitlement of the majority to more benefits; as a result, the minorities felt even more inferior. In the Soviet collective, we were the descendents of many great nations, but only one domineering ethnicity was chosen as the older and wiser brother. The movies and TV programs floated with characters that were disciplined, very moral, and unaffected by any impulses; they behaved as the monks in a monastery, genetically pure and very attractive. Those fictitious characters displayed enormous love for their homeland and were presented as the standards for the patriotism and bravery. This brainwash was confusing for everyone and caused the members of the majority ethnicity to feel unjustifiably superior. In actuality, it was a copy of the ideology of the fascists.

The radical ideology entitled members of the dominant ethnicity to intimidate and discriminate because they believed that minorities were the freeloaders and that only the majority ethnicity was the productive force. The drunk and irritable members of the elitist majority could, without any repercussion, call minorities by insulting names and cast out any of them from a public place. The minorities did not have any way to complain, because everyone understood that they were not entitled to equal rights.

In many instances, as Jews in the Soviet collective, we had more problems than the other minorities. The difference was that other minorities perhaps could learn their own language and history, but Jews could not. As Jews, we were not able to learn anything about our history and language. The collective found the way to rationalize it with a connection of Jewish language and history with religion. We were not allowed to learn our religion; it was strictly forbidden to teach Jewish history in school. We did not have the pride that we were the biblical ethnicity and that our history and language was part of many religions.

Professor Kryvoruchko says, "As a minority, we were not protected against harassment. In the Soviet collective as Jews, we had a little fictitious place, but it was not our historical region of habitation. The region on the border with China was without any of our historical roots. Instead of being a historical homeland, this place was established to keep criminals away from the big cities. It was a piece of land populated by mosquitoes and did not have any elementary conveniences."

After miraculous survival, Alexander Kryvoruchko did not want go with his family to Birobijan. He had lived through the atrocities inflicted by hatred and did not want to be an easy target. He did not know when any villains would come next, though his son did not mind having an ID card of the dominant ethnicity. In the Soviet collective the Jews, as victims of atrocities of the war, were not safe because hatred was infectious. They needed to split from their real origin to avoid intimidation, name calling, and physical and emotional abuse.

When we kept our identity, we had a life of continuous guilt and degradation, created by the collective and the shameful stereotypes of our ethnicity. In the stereotype of the collective, Jews were greedy and cowardly and were always betraying the trust of the dominant ethnicity. In the Soviet collective, the biggest insult was to be called a Jew. When we stubbornly admitted it, it was comparable to an act of suicide. Hate found fertile ground, and in those circumstances, we were completely right when we did not disclose our ethnicity. It was not an act of cowardliness—it was common sense when we did not put the self in the position of a target. To avoid discrimination, some minority members changed their answers about being a minority. We falsified the fifth paragraph of our identification documents so that we were members of the dominant ethnicity. The situation in the Soviet collective was not safe for us to disclose our original ethnicity.

We are the new generation of survivors

The children of survivors were not immune to the horrors of hate. From birth we knew what hate was about. Eventually we were able to stop the splitting and move away from hate. Because of our struggles, the world does not live in complete darkness. We brought to the world the hope for the love. We were brave and were not scared to unify with our painful past. In our families the past was deeply hidden from others. The process of dealing with the past required from us a lot of strength. We restored the memories of the shocking experiences and relived the horror of the traumatic events.

Until the right time came, we were scared. We continued to be split from loved ones, our own safety, and our human rights. Our psyche was losing the ability to trust anyone, because hate was everywhere. As a result of trauma, we lived in misery. Only some of us—the members of the new generation, and only after a special meeting with love—were able to unify our psyches. Those lucky few were able to use their lives for love. When we are surrounded by love, we fly to highest level of our aspirations. We show our creativity and desire to work, to build something, to acquire professional skills, and most important, to meet a partner in love.

Lyonya was a good worker, well liked by everyone. He spent all his free time with Marinka, who helped him with his studies. After finishing high school, Marinka entered medical school, while Lyonya attended evening classes at the technology university. But most important of all, Lyonya and Marinka, who had known long ago that they could not live without each other, finally revealed the news to their parents. There were of course no objections.

The birth of their child brought happiness to all of them. The boy was named Stepan after his grandfather, partisan Stepan Luchko. The baby belonged to the new generation of love. As a new seed, our new generation had one very special quality: we were not easily intimidated and scared. The hate did not have strength to get us, and we were able to unify with love. We were heroes and got into history as the brave generation. We were not afraid, leaving the life of comfort in the Soviet collective. Many left because our life was poisoned by the lies and intimidation of the hate. No reason was strong enough to make us to stay. The new generation of the survivors were also immune to the fears of unknown, and our destiny is to be saved.

Stepan Kryvoruchko, the son of Lyonya and Marinka and a member of the new generation, was fearless and was not afraid of reliving the horror of the past. We became the fighters against the hate and changed the collective society to make it more flexible. We made a lot of public protests and endured a lot of harassment. Eventually, we wanted to leave collective, went away from the worker's paradise, and built our new reality. We were not afraid of jail, intimidation, and persecution. We did not have fears and were called "refusenicks," who were refused the exit visa from the Soviet collective. We did not want to be stigmatized as second-class citizens and carry the guilt of offenses fabricated by monsters. Our psyche preferred unification to safety, and we felt safe because we were not afraid of torture. The Soviet collective ruled by fear but was helpless against our fearlessness. Now, we are equals, unified with our history and language, with our honor and dignity, which were looted by the Soviet collective.

The war created the big split in our morals

The war, which was the extreme hate, created the big split in our morals. During the war there was always a split between the front-line heroism and criminality. After the unthinkable time when citizens were killed, tortured, raped, and robbed without any second thought and fear of justice, the morals in the collective were very low. The war split us from humanity, tenderness, consideration, care, and most important love. We had to be very strong to resist the split.

During the war women became a leading power and sacrificed everything. They lived without intimacy because their only thoughts were about supporting the fighting men. After the war many men were dead or were placed into labor camps; the motherland was suffering from the losses. Everywhere was ruin and poverty, because there were not a sufficient quantity of healthy men. The country did not have enough manpower to satisfy lonely women. The war ended, and after the atrocities and fears, we wanted to have fun. For a woman the biggest dream was to have a husband with all his extremities intact.

Men were a big commodity. One surviving man may satisfy many women, but during the war he learned to live without a woman's love. In wartime men lived in the company of other men. After the war they often drank in the company of other men and told war stories. Many men released from military service did not work because they were always drunk. At night time they did not do the much-needed man's work. When we are deprived from the most important necessities such as sex, we get angry and violent. Our morals get weaker, and we became the carriers of hate.

In the Soviet collective, a new crime was on the rise: the rape of men by women. The women hunger for sex kept a man's penis tight by rope, and did not allow him to ejaculate. In this kind of raping, a man had the ability to please a group of women but then needed hospitalization for internal damages to his penis, and after recovery he may not be able to have children. In several cities the women refused to work because there was not even one man in the area. The government placed military bases in some metropolises with only one goal: soldiers could satisfy the working women. The women lured the soldiers into their houses with drinks and good food as a payment for sex. A man could get lucky everywhere, because he was a rare commodity. Lust replaced the love, and single mothers raised children without knowing the name of the father. The ruined collective after the war was a sexual paradise for a healthy man, because there were many needy woman. The country also was filled with the abandoned and crippled, the casualties of war, but no one needed them. The number of cripples increased because many youngsters lost their extremities when playing in former battlefields, stepping on hidden explosives. Many displaced and desperate cripples from occupied territories moved to low-populated islands, because their cities and villages had been burned during the war.

Professor Kryvoruchko affirms that the members of the worker's paradise were completely insensitive to cripples, because for a long time there was a shortage in all necessities, and members were not generous enough to share anything with anyone. The misfortunate saw only struggles and misgivings; they were everywhere begging for a small change, and they brought the heartlessness and injustice of war to the cities that were miraculously spared from physical destruction. They brought misery and qualms and carried a split from the love of the survived land. They were just ordinary casualties of the patriotic war.

Someone ordinary was called an anti-hero

After the war the stereotype of the anti-hero was someone average who did very ordinary things and was unimpressive. The anti-hero would not say to everyone that he was the bravest and stormed enemy citadels. Every day he went to his ordinary and unattractive job, which had no glory. Instead the heroic characters were the too many drunk heroes reveling in their fabulous stories. They told so many extraordinary things that anything ordinary was not popular. The anti-hero was a family man who did not want to fight for glory and who cherished the stability. In the Soviet collective those feelings were shameful. The anti-hero was a carrier of reprehensible feelings, only because he did not want to spread any lies. His aspiration was to raise his family in comfort and to be a good provider.

The collective had a skeptical view on the desires of the family man and projected him in the media as unattractive, because he did not make any sacrifices. It projected as shameful that a man only loved a woman and raised his children. In order to unify with the ordinary, family men needed to pay a heavy price by splitting from the attractive stereotype of the hero. Many members of the Soviet collective pretended to be heroes, and as a result so many youngsters had a desire to be one. The stereotype of the hero was someone extraordinary who had enormous patriotic feelings and risked his life for the collective. The appearance as a hero was flamboyant and extravagant, and the most important quality for a hero was winning—the price did not matter. Definitely he did not look ordinary. The members of the Soviet collective had to have a lot of guts to embrace the ordinary. Nevertheless, many ordinary people provided the groundwork for a country to move ahead.

Professor Kryvoruchko wanted to unify with the image of a family man, the same as Grandfather Alexander did. His desires came from the deepness of a big heart, and he was a part of the universal love. He believed that to find a soul mate was the most important task of his life.

The Kryvoruchko family was physically well and happy. They were glad to be alive and delighted in the fact that they had found each other. They were careful enough, did not criticize the government, and avoided any repulsive feelings. They understood that they could appreciate soul mates only in love. They asserted the self to be successful in love and knew that they could not recognize love in the abhorrence. They were grateful for someone special in their lives and did some groundwork to get in touch with the love in their hearts. With a solid identity, it is much easier for us to be in harmony with the self; we do not have any disturbing turbulence inside and feel good about our choices. When we are rigidly fragmented and split, love is a challenging task.

We can see somebody every day and do not know that this is our soul mate. To meet a soul mate is an arduous task. We see with our eyes, but we meet with our soul. The sad fact is that we can meet our soul mates when it is too late and they are not available, so we cannot express our love. For anti-heroes the ordinary desire to find love became an extraordinary one. The achievement of manhood was to meet the match, start a family, and establish the self as a family man.

The cover-up of secrets

Our secrets, and the efforts to cover them up, create mistrust and suspicion, and our secrets are part of the splitting force. Maintaining secrets is a pure splitting, because it creates inside our psyche a lot of fears, anger, and resentment. In order to keep a secret, we split from many of our fragments, and as result we reject a big part of ourselves. In many instances the fragments from which we are splitting need our protection and help, but instead we dump them. We hide from our consciousness the part of ourselves that is most vulnerable and fragile; as a result we pretend and want to appear to the world like we are not who we are. The secret also splits us from others because the process of keeping a secret is very demanding. We need to protect our secrets, and because we are afraid to reveal them, we are not frank with others.

The secret may be our own or a family secret. The family secret puts a lot of responsibility on all family members. Because of secrets, the aged members get tired from the constant altercation and just want to enjoy steadiness and comfort. The secrets of the older generation are preserved by the youngsters and bring a lot of clouds over the supposedly bright childhood. Despite family secrets, the young Professor Kryvoruchko had a good childhood because he was a child of love. As he grew older, he became a happy man who was proud of the self. His love force got stronger and brought him to the universal circle of love; he was an addition to the cosmic goodness. Unfortunately he had a big secret and needed to pretend. If at one point in his life he did not stop to pretend, his psyche may not unify. He had a long way to establish his identity as a solid one, and one day he needed to open up about his family secret. This secret and need to cover damaged his psyche and caused a big split, but he brought it to an end.

Unlike the older generation, who wanted peace and stability, the new generation had distinctive ideas. The youngsters created very challenging goals and did not want any ghosts in their closets. The fight to achieve those goals required a lot of uncomfortable movements and changes to the existing structure of their psyche.

The split between external and internal

The split between internal feelings and external appearance cause a life of misery. It is an old controversy between forms and essence, and it is about the split inside and the cover-up outside. We pretend to cover up our internal split, and our fragmented identity causes a lot of dissatisfaction and resentment. Our ethical fragments are united against the one that we considering weak, dishonest, and conforming. When our negative feelings are strong and we are dissatisfied, we are against the fragment, which is a conformist. We feel split in all our diverse manners of expression. Our mind organizes the unique combinations of splitting sizes. When we feel content, we are against the rebel who is not happy. The split in our psyche may be against the rebel or conformist, and it provides us with diverse responses.

When we display the presence of a split in visual form, we avoid eye contact, evade conversations, project uneasiness of being in public places, and feel a challenge in participating in activities. The splitting in audio and kinesthetic styles can be seen in the avoidance of conversations, uncommon pitches of voice, tightness, and general anxiety.

In St. Petersburg the young Stepan Kryvoruchko was returning home on a warm spring day. His school uniform looked neat. and he was an excellent student and had many friends. He was involved in helping fellow students who were unable to keep up with their schoolwork, and he had confrontations with delinquents who were unwilling to wear appropriate attire to the school. Such students appeared at school wearing striped jackets, bell-bottom trousers, and platform shoes. Schoolwork was of no interest to them—their main concern was the impression that they made on the girls. Stepan also owned some fashionable items, and he bought his shoes at the government store, with platforms added by a private shoemaker. He had Italian shoes but did not see a reason to show off at school.

The girls in his class noticed him anyway. He did not have any difficulty in finding a girlfriend, but he felt that it was not yet time for that. Meanwhile, his spent his time fencing, a sport in which he excelled, and he could perhaps become a champion. Nevertheless, he was not a happy child. In his psyche the split was on diverse modalities and was internal and external. On the outside he was splitting from the rebellion fragment and conforming to his surroundings. In the inside split, he was a rebel. His psyche needed pretending and sided with conformity, because the unification with rebellion probably could put him in the danger. In the meantime, the process of covering up the split drained a lot of his energy and could be a reason for his emotional turmoil. The one split in his psyche caused the other. In his exterior, to cover splitting from the rebellion fragments, he emerged as an ordinary individual who conformed to the norms of the surrounding. In his interior the splitting between a conformist and a rebel produced feelings of misery and anger.

On the eve of his sixteenth birthday, he was beset by anxiety. He was about to become the bearer of his own identification card, where he needed to put his ethnicity. Any carelessly spoken word could upset him; he was especially miserable during the "current affairs" discussions at school. Although he felt quite comfortable when the discussion centered on American imperialism, any mentioning of Israeli aggression and of Zionist racism made him shudder. His split was triggered by audio stimulations, which were the current affairs discussions. The split had something to do with the belief and general position of the collective government, which for many years was anti-Zionist; in the eyes of collective, the Zionist movement looked very unattractive. The condemnation of this movement by ordinary citizens was a sign of devotion to the collective.

When, as members of soviet collective, we felt good about the Jewish state, we also had feelings that we were betraying our beloved collective, because we embraced a structure that was, in the opinion of the collective, was ugly and inhuman. The official logic was intolerant about it. The collective did not allow us any deviation from an approved directive. If we loved something that in the opinion of the state was ugly, then the conclusion was that we were in danger of being perverts and possibly retarded. To confirm with the official directive, we learned to restrict our appearances and covered our internal turmoil.

We cannot get rid of the fragment in our psyche

It does not matter how hard we try, we will not get rid of the rebellious fragments in our psyche. We are not able to run away from the self. If we do not have peace within, we might not find it outside. The split can catch us everywhere, even in dreamland. Our desire to run away from one of our fragments can possibility destroy our identity by creating disassociation and splits between other fragments. The fragment is ugly and makes us feel ashamed. Nevertheless, we put a lot of energy into the hope that we are capable of getting rid of it. When we understand that it is impossible, we protect our secret about having a hidden fragment. We keep our secret from others, even at the expense of our happiness. When we do not have strength to do it anymore, then it is time to deal with the secret, otherwise we will be powerless from keeping it inside.

Our identity has a hole, and in order to become solid, we need to patch it. We do this by having a dialogue with a fragment that we were hiding. The world lives through big changes, but still for every lowlife the Jews were scapegoats. Instead of calling the Jews by dirty names, they called us Zionists. To be sure that no one would defend Jews in the Soviet collective, ideologists made up stories of Jewish cowardliness and equated Zionism to fascism. Many people did not feel safe admitting they were Jewish; after the Holocaust, no one wanted to be a martyr.

Some changed their ethnicity on identification documents. They also knew that in the Soviet collective, any discussion defending Jews and Israel would bring only troubles. If some snitch reported to administration that someone were defending Jews, that person could lose his job and other privileges, and would be questioned by the Department of Security. Cruel people would say, "If you love Jews so much, why do you stay in our land? Go to your Palestine because otherwise we'll take a whip and will throw you out from our Motherland." In the worker's paradise during Stepan growing up, everyone had the power to slur Jews, put them down, and not be afraid of any consequences.

The scams and drunks yelled insults on the streets, and when they were offended, they'd call others a Jew. This appeared to be one of the biggest insults and caused fights. Definitely the person who was called a Jew was insulted. The police never stopped any mudslinging and verbal abuse related to Jews. In the Soviet collective the ethnic hater was skillfully promoted. It was no secret that Jews in the collective felt as second-class citizens, and in the presence of the majority opinion they often acted cowardly. It was very seldom that we would declare ourselves a Jew, and we avoided it if possible. It was like confessing to being a thief. Many of us hid it as a deep secret.

Professor Kryvoruchko confirmed that the crucial point was to get in touch with his fragments, acquire a unifying psyche, and feel good about the self. When he was young, he did not believe in the rumors and lies. He lived a double life and was not proud. On the surface he was a very handsome, bright member of a youth political organization, but inside he was overwhelmed with doubts. Legally in identification documents he belonged to the dominant ethnicity, and so he did not go through any major humiliations. He had a bright future in the collective if he would be able to forget about his roots—although if he did it, he could be involved in the process of a bigger splitting. He would have to give up any hope of having a solid identity. From any perspective, if he complied, he always would have a fragmented identity, because it was not possible to get rid of one of his fragments, which was also a very well-guarded secret.

The fragments are hidden in a closet

Fragments which kept in a corner of our minds strive to get out and create painful feelings in our psyche. Unification sometimes is not possible, and when we resist it, we are just torturing the self. The fragment that is our deepest secret creates a big discomfort, like a blister on our skin, and it does not give us a chance to enjoy life. Perhaps the reason is that a time is coming when this fragment is supposed to come out from the closet.

Similarly, the fragments of the victims of atrocities of the war were crying for action. Because the fragments of their dead relatives pushed out from closets, the thousands of "refusenicks" were obsessed with the goal of leaving the collective. In many instances the push was beyond their conscious awareness.

This situation is comparable with the turmoil that the childless woman has in her psyche, when she gets to the limit of her childbearing time. At this particular time, the fragment of an unborn child becomes active and pushed the psyche for action. Some childless women want a child, and without one they perhaps may not assert the self as a whole individual with a solid identity. They will always suffer from a split from the fragment of motherhood. This fragment may perhaps be on an audio, visual, kinesthetic, or olfactory sensor. The pain of split from motherhood and an unaccomplished life may be triggered by the look of someone else's child, the voice of a child, a hug from a child, or the smell of a child.

In the same way, the thousands of people that were on the streets when the Berlin Wall fell were pushed out by the liberated fragments. The fragments were the images of loved fragments that wanted to be free from the closet. There are moments that are very significant for the rest of our life. Stepan was in a critical moment of making an important decision. This time in his life was crucial because it set up a mission for the later time. He tolerantly waited for the right time, but otherwise his future was looking bright. He was very competitive and could expect prizes in fencing, but he was burdened at the same time by thoughts that robbed him of peace of mind.

Who was he? Why were his father and grandfather, both Jews, registered in their passports as members of the dominant ethnicity? Why were his Jewish acquaintances embarrassed when they were asked about their ethnicity? From where did all these wartime stories about the cowardliness of Jews come? What was the origin of these anti-Jewish jokes that depicted Jews as greedy? Why was a monument mark not set yet in the place where his grandmother, Riva, and Lizochka were murdered?

Stepan's grandfather, who had Ukrainian ethnicity, had been honored with a monument as a hero partisan, and everyone respected his memory. The school where his grandfather had taught now bore his name, but the martyrs of Baby Yar remained unmentioned, as if nothing had happened. His grandfather had been a partisan and died in military duty, but all of those massacred at Baby Yar were civilians, and their only crime was that they were part of the Jewish race. The memory of the Holocaust victims seemed to be blotted out deliberately by all the possible means. Stepan felt that the memory of the innocent who perished by the hands of monsters were as important as the memory of heroes. The thought of this injustice and the ardent wish to rectify it led the young man to take the following step: he would let the monument to his natural grandmother, Riva, and his aunt, Lisochka, who died as a baby, be erected through his decision to register as a Jew. Let the plant that was burned and stepped upon take new roots in his family.

Stepan told his intentions to a pragmatic man. His grandfather, Alexander, was not at all enthusiastic. "What do you need it for, my grandchild? Think of your future! You won't be accepted into the university or be able to go abroad with your fencing team, and what if there is suddenly another pogrom epidemic? I remember in 1953 in the Soviet collective during the Jewish doctors' trials: doctors were accused of poisoning patients, and mobs broke neighbors' windows. Who knows what might happen now and later. And what kind of Jew are you, if you have a Gentile mother? You don't know your language, history, and religion. I understand that many youngsters are facing such contradictions, but you technically are not a Jew. By education and upbringing, you are a bearer of the culture that belongs to the dominant ethnicity. You do not understand how lucky you are that you are not a Jew. Many Jewish youngsters are being held back because of their ethnic background. They are not permitted to be acquainted with their own culture. Many are ready to renounce their Jewish origin and disappear within the collective. I honestly believe that it is very difficult and unsafe to be a Jew. In the Soviet collective, never was there any basis for a spiritual and cultural revival of the Jews."

But Stepan remained adamant in his decision. When he brought his application to the identification card office, the woman in charge gave him a surprised look: "You state under the heading of ethnicity that you are a Jew. We cannot register you as Jew because according to your birth certificate, both your parents are of the dominant ethnicity."

"But the constitution of the Soviet collective gives every citizen the right to choose his ethnicity!"

"I cannot help you; I have my orders. If one of your parents were Jewish, then by all means …"

Stepan's survivor skills were a hereditary quality. He did survive the split and lived through the moment of unification with his inherited past. He had endured a lot of psychological pain until he let his secret out of the closet.

The rules of survival change us

The rules of survival change us because when we are splitting, we are reaching a limit. We split from the traditional rule of survival, and when we are in danger, we run away by cutting the losses. Our psyche splits when we do not have the opportunity to follow a map, genetically designed for us to reach a solid identity. In moments of menace, this map is scratched out. Our psyche is flexible, and under pressure we perhaps may abandon our identity, which is not needed for survival. In moments of danger we can become something else; to survive we change our psyche. We get diverse functions and make adjustments to an uncommon morality. When we need to survive, our universal translator stops the regular translation of the visual, audio, kinesthetic, and olfactory stimulations to common logic. Because we are splitting from previous frames of reference to facilitate survival, our psyche allows us to split from the obvious and create new meanings. During survival we are not concerned with losing our solid identity, because our goal is to salvage whatever is possible.

Many families survived the physical extermination and cared more about surviving than about their solid identity. Survival for them was the most important goal, and to be a survivor became their identity. They were ready to trade off a lot of their beliefs to survive.

Professor Kryvoruchko stated that in the collective, we, the new generation of the survivors, did not have a goal of physical survival because no one threatened us with a physical extermination, but our identity, which was inherited from previous generations, was on the verge of dying. The systematic pressure on us from the collective to give up our birth identity created a lot of resistance. The collective was involved in the ideological assassination of our unique ethnical awakening. Our rules of survival did change when our splitting reached a dangerous level. The collective never accepted us as equals, and the worker's paradise always undermined our indisputable achievements. We were unable to learn our language, our history, and our heroes. To survive in the collective, we were forced to split from our identity and to become an ugly hybrid, because culturally we had one face, but our IDs told something else. Eventually the continuous split in our psyche reached the limit of our tolerance, and we did not want to compromise the self any more.

The Muslim soldiers in the Red Army were forced to eat pork. The army did not want to carry any burden of respecting special dietary needs. Some Muslim boys h preferred to commit suicide than eat pork. The Jewish boys were supposed to be Kosher, but after years of slaughter in the Holocaust, they would eat pork. Inside, we had a deep resentment of the Soviet army's inconsideration. We probably did not say anything out loud against the draconian rules because we were registered as a part of the dominant ethnicity. Our silence created a lot of tension inside. As victims of the splitting, we wanted to be invisible and were hiding in the closets. Meanwhile, the majority ethnicity was not able to understand that we may possibly have resentment and did not wanted the pork-based foods. They were overconfident and full of pride by believing that we loved their lard, which they proclaimed was the best in the world. They were certain that we were looking for a chance to grab all their grease. They were not concerned with the feelings of guilt after Muslim soldiers committed suicide. They honestly believed in only one explanation: "Why a soldier kill himself for that? He was just a crazy person." Our need for unification was replaced by splitting to placate the big brother. In the collective the dialogue with minorities never started, and this was one of the reasons why we changed the rules of splitting: we did not want it anymore. The system finally fell apart, and the conflict became visible. We did not want to be the victims, and we got out from the closed and made a lot of noise.

The meeting happens when we are ready to recognize it

The meeting can only happen in due time, when we are ready to recognize it. To look for a meeting, we need an aspiration to have it. If we do not want it and are not able to appreciate it, that means that we will miss it and will continue with the split. We possibly do not have any ability at that same time to have a dialogue. Splitting and unification are complementary and cannot possibly exist independently—it is like day and night, which are impossible to have together. In the daytime we reach out to the world, but as the night comes, we crawl back to our burrows. It is not forbidden to dream about the light during the night, but our dreams do not always come true. We possibly dream about dialogue, but we also understand that dialogue requires two sides—otherwise it is a monologue. Dialogue requires openness, understanding, and compassion. Unfortunately, our situation in a collective was not good not only for a dialogue, but it was not appropriate even for negotiations. Our negotiations required the willingness of both sides to have an agreement. The light and dark perhaps were not agreed because they never met. The time of confrontation is when one side, by brutal force, gets rid of its opponents without any attempt to mediate.

Manipulation, when others are playing with our mind probably, is threatening and cunning. We are not able to negotiate with manipulators because they do not accept us as equal partners and would not respect any agreements. It would be foolish for us to start negotiations and open the self to destruction. To negotiate with the other side, first we need to have an atmosphere of negotiation. Before any negotiations we meet our fragments. The best situation for a meeting is in an atmosphere of being strong and ready to face responsibility. When we meet with the self, we do not have any place to hide from our real self, and we cannot pretend that nothing happened.

Stepan Kryvoruchko knew how to control his emotions. He also understood that by showing of his real feelings, he may probably jeopardize the well=being of his family. He wanted a dialogue, but at this time it was impossible to have a meeting and dialogue outside of his psyche. He would get an identification card that did not revealing his identity. Even thought he felt like shouting at the ID clerk, "My father is a Jew," he remained quiet because he did not want to ruin his father's career as a decorated partisan heading a department in an arms plant. If it was discovered that his father had given false information and had hidden his real origins, there would not be an end to his troubles, and he would probably be fired.

"I was only joking," Stepan said quietly.

"Some sense of humor you have, my friend," the clerk replied. "You do not understand, young man, what a blessing it is to belong to the founding nation. I suppose many Jews would be happy to register as a dominant ethnicity, if only we would allow it."

Stepan was not convinced by this declaration. "I shall be a Jew, just the same," Stepan said to the self as he left the identification card office. "There will be a time and place where I will freely call myself a Jew, and no one will be offended. I will leave this country, and I will do it not because of money or commodities. I will look for a place where I feel safe and where I will not need to lie." In other words, Stepan promised the self to resist splitting and to look forward for unification. To unify his identity, he needed to meet some conditions. He also needed to find a safe place where he was able to be proud of his identity. He started looking for a safe place.

When he found it, he needed to be sure that it was the right place for him, and then he had to overcome the obstacles on the way to reaching this place.

The laws of splitting and unification are universal

The laws of splitting and unification are universal, and they affect countries in the same way as they affect individuals. There are some organizations that are always in the direction of the splitting, even when they completely change the way they operate. After the war the Soviet collective steadily moved in the direction of splitting, and eventually this trend ended with a big crash. The collective missed plenty of the signs and ignored the need for internal dialogue. The worker's paradise was cautioned by many signs that the big crash was coming. The structure of the Soviet collective itself was involved in the splitting. The power structures manipulated the people, and without any shame they took from us everything they could. Taking wealth from one of the segments of society and redistributing it to another is part of the collective mentality. During this reign, the collective government took from us our property, hopes, and lives, our land and possessions. Throughout the period of industrialization, the collective arrested us and sent us to slave labor camps or the Gulag. The idea of taking from us and not giving back continued after the fall of the Berlin Wall. Grabbing wealth from the oligarch was on everyone's mind. The rich were stereotyped, and the concept of taking wealth from the rich and redistributing to the poor was very appealing.

Limiting human rights by taking away from the population the right to have possessions was very tempting for powerful leaders. To suppress the guilt of doing it, ideologists came up with a lot of moralistic excuses. Generally the idea of giving something to others was not as attractive as an idea of receiving it; philanthropy was not in favor. The reality was that one took something that in the first place did not belong to him, but somehow that person felt entitled to have it. The idea of receiving something without deserving it and without putting in an effort was a mentality of the dependent and antisocial, and lately the attitude spread throughout the main population. It became very popular all over the world but was exceptionally widespread was in the Soviet collective. The members of the collective were not motivated to produce because they were not used to having honest reimbursement for their efforts, and they did not want to take any risks. By working as entrepreneurs, they did not have any guarantee that they would ever enjoy the fruits of their labor. They did not take risks themselves, but they also had a strong resentment toward anyone who had the guts to risk.

Normally the ordinary person was motivated by an opportunity to get up to a new social economical level, but in the collective the richness was a shame. In the worker's paradise our wealth was usually not very attractive and was scary, because in many minds it was associated with crime, blood, and treachery. Productivity was compromised by association with the forced labor. The healthy part of society may generate a lot of wealth, but the people did not want to be ostracized for being involved in the murky financial transactions and for being associated with exploitation. It was a dead cycle: without entrepreneurs, the industry did not produce and did not increase the nation's growth, but population were not getting richer. It was beginning of the end of the worker's paradise.

The redistribution of wealth never worked, because the poor did not become rich from grabbing handouts. In fact it was quite the opposite: by keeping the oligarch respectable, the smart society showed to others the examples of success and the existing opportunities of becoming victorious. The goal of the powerful was to motivate members to increase efficiency and to broaden the wealth. Only when the time was right did the wise slow down some audacious investor who had acquired too much clout, because it could disrupt the economic arrangements. Nowadays the post-soviet collective does not want to learn anything from earlier experiences and continues to dream of the redistribution of wealth. They do not understand that the timing is wrong. The witch-hunting on the oligarchs is suicidal because it slows down the economy. By taking wealth from others, no one becomes rich and no one wins. The previous lessons did not teach them anything.

The post-Soviet collective is pushing business under its control. Regrettably, the powerful are not interested in learning good things from the American past or from the shocking stories of their own history. In America the old oligarchs were not better than the ones in the post-Soviet collective, but in time, when the first thoughts were about the increase of the nation's growth, the American government wisely decided not to go after them. They closed their eyes to some misdeeds of the oligarch. The government did not punish them for financial transactions because it was more important to create a new field of opportunities. The goal was not taking money from the rich, but quite the opposite: to create more oligarchs and widen the middle class. Only swindlers were stopped. The prime directive was to revive the economy, and the government punished oligarchs mainly for violence and inappropriate behavior. The post-Soviet collective is afraid that money is corrupting. That is not right. Instead of manipulation, monetary transactions teach us the art of negotiation and respecting contracts, which is the first step in stopping splitting and opening a dialogue.

When the economy gets stronger, a business using manipulation is somehow straightened up. The law of splitting and unification predicts the improvement in relations between diverse economical groups. Because of the universality of many issues, the mutual benefits of unification are obvious.

The fragile structure of the psyche might be reinforced

The fragile structure of our psyche may be reconfigured by diverse interventions, which include the identification of our fragments and the awareness of our strengths and weaknesses. The reinforcement of our psyche's structure helps, but it is not a guarantee of our stability because our psyche is in a rearranging state. Our individual psyche displays sophisticated and atypical designs, is represented by the consistency in the organization of the psyche, and depends on distinctive, expressive modalities and the fragments' flexibility.

Our psyche is a complex construction and has diverse organizational levels and substructures. The structure is built upon genetic hereditary, environmental conditions, opportunity for growth, flexibility, and sensitivity to changes. Some psyches fall apart faster than others, when a few configurations do not produce the needed support. One of the factors that we suspect is triggering breakdowns is the unevenness of our psyche. The fixated fragments cause problems with adaptations and restructuring. The instability of our psyche causes rigid structures, and we are not able to create a strong relational bond and prevent the crash of our system. The fixated release of brain chemicals are not regulated by any adjustments and exceptions, and they are the causes of the chemical imbalance. The rigid fragments are represented by fixated combinations of the brain's chemicals, which produce non-changeable reactions on dissimilar triggers. In other words, we constantly overreact and underreact to diverse stimuli.

The psyche's structures depend on the distinctive fragments in our psyche. Some fragments are tightly attached, but some of them are loosely connected. The brain's chemicals are always underneath our feelings, representing the diverse fragments. The fixated release of brain's chemicals is opposite the brain's plasticity, when the chemicals have a fluid release and allow adjustment of the release according to need. Even short interventions, which include the identification of the fragments, may stabilize the system. The process of identifying our fragments is present during times of negotiation. We are consciously aware of which of our characteristics may be an indication of our strength in negotiations, and we use them for that purpose. Plasticity is the most crucial characteristic of our psyche's organization. Without plasticity our psyche is rigid and fixated, and our adaptability depends on plasticity, as well as the release of unique combinations and quantities of the brain's chemistry for different stimulations.

Flexible fragments have fluid amounts of combinations and quantities of brain chemicals, which allows us to have an adequate reaction to the trigger. The flexible fragments are very valuable and are the building blocks of a solid identity. The goal of restructuring is enrolling the fixated and flexible fragments in genuine dialogue. By promoting genuine dialogue between fragments, we have the strength to reconstruct the dysfunctional design, and we create an atmosphere of unification and build our solid identity.

CHAPTER IV

Meetings with The Self

We can translate our responses

We have an ability to correctly identify our responses and translate them, if needed, to a diverse, expressive modality. When our responses represent rigid fragments, they are not adaptable and are hard to express. Our goal is to identify the response that we are ready to express. The responses, which are the rigid type, are not easy to identify; to facilitate identification, we perhaps need to translate them to a more flexible modality. The rigidity and flexibility of responses may possibly be on the audio, visual, or kinesthetic expressive modalities. Our psyches do not consciously set apart the modalities by the level of their rigidity, because we express them verbally. It is very important to identify our rigid and flexible modalities, because they determine special psyche organizations.

The capacity to understand stimuli is part of our response-forming processor. To verbalize the experience, we rely on the subconscious use of a universal translator. The universal translator is an interpreter of our responses, from dissimilar modalities to verbal expressions. We all have psyche organization that includes the flexible and rigid modalities, as well as fragments on diverse modalities. Plasticity is the most important part of the psyche structure. The internal conflict causes the splitting of the psyche on rigid fragments. In other words, the psyche acts like the library of responses on distinctive stimulations: we are able distinguish from our visual, audio, and the kinesthetic modalities which one is currently domineering in our psyche. The ability to identify and correctly translate our responses to the most flexible modality is a sign of the ego's strength.

The professor of engineering responds in an alternative way compared to someone else with a different domineering modality. His identity relies on the domineering visual part of his psyche, which responds flexibly on visual stimulations. He also is an athlete and a sexually active man, with well-developed kinesthetic responses. As someone who loves to poetry, he develops audio parts s well. His audio and kinesthetic modalities produce rigid responses, and he has an ability to translate them to more flexible manners. Just like our professor of engineering, distinctive individuals have diverse styles of responses. In the perfect situation, all those expressions are harmonious and flexible, but when the identity has many internal conflicts, it falls apart on fixated fragments. The professor's sexual preferences are not part of his visual expressions that distinguish him in engineering; nevertheless they are important in his everyday interactions. It is important that the professor's choices in music, which vary from classical to electronic, create an especially nice aspect of his psyche. His behavior becomes unpredictable when his rigid fragments take over his psyche without his conscious awareness.

One story about the professor of engineering was that he was madly in love with a student in his class: a young brunette with glasses who was not a good student. She listened to the professor, and it appeared that she was completely consumed by his knowledge. The naïve professor possibly was not able to understand that a young student was playing him. Another story was that deeply in the professor's heart was an enthusiastic composer, and he dreamed that he would resign from engineering, give up all his engineering books, and pursue musical publication.

Those stories reveal that the professor's psyche is not strongly resisting attempts of takeover by the fragments on various modalities. His fragments of sexual needs are connected with a kinesthetic type of expression, his engineering skills are visual, and his dreams of music are audio. To avoid a crash, he needs to identify the rigid fragments and what type of expression they represent, and then he can translate them to a flexible style of expression. The professor's identity is built on a visual modality, and he needs to translate the audio and kinesthetic responses to visual; then he will be able to see, feel, and hear.

The damaged psyche is splitting

The psyche can be damaged by internal conflicts or by external pressure. As a result the psyche splits on fragments with diverse levels of association and disassociation. Some psyches have a loose association; the mild damage occurs as a result of splitting caused by non-hostile disagreements. Moderate damage is a result of hostile confrontations, like divorce, custody disputes, and natural death of the family members. The psyche may have severe damages that deform the whole structure; severe damage can be the result of post-traumatic stress, seeing a violent death, mental illness, and dissociations.

Damaged psyches maintain loose association between fragments. Nevertheless, those psyches are poles apart from the psyche with multiple personalities, which have several completely dissociated and dissimilar egos. The diverse egos in multiple personalities split on fragments that fight to take over the psyche.

Contrary to multiple personalities, the loosely associated fragments do not have a notion of lost time, but they too suffer from the feeling of uncertainties and confusion. When dissimilar fragments take over our psyche, they change our behavior. The sudden changes are involuntarily and without conscious decision; we are not even aware that we were the objects of the ego's changes and fragmentation. Consciously, we do not know which fragment is taking over our psyche, but we feel confusion about others in our surrounding. When we fragment, our identity is very unstable. Other people have the complex task to understand what we need and what to expect from us. We have the task to incorporate the diverse fragments to one entity and to build a stable psyche. We need to solidify our psyche in order to have stable associations.

It is very important to identify fragments that are involved in hostility and feuds. We create a big turmoil by our inability to maintain a stable identity. With an unstable identity, our task to interact with others is very tricky; because of the internal disarray, we have a hard time maintaining feeling of self-esteem and self-worth. We are unsure of who we are and how we react in distinctive situations. The unpredictability of our actions and our unexpected behavior creates feelings of fear and uncertainty. If our identity is shaky and unstable, we can be exhausted by assignment that we are not able to accomplish. A life with an underdeveloped identity is similar to the life of a caterpillar that will never become a butterfly. All his existence the caterpillar is not able to fly and does not have the forms and colors of the butterfly, which we admire. With a fragmented psyche, we do not know much about the self. We are aware that we are at the mercy of some powerful forces, and we often feel possessed. We do not know that we are dealing with the forces of splitting. Fragments with distinctive levels of association and disassociation cause our discomfort.

We might be able to correct wrong responses

Our psyche is organized in a way that we have the ability to correct wrong responses. By using the universal translator, we translate responses to dissimilar manners of expression. If our stimulations cannot produce correct responses in one form, then we use other available styles. Sometimes we correctly respond in a dissimilar mode of expression to visual, audio, and kinesthetic triggers. However, when our psyche endures the severe trauma, we cannot process the stimulations correctly. Our rigid fragments constantly act as the trauma reoccurs, we release brain chemicals that are not congruent to the stimulations, and we disassociate from events comparable in stimulation. Our psyche overreacts or produces an insufficient response. When the stimulations reach our damaged substructure, we get confused and do not feel that we understand the others. It seems that others also do not appreciate us.

After traumatic events that caused the disassociation, our psyche can split from other associations. Our fragments resemble a damaged music record, which go in a circle, plays only one tune, and is not capable of continuing with rest of the song. Our damaged fragments have limitations and cannot process stimulation in a flexible way, producing only fear and anger responses. Because the process is on a subconscious level, we are not in control of our psyche.

In reality our responses depend on the release of the brain's chemicals, which are produced and released in diverse areas of our brain. The interactions of the chemicals are on the physiological level. The dissimilar mixture of our brain chemicals creates rigid and flexible fragments. If we had a cookbook that describes the release of brain chemicals, then we could have measurements of the fixated and flexible ingredients in our brain.

To be in control of our psyche, we bring interactions of our fragments to the conscious level. By bringing the unconscious process to the conscious level, we learn about the incongruence of our responses and are aware that our heredity also plays a very important role. It seems that our genetics plays a part in our stability and in the speedy recuperation from damage. Some psyches have the ability to recuperate and regroup faster after trauma, but for others trauma is very painful and rehabilitation takes a long time. Nevertheless, our psyche has some ability to correct abnormal responses.

We have an important ability to choose the manner of responses. By connecting the stimulations to the responses, the psyche processes the information on distinctive styles. Our fragments are associated with audio, visual, or kinesthetic expressions, and in many instances, the stimulations that belong to one particular approach trigger the same type of responses. When we have kinesthetic stimulations, our reactions are kinesthetic, but when we yell and make faces, then our quick responses are visual and audio. We cannot adequately respond to the stimulations because we have the only one way of reacting to dissimilar stimulations.

Our rigid responses include facial expressions, distinctive sounds, and angry gestures. We are connected to the universal translator, and all our responses became verbal. By using the universal translator, we are able to modify our responses and make them less rigid. To achieve our goal to have a flexible response, we use our diverse styles of expression, because the psyche provides us with many comparable responses. When the stimulations trigger the flexible responses, we are in control. To correct the damaged fragment that produces a rigid response, we can replace this rigid fragment with a flexible one on a different modality by using the more comparable type of expression to produce a distinct response.

Plasticity is one of the most important characteristics

Plasticity is a very important characteristic of our psyche. The plasticity of our brain is represented by distinctive manifestations. When we look forward to changes, then the plasticity of our psyche is revealed. When we have enough plasticity to alter the biochemistry in our brain, the psyche is not rigid. The one method of analysis of the psyche is strictly physiological. We understand the difficulty of learning physiology and the paths of the brain chemicals. Without extended knowledge and sophisticated equipment, we are not able to use this method. The other method is psychological, and we can perhaps evaluate the psyche through our observation. We understand that the most important characteristic of plasticity is our mechanism to cope with stress and our desire to be successful. We analyze how to make right decisions and how to act on the pressure.

The presence of plasticity is observed when the brain successfully deals with stress, correctly assess the situation, and finds the best solution.

The characteristic of the brain that is opposite to plasticity is a precursor of rigidity. The warning of rigidity can be observed when we act paralyzed by stress and do not have the ability to find the correct solution. One of the outcomes of our trauma is inflexibility in the release of brain chemicals, which creates a chemical imbalance; the disproportional discharge of the brain's chemicals causes confusion and stress. Some of us are very thoughtful and help others with priceless advice, but we lose those qualities when we solve our own problems. This is a warning of rigidity caused by stress, which makes us act paralyzed when we face our own problems. Our life changes usually go together with stress, and we are fearful of the changes. The feelings of fearfulness are formed by the expectation of discomfort after even minor changes. Our negativity is an indicator of low adaptability and a lack of plasticity, which are triggered by anticipation of the worst.

Everyone has at least some stress. The charges for dealing with diverse life stages, deteriorating health, marriage, children, and more are often very costly. The anxiety and fears cause a splitting in our psyche, and the lack of adaptability deprives us from environmental support. Resistance to the change creates fixated fragments, causes the strenuous pressure on the brain, and prevents the release of congruent brain chemicals. Our painful sensitivity to stress is a precursor to deficiency in coping ability. Fearfulness and discomfort are indications of rigidity in the releasing of brain chemicals. The psychological side of inflexibility appears when we are reluctant to accept challenge and display abnormal behavior, such as avoidance, anger, discomfort, and irritability.

It is very important to develop plasticity of our fragments, because plasticity is a most desirable characteristic of our psyche. We assume that our plasticity on the biochemical and psychological levels is present when our brain chemistry can easily regroup and our responses are congruent to stimulations. Our plasticity is present when we feel adequate.

The level of abnormality in our responses

The abnormality of our responses may perhaps be estimated by the severity of splitting. Our psyche has a tendency for both splitting and unification. Our healthy fragments are flexible, exhibiting plasticity and having good coping skills. Our fixated fragments lack flexibility and have a tendency to split and dissociate. The groups of our fragments that together produce our fixated replies are responsible for abnormal responses. Our surrounding environmental conditions are very important to understanding our special characteristics and responses. To survive harsh conditions in a stressful environment, our psyche creates more fixated fragments. Even though all fragments have access to the information stored in the memory base, our fixated fragments avoid particular areas, and our memories are selective. Some fragments are very loosely associated and are on the verge of dissociation. Based on hereditary and environmental conditions, our psyche has distinctive levels of stress tolerance.

Our dissociated psyche has an inclination toward splitting. Extreme stress can cause complete dissociation in the psyche; the detached psyche constructs the new structure from the collection of dissociated fragments, creating its own, completely new memory base. Because it does not have any access to the original memory base, it compensates for the lack of information by fabricating dissimilar memory data and creating false memory. Our new structure, which does not have access to the former memory base, is not able to learn from previous information. We make up the fabricated life histories, which are far from our real histories. The new structure presents the fabricated memories, which are not corresponding with bits of preserved images.

The new memory contains fictitious information about our life, including age, marital status, and information about parents and children. Our fabrication is a symptom of the dissociated constructs. The damages exhibit the self in our abnormal responses. Because of the harsh environment, our psyche develops a new organizational structure, which splits from the existed construction. If our new organizational structure passes the test of reality, then our new construct becomes independent. Sometimes our dissimilar structures are aware of others, and by competing for dominance they are hostile to others. They insist that they are using real information, but they use fabricated data and have false memories. In people with multiple personalities, the brain produces a unique cocktail of chemicals for atypical structures and creates new files for memory data; access to the independent memory bases is closed or restricted. Our level of dissociation is an indication of the severity of the damage.

Our responses rely on information

Our responses rely on our ability to properly receive and translate information. Because of incorrect translations, we get inadequate reactions, and others judge us by our replies. To be valued, we need to be sure that the stimulations translate correctly and that we generate the appropriate responses. By our level of congruency between stimulations and responses, we have been graded for smartness and geniality. Unfortunately, we do not consciously know what triggered the abnormal responses. We also are not aware of the consequences when the stimulations translate in an abnormal way. Until we get into big trouble, we do not even concern ourselves with what went wrong with our responses and why others get offended. We do not know that our interpretation of stimulation might perhaps be affected by chemical imbalance, heredity, environment, faulty parenting, and psychological and organic damage. Our ability to translate received information also depends on our traditions and backgrounds; we wonder why we are always wrong and why our replies are not congruent.

If supplied with faulty translation, even a brilliant mind cannot arrive at the correct response. When we do not produce an accurate response, we feel bewildered, are uncertain about our abilities, and experience a feeling of helplessness. We get confused and are not certain that we will ever be able to arrive at the correct response. The whole stability of our identity depends on the correctness of translating stimulations. Because we produce abnormal responses, others avoid us, though we do not understand why. There are diverse reasons why we generate wrong responses. We feel the most pain when our process is correct but for some reason the stimulation is wrongly submitted. Sometimes the stimulations are damaged on intake by our perception apparatus, so already deformed stimulations are presented for translation. Our identity depends on the individual manner of the receiving and translating of the information.

Depending on the approach, our psyche is divided into several groups, where each group organizes matching fragments. The comparable responses may perhaps be on diverse manners of expression, which include visual, audio, tactile, kinesthetic, olfactory, and mixed senses. Each style triggers the release of diverse brain chemicals. Each group of fragments has unique areas in the brain for processing similar information and producing similar responses. After receiving the psychological trauma, we realize that the environment does not support our desire for unity, and our psyche falls apart and restructures the previous organizational arrangements, creating new dominant areas. Because the previous method of receiving and translating the information brought enormous stress, a victim might avoid common ways of processing information.

The victim's responses now rely on uncommon ways of receiving and decoding information. When our responses change, we need to understand the new changes. If the previous identity was built on visual responses, and we gathered information through visual stimulations, when we face a disastrous situation, our new identity may decide to abandon visual processing and focus on the audio and kinesthetic. A woman prior to a date rape attack may have wanted to impress handsome men, but after being attacked she is no longer interested in visual stimulation, and she does not use tight clothes to impress her dates anymore. Now the victim is firm in visual responses and relies more on the processing of audio stimulations for detecting expressions of compassion and tenderness instead of good looks. She observes the kinesthetic manner of the man, detecting by his posture if he has criminal intent, and she also keeps her own feelings in control.

Because our identity is based on our responses to stimulation, we bring unconscious processes to our conscious level. When we deal with incoming information, and our formation of response are on a subconscious level, we are not capable of changing our way of processing information. To avoid overreaction, underreaction, and confusion, we bring information to the conscious level. We are in control when we knowingly evaluate and translate stimulation, consciously choosing our responses.

An opportunity to grow is essential

An opportunity for growth is essential for the development of the psyche. Establishing of our identity is not an finite process and continues our entire life. In old age we are supposed to be more comfortable with our past and our old sufferings, and we expect to have peace with our internal demons. When we talk about maturity, we assume that near the end of our life, we get wiser and softer. The need for dialogue and unification is stronger as we age, because we come closer to the time when we are ready to unify with eternity. In old age we intuitively look for real meetings with loved ones. In many instances during our life, we failed the complex assignment to meet our loves. Perhaps the meeting with the loved one occurred when the loved one was very sick or perhaps could not be an equal participant. In many instances we really meet famous artists and scientists only after their death; they could not benefit from our recognition. Only if we are fortunate do we get real meetings with loved ones during our active life. If we grow up with a unified psyche, the splitting forces are not able to prevent our real meetings.

Nourishing the formation of our psyche is associated with developing plasticity of our fragments and with the atmosphere of real meetings and dialogues. Our healthy psyche successfully resists splitting and strives for unification. When our psyche is in the process of unification, then we have an opportunity to develop a solid identity. The opportunities for growth create congruency in the release of the brain's chemistry. Our fragments are the representation of released brain chemicals; when the combinations of the released brain's chemicals are congruent to stimulations, we respond according to the intensity of the stimulation. Our flexible responses can match the stimulations.

The process of unifying our psyche is not an unvarying one. Our psyches also are constantly under the attack of the forces of splitting. The fragments with fixated and suppressive responses put pressure on our psyche to stop unification and to split. The splitting can limit our opportunity for growth or may entirely block our maturation. The lack of opportunities and stresses, life in oppression, and hereditary aspects can cause fixated fragments to develop.

Fixated fragments conflict with and sabotage self-growth. Flexible fragments are responsible for building the atmosphere of unification and maturation. To avoid conflict between the fragments, we can identify similar fragments on uncommon forms of expression. We need to carefully translate the stimulants to different modes of expression and consider how the fragments on various manners of expression would respond. Depending on our needs, we can utilize both the fixated and flexible fragments. We can transfer the response from a visual fragment to audio, kinesthetic, or olfactory, and vice versa. We create the atmosphere of meeting and dialogue between our fragments on all available styles of expression, building a background of internal peace, and our identity becomes more solid during real meetings and dialogues. We have an opportunity for unification and feel good about the self and the environment around us. The opportunity for growth is essential to have a solid identity. Flexible responses are the solid parts of our psyche and keep the psyche united.

Tolerance to stress is a very important factor

Tolerance to stress levels is a very important factor in the development of a solid identity. Without tolerance our identity can easily split apart. The tolerance level is an indicator of our endurance and the presence of flexible fragments. If stress gets stronger, our psyche can give up, and our system cracks down in the situation when the stress level gets over the maximum tolerance. When our psyche falls apart, our identity shatters. Our psyche needs to survive, and it creates fixated fragments, which are narrow in their responses.

The fixated fragments are loosely attached and display the limitation of our functions, having only survival as a goal. The loss of flexibility is similar to the process of intellectual castration, when we do not have any power to generate unique ideas. Our fixated fragments are restricted and produce specific responses, perhaps not creating anything distinguishing. The fixated responses are very predictable.

The splitting is a product of the reorganization of our psyche. It can be a result of real or imagined trauma. The splitting perhaps may be an effort to adjust our psyche to different circumstances; it is an attempt to salvage part of our identity. Frequently splitting happens when the whole system is in danger of destruction. Our psyche can split to preserve our identity from complete obliteration. In a harsh environment, our identity is falling apart, but because of splitting, the psyche leaves intact a few fragments as part of the crushed identity. In other instances the reorganization by splitting is an effort to break away from our old patterns, which are unhealthy and unproductive.

The splitting actions can be very dangerous. Sometimes they are similar to hitting a fly on glass with a metal hammer. The damage from breaking the window is not compatible with the victory of chasing the fly away. We use less damaging tactics to avoid splitting and get stronger, acquiring the desired skills and changing unhealthy habits. Instead of splitting we have a dialogue and unify with the existing fragments, creating new responses. We alter the psyche without any danger to the existing system. This approach of rearranging our fragments requires some tolerance to unwanted responses. When facing unwanted responses, many psyches exhibit signs of prejudice and narrow-mindedness, which are prerequisites for splitting. However, tolerance as a response may perhaps be built through meetings and dialogue. Without tolerance our psyche is always on the verge of splitting and encounters stumbling blocks in developing a solid identity. By using tolerance we stop splitting forces and create a durable identity.

The fragmented identity represents the brain's imbalance

A fragmented identity is representative of the imbalance of the brain's chemistry. We display this manifestation of chemistry imbalance by our incongruent reactions to ordinary stimulations. When we are stressed, we produce more fixated fragments and lose the flexibility of our responses. The fixated fragments produce similar, repetitive responses on dissimilar life events. When our psyche falls apart, then our identity breaks into fixated fragments. As a result some fragments still are strongly connected, and others are loosely associated. The tight fragments represent our identity, but others are disassociated. The wholeness of our identity is closely related to the level of fragmentation and the degree of association between our fragments.

When we have a fragmented identity, we repetitively display fixated fragments, and our reactions are easy to predict. In bipolar disorder the fixated fragments with the opposite responses take over the psyche. Those fragments feud and function in opposition to each other. The actions of our fragments are similar to a new administration that comes to the power after the revolution and does everything to reverse previous rulings. The fragments in bipolar disorder take over the psyche in the sequential order and produce predictable, extreme polarities in responses.

Our fragments move by sequential order to become dominating and can be associated with a special time and schedule, though the sequence of order may be constant or random. Understanding the bipolar process is important to figure out all forces that are pushing our fragments to become domineering. Some changes affect our psyche by particular sequences, which perhaps may be time, magnetic compositions in the atmosphere, or a variety of other prompts. The change in our mood comes together with changes in our perception and attitude. The disparity is so sudden that it seems we become dissimilar even though we have the same memories and the same habits; we also modify our interpretation of past, present, and future life events.

The change of our responses is also observed when we suffer from borderline personality disorder. As borderlines, we can experience gloominess to produce stable responses. When we have mood changes, we change our attitude toward others, which becomes evident from our responses. With borderline disorder and cyclothymiacs, we have the complexity to identify sequences of behavior and triggers of mood swings. The sequences and triggers are not as evident and predictable as in bipolar disorder; They become explicable when our domineering fragments change and our confused psyche can display loose associations. With loose associations, the fixated fragments can take over our entire psyche. Our psyche exhibits reactions that are complicated to predict, and we can suddenly display unprovoked anger, hostility, suicidal feelings, and self-mutilation.

Our complete disassociation from the previous organization becomes evident when some of our fragments arrange in a new, independent structure that does not contain many shared memories with the preceding one. The disassociation of our psyche is the result of an escape from the old organization to the new and independent structure. The complete splitting happens when our previous structure is unable to keep our identity unified. In a hostile environment and with the goal of surviving, our psyche needs additional formation with the completely new memory. To deal with our disassociated personalities, we want to acknowledge our new identity and find the truth: that we do not know the self. Multiple personalities are a result of the splitting and termination of associations. To be aware of different personalities, we need to identify the changes in our structure. We do not know too much about the self and suffer from the animosity. We blame and feud with the unstable personalities that rule over us.

Loose fragments are a sign of the brain's imbalanced chemistry. By unifying our fragments, we balance our brain's chemistry and begin to understand the self. The unification of our psyche is a complex process and requires knowledge of some of our fixated fragments. Our whole psyche is built from little blocks; one fragment is only one block of our psyche. To understand the whole structure, we need to identify the building blocks in our psyche. When we deal with the entire psyche, failures in communication arise. In many instances to help the self and to be more successful in the reconstruction of psyche, we do not work on the whole psyche but only one block. It is much easier to deal with one of our fragments instead of the whole psyche. Our mental problems, addictions, pains, and difficulties can be treated more effectively when we deal with a single fragment as a substitute of the entire psyche.

Some areas of our brain are overused, but others are underdeveloped

The release of the same amount of neurotransmitters on divergent stimulants is a sign of our fixation, and our responses are rigid. Certain areas of our brain receive stimulations and then form a response, and we react to the stimulations. With a fragmented identity we keep a few areas of our brain overused; other areas are underdeveloped because of low demand. We produce quick and similar responses that are responsible for our feelings of anxiety, fears, and anger. We have tormenting reactions and become destructive without any stress-provoking conditions. In this situation our fixated fragments are activated, we are driven by feelings that represent our incongruent release of brain chemicals, and we have responses from the anxiety-producing area of our brain. The brain's areas that generate fears and anger are usually overused, but areas with anger control and stress management are underdeveloped. The congruent release of our brain's chemicals is very important.

One can characterize the process of rigidity by the release of an inadequate amount of chemicals during complicated life situations. Our fixated fragments stock our brain with rigidity and limit our brain's ability to have appropriate responses. By a level of congruency to our responses to stimuli, our psyche provides us with the analysis of our brain's condition. Chemical imbalances cause our brain to overwork in certain areas; in the mean time we do not utilize adequately the available resources in other areas. We are confused because our responses are unrelated to stimulations. Our psyche is not a simple one, and when the emotional chains break, we are left with turmoil. We do not understand where our responses came and are unable to compose ourselves.

Our responses can be visual, audio, and kinesthetic. With strange responses, our psyche provides us with explicit information: that the responses to stimulations are wrong; they are not coming from the correct part of our brain, where we expect them to be generated. In a fragmented identity the fragments are loosely allied with others and are not in agreement. Some of our fragments distort our responses instead of support us—we call those fragments the troublemakers, because they also affect our brain. We have great ideas and thoughts, but we have not benefited from our ideas and never see the development of any of our plans; those disappointments are evidence of the fragments that sabotage us. Our fragments provide views of the variety of areas in our brain. Through our fragments, we can understand what kinds of brain chemicals are released and whether they show plasticity or rigidity. When our psyche has fixated fragments, then when triggered by stimulations, our brain does not release the appropriate chemicals. The split of our psyche leads to a disproportional use of areas of the brain that released the same chemicals for unrelated stimulants.

When our fragments have plasticity, the brain properly processes stimulants and receives the correct responses, which are sent to the appropriate area of our brain.

A solid identity is characterized by the chemical process, when the brain works in balance. In the appropriate areas the brain releases the proper amount of chemicals; feelings of anxiety and anger perhaps can be appropriate. When we have a sudden and disturbing stimulation, then we delegate the response to the fragment, which releases anxiety-provoking chemicals. The stimulations disturb our balance, and the anxiety response is somehow congruent. This response is a kind of an alarm on unusual stimulations and is appropriate.

If we become anxious without any anxiety-provoking stimulations, however, we should be concerned about our reaction. It is an indication that our brain overuses the areas that are associated with anxiety, and our fragments unnecessarily trigger anxiety responses. In an anxiety-driven psyche the areas of the brain that provide the anxiety responses are overused, and the areas where relaxation responses are produced have been underdeveloped.

Rebellious and vicious fragments are the main point of self-analysis

The main point of self-analysis is to identify our rebellious and vicious fragments and bring them to our conscious awareness. We must not overlook our troublemaker fragments, which sabotage all our efforts to unify and to be happy. When we analyze our psyche, we need to be sure that we clearly see these fragments; otherwise our analysis may be misleading. Our obscure life and unstable environment affect the normal development of our psyche. The stressful changes during our life span can cause splits in our psyche; these changes include tragic losses combined, unpleasant life experiences, and the development of rebellious fragments.

The rebellious fragments are usually in confrontation with the dominant fragments. In many instances only after a long self-analysis do we have information to identify our rebellious fragments, which probably will revolt against our existing structure. Our rebellious fragments are not the multiple and dissociated one—they are just loosely associated fragments of the same psyche, and they generate conflict within the main structure. Our rebellious fragments are unstable and create unexpected disturbances. Because of our unstable psychological structure, we feel stressed and confused, and we need effort to understand the self. Our unstable psyche's configuration lowers our self-esteem and is an obstacle in our desire to achieve our goals. Note that our brain stores the information like rings on a tree stump, which shows the presence of hardships during the life of the tree.

The fragments, which correspond to stressful times, take over our psyche and become our dominant fragments. The other fragments are semi-independent blocks of our fragmented psyche, and they have the capacity to align and separate from our dominating fragments and become rebellious. Depending on our ability to process information and communicate the right messages, either we are in agreement or our life is in turmoil. In pathological psyches the domineering fragment represents the abnormal responses of anger, paranoia, or delusion. In the meantime, the dysfunctional fragment skillfully manipulates the other fragments with threats and intimidations, and it builds a deranged identity. In this situation the rebellious fragment can be helpful by fighting the viciousness of a dominant configuration. There are instances when an insane fragment makes reasonable decisions. Because of the rebellious parts, our unstable identity generates the appropriate responses. To our surroundings, our abnormality can be very confusing.

Our rebellious fragments fight the dominant structure and help the psyche to have appropriate responses. However, there are times when the rebellious fragment sabotages the appropriate responses. The key point of self-analysis is to recognize the troublemakers, the unruly or brutal fragments, and to transfer them to the conscious. Several our fragments probably are in agreement, are well integrated and solid, but others can be in confrontation and be splitting. With few exceptions our identity is maintained by domineering parts of our psyche. Our dominant fragments are the mirror that projects our identity to outsiders. With appropriate forms of communication, we can present a cohesive identity.

We use rebellious fragments to resist the power of the disordered, domineering structure because we have the hurdle of dealing with mental problems. We may assume that we interact with the whole psyche of the mentally disordered, but it is not exactly true. We are in contact only with one area of the psyche, interacting with only one fragment. We leave the other fragments, which maybe rebellious, out of our view. When we deal with attention deficit, our fragments sabotage the self. We are not sure if attention deficit is associated with disturbed audio, video, kinesthetic, olfactory, or rebellious responses to stimulation. When we interact with the kinesthetic-based fragment, we need to be sure that we are not ignoring the audio- and visual-based fragments, which have the same problem. It is important that we are aware of our rebellious fragments, because they may use our inattentiveness to fight the dominant fragments. Only the identification of kinesthetic fragments, together with the audio, visual, and rebellious, may bring to conscious awareness the full picture of the mental disorder.

Releasing a variety of chemicals

The diverse regions of our brain produce variations in chemicals. Behind the fragments are the numerous areas of the brain, which like a factory produce the brain's chemicals and mix them in a variety of combinations. The response to stimulation is affected by the amounts and the ingredients of our brain's chemicals. When our responses are driven by anxiety and interprets all stimuli as anxiety provoking, the brain uses chemicals that align with our kinesthetic sensors.

Through different combination of brain chemicals, our feelings can be characterized by worries and physical discomfort, resembling heart attacks and including shortness of breath and a choking sensation. The symptoms might include increased heart palpitations, a problem with vision where static objects appear to be moving, dizziness, a lack of coordination, a sensitivity to the sounds, an expectation of catastrophe, exaggeration, and overreaction to insignificant stimuli.

. The audio and visual areas of the brain can interpret information as mood suppressors. Some of our fragments are associated with traumatic stress and use combinations of the brain's chemicals that were derived from visual, audio, and kinesthetic areas. The fragments, which exhibit a lack of control over the stimulations, offer only a few fixated responses. In some instances our need for survival command our psyche, splitting us and making more fragments. Our surviving fragments can be a guard who does not trust anyone and constantly checks if a traumatic event can reoccur.

Unfortunately, the alarm is often falsely activated. Without a threat we did not need to prepare for stress. Nevertheless, our fragmented identity provides fixated responses like we are in danger. The destinations of the fixated fragments were set long time ago; by using the same brain areas, we pick up the chemicals to a response for danger. Our domineering fragments interpret the incoming stimulations as danger and prepare for intrusion. We transport the stimuli to the brain area where the fixated responses form. When our flexible fragments represent the use of the chemicals from diverse areas, unfortunately the fixated fragments restrict them, and our flexible responses do not form. In a fragmented psyche the interpretation of atypical events depends on the fragment that dominates at that particular time. The restricted, fixated responses are usually complicated but also may be simple.

When our psyche produces a mainly kinesthetic response, it is connected with obsessive compulsive behavior, which uses chemicals released by kinesthetic, audio, visual, and some hormonal areas. The fragments, which are allied with paranoia, are driven by the brain's chemicals from the visual, audio, and kinesthetic areas. The fragment associated with schizophrenia uses a cocktail of the brain's chemicals from hormonal, audio, visual, and kinesthetic areas of the brain; the various areas produce diverse chemicals. The fragment of schizophrenia is restricted to the area of the brain that produces delusion, and it produces restricted chemicals. The solid psyche has a flexible structure, has easy access to any diverse areas of the brain, and has plasticity in releasing chemicals that arrive from any area of the brain and accurately matching the stimulations. The solid identity has the ability to generate flexible responses.

Remembering the diverse amounts and ingredients

Our fragments trigger the release of the brain chemicals and have the ability to remember distinctive amounts of the ingredients and where to pick them up again. They also remember where certain chemicals are detected. Our fixated fragments repeat the same emotions because they are unable to change routes to the area where the responses formed. Our fixated fragments memorize the incongruent amounts and generate a release of excessive or inadequate chemicals. They have restricted access to the area and can get only a particular amount of chemicals.

In contrast, our flexible fragments get chemicals congruent with the stimulation. They use the flexible recipes of our brain's cocktails and produce adequate responses. The flexible fragments have access to many areas of the brain and use chemicals in the accordance with the situation. The fixated fragment can release an excessive amount of chemicals, which is associated with an increase in heart rate and can be the result of audio, video, and kinesthetic stimulation. The word "police" is an audio stimulation and is a package that includes audio, visual, and kinesthetic pictures of perceived brutality. When anyone yells this word, the brain releases a lot of chemicals and triggers fixated responses, which are responsible for increasing heart rate, tightness of muscles, and the urge to hide. The inadequate amounts of chemicals from the same areas of our brain are associated with feeling of tiredness, numbness of the extremities, and psychosomatic pain. If we suffer from dissociated disorder, then when the psyche splits into an atypical structure, the connections between stimulations and responses are transferred inaccurately because in the new, independent structure, the areas of the brain activate differently.

The new formations change the previous combinations of chemicals. Fragments from the new structures create new cocktails, which produce unusual feelings and thoughts. Even when they access the same areas of audio, visual, and kinesthetic processors, they release various combinations of chemicals. In the range of structures, the fragments learn to respond to the same stimuli with new emotions. They use new amounts in combinations, and we have new responses to the situation. Our new formation may have a fixated or flexible release of brain chemicals.

The particular combination of brain chemicals

Our reaction to stimulation corresponds to a particular combination of brain chemicals. We create a fragment when the combination of chemicals corresponds to a particular type of response. When our identity is fragmented, we are overwhelmed with emotions that are incongruent with the stimulation; our brain releases a combination with an excessive or inadequate amount of chemicals. Behind our reaction is a domineering fragment that monitors the release of specific combinations of chemicals. Our psyche remembers how many chemicals were released during the painful stimulation. After the trauma, even when it is not needed, our fragments continue to provide traumatic responses for other events that are completely unrelated to the trauma; the process is similar to the sudden activation of an alarm system without any intruder. In our psyche, we also have fragments that trigger unneeded responses like the false alarm does.

We may proceed in the same way as we deal with falsely activated security: we shut down the alarm and reprogram the security system. By reversing our fragments' trend from splitting to unification, we can change our responses. Our fragments are activated by fixated combinations of brain chemicals, but they become more flexible after our intervention. Our goal is to recalibrate our psyche and shut down the false alarm. When we are not changing our responses, our psyche is possibly stocked with fragments, and we have a false alarm. Our fixated fragments create the struggle and release fixated combinations of chemicals. Those settled combinations get released again and again, until we need move away from the area affected by trauma.

The fixated fragments are rigid and remember the distinctive combination of brain chemicals. In contrast, the flexible fragments can adjust the combinations according to the current stimulation, creating different modes of expression. When an area of the brain is in a dissimilar form of expression and produces congruent responses, then it is probably not affected by a traumatic event. Those flexible responses can be activated by the audio, visual, or kinesthetic stimulations. We search our psyche for flexible fragments that produce chemicals congruent with the stimulation. We translate the incoming stimulations to our unaffected ways of expression and release the brain's chemicals that match the situation.

The goal of solidifying our identity

The goal of solidifying our identity is the same as achieving chemical balance in our brain. The process is based on the concept of the unification of our fragments, and the combinations of the brain's chemicals are the driving force behind our feeling and emotions. Because we cannot yet permanently change our psyche's organization by just prescribing medication, we must change the damaged system with psychological means. In dealing with fragments instead of the brain's chemicals, we can slightly touch the physiological base and the whole chemical system, and introduce the more simple explanation of the chemical imbalance. We are not ready to discuss the complicated physiological specifics because it is very complicated to get a list of the chemicals involved in each response. We deal with physiological processes through psychological analysis and identify what caused the fragmentation and how we can use our intelligence in this process of solidifying our psyche. By using psychological interventions we give the psyche the opportunity to use our insides to reorganize the self. We change the regulatory system. In our view the brain is a combination of many fragments. We do not deal with our brain as a monolith structure; we deal only with the brain's little parts. Instead of direct control by chemicals, we introduce the feedback approach from various areas of the brain. In this approach we promote change from within.

Hopefully by working with psychological means, we alter the chemical combinations and achieve adjustment in the chemical processes. By reorganizing our fragments, the psyche changes the unwanted and destructive pattern. The fragments are the psychological representation of the physiological processes, and by bringing the chemical processing to the conscious level through the concept of fragmentation, we get conscious control of the release of the brain's chemicals. We can achieve the desired chemical balance by using psychological interventions and by analyzing the relationships between the fragments, which lets us become aware of the appropriateness of our responses. Our goal is to build a solid identity and achieve chemical balance.

When the psyche is solid, we react properly to any stimulation, and the brain releases chemicals appropriate to the event. The solid structure of the psyche depends on the chemical processes in distinctive areas of the brain, which provide us with the congruent responses. It is similar to the construction of a building, where all areas of construction are very important: if built accurately, they are the complete representation of the design. Our responses are products of the brain's stimulations and are not as visible as a construction site. When our identity is fragmented, the chemical structure of the psyche is unstable and displays the lack of interaction between loosely associated fragments. By encouraging interaction, we unify the fragmented psyche and correct inappropriate responses. When the fragments are properly identified and develop a common goal, then the interactions start. By unifying the various fragments in the solid entity, we achieve a balance of brain chemistry.

The psyche and computers

The psyche's organization of responses is similar to a computer program. The stimulants follow the already established routes, reaching the area of our brain where responses are formed. Another way of presenting our responses are through combinations of chemicals. Our brain remembers the types of the chemicals in the combinations and knows how much can be released for the particular stimulations. It uses the already created database and retrieves the necessary information before combining the existing information with incoming stimulation. The brain calculates the needed amounts of the chemicals, releases them, groups them together in combinations, and stores updated information in the memory. When our chemistry is well balanced, stimulations do not have any strangeness and finding the needed area, where our brain produce and put together the appropriate combinations of chemicals. In our psyche we have a cookbook of the recipes, including the flexible and fixated combinations.

Psychology helps to deal with the physiology. The knowledge of the brain's chemistry requires a broad knowledge of physiology. We substitute extensive physiological knowledge with the analysis of the fragments. The physiology of the brain is comparable with the machine language in computers, but fragmentation is like a high-level computer language, which does not require the knowledge of machinery and uses common languages. Instead of physiology, we use self-analysis the theory of fragmentation to unite our fragment. We transfer our fixated fragments to be flexible. By analyzing the fragments, we find a way to build a solid psyche.

The solid psyche is associated with the release of the appropriate combinations of brain chemicals and is similar to flexible fragments, which produce responses congruent to the stimulations. It may possibly be compared with the well-written computer program on perfect database. In the computer work, every programmer does not know the machine language. Like computer programs, the calculation of the combination of brain chemicals, which is done on a subconscious level, is a precise work, because any deviations in the amounts of ingredients can change the response. We are not aware of the amounts of imbalanced chemistry that the brain is producing, but we know that our fragments become fixated because of psychological traumas and developmental problems.

When our psyche is not yet recuperated from a trauma, it continues splitting into rigid responses. Our inappropriate responses are formatted when the atypical stimulations get access to the area of our psyche where normally they are not supposed to be. Because of the distress, our brain produces dissimilar chemicals, which causes our responses to be fixated, and our psyche falls apart. As a result of damage from trauma, the fragments provide similar responses to completely different stimulations. The fixated fragments can provide anxious and angry responses to stimulations that do not have any intent of provoking those emotions. There are symptoms of the fixated fragmentation in the form of flashbacks, tightness, and fearfulness, as well as excessive reaction to noise, unpleasant feelings, and anger.

The fixated fragments are similar to a damaged computer outcome, which is not congruent with the inputted data. Our psyche uses the wrong data and does not rely on updates. Instead of flexible doses, it produces fixated amounts of chemicals in the combinations, which causes inappropriate responses to stimuli. The splitting is on the subconscious level, and the release of fixated combinations of chemicals is a response to the glitch in the program. It is nothing major with a computer, but we need a programmer to change the faulty parameters. To fix the trouble with fixated fragments, we need to bring the problem to the conscious level, and then we gain ability to change the faulty program in our psyche and remove the glitch.

CHAPTER V

Meetings with Fragments

The dissociated psyche and fragmented identities are dissimilar

The dissociated psyche is split on several personalities. The alter psyches are not connected and are in the process of dissociating from the past life's events. The dissociation can be a result of narcotics or genetics and occurs when the psyche was in an extreme situation and was unable to handle the stress. When the trauma is very strong and happened to a fragile psyche, the psyche got completely dissociated and did not know about the existence of others. In the previous frame of references, the operating system of the psyche saw the circumstances as insurmountable. In an attempt to survive, our psyche is organizing the new, independent structures with dissimilar frames of references; there are the new sets of norms, values, and ideas that affect the interactions. Each alternative character is fragmented, but within the personality its fragments are not dissociated. In the process of organizing a dissociated psyche, some fragments are loosely associated, but others may be interrelated and clearly present fabricated events from a nonconforming viewpoint.

The new system is completely distinct and allows us to continue to do what previously was impossible. Perhaps our original character was a victim, but the new alter ego is a villain. Our disassociated structure is falsifying knowledge of the past, which is not congruent with real facts, and it uses uncommon approaches. Our personalities may not have any shared memory and can lose access to life events, including weddings and sexual interactions. Sometimes alter ego personalities are aware that the other had sex or got married, but because of loose associations, they are separated from feelings about the event. Sometimes they are aware that other fragments of the personality are around and sharing the same physical body.

People with multiple personalities have unique psyches; even they exist without any involvement in the lives of others personalities. Usually the personalities have no communication, but sometimes they may have a little interaction.

The fragments of every personality are parts of one identity and share the same memory base. The fixated fragments are in the process of rearranging their connections—they are unstable and produce a fragmented identity. They have access to the current life events but produce inadequate responses. Our psyche can be taken over by fixated fragments, which produce restricted responses on distinct life events. They continue to use the same dysfunctional and persistent patterns, and they are the parts that were left over from other experiences. They fight to take over responses from other events because they want to dominate in order to save us and to go after the entire psyche. They associate with the repetitive responses and react again and again like the traumatic event has reoccurred. When they take over, they confine our psyche to the predictability of responses. They can act as a result of the learned behavior as well as the inheritance. When the events are not fearful, they exhibit fears anyway and repeat the fearful responses.

Our psyche survives the trauma by restructuring our previous responses. The first defense happens when our fears does not go away. We believe that at any time, we can have the trauma again; it is one of our learned defenses. Our fears became a domineering reaction and suppress our other responses, becoming the center of our identity and continuing to repeat the fearful responses. As a result of trauma, we live in constant fear.

The second learned defense disregards the previous sufferings and denies the fact that the traumatic experience existed. The denial of the trauma makes us reckless, and we ignore safety precautions. The reckless behavior can spread to other areas of our life, and very soon we are in danger of another trauma. The previous functioning becomes impossible because the stress is unbearable. The psyche needs to survive somehow, and to save ourselves we dissociate to a character that does not remember our past but somehow has fragments and continues functioning.

Dissociation from audio and visual memory

Our amnesic disorder has its origin in losing contact with audio and visual memory. During amnesia our psyche is dissociating from previous visual and audio experiences; it has a blockage to the part of our memory where needed information is stored. Our psyche has restricted access to areas with information about our past, and the restriction may be a result of physiological, emotional, psychosomatic, or substance-induced processes. Our access to the database is locked, and the loss of memory may be voluntary or involuntary. When we experience something bizarre, then our voluntary restrictions have begun. Our psyche possibly did not accept that we committed a crime or saw some other terrible action.

Our involuntary restriction happens when we become a target of brutal environmental or organic conditions. When our psyche experiences a strong trauma, as a defense we can experience amnesia. When we are poisoned or injured, we can develop amnesia, experiencing blockages to the access of the traumatized memory. When our memory comes back, we view again the memory's data but see our past distinctly. Our lowest level of access is represented by the loose associations and memory lapses. We appear confused because of blockages in access to our memory. For our protection, the psyche creates a fictitious memory; when our fragments became more flexible, we do not need protection from the past anymore and acquire full access to our data. Our atypical level of fragmentation or reaction to the traumatic event might have a genetic underlining. The psyche has diverse responses to stress: some psyches stay solid, others get fragmented, and still others become amnesic and disassociated. The answer is in the genetic organization of our psyche.

When we regularly use alcohol, we risk becoming alcoholics. Not everyone who consumes alcohol becomes dependent on it. One of the factors behind the chemical dependency is an imbalance in the brain's chemical. Our addiction is also the result of the presence of fixated fragments that are taking over our psyche, limiting our accesses to the learned memory, and forming our fixated and repetitive responses. The fragments suppress our common senses, and as a result we overlook previous unpleasant experiences. In the psychological or physiological infatuations, we can see the process of fragmentation. By being far away from the object of our infatuation, we can be very reasonable and talk sensibly and sincerely about the wrongs of our infatuation. The rigid fragments can cause detachment from our learned memory.

Psychological addiction depends on our brain chemistry. In the same way as chemical dependence, some of us stop gambling after big losses, but others continue to put money on the game. If we suffer from an addiction, we do not make the right choices. In the casino all our common senses are left at the door. Our fragments that represent our common sense are replaced by fixated fragments that seem loose and detached from our common sense. The change in our attitude is very sudden, and sometime it is impossible to believe that we are the same people. We choose to ignore our previously learned memory. Our psyche does not provide an access to our common sense, and we have blocks against retrieving needed information. Behind our psychological addiction is amnesia. We detach from our learned audio and visual memory and leave them to the control of our kinesthetic urges.

Gambling has both physiological and psychological roots

In the same way as alcohol and drugs, gambling addiction can have genetic roots. At first look, gambling appears to be a psychological addiction. The separation of our psychological and chemical addictions helps us to deal with each of them separately; this way we have more understanding of the process of addiction to address it in treatment. The physiological part is clearer when we deal with the psychological. The roots of our psychological addictions are in the inability to have congruence in our responses. We can have more than one psychological addiction, but the roots of them are in the incongruence of our responses. The need for congruence is based on our drive for unification; we split and cannot live without any pretensions. When we are addicts, our fragmentation is very visible, and our responses include denials and promises that we are not planning to fulfill. We lie to everyone without any remorse and cannot be trusted.

Treatment is successful when we take our addiction under our conscious control. Consciously we must meet our fragments by their responses and deal with them. We can identify and have a dialogue with any of our fragments. When our fragments stop lying and pretending, real dialogue becomes possible. Right away it is impossible to achieve real dialogue between our fragments. As a temporary intervention, we can negotiate. The process of identifying fragments is our goal, and building an atmosphere for honest dialogue is time consuming. To stop our pretensions and our desire to deceive, we need time. We must unify a majority of our fragments and have congruent responses. The unified fragments characterize our identity, and our real dialogue is the healing factor.

Our psychological addiction is a result of our fragmented psyche. Our strong and aggressive fragments cover the hopeless and helpless. The main purpose of the fragments in the gambler's structure is the protection of his psyche. The fragments preserve the appearance of functionality and the presence of the congruence of the expressions. Many of our fragment are weak and damaged, and other fragments cover up for them. In diverse psyches we have dissimilar structural organizations, but in all of them the more functional fragments cover for the dysfunctions of the damaged fragments, which display a lot of pretension and stubbornness. Our damaged fragments do not function properly, and as result, we have incongruence in our responses and lose to the gambling addiction. We cover up our imperfections and are involved in the process of pretension.

Our pretension is an attempt to keep together our fragmented psyches—we want to be together despite the stress and struggles. Pretension protects us from admitting that we are losers. The gambling addiction is a result of incongruence in translation of our kinesthetic, audio, and visual stimulation. When we sit at the card table and play cards, we feel a nudge to leave, but we stay. When we lose, we have some expectations that our lack will change for the better. When we are winning, we have the feeling that the luck will continue forever. Because of faulty assumptions, we are disregarding our audio messages, like the one that gambling is unpredictable and that luck changes. Eventually we lose much more than we win—we become losers. However, when we are not losing too much, we are more congruent in our audio, video, and kinesthetic responses; nevertheless, we still do not have the strength to leave the card table.

As typical gamblers, we are pretenders and do not leave a table when we endure a significant loss. We do not accept our visual imperfection and feel insecure, unattractive, and unpopular. We do not admit to being unlucky and continue gambling despite significant losses. Our gambling addiction reflects the incongruence between audio, visual, and kinesthetic modes: we become gambling addicts when we pretend that we love the self, but really we do not love. When we do not have the strength to admit the visual, kinesthetic, and audio imperfections, we become a target and can be converted into an addicted gambler. Just like businessmen who are not able to admit their mediocrity, or middle-aged people who have lost their sexual attractiveness, we are not admitting reality. We get on a shaky road to be losers in gambling. We lay bets despite heavy losses. When we cover our natural face with a mask of pretension, we are at great risk of becoming losers. If we are victims of the illnesses of depression, attention deficit, obsessive compulsion, and impulsivity, we are at high risk of becoming fascinated with gambling and its atmosphere of unstable emotions.

In many instances gambling is our substitute for sexual satisfaction. Our sexual dissatisfaction can be an echo of prior sexual abuse or another psychological or physiological injury that prevented us from future sexual pleasure. Gambling provides us with a needed emotional discharge. Our desire to get satisfaction can be strong enough to forget our common sense and do very foolish things. Our drive for gambling is comparable to the strong desire to be around our sweetheart. It is our love affair. In both instances we have a yearning for satisfaction and to be real without any pretensions. Gambling addiction is a masqueraded attempt to love the self and to be real. The life of pretension brings us to gambling, which is self-medication in the same way as alcohol and drugs. By dealing with gambling addiction, we explore our desire to escape from the splitting of our psyche.

Addicted gamblers continue to play despite of the reality losing everything. The most amazing conduct for us, as addicted gamblers, is our unchangeable belief that bad luck will miraculously change and that our winnings would cover the losses. The fragment that believes in winning is united with our neutral fragments. The brain supplies us with a chemical cocktail that keeps us believing in our good fortune and motivates us to continue gambling. Our impulsiveness takes over and suppresses our more reality-oriented fragments. Our brain has a task: to keep us gambling in a losing game and to constantly release the same cocktail of chemicals. The chemical combination is similar to the one we have when we are winning— addicts do not feel any change. We do not adjust to special circumstances, and the desire to win suppresses all other opinions. Our motivation is stronger than our common sense.

The act of vigilance contributes nothing to justice but can help retain an illusion of fairness. As a result, at the end we hurt the self more than others. We cannot understand that when the psychological trauma is hurting so much, the act of vigilance will not help. The pretension continues despite any common sense; the gambling helps us to forget about trauma. Our gambling is our self-medication and helps to prevent disassociation, keeping our fragments together. As a result of gambling, our vigilance decreases, and our vigilante feelings are usually the result of abuse and post-traumatic stress. Our flashbacks of abuse, and the effect of those flashbacks, reproduce the feelings of the traumatic event. For us gambling is associated with a desire to have a congruent visual experience, and our fragments get connected to visual stimulations. Our gambling is a deception, a chimera and farce, and our desperate minds believe in the illusion. Underneath we pretend that we can somehow return back to the traumatic experience and change it to our advantage. In reality the gambling takes us far away from the trauma; somehow it can protect us from becoming vigilantes. It offers a false impression of congruence between visual, audio, and kinesthetic stimuli, granting us with escape. We pretend that we are keeping the self in balance and are preventing dissociation.

We are potential gamblers when we feel guilty without any offence and suffer from intense feelings of culpability. The punishing fragments gamble on the big bets, and we honestly believe that we have a winning card. The big bet needs to have a desired winning. We punish the self by avoiding playing minimum bets. As soon as we win some money, we put all the money back into the pool for the next bet. If we win on the small bet, we would feel guilt and hate ourselves for not playing big. We are not afraid of losing a game—we are scared that, instead of getting a maximum win, we will win too little.

When we are scared, we can become addicted gamblers. The internal pressure of our scariness and the desire to prove to the world the opposite creates a very aggressive fragment that pushes us to play recklessly when it is not reasonable. It encourages us make irrational bets and to take part in the high rollers' game when it is obvious that we do not have the required qualifications. We can easily be addicted to gambling if we feel angry and intimidate others. Our biggest self-deception is in belief that by instilling fears in others, we can insulate the self from a victim's role. Gambling creates the illusion that we are protected; it helps us to express our emotions.

The pretension is one of our desperately invented tools to resist emotional trauma. We subconsciously know what is right and what is wrong, but we pretend anyway. We talk about casinos as evil, but we gamble during all our free time. The need to pretend has a base in our crippled structure; it shows everyone that our fragments are in disarray. The pretension dominates our audio, visual, kinesthetic, and olfactory functions. The sexually abused victims have a fragment that is very sensitive to kinesthetic stimuli and touch. They overreact on touch, and the kinesthetic fragment activates their alarm system, making them tight up and tense. Our alarm system can influence us to be hyper and arrogant. We are very sensitive to our visual stimuli. As victims of violence, we struggle when we see hostility on the TV and in movies. We resist giving up our images of revenge. Our flashbacks are the images of abuse, and the chemical released is unconfined and can get out in unpredictable situations.

When we are gamblers traveling to a casino, our fragments agree to gamble, but only a few have a real problem. Our psyche can have diverged fragments; it can be a representation of an old or a young woman, or men at different ages. The man may gamble often, but he comes to the casino only because his family is coming. Another man is asexual; he is an impotent and has a lot of fears in him, so he plays unreasonably and loses a lot, but he is in casino to prove to himself that he is not a coward. One woman comes because she has gambling addiction. She is addicted and releases her deep bitterness; she really believes that she can beat the odds of the game.

All our fragments can be gamblers, but only a few are influence others to gamble, and we cannot be persuaded to stop gambling. It is impossible to stop us from coming to the casino, because our fragments agree to gamble. The spokesman of the psyche is one fragment with the psychological addiction. When other fragments bring some convincing evidence against gambling, the spokesman ignores them. Influence from the outside is not too effective with our inside structure. The best way to reach our fragments is by getting them engaged in internal dialogue, which will help restructure our feelings about the self and others.

An old woman goes gambling because she does not want to be alone at home. She is always winning because she never gets involved emotionally in gambling. The gambling for her is not a problem, and she would not gamble if she had something else to do. She has had a traumatic experience: she was physically abused as a child. Her father was a despot and always dreamed about a son who would continue his bloodline. His son died, and instead of the son he had a daughter. He treated his daughter as unwanted and beat her without any reason. He did not allow her to wear shoes and ordered her to walk barefoot through the forest. When she got splinters in her foot, he did not allow her to stop and remove them. The grown woman does not have the ability to verbally process her traumatic experiences, because all her experiences were kinesthetic. All her life she had pain and discomfort. She did not know any pleasure and satisfaction. She can translate her experience from kinesthetic to audio and visual. Her audio experience is crying and yelling. She looks in the mirror for her visual experience and to express her bitterness, she makes faces. Her life was about pain and suffering, and she did not grow up to be mature and flexible but became opinionated and stubborn. Her fragments are loosely associated. Gambling is her intuitive way to get positive emotions; to deal with pain and suffering, she needs a positive incident. The new kinesthetic experience pleasantly moves her. Unfortunately, she gets addicted and continues gambling despite the losses. Nevertheless, if she debriefs her trauma after the emotionally painful experience, she can avoid the fixation of her fragments.

Another woman, in her forties, sometimes wins or loses but does not cross the line of normalcy. She likes to come to casino because she does not have anything in life of which to be proud. Her lover left her many years ago, and she is raising two boys. She does not trust anyone, and for her gambling is a substitute for sexual interaction. She continues suffering from her trauma. When she was seventeen years old, she fell in love with a married man who was twelve years her senior. The love was very strong, and the man wanted to marry her. He went to her parents and told them that he was leaving his wife and his child to marry their daughter. Despite cautions from her parents, the seventeen-year-old trusted her lover, and they became intimate. Very soon she got pregnant, left her parents' home, and lived with her lover. Her lover was a gentleman with soft manners, and he always nicely explained that he had problems with divorce. One time he said that he hated the obscure paperwork. The next time he said that he had stupid lawyers and that his wife's excessive demands needed mediation. He was financially secure and stable in his work, but he also needed to travel a lot. He always called her from his business trips.

Shortly after delivering the first boy, the woman got pregnant again and had a second son. She enjoyed her motherhood until a mutual friend told her terrible news: her lover had been seeing another woman in the city when he was on business trips. The woman questioned her lover, and he denied everything, but the facts came out. The reality was that he had never filed for divorce papers, and as a matter of the facts, he did not even stop living with his wife. He was a pathological cheater and lied to both women.

The woman clearly understood that she always was a mistress and that her lover would never leave his wife. She immediately left her lover and came back to live with her parents, who took in her and her two sons. The woman now does not trust any man. Her emotions are tightly locked away, and she does not express them. Gambling gives her a chance to express her emotions. She was deceived by a man whom she loved and completely trusted. Years after her trauma, she started to believe that she was too naïve and probably deserved her fate: she got involved with a married man, and she did not listen to the voice of common sense coming from her parents. Eventually she believed that she was not smart enough to deal with any man and saw them as dangerous liars. In the casino she gambles and loses money. She still continues losing because she does not believe that she deserves to win.

Our flexible fragments are getting replaced by fixated ones

As soon as we get into the casino, the fixated fragments replace the flexible ones and provide us with the fixated responses. With a fixated processor we continue gambling despite the heavy losses, and we make decisions that are reckless and repulsive. We lose our own money and money borrowed from others. As addicted gamblers, we do not have the strength to stop the process of gambling until we lose everything. We suppress our feelings of being in danger and do not listen to any of the precautions against unnecessary risk. The gambling rush takes us over, and we place bets on unreasonable odds. After losing a bet, we do not have any money left, but we continuing with someone else's money and then lose again. It is amazing that when are not in a situation related to gambling, we are very reasonable with money and might even appear stingy. During gambling, however, we lose our common sense and fail to remember the promises we gave before the game.

In times of gambling, our common sense is absent, and we operate on dissimilar parameters than when we give our promises. We split from our wisdom and became irrational. Our life is distorted, but we do not dissociate. In fragmentation we do not have any feelings of lost time, and our life data is not missing from our memory. We split into many fragments but do not have diverse personalities. As a result of the split, we disregard everything that we said previously. We forget our criticism of the gambling, which we expressed outside of the casino.

When we criticize gambling, we have a change in our perspective. It is the result of the transference of our fixated fragment to a flexible one. The noticeable changes, which arise from new configurations of our fragments, can be observed by the changes in our energy level, expressions, and appearance. Our new flexible fragments change the interpretation of the stimulation, and we use the new references and are not affected by old stimuli the same way as before. In the past, when we entered a casino, the new chemicals were not included in the processing of information, and we were limited in the interpretation of the memory data. With flexible fragments everything changed. In the new regime the flexibility replaces the previous rigidity. Now, when we enter the casino our processor retains all memories and data. Our interpretation of the incoming data changes because the neurotransmitters work in the new regime. The firing of the neurons is comparable to a firework salute during holiday festivities. We do not believe anymore in being reckless, because the new interpretation of the data pushes us to be more cautious.

The new responses, which utilize the excessive release of new neurotransmitters, create restraint for gambling activities.

Recreational gamblers

Recreational gamblers with a solid organization of the psyche are not the same as influenced gamblers that have a slack organization. We know that the addictive gamblers have an obsessive psyche with the fixated fragments. We need to separate the obsessive, influenced, and recreational gaming activities. Simply put, gambling is a process of making a bet. We are infatuated with the bet and also need to acknowledge that not every person who is gambling is captivated by passion. It is important to distinguish an addicted gambler from a recreational one who just loves the game or who is influenced by others.

Many of us are gamblers, but we are not addicted gamblers. Even when we make bets and play numerous games, we are not addicted. As recreational gamblers we have a solid psyche; we love the game and appreciate challenges. We are not doing anything destructive to continue gambling, because we can stop at any point and do not have any uncontrollable urges. We do not gamble to the point that we lose everything. We would not give in to recklessness, and we have the ability to use a variety of responses. We do not give in to the urge to place a bet every time.

We may not be a compulsive gambler, but because of influences we can act as one. As influenced gamblers we have a wobbly organization of our fragments and are very susceptible to the pressure of making a bet. We copy the behavior and attitude of the addicted. The pressure on us, as influential gamblers, is from the messages from recreational and addicted gamblers: that gambling is somehow beneficial. The influence is like a virus that is transmitted to us.

As influenced gamblers, we are victims of pomposity, pretension, and grandiosity. Our psychological structure is predisposed to be dominated. While we are in close proximity to the generator of the influence, we show a sign of the addiction. As soon as we are outside of danger zone, our gambling urge stops. We are not addicted but under a terrible pressure from an addicted gambler. We do not control our obsession as soon as the galvanizer is around. By being influenced we can display a variety of addictions that are distinctive from gambling, such as alcohol and drug addiction. As influenced addicts we involuntarily act as addicted, and we always appear be under pressure. We stop acting on an obsession as soon as we change our surroundings, and our addiction stops. At the influence from a person, we change our psyche's organization. It is a symptom of our fragmented identity: our lack of solidity and incongruence in our responses is an indicator of the submissiveness of our psyche to external influences. It is also an indicator that our psyche does not have the ability to resist influence. We are not motivated to unify and split; our conformity leads to submission to external structures. Our structure is a copy but appears very natural, and the external control is not durable and falls apart when the influence stops.

Because we were taken over by a dangerous structure, we endure a lot of damage. By reason of the looming interaction between our fragments, we are not aware of our situation and put the self under another structure that is assumingly stronger. As traumatized victims, we also have a wobbly organization of our psyche; because of our turbulent life, we need safety. Our new structural order is based on the subconscious copy of someone powerful, and reorganization is crucial for our survival. Because of the uncured trauma, we alter our psyche by incorporating reckless behavior. Our fragments rebel against our own domineering fragments, which are not providing our needed security. The pressure of gambling, as well as other influences, happens when all our structures are shaken. As a result, our fragments are tentatively linked, and our whole system wants a new structure.

The influence for our reconstruction can be from peer pressure, respect, hate, and emptiness, side effects of medication, criminal lifestyle, or pretension. Often the influence happens when we have our incongruent response system. We can hate the uncommon structures but consider them safer than ours. Unconsciously we pick up the structure that we hate and, as a result, become influential gamblers. We are influenced without any persuasion, and our fragments have a loose organization and want to change the domineering rule. When our psyche voluntarily agrees to be influenced by other structures, then the influence is strong and stays for a long time. Nevertheless, as influenced gamblers we are not the addicted. It is very complicated to distinguish us from addicts, but we are on opposite poles from addicted gamblers. Usually we are the main benefactors of rehabilitation programs and respond to any help for resisting the influence.

Sexual addiction is another example of infatuation

Another example of infatuation is sexual addiction, which easily illustrates fragmentation. In our fragmented psyche, one of our fragments is a loving and a caring husband and father, and another fragment is a reckless adventurist who can put at a stake his and his family's well-being for a moment of sexual gratification. The conflicting fragments provide us with special responses. Our fragment of the loving husband criticizes the womanizing behavior, but our fragment of the sexual addict defends it. The process of fragmentation shows how the opposite responses emerge and cause our internal conflicts. Our fragment of the caring husband accuses the sexual addict of shaking the long-standing stability of the family for a short moment of sexual gratification. On the other side, the sexual addict talks about the joy of having this moment of fulfillment because life is very short.

Our points of view and justifications change according to various conditions. The circumstance of acting out varies from one situation to the other; it is the common tune in the responses of sexual addicts, who try to convince us that their behavior is normal. When the fragment of the sexual addict takes over, it looks for unification with various other fragments. We have intense, sexually arousing fantasies, and even sexual urges toward generally non-sexual stimulations, justifying any perversions. As fetishists, we argue that our responses are normal. An addict who has sexual urges looks for approval and unification with the whole psyche. Our addiction is a dysfunctional way to unify our psyche.

Prostitutes are always careful because they are well aware that we, as their clients, possibly are sexual perverts and could have an intent to inflict pain. We do have fragments built on unusual combinations of our brain's chemistry; as a result we give in to pomposity, pretention, and grandiosity. Our brain's chemistry is not balanced, and our impulsivity and overreaction, as with many other deficiencies, are a result of an imbalance in our brain chemistry. The atypical responses result from the work of neurotransmitters, which process information in a pervasive regime. Sexual and other hormonal chemicals are released in distinctive areas of our body; the problem is that our fragments affected by perversion view the pervasive data as neutral. Because of traumatic experiences or genetic damage, we do not have any flexibility in our responses. We cannot detect perversion in stimuli and provide responses in dissimilar propensity. Our fixated fragments also provide pervasive responses to ordinary stimulation. When our perversion occurs, we justify our pervasive behavior; our fragment of the addict splits from the previously domineering neutral fragment and, as a leader, takes over our psyche and accepts our pervasive responses.

When the sexual triggers are absent, we suspend the fragments of the addict and troublemaker, and we act with restraint. During sexual stimulations, our addict fragment becomes domineering. Our pervasiveness takes over only for a very limited time, and our pervasive responses may perhaps be very short. The fragment of the caring husband splits from the fragment of the sexual addict. As soon as stimulation is not present, our neutral fragments replace the fragments affected by perversion. The prostitutes know it—for their services they take the money up front. The customers lose appreciation for the received services as soon as they achieve sexual gratification, and they will not want to pay. When the stimulation is not active, our fragment of the sex addict unifies with other domineering fragments. When stimulations are not active, we act in front of the prostitutes as very respectable gentlemen who also like to moralize about the wickedness of others, and we believe that we would not pay for sex.

Our sexual addiction is probably the result of an influence, such as peer pressure. The pressure can be substance induced; it may quickly stop when our surroundings change and the substance is not present. The sexual addict is not someone who suffers from obscurity in his relationships, causing a change in partners. Only when we have an impulsive infatuation with sex are we sexual addicts. We pursue sexual gratification, exhibiting our impulsiveness and a reckless behavior by interpreting even non-sexual stimulation in a sexual way. The signs of our sexual addiction are the sign of our fixated fragmentation. To resist pervasiveness, we must restructure our psyche. By increasing our plasticity, we reduce the effect of our fixated fragments. When our brain releases chemicals congruent to the stimulation, then we achieve cohesiveness in our responses.

We compare our fixated response to our flexible ones

We do compare our fixated and flexible responses. Although they originate from stimulations that are miles apart, we still can be consciously aware of them. We do have an ability to compare kinesthetic responses to audio and visual ones. When we have flexible fragments, they help us to restructure our psyche. In our conscious mind we can learn many things from our flexible responses and keep our psyche solid. The biggest danger to our solidity is that after a trauma, our flexible responses are altered and can become fixated; the structure of our traumatized psyche gets fixated, too. To remedy this, we identify the fragments affected by fixation. After identifying fixated fragments, we can restructure them back to flexibility. We look for the flexible responses even on unusual ways of expressions. Flexible fragments help us to deal with the fixation.

We use a powerful lexicon that has the strong, forward-moving words: the forceful expressions sound like do, go, take, and move. We get stressed and get in altercations, and our dominating fragments produce many kinesthetic responses. With domineering audio fragments, we offer a world of sounds and use of words like: please, listen, and good. When our domineering fragments are based on visual responses, we use words that are dissimilar. As adults we also have children's responses. We express the self as children in our distinctive modes of expression. The children have more visual responses and respond better to visual stimulation. They ask questions like what kind of color, who is the blond, is the really moon so big, and more.

After psychological trauma, our body gets tense and prepares for other attacks, and our kinesthetic responses become limited and rigid. We consider the environment to be unsafe and restrain the self; our responses becoming altered and fixated. We use expressions like "leave me alone," "go away," "stop bothering me," and more. The change can happen even after a low stress level. We experience adverse reactions toward the light and bright colors. We hate some forms and objects without any reason. Everything that we see is ugly, too dark, nasty, messy, or worse. With olfactory-based fragments, we might say, "Is something fishy here? It smells so bed. What if the smell stays forever?" With tactile fragments we are say, "Do not tickle me, do not touch me, do not come too close. If you touch me, I will vomit." After trauma, adults get tense and frozen, but children often fidget and shake.

Our brain is better at responding to already learned stimuli triggered by familiar brain chemicals. To restructure our psyche, we analyze our audio, visual, kinesthetic, and olfactory responses to find the dominant responses. We discover that the responses in a particular area of our brain have been altered. In our analysis we pinpoint to the event when our responses changed. We translate our flexible responses to our diverse styles of expression, where we have fixated responses. To restructure our psyche, we compare the flexible responses to the fixated responses on our traumatic life experiences.

Fixated fragments are the result of psychological struggles

Our fixated fragments formed as result of the luck of our conscious clarity about psychological struggle. When our brain has an impediment in adequately processing information, we rely on a fixated combination of chemicals. The release of brain chemicals is not congruent with corresponding audio, visual, and kinesthetic stimulations. Our responses are confusion, fear, and agitation, and e make an assumption without any evidence and even against the facts. Without any evidence, we feel that the stressful event will reoccur, and we activate the fixated fragments. Our brain processes our new information in the previously used part of the brain; we are responding in old way to the new information. The fixated fragments are a result of the physiological impairments in our brain. We trigger the faulty learning, which is a result of our inability to decode, transport, and process specific information, and we cannot distinguish dangerous signals from ordinary ones. This is the cause of our psychological and physiological impairment.

We process all incoming stimulations in the same way as we have before, with the same brain chemicals. Our failure to handle the information on an individual basis supports our confusion. Our psyche is confused and provides us with atypical and bizarre responses. We are shocked and frightened and scared in the same way as viewers of horror movies. In scary movies we hear a very intense sound, but we do not receive any confirming visual information; we see the killer's foot, but we do not see his face. We suspect that everyone in the movie is a killer. The scary scenes accompanied by the sounds, like the telephone ringing, prowling steps, and a tea kettle whistling are loosely related to the plot of the movie. The incongruities create uncertainty and fears, and the intense, repetitive sound prepares us for an alarming situation. We experience the frightened feelings because we are confused.

In movies, when we do not have enough visual information to process, we jump to conclusions by using our imagination about how the crime would be committed. Meanwhile, we are frightened if we see that a cat or dog was also killed. The human is still alive and the mystification continues. The director does not need to do much to scare us, because we are already baffled by incomplete information. To stimulate our imagination, the director forces us to process audio stimulation without the visual stimulation. When the information lacks clarity and is mystifying, the responses are our feelings of terror, nervousness, rage, and emotional volatility. The incomplete information also triggers the desire to run away and to close our eyes, because we have do not wish to face the unknown. We have a hurdle to proccss the information, and because of our confusion, we receive the bewildering stimulations and get scared.

In the same way, if we struggle with our coordination, we are scared of dancing. If we suffer from dyslexia, we are scared of spelling. The restructuring of our psyche allows us to change our perception about the psychological struggle; it gives us the unique approach to process information, reduce confusion, and reinstall confidence in our ability to hand out information. In restructuring the fixated fragments, we clear up confusion, reduce fearfulness, and bring traumatic events to consciousness awareness.

By debriefing we bring our traumatic event to our consciousness. After regaining our consciousness awareness, as the next step we create plasticity in the release of the brain's chemicals. By translating our information to special modes of expressions, we avoid fixation, increase the plasticity of our fragments, and restore a congruent response to other events.

The psyche produces expressions unrelated to the stimulations

When our psyche splits from plasticity to fixation, we produce expressions that are unrelated to the stimulations. Our emotional instability is visible when we display our emotions in an inappropriate manner. Our emotional frigidity takes place when we display emotional unresponsiveness and numbness. When we express anger, agitation, aggravation, and irritability without any provocation, then the inappropriate arousing is associated with a lack of comprehension and attention, and also with the presence of atypical distortions.

The roots of our emotional dysfunctions are in the faulty organization of our psyche. We have incongruent responses on the same stimulations; some of our fragments dramatize our responses, and others do not act enough to produce a valid response. They are in the constant confrontation when one fragment overreacts and another does not react enough. Our psyche never feels content, and the other fragments can sabotage our relationships. Our feuding fragments push us to be aggressive, and perhaps we squeeze our girlfriend's breast in an elevator. She feels offended and scolds us. We also fail to have appropriate attire on a special date, and we forget to bring flowers. Our significant other gets upset again, and we feel upset too. We are not satisfied with the self, because we did not have the ability to express our emotions in an appropriate way. We are in love but do not show our feelings.

We feel distress when our emotional expressions do not produce the desired result. When we receive a negative reaction from our significant other, we feel unsatisfied and lost. Our emotional dysfunction is created by our inability to provide emotions that are harmonious with stimulation. When we do not feel emotions, we cannot produce appropriate responses. The split is shown in the fixated fragmentation, when our psyche produces only overreaction or inadequate reaction. Our psyche is not able to tune to the stimuli and produce an appropriate reaction. Our incongruent, repetitive actions are a sign of splitting.

When we are always late, it is a sign that we suffer from a split and a presence of a fixated fragments in our psyche. We ignore stimulation and always respond in the same manner. We are late for many occasions and feel bad, but we do not have the strength to change anything. Because emotions are on a subconscious level, we are not able to change our fixated fragments. We also do not know how to manage our emotions, denying that we have the troublemaker fragments in our psyche. The troublemaker fragments seduce us to be late to appointments and then torture us for being late; they constantly release unpleasant feelings and suppress our joy for life.

We need to restructure our dysfunctional psyche. We must bring to our consciousness our dysfunctional emotional structure and provide a verbal correction. When our fragments are united, we understand that our lateness is not related to our whole psyche but is caused only by our troublemaker fragments. By having a meeting and dialogue with our fragments, we can identify the troublemakers and deal with them. On a conscious level, together with other fragments, we are able to supervise them and achieve internal tranquility by creating the dialogue between dissimilar fragments, allowing them to inject plasticity into our emotions. As a result of the correction, we arrive on time to our meetings and do not need to continue with our usual misery.

The shortness of harmonious interactions

The shortness of the harmonious interaction between verbalization and our expressed emotion is a sign of the presence of the fixated fragments in our psyche. We are stocked with emotions and perhaps do not have the ability to get them out. This inability is not related to a deficiency in our education; it is a physiological impairment. Our incongruence between verbalizing and expressing our emotions contributes to our lack of sophistication in our verbal and emotional intellects. Our brain does not recognize and is not adequately translating the stimulations; our spoken deficiency is associated with the trouble to produce our verbal response. It is imperative for the verbal intellect to have an ability to focus on the topic and to avoid circumstantialities. When we have impenetrability in verbal communication, we can process our emotions in distinct approaches.

The expressions of anger, agitation, aggravation, and despair are best expressed in kinesthetic form. Our kinesthetic expressions get exaggerated because of a perceived lack of understanding. Expression of emotions in exaggerated kinesthetic form indicate the presence of fixated fragments and a lack of verbal capacity. If we suffer from intermittent explosive disorder, then we display exaggerated forms of our aggressiveness and express completely incongruent emotions during episodes. The reactions are grossly out of proportion and do not match any preexisting stressors. By our movements we express our most offensive emotions, which have a goal to scare, intimidate, and push others into submission. We express our explosiveness in kinesthetic forms, including assault and destruction of property.

As patients in mental hospital, we often display explosiveness. When we are talking to another patient, and the nurse interrupts our conversation, we get an explosive reaction. We are upset that the nurse interrupted our conversation by asking us to take medication, and as a result, we wants to hurt the nurse. Our reaction is not congruent with the stimulation; the nurse's actions were not asking for a violent reaction. It is important for us, as the patient in a hospital, to take medication at a particular time. This is the reason that the nurses act very directly when they administrate medication. The straightforwardness of the nurse upsets us, but it is not a reason to hurt her. When our verbal intellect is suppressed, and we do not provide an exit for the emotions, our psyche uses kinesthetic expression to substitute for the verbal. Our exaggerated expressions of rage are often kinesthetic, and we are always ready to express them. Our expressions of being annoyed, irritability, and anxiety are involuntary; when they are incongruent to stimulation, they create a lot of disturbances.

Our emotional astuteness can be presented by our capacity to experience bottomless feelings of love, compassion, and trust, and also by our ability to express them verbally. If the fragments have plasticity, our emotions can express harmoniously and in a variety of forms. Our harmonious expressions are congruent with stimulations: usually we use kinesthetic expressions when an immediate response is required. Because verbal expressions require a longer time to prepare, we express emotions right away by using our movements and our posture. Our vocal aptitude is linked to the richness and deepness of our emotional articulation, and our verbal intellect is associated with the ability to understand and separate the important from insignificant. By using meetings and dialogue between fragments, we restore our harmonious interaction between verbalization and emotion.

The congruence between our verbal and kinesthetic expressions restores our emotional balance and helps us achieve emotional stability. In our interactions with others, we harmoniously express our emotions appropriately. Because of various physiological complicatedness, language barriers, and inadequate education, we do not have ability to express the self. An indication of the fixation of the psyche is the hurdle to verbalize our emotions and the struggles to match incoming signals with emotions.

The restructuring of our psyche

If we want to restructure our psyche, we bring our traumatic experiences to conscious awareness. By verbalizing a traumatic event, we experience our emotionally shocking encounter in a safe environment. Eventually, after several repetitions we can achieve equilibrium between our verbal and emotional expressions. The restructuring is a regulatory process that is available in our conscious mind and allows us to regain control over our expressed emotions. When we verbalize our traumatic experiences, we transport our emotions from the subconscious to the conscious mind. In many instances our conscious mind does not accept the gravity of our trauma and pushes it back to the subconscious. We receive involuntarily replays of the traumatic event because our subconscious mind sends visual and audio reruns. When we have our flashbacks, we see and hear distinctive voices or even noises related to the trauma. We re-experience distress, and our trauma reoccurs again.

By comparing our feelings on the diverse manners of expression, we understand our strength and weaknesses and estimate our capacity for handling the pain and the deepness of our emotions associated with this ordeal. We use comparable forms of expression and achieve congruency while processing the damages. We reduce our overreaction by opening a dialogue within various ways of expression. Our sensations have kinesthetic, audio, and visual forms, and our function is to understand our feelings on different sensors, translate our sensations to the verbal expression, and then compare our reactions. We can perhaps correlate them to discovering the existence of our overreaction. We correct our overreaction by using **self**-awareness and self-regulation. We stabilize our increased heart palpitations and regulate the shortage of breath.

Because the fragments are a part of our psyche, we are consciously aware of dissimilar chemistry between our fragments. Our feelings and reactions are affected by splitting—when we deal with our pain and suffering, we have dialogues with our fragments, and we become united when we have meetings. To be prepared for our internal meeting, we consciously identify our fragments and engage them in dialogue. Within the self we can accomplish our unification. This is a way to tune up the parts of our psyche and to remedy our traumas and splits. Our internal communication becomes a balanced system, and our psyche can be whole. Unlike internal dialogue, external dialogue cannot happen very often, because we rely only on our intuition to validate the intentions of others.

Dialogue with others has an impediment, because we cannot know for sure the feelings of others. Even when we are close to them, we do not know much about their fragments; they have many chemical reactions that we have not experienced. When we are communicating with the fragments of others, we may not experiencing dialogue and meeting. Nevertheless, we can enroll in successful negotiations to avoid misunderstanding and more damage to our relationship. Through negotiations we can successfully communicate with others, and our styles of expression can be verbal, kinesthetic, and visual. When we are completely open to others, we can have intuitive forms of dialogue with them.

External dialogue mainly depends on our intuition because it is too complicated for us to completely understand others. The dialogue is an exchange of our feelings; we form a dialogue when we understand others. Being aware of the sensations of others is a form of dialogue. Sex is also an external dialogue: we achieve unity by giving each other pleasure. In sex we have a moment of external meeting, which occurs on the intuitive level. Unlike our external dialogues, our internal dialogues require a conscious awareness of our inner feelings.

The kinesthetic expression is domineering

When we experience anger and frustration, our kinesthetic reactions take over all of our functions. We express the self on the body's automatic level of functioning, which includes increased heart palpitations, muscle tension, and rapid breathing;

in this highly intense situation, our verbal and auditory resources become very limited. The splitting occurs when the flexible releases of our brain chemicals are replaced by fixated combinations. When our trauma is strong, we are in a state of anger and frustration, and our psyche works on autopilot. All manner of communications—which include our complicated movements, spoken, and audio expressions—get shut down to a very simple level. We use simple movements, have inconvenience using our verbal expressions, have trouble understanding audio information, and react only to simple audio signals. We are in a state of being shutdown from our sophisticated communications and are descending to our basic level of expression, which does not include our verbalization of feelings. We switch to altered levels of expressions; it is like changing speeds by switching gears in an automobile, and the car's speed decreases. At low speed the car cannot cover the same distance compared to running on a high gear. At the low level our psyche does not accommodate our high-functioning verbal fragments, and we rely more on our kinesthetic fragments. In our affective state of mind, all of our capacities of communication are shut down, we are left with the choice of flight or fight, and simple audio sounds are our only available resources.

Our physical pain is a kinesthetic feeling that comes from our body. The response to pain triggers specific ways of expression. When pain is at a significant level, the psyche focuses only on the area where the pain is generated. When we win a lottery but are in pain, we do not care much about money. When we are hurt, our natural responses mostly depend on the intensity of our pain, and we yell and cry. By knowledge from our birth, we make sounds with apprehension. When we match the intensity of the produced sound with our pain, we let others understand our suffering. When we are in pain, we are on the most basic level of our functioning; we have obstacles to identify our pain by our verbal expressions, because the verbalization requires a distinct level of functioning. Our talks about pain do not help; the verbalization requires time and takes our attention away from our pain. The verbalization of the pain, in many instances, is not a distraction from pain but quite the opposite: it expands our pain. We distract ourselves from the pain by listening to someone's pleasant voice or by being with a loved one. When we visualize a variety of colors and match them with pain intensity, we also have some decrease in the pain.

Our psyche has diverse levels of functioning, and on every level it activates diverse fragments with dissimilar responses. We restructure our brain to have congruent responses, apprising and matching our feelings. We rely on audio, visual, and kinesthetic forms of expression to respond adequately to new situations, and verbalization helps us to restructure our fragments according to the new situation to find an appropriate way of expressing our feelings. However, identifying the divergent expressions is not the end of the task—we also need to match stimulations with our capacity of anger management and impulse control. We identify the other options, and fighting can be avoided if we generate suggestions as to how to negotiate and look for more peaceful solutions. We rely on these various approaches, which are distinctive from kinesthetic forms.

If we have a solid identity and become angry and frustrated, our verbal and audio forms of communication are adequate and match the kinesthetic. We do not rely only on the kinesthetic styles of expression; we control our reactivity and tune our emotions to the intensity of incoming audio, visual, and kinesthetic information. We create equilibrium in the processing of information and do not overreact. The stimulation that seemed not tolerable for others is controllable for us.

Olfactory stimulations seem unendurable. When we express unpleasant odors, we react kinesthetically because it triggers in us a reaction of jumpiness and anger. Our anger subdues when we observe that others feel the same uneasiness and the odor endures. The verbalization of our discomfort and validation from others makes the discomfort more tolerable. The kinesthetic functions stop dominating our responses, and we allow the verbalization of our audio and visual sensations, which may trigger a humorous exchange of jokes. We see the completely changed responses and notice expressions that change from anger and frustration.

The psychotic process is characterized by incongruent responses

The psychotic mind can be described by the incongruence and the loose connection inside the psyche. Our communications are incongruent with others who saw the same thing, and our reactions on the same precipitated factor can be far apart. We reply differently to the same stressors, sometimes with accelerated movement and a loud voice, and sometimes we have nightmares and flashbacks. Our psychotic symptoms include hallucinations, which are the manifestations of the split. Our imaginative forces create the split, and these processes are not simple. To solidify our psyche together with the restructuring, we may require pharmacological intervention.

Our distortions and psychoses are symptoms of splitting and are a demonstration of the disproportionately elevated incongruence of our internal processes. The precipitating factor can be completely imaginative and may be psychotic by nature; it also can relate to a real and stressful situation. In our psyche organization, the audio and visual hallucinations and delusions take over all aspects of our life and present us as psychotics. By understanding the psychotic processes, we can learn a lot about the function of our mind.

Our symptoms and atypical distortions are a mark of incongruent organization. We have psyches that include the stressed and depressed fragments. We experience the flashbacks, intrusive thoughts, and nightmares, and we have exaggerated kinesthetic functions. Our symptoms include the inability to control the repetitive accelerated movements, restlessness, fidgeting, fears, panic attacks, and rapid speech. We react on insignificant details, detaching and daydreaming. The stimulations that trigger our exaggeration are visual, audio, kinesthetic, and olfactory, and they commonly trigger incompatible reactions. Our incongruent responses are indications of fixated fragments, which can display hallucinations or hyperactivity and are distinct from flexible responses that match stimulations.

After balancing and restructuring our fixated fragments into flexible ones, we realize that some of our reactions are exaggerated. By translating our responses in a discrete manner, we lower the intensity and exaggeration. Our flexible fragments do not support any kind of fixation and include the hyperactivity and hallucinations. We use the same reality testing used everywhere for reducing psychosis. Via congruent responses, we send the message to our brain through various types of communication that the hallucinations, flashbacks, and nightmares are not real; they are about the dangerous past and have nothing to do with our safe present. By restructuring our psyche, we adjust our kinesthetic responses to our congruent reactions. The vigor of our reaction decreases when the audio, visual, and olfactory information does not support the intensity. In restructuring, we balance the exaggerated information from our audio, video, kinesthetic, and olfactory areas of our brain. The process of decreasing incongruence is also very helpful in the reduction of our psychotic responses. The route of creating congruent responses is in a process of balancing our exaggerated reactions. The process of decreasing incongruence is universal and helps us reduce our psychotic responses.

The result of splitting is overreacting and a loss of tolerance

Anyone can split, but as the victims of numerous psychological traumas, we suffer from constant splitting. We lose tolerance and overreact about any threatening stimulation. If we are victims of robbery, we overreact to visual stimuli, becoming fixated on the adverse stimulations during the robbery. After being pressured to give up our jewelry and money at gunpoint, we overreact. We also get very sensitive to kinesthetic stimulation, because the assailant's posture was very frightening. If we were in an auto accident, we become very sensitive to audio stimulations—the noises from car motors and brakes. We also have an excessive reaction when we see racing or clashing cars. We have a number of fixated fragments that generate fear and despair. Any of the fixations can cause a split in our psyche. Our split has many warnings, including tension, fearfulness, and anxiety. In our psyche we can identify numbers of our fixated and flexible fragments; we understand that our problems started when the fixated fragments became a domineering force.

To have stable responses, we use our strengths instead of weaknesses and reorganize our psyche. We restructure our fixated fragments to have flexible responses. If our psyche still has plasticity, we chose an appropriate response and use various means to respond to the stimulations. With the presence of plasticity, we can control our overreaction and decrease fixations. We mobilize our flexible fragments by switching the internal force from splitting to unification, and we form an atmosphere of tolerance and respect. The process is on our conscious level, and to avoid overreaction we balance our responses in a discrete manner of expression. The process of unification generates great feelings of self-satisfaction, respect, content, and healthy self-esteem. If our kinesthetic responses are more stabile and do not produce exaggerated reactions, then our visual and audio information gets tuned into a kinesthetic response.

Our aversive olfactory stimulations do not create agitation if they are not supported by other forms of expressions. As workers on a chicken farm, we are exposed to intense smells. We are informed that intense smell does not do any harm and is one of the routine demands of our job, so it needs to be tolerated. We know that chickens are harmless, and the visual and audio information does not support any danger from the odor. As a result, we are not disturbed by the stink and do not wear cotton masks; nor do we experience any threatening emotions, because domestic fowl are very peaceful birds. We do not sense any discomfort.

In places where we are not informed about the harmlessness of smell, and we are not trained to tolerate intense olfactory stimulations, the odor creates an uncommon response. We get angry when we detect even slight odor in the sauna. We are in the sauna to relax and do not expect any disturbances. As workers of the chicken farm, we are more tolerant to smells because our mental process forms a flexible response. To investigate any of our discomforts, we check our vital signs: if vital signs do not support our worries, we better tolerate our discomforts. If we have plasticity in responses to olfactory stimulation, we are more tolerant to other stimuli. As chicken farm workers we have tolerant responses also to verbal and visual stimulation; we do not make a big deal of unusual verbal comments, because we are already trained to control our reactions. Our behavior is congruent with the tolerant responses to the intense olfactory stimulations. Conversely, when we did not have tolerance training and are called a "mama's boy," we get angry and get insulted because we did not learn any restraint of our emotions and want to start a confrontation right away. Instead of laughing, we are fighting.

To ignore provoking stimulations, we do not need to be trained at a chicken farm. We may achieve the same result by relying on our flexible styles of expression. Before responding, we should assess how our various types of expressions react to the stimulation. We empower the flexible fragments, which do not support overreaction. We do not hold up to the anger and anxiety, and as a result we avoid splitting and fixation. After the trauma, if we are able to restructure our psyche for flexibility, then instead of the misery of overreaction, we enjoy unification and tolerance.

We avoid unneeded and incomplete responses

In order to have balanced responses, we avoid unneeded and incomplete replies. Usually our unbalanced responses can be categorical, demanding, passive, and automatic; they already set us to explode easily, to be very limited and deviant, and to not have any analytical capacity. We appear to be inflexible and tough, and while producing dictatorial commands, we are frequently too quick with replies. The first responses of our psyche represent our fears, anger, and worries; they are usually accompanied by physical reactions such as increased heart rate, shortness of breath, and chest heaviness. Often our incongruence happens when our stimulations are atypical for us in the manners of expression. Our visual or audio stimulations request the kinesthetic responses, and vice versa. The incongruence between the type of the stimulation and the response creates overreaction.

We are worried and fearful when our child is unexpectedly late from school. All these problems occur because our audio, visual, and kinesthetic experiences are not congruent and do not produce the needed information. We can visualize that our child stayed in school for an extracurricular activity, and for an audio form we recall a sports event in which our child participates; then our worries and fears decrease. In order to have flexible responses and to avoid overreaction, even if it takes time, it is important to check stimulations from all possible angles and translate them to discrete methods of expression. We were traumatized when we were placed in an elevator that fell from the tenth floor, and we miraculously survived due to the shaft's emergency brakes. During the fall, we thought that we definitely would die, and we experienced a shock. The only recollection we had was a kinesthetic reaction of grabbing something to hold on to. We have flashbacks about the fall and the screeching noise of the elevator's brakes. We are really distorted, sustained some physical injuries, and experienced a strong psychological trauma. We need serious mental work to deal with the trauma. We visualize the brakes that slowed down the elevator and saved us, in order to regain control of our life and get over the shock of this experience. We recall the noise we hear during the fall and realize that it was the noise from the brakes that saved us. Our kinesthetic experience was adjusted by audio and visual experiences, our heart palpitations decreased, and respiratory function returned to normal.

In times of worries, instead of thinking about horrible things, we have ability to visualize something pleasurable. If we are alone waiting for a bus in a dangerous area, and the bus is running late or may not arrive at all, we are aware of danger and pace, feeling worried and unsafe. Conversely, if we visualize a relaxing walk, think about nice scenery, take the opportunity to have a relaxing exercise, and listen to soothing music, then fears and worries decrease. Even if one of our responses is very deep, but the others around us are not validating the intensity, then the worries and fears are significantly reduced. We experience a change in our physical responses such as deepening our respiration and regulating our heartbeat. By using plasticity we can enhance the process of unification and balance our responses. The flexible fragments provide us with an array of balanced responses to various stimulations. The formation of the best one takes time, and we produce the response that exactly matches the stimulation.

Overdevelopment in the kinesthetic area

The overdevelopment of our kinesthetic area leads to our confusion in understanding the audio and visual stimulations and, as a result, causes inconvenience in negotiations with others. Our psyche, with domineering kinesthetic fragments and splits from our other modalities, excludes them from processing information. When we cannot properly translate our visual and audio responses to kinesthetic form, our negotiations with others are only on the kinesthetic level. The exclusions of other forms bring our negotiations to a more primitive level and usually results in a split. The overdevelopment in our kinesthetic area leads to feelings of grandiosity and superiority; it accounts for our more primitive view of the world. Our disturbance in attention and concentration is related to kinesthetic overdevelopment; our brain's chemicals are distributed only in limited areas of our brain and cause them to overwork, so we lose our ability to process stimulations. We do not use reality probes, which come from our visual and audio sources. When we negotiate from the kinesthetic form, and our opponents are on the audio and visual level, we do not understand them.

We use the kinesthetic way to solve our grievances. We make some body movements and show our strength to our negotiators. We have an opportunity to show our strength, but we need to do everything in accordance with our honorable agreements and without physically hurting others. As bullies, we are usually overdeveloped in kinesthetic area and want to fight, so we challenge our surroundings. Some of our opponents will take our challenge, but a lot of them will not and give up.

If we are not bullies, we might fight sometimes, but we do not feel like fighting. We do not have many choices and prefer to split from our internal aggressor, because we still hope for unification. We are not violent, but we face a predicament on how to avoid fighting and to prevent more splitting. We hope to succeed in negotiations and to avoid confrontation. Behind every split is unhappiness, and we find no benefits in physical confrontation. The fight is a split and includes the use of force. In our negotiations a dilemma is always present: to fight or not to fight. It really means whether or not to have negotiations. The clash starts when one of the negotiators refuses to bargain; h does not believe that a bad peace is better than a good war. The fighters rarely deal with reality and rely on their kinesthetic abilities.

We are targets of bullies and rely on negotiations. The negotiations with bullies are dirty, but we expect fairness, and as usual we fail in our negotiations. We do not have enough flexibility to prevent the fight, and very soon we split and settle our differences with brute force. In the animal kingdom the animals negotiate before a fight: they make some sound to caution the opponent of the consequences of the fight, presenting distinct postures to demonstrate that they are determined. When the differences are not resolved by talks, our failure of compromise is the start of confrontation. Our opponents are too driven by the splitting, and soon the fight starts. Often the others are the initiators of the fight, and we only reluctantly enter conflict. The fight usually has the goal of harm, and we detach from other feelings. The attackers do not have empathy and show a clear indication of emotional instability. The worst scenario happens when we run away from a fight, and then during the chase the encounter gets bloody. In many instances, when we ask for help and no one responds, we must survive in any way possible. We can be destroyed when we continue to fight without the proper strength. If during the fight our opponent appears stronger, then we need to surrender or expect to be seriously injured. In the fight our opponent wants to hurt us, and to survive we split on all levels of functioning. The winner is one who hurts his opponent more, but if no one wins, sometimes negotiations can start again.

Our solid psyche is more inclined to settle for negotiation. When we have an internal split, we are more driven to fight. As successful negotiators we achieve congruency in our perceptions by learning new ways of interaction. In negotiation we send probes to understand the intention of the other psyche. We need to be sure that the opposing psyche is ready for agreement but does not cover the goal of manipulation and confrontation. To negotiate agreement both psyches should have a sincere desire to work together. If we are pretending to be negotiators but are just taking the time to restructure our forces, then the negotiation fails. If we refuse to negotiate, then we have another fight. Sometimes it appears that we reach an agreement, but this agreement is only on paper and the splitting is unresolved. The peace does not stay for long if we are not satisfied, even if we have a written agreement. If we have the better negotiating position but do not understand the turmoil in the opponent's psyche, we can lose. If we are just enjoying the better terms and are getting pleasure from winning, we can lose. Sometimes our negotiations are a gamble, and it can turn out that our opponent is not yet prepared to cooperate, in which case the split resurfaces and leads to confrontation.

When the neurological paths in the kinesthetic area of our brain are impaired, we focus on other areas and emphasize the audio and video experiences. Contrary to the kinesthetic, in our audio and visual processors we rely on the history of our verbal and written agreements. The real negotiators don't go for a short-term solution but aim for long-term understanding. If we are suffering from emotional instability or attention deficit, and we have trouble recognizing and identifying our feelings, then we need to restructure our psyche. The modification of our psyche to be a better negotiator effectively helps us. Without wasting time on the physiology and pharmacology aspects, we help our brain to achieve a balance. We are not exercising excessive knowledge of the neurological passes, through which the brain's chemistry moves. In our psyche we transfer the kinesthetic responses to the audio and visual areas. To restructure the overdeveloped kinesthetic area, we explore visual and audio feelings about all kinesthetic activities, including tactile experiences. In our psyche we process our conscious awareness of our audio and visual feelings and how to resolve our grievances without a fight.

The constant overstimulation of particular areas of our brain

The overstimulated areas of our brain produce a split, and as a result, our psyche creates fixated fragments. We are overstimulated when our brain disproportionately uses only a few areas. The root of psychological addiction is genetics and chemical imbalance, and it results in the creation of overstimulated and out-of-balance areas of our brain. When we have too many gratifying stimulations, we get out of touch with reality and do not recognize our dependency. We also carry a lot of misery—we continuously lose at gambling, and others think that we are dejected. We cannot recognize that we are acting foolishly. We do not care about the opinion of others, and against all rules of reality, we never accept that we are losers. We have a stumbling block to a realistic perception of our abilities, and we hold back audio information and use fixated fragments. Our incongruent responses are a result of overenthused areas in our brain. We lack congruency between audio, visual, and kinesthetic responses. In gambling we rely on luck and make too many bets; we are fascinated with our relationship with fortune. Our responses have patterns of fixation.

As gamblers we are servants of luck and follow all the superstitious rules to keep chance on our side, but our responses became contradictory. When we are away from gambling, we reject gambling as a money-wasting activity, but we do not reject our relationship with luck. We do not see the self as a failure. We believe that luck is on our side, which is common for all gamblers. We consider as fact that for a short time, luck can turn away, but we also believe that eventually fortune is on our side. We reject the opinion that gambling is a sickness, that we are under control of the fixated fragments, and we reject the external reality to follow our internal feelings and eliminate outside criteria.

Eventually we are forced by grave circumstances to have some recognition of reality, and we have a lot of resentments inside of us. We hate to be losers. The overindulged areas of our brain are not synchronized in the processing of information. In our overstimulated area we produce too many domineering responses. To satisfy those areas, we create fixated responses and become a servant of our overenthused feelings, behaving in the same way that spoiled children do. We get hooked on imaginative gratification and allow powerful, dominant fragments to rule our psyche. We do not care about anything but our own gratification.

We are bothered by thoughts of being unappreciated geniuses. By being actors, singers, artists, and mathematicians, we use the overstimulated areas in our brain. We get our main gratification from winning and are out of the touch with reality, because for us the most important thing is our games. For a few the life of others becomes a game. If we have leadership abilities, we can be leaders of revolutions, sects, and terrorist networks; we believe that we are saving world and listen to our domineering, fixated fragments. We spend all of our energy to suppress the messages of being a failure and use the fixated fragments to avoid external reality.

The underdevelopment of kinesthetic expressions

We can have underdeveloped kinesthetic abilities, but we do not understand the severity of the problem. Consciously we are not aware of our struggles, and we do not know how to remedy the problem and are playing games. While gambling we do not have any inconvenience interacting with others; we feel relaxed because we see the other players as our enemies, and our anger covers our impairments. During a football game we can hurt another player and do not think twice when attacking the other team. When we are not playing games and face real life, however, our behavior may be not similar to our game interactions. We are suffering from underdeveloped kinesthetic abilities.

We look tense, and our oral and visual abilities are not congruent with our kinesthetic. When we get upset, we can be violent. When we are angry, our vocabulary is poor, and we use offensive gestures. We are moving in the stereotypic patterns, which is a sign of fixated fragments. We also present timidity and restriction in our movements, do not feel good about the self, easily become confused, do not know what to do with our hands, and feel that we are inflexible. We often get upset without any reason, blaming the self for being different. In social situations and in school, we feel inadequate and want to modify our behavior, because our responses are incongruent.

As youngsters, the biggest part of our communication is through the kinesthetic expressions. Our kinesthetic impairments cause a strong split. Some of us do not realize the difference between games and real life; we are victims because we bring the aggressiveness of the game to the real life. We cover our imperfections in underdeveloped areas, but we cannot fool bullies, who somehow know who can be challenged and victimized, in the same way as wild animals intuitively recognize who can be prey.

The bullies do not care how intelligent and nice we are, because they evaluate only our kinesthetic abilities. Intuitively they know that we are scared, and we become victims. They also know that we are demoralized, weak, and not careful. We are the victims of bullies, because we have the intricacy to interpret and properly respond to kinesthetic stimulations, and because we do not believe in our own kinesthetic abilities. Our fixated fragments cause a split, and we avoid having congruent kinesthetic reactions. We split from kinesthetic to our visual and audio experiences; the split in our psyche is reflected in our antagonistic feelings toward others. We use the fixated fragments to hide our underdeveloped abilities. The underdevelopment of our kinesthetic expressions causes a split in our psyche and can be mild or severe. When we reject our kinesthetic reactions and rely only on our visual and audio feelings, our wrong processing of kinesthetic stimulation and mistaken interpretation leads to severe disturbances like paranoia and, as a result, sudden and unprovoked outbursts of anger. To balance our mild obstacles, we must reinforce our kinesthetic system and strengthen our existing abilities, challenging our beliefs that we cannot produce the appropriate kinesthetic responses.

We consciously understand that while we have major losses of our abilities, we are building a new structure to make our reactions congruent with stimulations. We restructure our fixations and create a plasticity to provide an array of our congruent responses so that we can have a deep understanding of our reactions. We open the new relationships with our underdeveloped kinesthetic fragments and express our feelings about kinesthetic imbrications and responses, having a dialogue with connccted fragments. Eventually, we become sure that we are capable of producing the appropriate kinesthetic responses, and our relations with others change.

Domineering and overstimulated responses

Our underused areas of the brain are straight, always criticizing our gambling behavior, but they are not strong enough to stop the destructive tendencies of overstimulated areas. Our underused fragments do not process information to their full capacity, and in many instances they can be torturous but lack the power to change our behavior. As gamblers, because of our underused areas, we are ashamed of the self and feel weak and inadequate. When we are losing in gambling, we cover it up and listen only to selective messages. We reject the honest messages, which come from underdeveloped areas of the brain, and we respond only to affirmative statements about gambling. The suppression of criticizing fragments drains a lot of power from our domineering fragments; as a result, our domineering fragments overuse their energy base.

When our psyche relies on overused fragments, we are always on guard, focusing on prevention of negative views on our weaknesses. We avoid the influence of any bits of reality, and our domineering fragments does not accept messages that are in the underused areas. Dominant fragments keep us insulated from emotional pain, which can be articulated by underused fragments. We have internal messages like "Luck will be good to me after midnight," and "I lost because someone next to me brought bad luck." We are nasty to others who challenge our perception: "You live your life the way you want, but I know that my life is short, and I want to have fun," and "I do not have any responsibilities for anyone besides myself, and I am sick and tired of being considerate of others. It is not anyone's business what I do with my money." We suppress our underused fragments, and they cannot change our behavior.

The roots of lasting gambling addiction are in our overstimulated fragments. We have many pleasurable thoughts, desires, and expectations about favorable activities. When we feel satisfied, it is similar to gratifying the crying infant who is demanding a toy. We even attribute the process of gambling to relaxation, saying that we use the gambling as an escape from stress. Our addiction to gambling can also be triggered by medication, alcohol, drugs, and genetic factors. Our gambling addiction continues despite the opposition of underused fragments, which are splitting and generating negative emotions. The underused fragments are honest, straightforward, and blunt, but we ignore them.

Underused fragments do not waste any energy on diplomacy, but they are not strong. They promise that they will not let us go back to gambling, but the domineering fragments again push the gambler to the table. In the meantime the underused areas produce feelings of guilt, depression, and inadequacy. Unfortunately, the underused fragments do not affect gambling addiction, even after heavy losses. The affirmative messages from the domineering fragments and overstimulated areas replace the messages from underused areas. The reason for our failure to stop affirmation is that instead of giving constructive suggestions, we are criticizing the self.

We constantly keep the self in a suffering state without providing an acceptable plan for recovery. We continue our distractive behavior despite our painful losses, because we narcotize our perception with overstimulated fragments, which attribute gambling to pleasure. Their message implies that to have pleasure, we need to pay. The root of our behavior lies in confusion: we are not dealing properly with our addiction and are mixing our perception and opportunities. When we accept the fact that we are infected with gambling addiction, we expect an imminent relapse. Our understimulated fragments are weak and do not resist any of our excitements and desires. Because our fragmented identity is providing us with fixated responses, we experience splitting despite any common sense, and our psyche loses plasticity and flexibility.

We have two faces: one appears happy, and the other is suffering. The happy face placates the addictive behavior and covers weakness. We suppress distressing messages and continue doing the same thing despite our heavy losses. The suffering face provokes internal turmoil; when our fragments are not producing placating responses, we are unhappy. When we are suffering from gambling addiction, we are aware of the incongruity of our audio, visual, and kinesthetic perceptions.

We see the similarity between our gambling addiction and unshared love, because we have parallel asymmetry in perceptions. We use the overused areas to suppress underused fragments. When we are heartbroken from love, we suffer from incongruity in perceptions of our abilities. We continuously fall in the love with someone who is unable to feel the same way about us. In school, as inexperienced boys, we fall in love with girls who are not attracted to us. We fall in love with the girl who is popular, and unfortunately she is already in love with somebody else. As boys, we are visual and want to impress girls by copying a strong appearance, but it does not work. Girls are impressed by audio messages from more mature boys; they are not impressed by looks, because they have a domineering audio perception. We do not attract girls because we rely on visual impressions, which are mainly underused fragments for them. We are admiring our love as a visual object, but girls are overusing their audio fragments. In many instances the asymmetry in our perceptions is the cause of our suffering.

The remedy for our unshared love and our gambling addiction is the congruency of audio, visual, kinesthetic, and olfactory replies. Common sense requires the congruity of our responses. In many instances, because of the interference of the perceptions of our peers and other factors, our overstimulated fragments lose their domineering role, and we restore the congruence of our psyche. We have the strength to resist any temptation and craving when the fixated fragments lose their domineering role. We begin listen to the underused fragments and stop the destructive behavior.

The oversexualizing and distorted perception

Our oversexualizing is the result of distorted perceptions in visual, audio, olfactory, tactile, and kinesthetic. The overstimulated fragments attribute sexual activity to the reason of our existence. We carry through all our life the belief that nothing can be compared to sexual pleasure. As sexual addicts, we feel that sex is the best thing that our life can possibly give us, and we enjoy it by all available means and as often as we can. By overstimulating our fragments with sexual thoughts and feelings of desire, we alter our perception of reality. We have a psychological addiction to pornography, sexually explicit material, sexual gadgets, and replicas of sexual organs. All our sexual infatuations have a base in our overstimulation. In our psyche we have a fragment of a young child. Conducts of our overstimulated fragment are similar to the behavior of the spoiled kid whose parents showered him with many toys, and now nothing may satisfy his appetite; his room is like a toy store, but he demands more and more possessions.

Our behavior as sex addicts is also similar to the behavior of an elderly woman who wants to drink from the fountain of youth. In a weird way, she is sexualizing her life, continuously denying the losses in her appearance and relentlessly suppressing reality. She covers her age like an offender hides his criminal record, and her behavior does not make any sense. The incongruity of her perception exists on her subconscious level because consciously she is not aware of her behavior; her responses became fixated when she overused the flexibility of her fragments. She suppresses audio and video information about her age, and when she sees herself in a mirror, she avoids signs of aging and uses selective visual information. She ignores question about her age because she wants to appear younger, and her movement and reactions become unpredictable. She suppresses age-related messages and losses. Her mannerism is not congruent with her real age but corresponds more to her imaginative age. She wears the fragrances of a young woman. Her fragments are overused and fixated, she blocks out unpleasant messages of her age, and she suffers from a split in her psyche. The woman may be beautiful for her age, but she still produces incongruity in her perception. She is separating her appearance from her perception.

Similarly, as sex addicts, we treat the sex organs separately from the relationship. We move away from human interactions, which do not satisfy our desire, and we are infatuated by sexualizing everything around us. Instead of intimacy with a partner, only the sexual act is an object of our desire. The sexual organ becomes a pleasurable toy. The fragments of the spoiled child and the elderly lady become our domineering force, and through overused, overstimulated, fixated fragments the psyche placates our thoughts. Our thoughts represent the overused fragments: "I did well, and many can give up their lives for a night with me. I feel like a millionaire because I kissed him. He is mine, and I'm jumping for joy." In meantime, the underused fragment sends an opposite message: "I probably have a venereal disease. If I get pregnant, I'll kill myself/ If my husband finds out, I'll be in trouble." Nevertheless, our underused fragments are weak and cannot stop the sexual addiction. Despite any negative audio messages, we continue to have the sex addiction. We switch to the visual or kinesthetic form of interaction and are not concerned with audio messages.

The process of overstimulation develops the incongruity in our audio, visual, kinesthetic, and tactile perceptions. We feel the incongruity between own perception of our ability and the norms that exist in our surroundings. When the internal perception of our abilities is equal to external perception, which comes from the outside world, we achieve a state of equilibrium. To change our faulty perception, we need to have flexibility of our overstimulated fragments. In many instances the sexual addiction does not make any sense, and the life of the addict is not pleasurable at all. The sexual addict is turbulent, always under the stress, and full of suffering from perceptual distortions. The addict needs to restore congruence in the audio, visual, olfactory, and kinesthetic perceptions to stop the perceptual distortion.

The incongruence between our and others' perceptions

The incongruence between our own and others' perceptions about our abilities can cause a split in our psyche. The split prevents us from having consent of our ability and from developing a common opinion of our skills. Our split may be intentional or unintentional; the severity of the split depends on the level of deviation between our own ability and the perceptions of others. We need to be careful to accept perceptions of others who, without any conscious awareness, split us with only one intention: to feel more powerful. They generate incongruence and confuse us. The majority of splitters consciously do not realize what they do; by ridiculing us and ignoring our abilities, they subconsciously want to show their own superiority and higher ability. They do not know that they have a strong need to manipulate and to feel powerful. When they are capable of splitting us, they feel good, like a very important mission was accomplished. They split us for their fervent hunger for dominance, without any material benefits. They are always searching for an opportunity to split. When splitters finished working on a genius physicist, he was perceived as a moron because he was wearing clothes that did not match by color, and his hair was not combed. It is interesting that negativity was damaging for a physicist but was absolutely not related to his job-related abilities.

We are asking the self a question, who we really are and what perception about us is correct, because our identity is not strong enough to resist pressure. We feel negative feedback from others and do not get a fair estimation of our abilities. We are confused. In lots of circumstances, the incongruence in perception is very puzzling and causes cracks in our character. The fragmented identity is extremely vulnerable to influences from outside. The confusion contributes to instability, and when we have an already disjointed identity, we experience a big split.

The students in school are graded by teachers and peers, but those evaluations are not always matching. The opinions of teachers and peers can be distinct; peers are not united in their opinions. We can find respect and admiration from peers who were not in our classes, but we may be the laughing stock in our classes. This situation is very painful for feeble identities, because in one place we feel good and supported, but in another place we feel unsupported and ridiculed. It is comparable to traveling between parallel universes in a dream world. It seems when we are moving to the discrete place, the perception of others become atypical. The incongruence causes a split due to the perceptual incongruence, and we suffer from uncertainty. With solid identities, we are less susceptible to a split.

Life in a homogeneous setting is easier. The mainstream environment is too rough and is a test of our strength; our psyche is vulnerable, and the split noticeable. When we leave the homogenous setting and get mainstreamed, we can experience a split. In many instances, the weak identities split because of the incongruence between our own perceptions and the perception of others. In a heterogeneous environment, the criteria to estimate our abilities depend on the atypical opinions of others. The mirror becomes streaked and now reflects a twisted image. When in our middle age we are associated with the youngsters and want to be like them, we feel that the environment is hostile because the young do not accept us. However, with a solid identity this pressure is not important because we are very sure about who we are and do not get easily confused.

When we live in familiar surroundings, we are less susceptible to split because we are evaluated by more settled norms. When we are middle aged and surrounded by others that are close to our own age and interests, we do not feel a big difference in our perception about the self; we also feel mutuality in our opinion with opinions of others. We identify the self with others who are in the close proximity, and we do not have any resistance to seeing and interacting with them, or accepting any imperfections caused by age. When the environment is homogenous, the surrounding protects our identity from split. We mirror the others and the others mirror us.

We know our domineering styles

We need to be aware of our domineering styles of expression, to be able to plan ahead in our life. Otherwise we get stuck, because in many instances, our domineering responses control our life. When we are fearful, anxious, and irritable, and we are surrounded by people who are calm, we do not feel comfortable. When we change our surroundings to be around the fearful, anxious, and irritable, we are protecting the self. Even though the fearfulness, anxiety, and irritability do not support our success, we are happy. We become losers because our life depends on the speed and appropriateness of our decisions. Intuitively we are scared of our future and are protecting our kinesthetic responses, which are more important because they control all our functions. To have success in life, we need to restructure our responses.

We focus on our strength to feel good and to be sure that we are processing information correctly. In contrast, others judge us by the way we manage our whole life. If we are spending our life struggling to become a singer without a good voice, and we ignore our exceptional abilities to dance, we are choosing a life of unappreciated efforts. The better outcome happens when our domineering functions develop naturally, without any struggle. With good visual skills we can become a successful cinematography specialist and artist. Our original vision brings a lot of admirers and influences and inspires others. By being a coach in a popular sport, we can lead our team with our kinesthetic abilities. With our skills we create dependence in others that lack our important talent. It does not matter if those proficiencies are based on our visual, audio, kinesthetic, or olfactory abilities; without any talents we spend a lifetime being a student. A lack of those skills damages our self-esteem and stops our life enjoyment.

Many of us have a gift, but not everyone can discover it, and we do not always realize our potential. With only a few abilities, we should know our strengths and rely on them. In uncommon styles of expression, we have diverse fragments, and to know our capacity we also need to be familiar with our dominant moods of expressions. First of all we depend on the exceptional and outstanding, because we need to know our power and be aware of our giftedness. We are rating the self by our profound understanding of the subject and the quality of our responses. If we choose one of our functions to be domineering, then we program the other functions to be servants. In many instances the gift can be a burden. When we have several distinguished qualities, we need to choose one of them to be a dominating one.

It is great to have many talents, but paradoxically if we have only one, we have a better chance to achieve success. Any of us has a chance to be good at something, but our abilities are not equal and are like the cards received from the dealer in the card games: they provide us with unique attitudes to life. Some of us receive the upper hand without much, but others who give an enormous attempt struggle. When we have the upper hand, we play only to win, but otherwise we play not to lose a game. It is easier to play with the upper hand, but with small cards we can enjoy the game too. We cannot find the self exceptional, but we prove the self as loving parents; by providing the needed love and care, we raise a child to be very happy. As gifted individuals, we may not be the best parents, because we are invested too much in our work and do not spend enough time with the family. We cannot be everything. To realize the self, we must plan ahead by knowing that our future will depend on our domineering qualities. We are driven forward by our talent and reach for our uniquely life.

The tactile experience

The tactile experience is very important because through it we can understand our responses. If we are not consciously aware of how our touch affects others, then we are ignoring how others respond to our touch. It is impossible to count how many times we are emotionally touching others and getting touched. When we are not connected with others or even with our own bodies, we become completely ignorant of ours and others' responses. The way we touch others and respond to touches becomes evident to our identity. Our reactions to touch mirror the fragmentation process in our psyche. When the shy and emotionally reserve fragments take over our psyche, we avoid any touch because for us it is not a pleasure. With emotionally sensitive, domineering fragments in our inventory, we are very sensitive to a touch; the touch may create a lot of emotions that we cannot handle. Our straightforward and less sensitive fragments do not show any special reaction to the touch, but can be sensitive to tickling.

If we sexualize all touches, including those that are not of a sexual nature, we feel sexual arousal when we have been touched. Depending on our attitude toward sex, the sexualizing is a sign of splitting in the areas of pleasure and shame. In contrast, if we are fearful of touch, it is because the touch triggers pain and vigilant feelings when we were angry and traumatized.

Touch can be energizing and paralyzing. After an energized touch we feel refreshed and aroused, but after a paralyzing touch we feel empty and powerless. Our nervousness and irritability associate with our tension as well as tactile discomfort. We have inconsistent responses to touch when we are hyper and impulsive. Sometimes we overreact and show our intensive reaction, but at other times we are lethargic and show a very low response. When we are inattentive and depressed, we exhibit our inconsistent responses, and our dominant responses are the feelings of oppression that hold back our secondary responses. We have a propensity to be manipulated and get easily victimized by others. When we are depressed, our translation of information is wrong.

We make our responses very predictable when we produce a similar response to a variety of unrelated stimulations. We have anger or sexual responses to stimulations that are not intended to be offensive or sexual. We get tearful and sad from a touch that does not have any resemblance to the painful experience. We can also get numb and detached from any contacts, or be susceptible to sweet talk and embraces. Our confused fragments are predisposed to suggestions, and we are manipulated by flattery and hugs that appear sincere. The advertising industry uses the knowledge of our responses, and we see many hugs and pleasurable touches in ads. To resist manipulation from others, the media, the environment, and our own fragments, we need to know our reactions and which are triggered by tactile experiences.

Our incongruity is confusing

The stimulations with incongruity between audio and visual perceptions are confusing. The casinos attract us by using confusion; they design the games to bamboozle our domineering modalities. It may explain why we continue to gamble despite big losses: when we enter the casinos, we see the gambling machines, which appear fascinating. The casino's environment creates a misleading message, with the noise of the falling money from slot machines, which are just the promises but not an indication of gambling success. In the meantime on the screens, the slot machines display movement and bright objects, which can be sequential or random. They affect our visual responses, having a hypnotic effect and diminishing our resistance to losses. When it becomes clear that luck is not on our side, the skillful design of the unusual movements on the screen of the slot machines takes away our concentration of losses and gives us an expectation of winning—we experience false hopes. After the losses, the comforting noise of falling money and figures on the screen restore the feeling of comfort, and the seductive sounds and movements smother the fact that we are in heavy loss. The environment of confusion and false hopes is responsible for the paradox that we do not leave the gambling activity after significant losses.

The slot machine gamblers are addicted to the game in the same way as children. The knob of the slot machine becomes a joystick. We push the spin button with increased speed and experience the excitement of being on a ride. The greed is not a dominating part of our gambling addiction. As gamblers, we do not benefit much monetarily from our addiction, nor do we feel good about the self. We put our loved ones through a financial burden and tremendous stress to tolerate our impulsiveness. We are usually in denial of our problems and do not accept that we are weak and powerless in front of our impulses. We suffer incongruity of our audio, video, and kinesthetic expressions, and we are good candidates to become addicted to slot machines and table games. We can have separately developed audio, video, and kinesthetic expressions, but as a system they do not attune and are disarranged. Our single demonstration of expression can be very good, but all together the representation is out of balance and needs alignment. The misalignment influences our psyche to split, creating chemical imbalance. Our vehemence and vigor during the games is also a sign of the split. Our system can be realigned after the removal of the influences, and the split may be resolved.

Addiction to table games is not distinct from our addiction to the slot machines. In the table games we are also impulsive and addicted to the extremes, but we act more independently. We are driven by a desire to fulfill the excitement and to experience repeated feelings of risk. We are very spontaneous, and because of our gambling addiction, we can also have an alcohol or drug problem, or an addiction to sex. Our impulsiveness pushes us to act without considering logical consequences. The protective areas of our brain are suppressed and are not functioning properly; in other words, the impulsiveness causes incongruence of our brain in the area of sensory perceptions, and deficiency in the processing of the audio, visual, and kinesthetic stimulations as a system. Our psyche is split.

The split from our sensory perceptions

We mirror someone else's sensory perceptions when our fragments split. Our dominant fragments usually have a ruling sensor, which is consistent with the developmental needs of our psyche. As a result of trauma, our fragments split disproportionately from the visual, kinesthetic, olfactory, tactile, and audio sensory bases. Our perceptions become unclear because our domineering fragments are not fair to our minor fragments. We are not sensitive enough to the fragments that pinpoint dissimilar sensory bases. Our visual fragments can be insensitive to the fragments that are part of our audio and kinesthetic sensory base, and vice versa. Based on the different sensory bases, our fragments perceive reality in a contradictory way. We are in disagreement about our feelings and do not express any compassion to our sufferings, but if we translate our altered reality to our other senses, our feelings becomes more acceptable by our other sensory bases.

The translation of our experiences allows our fragments to understand and relate better. With translation we analyze the other frames of reference of our experience. Our diversely framed expressions provide many new clues, allowing us to understand them and to have compassion. It is similar to soldiers from distinctive military branches that fight in the same battle but may not feel compassion to fellow soldiers in dissimilar uniforms. By using translation, we do not compromise the validity of our experience, because the expression of the experience is not bound by only one frame. After the trauma we need the translation of our experience to other sensors, because otherwise we can split into an opposite perception that is not ours but that is influenced and introduced from the outside.

As victims we suffer from very strong visual perceptions and have flashbacks. We also have kinesthetic reactions, which include very aversive kinesthetic responses. It is complicated to receive pleasure, to relax, and to engage in sexual play. We have perceived painful stimulations of the tactile, and as a result we get very sensitive or insensitive to touch. As victims of rape, we have many painful reactions. We can oversexualize all aspects of our life, or we can suffer from religious, persecutory hallucinations that are inflicted by feelings of fear and guilt. We become very sensitive to audio stimulations. We need to survive, and our non-domineering fragments split from the main structure. Our separation has a variety of reasons, but because of pain, we do not care much about anything. We do not have any reason to preserve unification, and we lose the main reason of unification: to protect ourselves.

After the trauma, we may use drugs and alcohol. Our fragments split from the present sensory base to become dissimilar, and they are not a representation of the self anymore. They represent a structure that is not needed and was abandoned a long time ago. We emerge as a part of the new domineering system, which is dysfunctional and needs alcohol and drugs to keep us going. After the trauma, our psyche becomes unstable and unpredictable, and then the question arises: who are we? After extreme troubles, we abandon our own responses and mirror our fixated responses, which push us away from our flexible perceptions and cause an arrival of the false self.

Splitting keeps us in constant turmoil

The process of splitting the self may be repetitive, but it has no limits and keeps us in constant turmoil. When extreme stress interrupts our normal development, it is harmful to us, and we may split. To satisfy our developmental needs, the new system of domineering fragments detach from the old system, so that our stressful experience is not needed. It is comparable with a change in the ruling structure, when the new authorities do not want anything to do with the previous ones. Our new structure forms, and the old structure continues to function in opposition, hiding like rebels in the mountains and doing guerilla raids, for a short time taking over our psyche.

Our splitting from the old structure has been caused by discontent, lack of support, not enough emotional nurturing, and neglect of other developmental needs. The fixated fragments feud inside our psyche and are an indication of the split, the lack of plasticity, and the harsh conditions of our structure. Our fragments feud because of the addiction, mental illness, and character's problems.

Within many of our fragments, we have a few with destructive abnormalities, like addictions and mental illnesses. Those fragments share our life, and we treat them with respect and dignity. We solidify all our fragments, including the fragments that appear dissimilar and have atypical experiences; as a result, they produce congruent responses.

Some of our diverse stimulations test the stability of our psyche. When fragments exhibit destructive tendencies, our domineering majority is always ready to have a dialogue or at least negotiate. We do not dismiss those responses as nuances when some of our fragments create fearful responses about danger. We acknowledge the validity of the fragments' concern about our safety, assuring the fearful fragments in self-talk that we are doing everything to take care of the danger. Our real gains are by calming the fearful fragments, which reduces stress. All our fragments benefit from a lessening of tension.

The job of integrating our loosely associated fragments to a solid system requires consistent effort. We must bring rigid fragments to our conscious awareness and understand them, helping them to be aware of how they benefit our wholeness. We gently take care of our dysfunctional fragments, which are not actively participating in the integration process. We are sensitive to how the less functional fragments react, and we have the responsibility and knowledge of how to properly deal with them. We do not push and humiliate our sick and dysfunctional fragments; if one of our fragments has uncontrolled cravings, then our other fragments use self-talk and get involved in negotiation.

We clarify the consequences for breaking our sobriety, finding activities to direct us away from our cravings. We repeat our goals and the benefits of sobriety. When we withdraw from the substance, we become aware that withdrawals require medical monitoring and medical intervention, and that we are taking a risk if we do it on our own. During the withdrawal process, together with the medical monitoring, psychological support of our fragments is very important. A similar situation will arise when, if we are mentally ill, we need our medications, because our mental illness requires medical compliance. It is not enough effort to take a few medications for a limited time—our mental illness is a lifelong illness and needs long-term treatment. The other fragments help us to get better by using dialogue and negotiation. Many of our interventions cause improvement when we integrate our psyche into a whole identity.

The split of identity disables our capacity and tightens our internal resources. The function of the splitting identity is to produce more splitting and more fragmentation, and to challenge our stability. The splitting is associated with manipulation and confrontation; if our splitting is not stopped by a process of unification, the cycle does not have limits and continues forever.

The temptation to use

When our urge to use a substance suppresses our previous promises to stay sober, we detach from feelings of discomfort from breaking the abstinence and from upsetting our significant others. As addicts we rely on the part of our brain that supports our urges and temptations. Our olfactory sensor is very powerful, is the biggest supporter of addiction, and creates strong cravings; it is superior to our visual, audio, and kinesthetic messages. Our kinesthetic, audio, and visual messages oppose and resist our urges. Our resistance to use is suppressed by our olfactory stimulations, and our temptations continue to be very strong. The fixated fragments support our urges and allow us to drink alcohol or use drugs without resistance, until we become impaired. Our level of indulgence of alcohol is considered abnormal by kinesthetic measurements, which consist of our incorrect execution of movements, our rhythm of breathing, and incorrect pronunciation of words. Our fixated kinesthetic fragments become collaborators and enablers.

To satisfy our urges, we listen to our internal, pre-recorded messages. The audio messages keep together according our general mental condition and are based on responses of our fragments. Without internal and external support, it is much harder to achieve relief from the temptations and to resist our urges. The prolonged resistance to our temptation works in reverse and increases the strength of our urges. In contrast, our destructive tendencies mobilize all possible supports from the submissive fixated fragments, and our urges to use the substance have many supporters. We suppress our unpleasant audio, kinesthetic, and visual messages, which encourage us to resist temptations. We glorify the indulgence in using. Without support of others, our urges become uncontrollable and we break our sobriety.

The group of an addict is organized spontaneously. When we are users, we keep to the rules of the group. The messages of the group infect us like a parasite and spread. The group can consist only of a few members or just one, who distributes the group messages and constantly looks forward to enroll new members. As addicts we can be estranged from others and operate alone, but the influence of the group continues to be with us. As group members we insinuate that sobriety creates a very dull lifestyle and takes out all the fun and friendships from our life. We stress that others who are not a part of our group do not know what is good or bad, and only the group knows the real truth. We block the other messages that imply it is very wrong to use the substance.

Our visual messages support our usage, and we caution others that they are not intimidated by the messages against the use of the substance. We submissively recall the faces of our drinking bodies, which are dear friends, and the pleasurable sexual encounters accompanied by alcohol consumption. Those visual messages increase the craving, because we attribute the pleasurable memory to the substance enjoyment. The messages are about using the substance as a pleasure. The group mentality supports the craving and constantly pushes us to break sobriety, working against our resistance.

The neutral fragments support addiction

Our psychological addiction is so durable because our pleasurable association is attributed to the use of substances. A few of our fragments are neutral to cravings but later become supporters of the addiction. The power of addiction is in our desire to change our reality and to experience a feeling of euphoria. We cannot tolerate any unpleasantness, stressful events, and painful encounters that bring a high level of discomfort. The benefits of substance use are in the transformation of reality. After using the substance, our feeling switch from discomfort to comfort. Our fixated fragments, which are in opposition to the unpleasant reality, push us to have cravings and break sobriety. Because of the common goals, the neutral fragments do not oppose it. Negativity to the existing unlikable reality pushes the neutral fragments to support the substance use together with domineering fragments. They become supporters and are in opposition to other fragments that do not want to change the existing reality. The dominant fragments of our psyche split from the fragments that are against substance use. Our destruction of opposition to use substance happens on a subconscious level.

When we bring all our conflicts to the conscious level, we are more prepared to fight cravings, and then we are consciously aware of our internal processes and can achieve success in resisting urges. We understand that it is not very wise to change the unpleasant reality to addiction, and we empower our neutral fragments to resist the cravings. We identify and translate the stimulation of cravings to the centers of opposition, and we clear confusion in our responses, translating our smell, which creates craving, to our kinesthetic expression. Our opposition to addiction decreases our craving. The new messages are that we lose coordination when we use the substance. We translate the smell of the substance as the distortions and as blurring in the eyes. All of those discomforts are real and do not support the temptation; they emphasize the unpleasant consequences of using the substance.

By translating stimulations to other modalities, we reinforce the opposition and advance forward in the struggle against using the substance. We win over time. Our confrontation with craving can be done on the conscious level of awareness, if we willfully and consciously oppose the pleasurable attributions to substance use. To win the struggle against forces of cravings, we must use all means at our disposal. We mobilize and solidify the obtainable fragments, and in dialogues we prevent the suppression of the reality. By unifying against our cravings, we build opposition and enroll the neutral fragments on our side, because they are valuable parts of our psyche. The outcome of the struggle between our domineering fragments and the opposition depends on our skills and how successfully we acquire the cooperation of neutral fragments. If done right, we can transform the fixation to plasticity.

We have only a few ways to deal with our cravings. We can give in to cravings and then suppress our dissent and continue using the substance as we did before. To stop cravings, we must reinforce our opposition to its use. To achieve a victory over the forces of cravings, our opposition needs to be stronger than the power of the craving. Only if a majority of neutral fragments help us will we become successful in stopping cravings.

CHAPTER VI

Meetings After Restructuring

Our psyche gets cracked by small fragments

Because of the strong stress that arises from traumatic events, our psyche gets cracked by rigid fragments. To unify the psyche, we need a systemized approach to assemble and restructure our fragments, analyzing and classifying our responses. The sign of the originality of our psyche is the unpredictable responses to similar stimulations. In contrast, after the trauma we have similar responses to diverse stimulation. Our similar responses are in the same form of expression and are called common fragments; they are a sign of the unstable psyche, which is copying similar responses from others.

In a computer language, our fragmented psyche is the combination of small files that form our responses. Our files are not combined together in a directory and are in various sensory forms. The processes have not controlled and generate similar or dissimilar responses. We are not consciously aware of our internal processes and do not know where and how our responses are generated.

Our psyche has groups that consist of the combinations of the fragments, and we need to identify them. Our fixated fragments are in dysfunctional groups and are based on distorted perceptions of video, audio, kinesthetic, tactile, and olfactory stimulation. When our fragments with diverse responses assemble in groups, we easily observe the discrepancies in our perception. Our fragments have atypical ways of interaction, and some of them are under the strong control of domineering fragments, but some are loosely associated. When we have a loose association, we do not accept commands from the domineering fragments and are driven by a desire for independence. We feel guilty after our loosely associated fragments act out against our domineering fragments. When loyalty to the domineering fragments takes over our psyche, the devoted fragments are subservient to the domineering fragments.

Our psyche has a complex structure. To understand it is important in identifying the power struggle between our fixated fragments. A more stable identity consists of several groups that actively interact, cooperate, and exhibit plasticity. To reorganize our fragments, we need to identify all groups. When on a conscious level the draft of our psyche is complete, we can rearrange the relationships between groups and the relationship of our fragments within the groups. In our cohesive groups, we restructure our individual responses. The process of unifying the psyche creates a conscious awareness of the differences. We achieve the unification of the similar responses to the common groups.

The congruence of the translation of stimuli to various styles of expression is the most important task. We do not want our stimulations to be lost in translation. A proper translation is a basic rule for having congruent responses. We assemble our distorted responses in common groups, get them under conscious control, and rearrange them. Our goal in the restructuring of our misdirected and isolated groups is to establish the relationship between them. Even thought we act intuitively, we are stronger when we have congruency in our responses. Our identity gets more solid than a psyche with contrasting responses.

The link between the body and mind—The story of Lola

In many studies the emphasis on dialogue between the body and mind is very important and is a recognizable topic of discussion despite the difference in the systems and approaches. One of Lola's fragments belonged to a sexually abused little girl who was very frightened and experienced a frozen sensation, when she was in front of perceived danger. Lola was aware that her responses were wrong but did not have the strength to move. She was a very depressed and unhappy woman; she was not able to identify fragments in her psyche. She could not bring her fragments together and did not have dialogue between her body and mind. Lola lost cohesiveness and was driven by loose fragments to a split of her identity. Her rigid fragments affected her with very painful and depressing responses, and she processed stimuli with damaged structures. Her decisions were built on forces of split.

To overcome her problems, Lola translated her kinesthetic feeling to a visual modality. The translation of her responses appeared to be similar to the feeling of driving a car without brakes. Lola also translated her kinesthetic response to the olfactory form, like being in a burning house without any available exits and exhaling the fumes. She processed her feelings by identifying the fragments, meeting with them, and having dialogue between fragments. She took conscious control over her mind and over her reactions to her traumatic past, using the dialogue between body and mind to get relief from the freezing kinesthetic sensations. Lola synthesized her body's reaction and the struggles of her mind. In the past her fragments were operating on a subconscious level, but now she consciously identified her fragments.

Similarly, a computer has a unique level of operating and processes the low-level and high-level languages. If we work on the computers with high-level languages, we are not concerned about the machine's low-level language. The restructuring helped Lola get relief from her freezing through a restructuring of her fragments. After becoming consciously aware of her responses, Lola provided the translation of her responses and used the dialogue between body and mind to move from the kinesthetic to the audio and visual experiences. Lola translated her kinesthetic reaction from the frightening event, from the domineering modality to other modalities. Lola achieved the restructuring of her brain's chemicals by the psychological analysis of distinct fragments. Lola translated her freezing sensation as similar to stammering. Lola felt like she could not achieve proper pronunciation of words, and she couldn't say much. The analysis of fragments created opportunities for Lola to receive help to restructure her fragments without pharmacological intervention. In the past Lola was not able successfully treat psychological sicknesses, but the new knowledge opened up a new frontier.

The fixated fragments in the story of Lola

Before the trauma, Lola's flexible fragments communicated with and supported her main fragments. After the trauma her fixated fragments become loosely associated and were no longer under the control of her domineering fragments. Loose fragments easily replaced her old fragments. Because it was hard to adjust to a painful experience, Lola's psyche split. She suffered from low self-esteem and unhappiness, and she had many fixated fragments. Her fixated and loose fragments spontaneously took over her psyche and became her main fragments, but they looked like generals without any army and were in power only for a short time. The main fragment was the one who at a particular time dominated Lola's psyche and provided directions for her responses. In Lola's life her fixated fragments were a disturbance; they were associated with overreaction and the deformation of responses. The fixated fragments in Lola's psyche drifted away from other fragments and functioned semi-independently, ignoring other fragments. Because of the traumatic experience, her loose fragments created a lot of turbulence in her psyche in the form of flashbacks and intrusive thoughts.

The turmoil in her psyche was a result of her inability to have peace between her fighting fragments. She achieved coexistence of her fragments by engaging in a dialogue after her fragments from her subconscious mind transferred to her conscious. She was able to facilitate the meetings and dialogue between her fragments in order to keep them together. The process of unifying her psyche was based on her recognized needs for reconfiguration and restructuring. Her damaged psyche was reversed and in several steps regained its lost abilities. Lola achieved unification of her fragments in a solid identity with newly obtained flexibility and plasticity. The flexibility and plasticity of fragments is a link between a split and a solid self.

We are becoming plastic surgeons—
The story of an uncertain mother

The mother of a small child unifies her fragments. She is the plastic surgeon of her psyche and establishes new goals for her whole self. She brings new, dominant fragments to be in charge and changes the configuration of her psyche. The new goal for the mother is a better life for her child. When her goals change, her previously insignificant fragments become domineering, and many unique surprises appear. Her dominant fragments, which are based on her audio sensor, have changed. Because her fragments are unified with a common goal of providing physical protection for her child, the fragments with the kinesthetic sensory modality are in charge. Her kinesthetic base becomes dominant, and her other modalities become subservient.

Her kinesthetic fragment represents a grandmother who is very powerful and takes over her psyche. Her fragment of the grandmother provides the psyche with a response for protecting her child. At the same time her domineering grandmother's fragment takes away all fun from her life. The mother, a young woman, talks and acts like a powerful grandmother. When her behavior comes to her conscious awareness, she is not happy about her new structure. She develops more realistic goals. Her new goal is to reinforce her strength, but she also does not want confrontation with the grandmother fragment. She only wants a structure where all her fragments are actively cooperating and participating in common goals. Her rearranged fragments have enough flexibility and plasticity, so she is involved in the reconfiguration and restructuring of her fixated fragments.

She decides to expand her goal of the physical safety of her child to a bigger goal: the future emotional stability of all her family. She engages in a dialogue with her fragments. Unfortunately for her, as a child she did not have a good life because of her overprotective mother. Her desire is to have a better life for her child. Her fragments participate in the meetings, and she defines the meaning of what a good life for her child means. She changes the configuration of her psyche and brings the subconscious structures to her conscious awareness. On a conscious level she identifies her various fragments and initiates dialogue between them. When she is not engaging them in dialogue, she involves them in the negotiations and then switches to dialogue. Her work is as exciting as the work of the plastic surgeon of her psyche.

Loosely associated fragments—The story of Ola

Ola was a Norwegian male in America who came from religious surroundings where the topic of sex was taboo. He suffered from his low self-esteem and did not feel that he was attractive and lovable. He did not feel like a real Norwegian. He mentioned that around the world, the stereotype of a Norwegian was a strong, stable, and confident man. He mentioned that he always ran away from the spotlight because all his life he felt as an impostor. He was unhappy because his fragments were loosely associated and were in disagreement with others. As a result of his unhappiness, all his life he was sexually frustrated and lately became addicted to pornography. His responses were based on his moral and ethical rules, which condemned pornography and masturbation. His main fragments were not aligned with the others; he had responses characterized by shyness, fearfulness, avoidance, and also a manipulation of others. His domineering fragments were kinesthetic and exhibited his feeling of sexual immaturity, frustration, shame, and guilt.

Ola disclosed that his mother actually was not a Norwegian but an East European woman who spoke accented Norwegian. He added that during his childhood the majority of East European women in Norway were working as domestics and were considered a second class. He recalled that his mother was a farm laborer before she had met his father, who came from a well-to-do family. He also believed that his father's actions were reflected on him, and he felt responsible for the decisions of his father, who married out of his class. He had a Ukrainian mother and never defended her because he was scared that others would talk about him as an ugly hybrid. Several times he overheard his neighbors having fun by imitating his mother's accent. He did not confront them even though he felt very offended. Nevertheless, he did feel that he had done something wrong and felt guilty. Because of constant discomfort and fears, he did not feel comfortable and did not feel equal to others; he often thought that something was wrong with him.

Ola said that his responses to distinct stimulations were shyness and timidity, and they were established in his kinesthetic sensor. He also reported that his reaction included tightness in his body and a restriction of movement. He was troubled when he needed to express himself verbally, the same way as his mother was, and he was uncertain of his abilities. The name of one of his fragments was Oleg, which was the nickname his mother had called him in childhood, and it sounded more like the East European than Norwegian. Because he had a secret, Ola stayed away from girls because he was afraid that when they got closer, they would tease him or get him into trouble. He was scared of many of his body's sensations. He was unhappy and was constantly in internal turmoil.

Running away from danger—The story of Ola

Ola was able to identify a fragment that he described predominately as the kinesthetic response. This fragment had the kinesthetic response for every stimulation. On the influence of this fragment, Ola ran away from numerous troubles to save the self. He realized that in his life he ran away from danger and was not strong enough to face unpleasant events. He attributed his feelings to his childhood experiences when he was afraid of his father, who physically abused Ola's mother in front of their children. Ola mentioned that his fears were stronger than any other feeling because they were more eager to get out of any tense situation than his curiosity wanted to see what kind of new development would happen. He declared that his attitude of running away saved his life. Ola added that many times in his life, when was not in danger, the running away fragments took over his psyche. He felt that these fragments were beneficial and helped him get out of Norway and eventually brought him to America.

Because he was very lonely, his life in an American big city was contradictory and unpleasant. He disclosed that he didn't know the language and lacked any marketable skills to have a social life and advance himself in America. He was crushed by his unpleasant feelings of sexual frustration and the danger of losing himself in the big city. He ran away from the big city to the forest, which remind him of his native Norway.

He worked as a lumberjack for an American timber company in Canada. He lived with primitive villagers who were drunk more often than sober. After work the biggest fun for them was playing cards. He did not talk to them, and they did not bother him. He read a lot of books and studied English. In the forest he used adult publications for sexual gratification. After being in the forest for a while, he went back to the big city. He emphasized again that running away from the city did something good for him: in the forest he found a good use of pornography and of gratifying himself. With masturbation he did not need to get close to real women. He felt that running away from danger was an important and beneficial part of his makeup.

We are pretending—The story of Ola

Ola was not pleased with a number of his fragments, but he pretended that he was happy with the self. He was covering up a fact: that he did not achieve a wholeness of his psyches. Nevertheless, he was proud of some of his fragments, which were based on his kinesthetic sensor and provided positive responses of him being a hard worker and having a good work ethic. Before running to America from his native country, he was a soldier, and he considered himself to be a good one. He also was a skillful lumberjack in the forest and a construction worker in the American big city; he was paid top wages for his job.

Ola also recognized another fragment that was based on his visual sensor. This fragment represented a calculating and manipulative part of Ola's psyche, and it looked like a smart aleck. He was not ashamed of this fragment and was very thankful that he had it. Ola recalled that he became productive because of this fragment, which helped him to find optimal solutions to problems and provided him with very practical responses. This fragment was free from fears, and because of this fragment, he was able to marry a good American woman—but he was not able to keep their marriage going for a long time. He loved his wife, even though she was not a beauty queen. She was very stubborn American but did not have any intention to split him. Her stability helped him to build confidence and keep all his fragments together. On top of that, his wife was wealthy, professional, and smart, and she helped him get an education. She gave birth to his handsome son.

Because of his wife's influence, he developed self-reliance skills and was able to prove to his employer that he was very valuable. In America he was financially stable. Later in life he hired an agent who watched out for his business and helped him in his old age. He mentioned that in financial areas the manipulative fragment always took over his psyche and helped him manage complications and thorny circumstances.

Ola also had a troublemaker fragment that did not help him at all and actually sabotaged all his endeavors. This fragment was very negative and operated on the visual sensor. Because of him, Ola saw himself as ugly and unworthy of love. He mentioned that his father was a butcher and had inherited a butcher shop, but his mother was a peasant East European woman. His father was a wealthy man who married out of his class. He felt that his father's behavior was very irresponsible and was a weakness. He believed that his father put a big burden on his children because they came from a mixed background. He assumed that because of his shameful situation, no Norwegian woman would love him. Nevertheless, he was very close to his mother and felt that only his she loved him. From America he called her every week Norway to talk.

When Ola's mother passed away, his sister took his mother's place as his confidante, but it was not the same. He mentioned that his sister was a favorite of their father and did not remember their father as a scary person, like he did. She remembered their father as very nice and their mother as very stubborn. His sister did not have any negative feelings toward their father, but he still remembered his father as a horrifying man. He remembered that his father tenderly kept his daughter on his lap and swore at his wife. In his memory his father was fondling his daughters, but she denied it.

After Ola's parents passed away, he continued his calls to his relatives in Norway, and they argued about their differing memories. He realized that he did not have anyone to whom he could relate. He believed that, as a young man, he ran away from his relatives because around them he could not have stability and a wholeness of his identity. He believed that his relatives were disturbing his peace. Later he understood that he did not achieve wholeness because he was pretending that he was happy.

Luckily for him, Ola relied a lot on his intuition. On an impulse he married a woman who wanted him too, and that helped him keep his fragments together. He also knew that he did not have a real unity of his fragments, but in the front of his wife he pretended that he was a real man. Somewhere inside he knew that he was damaged goods, and he was afraid that his wife would find out.

Eventually his wife realized that he was avoiding real intimacy, and sex for him was only a mechanical exercise. Because he did not expect any rejection, he felt real and did not need to pretend. When his wife became sure that he was not open to her love, she made a move. His wife was a free spirit, and she left him. He never remarried and did not really feel happy, but he continued to pretend that he had achieved wholeness.

Pretension is the ruling force—The story of Ola

Pretension became the ruling force of Ola's psyche and was based on his false beliefs. Without any big commotion, he accepted the news of his wife moving to another state with a man, and she took their son with her. He was separated with his son, but Ola pretended that nothing terrible had happened in his life by detaching from his feelings. Deep inside, Ola did not believe that any woman would be attracted to him. He did not have any evidence of this, but he suspected that his wife had never loved him in the first place, and he meekly went along with her decision to leave him. His belief was based on the conviction that he was not a loveable person. Because of his thought that he couldn't be loved, he never let anyone get close and pushed others away. He did not permit any woman to love him.

Emotionally he ran away from women because he did not trust them. He remembered that as a young man, he ran away from his Norwegian sweetheart. He only trusted his mother and his sister. As a child he unsuccessfully competed for his father's love. Ola knew that his father loved his sister more. He also doubted his mother's love and felt that deeply in her heart she loved his sister more. To get his parents' attention, he pretended to be scared and sick.

Ola left Norway for America because he did not trust his family. The most important achievement was that in America, he did not need to pretend. He said that he loved his family, but by being far from them he felt at peace. All his life he ran away from every significant woman, which included his mother, his sister, his wife, and his girlfriends. Despite the fact that he deliberately abandoned any ties with significant others, he felt lonely and empty. To escape from his misery, he was good with philosophical abstraction, books, and art. He was deeply involved in the English language and spoke it without an accent. Ola had a very good verbal capacity, which helped him to be popular with his friends and colleagues. He expressed very eloquently new theories and passages of scripture. Ola was religious but did not replace his entire life with religion. Religion was his escape, and he often was involved in talks about religion because it was a part of his expertise.

The escapist, one of his fragments, operated predominately on the audio sensor. His verbal fragment helped him to be a valuable contributor to any intellectual conversation. Because of his skillful way of pretending and deceiving, he felt comfortable in the company of the young and naïve. In his conversations he pretended that he had achieved wholeness.

The roots of psychological addiction are in the fragmented identity—The story of Ola

As with other addictions, Ola's psychological addiction of going to prostitutes had roots in his fragmented identity and represented his impulsive behavior. By going to prostitutes, his domineering fragments wanted to keep his psyche together; on the subconscious level, they wanted unification with the loose fragments. It seems that for some the use of a prostitute's services is a positive reinforcement and is a symbol of being powerful and successful. As gamblers, after winning we sometimes go to the prostitutes because we want to celebrate our luck. The psychological addiction is also chemical and is on the level of our neurotransmitters.

Our addiction to prostitutes in many instances is a complex one. It is based on impulsivity, which includes addiction to dangerous behavior (including rage, recklessness, gambling, stealing, addiction to alcohol and narcotics, etc.). In Ola's case the addiction to prostitutes skillfully covered an unstable structure of his psyche and kept together his loose fragments. Complete disregard of the roots of the addiction caused a low success rate in the treating of the addiction. Our addiction to prostitutes is equal to machismo and to our big egos. The root of addiction is a pretension that our psyche is whole instead of being fragmented.

Our addiction is a powerful tool for covering up the presence of limited responses in our fixated fragments. Only a few of our fragments support the addiction, and they become dominant by controlling our neutral fragments. Because they do not experience any resistance, they keep their domineering position. Our psyche does not know how to keep together the loose fragments; to keep psyche unified, we keep the substance-dependant fragments as domineering and do not want to get rid of them.

In some dysfunctional manner, our domineering fragments want only good things for us—they want to keep unity in our psyche. An addicted fragment always has a counterpart, a fragment that is clean from addiction and has a lot of common sense. Unfortunately the healthy fragment does not have real power, because it is presented in an uncommon sensory. This fragment has a mission too, and it covers up the secret of our psyche, pretending that our psyche is solid. Because it is clean, it easily deceives others.

One of Ola's fragments was a physically abused boy, and even with a little stress he recalled a very distorted past. His fragment was built on the visual sensor and contained the traumatic memories of his child abuse. Ola also had an abusive, ignorant, and macho fragment that operated on the kinesthetic sensor. One of Ola's fragments covered up his fixated fragments and his impulsive behavior. Ola's addiction to prostitutes was an attempt to detach from trauma—it was a process for unifying him with his neutral fragments.

The first step of recovery is translating the responses—The story of Ola.

In order to get control of his addiction, Ola needed to achieve cohesiveness. He translated his responses to his other sensory modalities. Because of his desire to escape reality, Ola's fragments were loosely associated and had fixated and neutral responses. His fixated fragments spontaneously took over his psyche. The fixated fragments did not have any flexibility, lacked the common goals, and did not have any agreement in perception. They did not communicate and opposed other fragments on the other sensory forms. The fixated fragments of the kinesthetic modality humiliated the audio and visual fragments, and vice versa.

Ola's distorted perceptions were caused by the incongruence in communication between his fragments. He had a lack of desire to understand the differences in the sensory experiences, which complicated his efforts to get all his fragments together. His fragments lacked references as to how to translate one type of sensory experience to another. His kinesthetic fragments were incapable of understanding his audio and visual stimulations. Only the addiction to pornography kept Ola's fixated fragments together. His psyche strived for unification but would not give up the pornography, which was a main partner in keeping everything together.

The work to change associations of distinct fragments is similar to a plastic surgeon's work. Ola was able to consciously identify and rearrange the structure and composition of his fragments in order to build relationships. He translated his experiences to discrete sensory modalities, and his fragments agreed with the common goal. The destructive behavior stopped when he rearranged the fragments in his psyche. The destructive tendencies were part of an old system and did not have any place in the new system. Ola's psyche did not keep the addiction to the pornography. To keep his fragments together, he appointed distinct, domineering fragments. Until the psyche was reconstructed in the cohesive system, he had the strong need for the psychological addiction, but now the addiction was not needed.

The domineering suppressing the neutral—The story of Danila

Danila was married to a Ukrainian woman and had children. In Danila's fragmented identity, the domineering fragments suppressed his neutral fragments. He was the son and grandson of alcoholics. The domineering fragments supported his chemical dependence, and the responses of his fragments were fixated and provided only limited feedback. His psyche fell apart because his fixated fragments disintegrated and dissociated, and only his addiction kept the system from complete disintegration. He was a good provider and kept his work as a car mechanic for eighteen years. He did not drink during the business hours, but in the evenings he consumed alcohol until he was in a stupor. Despite his alcoholism, his fragments on the audio sensor had a good working ethic, and some visual fragments supported his need for stability. His psyche functioned as a productive one; he was the type of alcoholic who did not have any desire to stop drinking and become sober. He hated violence and did not want to abuse his wife. Nevertheless, he drank and was an abusive husband.

Danila was motivated to restructure of his psyche. He brought his conflicts to his conscious awareness and balanced and aligned his audio and kinesthetic fragments. In restructuring his psyche, he had two goals. The first goal was to find a way to verbalize his experiences. The second goal was the translation of the visual experience to other sensors. Danila was translating his fragments to the kinesthetic sensor to help him. The abused little child on his visual sensor was protected by the strong fragment on his kinesthetic sensory modality. The translation of his experiences from one approach to another created in his psyche the atmosphere of understanding and support. He verbalized his experiences in a distinct manner, and his fragments realized that their first priority was to keep them safe, because their emotional structure was damaged. It was the first step in the process of dialogue and unification.

Danila visually relived his experiences as the main way of representation. The balance of intensity of the visual, audio, and kinesthetic responses created an alignment between fragments that shared the same information. The visual experiences of him as a victim of violence translated to the audio experience, which allowed him to reach an understanding between dissimilar fragments. He translated his visual experience to sounds and created a better understanding of being a victim. The visual stimulation triggered a strong response, and he cried. He was recording the sound that later he was translating to the kinesthetic experiences. He then translated his visual experience to the kinesthetic, understanding that he needed to keep his fragments safe and to avoid unnecessary stress. He translated his experiences in steps, which was safer and less intense, and he recorded his yelling and crying. To stop his addiction, he worked with medical doctors, who monitored his withdrawal stages and his translations.

Danila recorded his audio experience in the dissimilar intensities. He also translated the sound to movements. He listened to the sound and visualized the matching movements. When he was ready to reproduce the kinesthetic experience, he hit the pillow and yelled at the same time. He beat the mattress with all his force. He had enough strength to avoid bruises, and he felt strong relief from the temptation to use alcohol. The alcohol was a means to keep the structure together, but he didn't need it anymore. The important fact was that the withdrawal, if not controlled, could cause physiological damages and may have lethal consequences.

The work on chemical dependence can be successful when the needed precautions are observed and the subject is closely monitored by a trained physician.

After Danila completed empowering his suppressed fragments, the dominant fragments did not need alcohol to keep the others together. His fragments were released from the suppression of the domineering fragments to keep his psyche together, but there was more work ahead.

The way to reach understanding between fragments

The translation of responses to diverse manners is the more simple way to reach an understanding between fragments. Danila's fixated fragments had several sensory bases and were not aligned and balanced. The modalities were audio, visual, kinesthetic, and olfactory. When he dealt with his inhibition, his addiction was better controlled. The factors of suppression were not on the way, and Danila felt that his chemical dependence was easier to manage. He focused on various modalities, where fragments were misaligned and detached from the experience; the translations helped him to deal with his addiction. He translated his experience to the audio modality from the fragment on the kinesthetic sensor. Some of his fragments responded with violence and physical dominance, inciting him to be a macho man. His psyche had fixated fragments that were violent, were aggressive, and expressed his emotions in sounds.

By recording his expressions, he was able to listen to his audio translations of his kinesthetic expressions. The audio match for his kinesthetic experience was mainly the yelling and swearing that he did in the translation of his audio experiences to visual sensors; in other words, he was visualizing his recorded audio experience. Danila's translation to visual experiences was unique and tough because he saw many horrible images. Danila mentioned that it was problematic to estimate how long it could take him to complete those tasks. He added that was impossible to predict what kind of visual experiences he would encounter. He acknowledged that, to be on the safe side, visualization may well be done together with relaxation exercises. He needed more time to have a translation of his experiences, because after the emotional turbulences, many fragments in distinct sensory styles suffered from psychological and physiological damage.

Because of the painful ordeal Danila had in his past, some of his fragments were terrified, handicapped, wounded, and not mature enough to sustain the stress related to translation. He needed to assess the damage to his fragments and move forward in his own pace. He relied only on the fragments that were mature and able to participate in the restructuring. By translating his experiences back and forth, he stimulated the process of balancing and aligning his fragments, building the relationship with the fragments on separate sensors. The new relationship between fragments provided the needed strength to overcome his stress. His psyche did not need any more addiction to keep the system from falling apart. He dealt with his addiction by restructuring his psyche; he had a lot of pain and suffering in his life, and he benefited a lot from the process of alignment. All his fragments shared the same psyche and learned to treat each other with respect and dignity. After achieving a state of dialogue and meeting, he experienced relief from the stress of craving. When real dialogue started, his psyche did not need any cover-ups or pretensions. He also felt that his fragments translated to the special sensors and that dialogues were going well. Now, the process of recuperation from addiction was unstoppable.

Psyches with comparable domineering sensors

Other people can have comparable domineering sensors, and there is a similarity in processing information. The similarity in domineering sensors, which can be audio, visual, kinesthetic, and olfactory, provides a better chance for others to understand us. Their domineering responses are in the same style of expression, which is a very important psychological factor. We deepen our relationships when we understand others better. When we have the domineering fragments on the same sensors as others, we are more tolerant and have a better chance to reach agreement on numerous issues. When our experiences are translated from one sensor to another sensor, the interaction between fragments becomes more productive, and we can more easily overcome disagreement when we translate assorted domineering sensors to one common sensor.

Without dialogue, it is not possible to achieve wholeness of the psyche, and we have a goal to get all our fragments engaged in dialogue—the self-actualization process has begun. The dialogues are between homeostasis and the desire for change. Our dialogues are in sounds, in images, in movements, and on a conscious level. Even our psyche structure resists any changes as we make an effort to keep fragments together. We use addiction, fetishism, and other things to resist splitting.

Our addiction keeps the pretension of wholeness, protecting our psyche from falling apart and resisting dissociation.

Our various addictions cover up the split, because we are not willing to deal with the lack of balance and alignments. In the self-actualization process we do not pretend, and our psyche does not need to use addiction because, besides being a verbalization, there are other ways to process feelings. We translate our experience to the audio and kinesthetic form in order to have a wider area of interactions and to become aware of others who have the same domineering sensors and exhibit a similarity in processing information. We successfully identify the others with the resemblance in our domineering modalities. When we have similarity in the processing of information, we are able to have more meaningful interactions.

New fragments are a domineering force—The story of Karine

Karine, a middle-aged Armenian female with changing perceptions, was addicted to the gambling. New fragments took over her psyche and became a domineering force behind her responses. In order to be aligned with new responses, the new dominant force altered her view on existence. When her new domineering fragments had cheerful responses, Karine's existence appeared bright; when her negative and irritable fragments took over, her psyche and existence was dark and uncomfortable.

The dissociated fragments were atypical because they had a loose view on the past and present. Often disassociated characters were not aware of others. There were loose associations between Karine's fragments, which continued to confuse her. Because of the recurrent changes, her perception was unstable. Nevertheless, her behavior was not completely dissociated, and she didn't block the feeling of existence. During the process of separation from her domineering fragments, some fragments did not dissociate and shared the same past and present. Karine had a fragmented psyche; she did not have a feeling of lost time, and she remembered all of it, but she had feelings of detachment from the present and the past.

When Karine had internal conversations, she always addressed it to some unknown fragment in her psyche. Her psyche presented an unstable structure, and she appeared very confused. When her fixated fragment, which was carrying an addiction, became domineering, her behavior changed and her responses became unreasonable. Karine did not understand that her responses were abnormal and that they were out of the limits of common sense. She had a tendency to present absurd ideas and was constantly losing money by gambling, but he always went back to the casino and indulged in gambling. Her behavior did not make any sense.

If Karine did make a right bet and win, she immediately risked again all her winning. She played recklessly and was unable to stop until she lost all her money. When she talked to others, her logic and her train of thought did not conform to common sense. She said that she did not need to save money, explaining that even though she was not young, she did not care about old age and may not live to see it. Our common sense would say that a healthy individual should work and save money for old age, because when she is old, she cannot work and needs to buy things. Karine expressed the exaggerated logic of the extreme. Her logic was not popular because it did not confirm to the general view—it was extremely blown out of proportion because the fixated fragment, which had an addiction, took over her psyche and became a domineering force for all her responses.

The process of splitting is resistant—The story of Karine

The splitting process in Karine's psyche prevented her from having genuine dialogue between fragments. As a child she was very sensitive to neighbors' gossips, which she overheard. She had a fixated, domineering fragment on her audio sensor that was very disturbing. She reported that when she was a child, her father left her mother for another woman. She recalled that her mother was always questioning the neighbors' words and did not trust them; she always tried to find vicious intent in the neighbors' idle talk.

This domineering fragment, which represented part of Karine's psyche, was suspicious, insecure, and very sensitive to all audio responses. A little increase in the pitch of someone's voice made her feel uncomfortable, and she felt disrespected. She depended on her audio sensor, and to have a stable mood, she could not hear anything disturbing. She easily became depressed or agitated when she heard something negative.

Karine also had fixated fragments on her visual sensor and had recurring flashbacks. One of the fixated fragments contained her childhood experience of being an abused little girl; other fixated fragments reflected other traumas. She was frightened because of the incident in an airport, where she was detained for taking out her family jewelry from the worker's paradise. She was threatened with arrest and was separated from her son, who at that time was a young boy. She remembered his cry and how he called her, and she had the flashbacks about those traumatic episodes.

On the kinesthetic sensor Karine had flexible and fixated fragments. One kinesthetic flexible fragment helped her a lot, because she was a good healthcare worker and had good relationships with her patients. She was a divorcee, and her fixated fragment contained painful responses about her painful losses. She mentioned that all of a sudden many people were dying around her, including her father-in-law, her mother-in-law, her brother-in-law, and several friends, and she took care of them. They all died in the span of two years; she still remembered the sound of their heavy breathing. She detached and had difficulty remembering things. Every time she tried to remember, she was sick in her stomach, felt pain, and was very anxious.

Karina's psyche split and she fell apart. She appointed the abusive audio fragment as her front. She was abusive to defend herself. Her mother was listening and telling her neighbors' gossip, and they implicated Karina in those deaths, but she did not give her neighbors any room for gossiping in her presence. She was physically strong, angry, and intimidating to others. In the meantime she lost her fragile femininity and acted as a bully. Her false pretension of toughness and an effort to keep her fragments together influenced her to make stubborn bets. She was addicted to gambling.

She was able to realize that her life was built upon false pretenses. It was a first step to achieving self-actualization and unification of her fragments. She was able to identify her fragments and understand the benefits of translating her responses of traumatic experiences to other sensory forms. She translated her experiences from visual to the audio sensor and recorded them. She produced animal-like sounds that were a precise illustration of her visual emotions. Her experiences also translated to the kinesthetic sensor, and still other experiences translated from the kinesthetic to visual and audio sensors. The translation of experiences opened the door for dialogue between atypical fragments. After the translation to distinctive forms, some of her experiences that suffered from loose association became less threatening. Her responses became clear and less distant, and she regained control of her emotions. Dialogue replaced the previous coping skills, which included dissociation and false pretenses.

The process of self-realization for Karine included the mutual understanding that all fragments were part of the same psyche and needed to be tolerant. The real meetings and dialogues were the way to achieve wholeness for the fragmented psyche. The suspicions and hostility between fragments was replaced by openness and trust. The desire to have a dialogue and a wish for unification are including in the ground rules of acceptance, embracing experiences, and compassion. Genuine dialogue between fragments is very important because through dialogue we can consolidate all of the fragments in a solid identity.

The psyche clarifies, simplifies, and desensitizes experiences—The story of Karine

The psyche clarifies and simplifies our experiences by bringing them to conscious control. Karine translated the responses from one form of expression to the other modes of expression. Her fragments were already identified and sorted in a special style of expression. If one of her fixated fragments had antisocial, psychotic, impulsive, or oppositional behavior, she was able to translate the experience to distinct sensors without judgment. The new understandings provided her with the opportunity to understand the splitting and to be aware how it affected her responses.

The need for unification became clearer and more convincing. By translating the responses, Karine's psyche gained the strength to overcome splitting and was motivated for self-growth. She became aware that her fixated fragments had destructive tendencies. Her other fragments dealt with delinquent fragment in the same way that a healthy family dealt with a member who got sick. Usually the family looked after the sick one with compassion. The good family wanted to be sure that the one who was sick had appropriate care, a healthy lifestyle, and a supply of necessities. If the fragment was violent and antisocial, the response was translated to the diverse sensors, and the fragments in the various approaches were able to record and correct the undesirable behavior. The main motivation of the other fragments, to care after the delinquent one, was based on the understanding that the misbehavior of the delinquent fragment affected them, too.

Our antisocial and immature fragments can be on the any of the sensory types and can hide behind any type of response. Being addicted to gambling creates confusion. The fragments were manipulating Karine, who was able to convince her neutral fragments that the beliefs of addiction were temporary. Before she had recklessly relied on the delinquent fragments, which were destructive by nature and could easily ruin the structure of her psyche. The reckless fragments could achieve splitting and hid behind very manipulative, demagogic responses. Those responses masked splitting tendencies by the seemingly appropriate contents. Karine's psyche was consciously aware of this situation; she had prevented the delinquent fragment from confusing the neutral fragments.

We cannot confuse the fragmented identity with multiple personality disorder. Both of them in the eyes of the law are equal and have the same responsibility to follow the rules and regulations. When dissociated fragments become multiple personalities, nothing changes. Law and the system of punishment in society does not distinguish between loose fragments and dissociated identities—it punishes only the physical body. In the fragmented psyche the fragment are supposed to be aware of what is going on. The law, unfortunately, does not care about the loose fragments and indiscriminately punishes all fragments and all personalities that are part of the same psyche. The incorporation of multiple personalities to one personality helps to avoid undeserved punishment. Nevertheless, the multiple psyches endure a lot of splitting in the process of incorporation and become fragmented.

Karine felt proud of her work in self-actualization, and her self-esteem increased. Her psyche controlled the delinquent, immature, and antisocial fragments and helped the rigid, sick, and abused fragments to deal with the trauma. Her self-actualization became a success, and false pretenses were not needed. Her fragments involved themselves in the genuine dialogue. The translation of her experiences to distinctive sensors created more opportunity for her fragments to understand her struggles. The work to solidify the all fragments of the psyche became her main goal.

We use the art of negotiation with others

In dealing with others we learn the art of negotiation, but in relationships with our own fragments, we want to achieve meeting and genuine dialogue. To find middle ground with other individuals is a big achievement, but with our own fragments we push for dialogue. We do not want any scapegoats inside our psyche, and we do not call our fragments by derogatory names. We are on a mission to be nice to all our fragments, even with the few that are rebellious or damaged. Our motivation is to engage our fragments in dialogue. We understand all of our fragments, because they are part of the same psyche. All our fragments suffer if we get sick or incapacitated.

Some of our fragments are in opposition to dialogue and sabotage the healing process. The process of persuading our fragments is a very delicate one. The neutral fragments can also be convinced to join a dialogue and achieve congruence. We want a dialogue with our own fragments because the inner negotiations are a confirmation of the unresolved splitting. The meaning of the dialogue is a willingness of all our fragments to discuss the problem and to find a solution. If they are forced to join a dialogue, the partners are unreliable.

When fragments realize the importance of the dialogue, then eventually they become facilitators of the dialogue. This process has two steps. In the first step, the job is identifying, translating, and enrolling the fragments in a dialogue. In the second step, through the dialogue between fragments, the spokesman for the fragments can be elected. The spokesman for our psyche can be a real representative of all our fragments and must honorably represent our solid identity. In our relationship with others, we look for negotiation; with other individuals we do not share the same emotional memories. The recognition of our own fragments helps us to recognize fragmentation of other individuals.

In our life we are responsible only for our actions; society practices collective punishment for all our fragments and personalities. If one of them has destructive tendencies, all will suffer. Normally we cannot have a collective punishment. In the lawful society we are not punished for others' deeds. We get punished only for our own, because we are responsible for dialogue between our fragments.

We can be very happy if we have dialogue with others, but it does not happen very often. In our relationships with others, our first goal is negotiation. If we eventually can be congruent with others, then we will be able to have a dialogue with them—otherwise our genuine dialogue with others happens on an intuitive level. In dialogue we feel unification and have a real meeting; we also know our limitations. It is very sad that in many instances, we do not have the ability to have a dialogue with others. We also cannot be accountable if we are not able to have dialogue with others. We do not share with others our thoughts and beliefs, and at least it is good if we know how to negotiate with others. The main reason for problems with others is our unwillingness to create an atmosphere of negotiation.

Before we have a dialogue, we need to learn negotiation. If we are involved in the negotiations, then we are successful in relationships. We do not ignore the fact that negotiation is not easy, and we need to learn the art of negotiation. To understand others we may well make an attempt to see the world from another's point of view. To be a good negotiator, we identify the strength of sensory styles of others and then choose which sensory form in our own experience is more acceptable for a negotiation. The main purpose of negotiation is to understand the experiences of others.

In many instances we translate our experience to others' sensory approaches, because it is easier to understand others from a variety of sensory perceptions. The willingness to translate our experiences to a distinctive sensory style is a sign of flexibility, which is a prerequisite for our successful negotiation. In translating our experience to diverse sensors, our skills become more transparent. With the translation of our experience to the sensory experience of a partner, we transcend insignificant barriers. The negotiations may not become a dialogue, but we make progress in our interactions with others when we have a successful negotiation.

The verbal, nonverbal, and mixed way of expressions

When we learn the art of negotiation, we also understand that our fragments have a visual, kinesthetic, and audio sensory base and have verbal, nonverbal, and a mixed way of expression. In kinesthetic form we appropriately use a lot of our nonverbal responses, like nodding our head or waving a hand. We use the verbal together with the nonverbal responses. Our flexible fragments translate our experiences to verbal expressions and help our domineering fragment with the verbalization of feelings. Our domineering fragments direct many of our responses, which stand in the front line as spokesmen for our psyche. Our domineering fragments usually align with others that are on the same sensory style.

When we have fixated, nonverbal fragments, we do not understand what kind of experiences they express. It is important to identify those fragments and to engage them in dialogue with our verbal fragments. Because of various reasons, we are challenged to express the self in public, but we don't do it only verbally, kinesthetically, and visually. When we are confused and are unable to express the self verbally, we use our posture; as a result, we express the self with weird movements, which sometimes reminds us of strange rituals, or we produce bizarre noises. It is the result of the fixated responses. We also use self-made rules and get a freezing effect that makes our bodies too tight, so that we seem to be in a stupor. We use fixated responses in numerous stimulations, not only expressing the self verbally, but often making sounds of crying, yelling, or mumbling.

When we deal with our own atypical responses, we are aware of which sensory manners the deviations exhibit the self. The exaggerated reaction shows the excessive release of our chemistry, and the restriction shows that our brain is not releasing enough chemicals. It indicates that there is a deviation from the mean. We realize that one of our sensory styles, where the abnormalities are present, has fixated responses.

We have an abnormal kinesthetic sensory base when we display excessive or restricted kinesthetic responses. Our excessive kinesthetic responses exhibit many unneeded kinesthetic motions, like when we spend a lot of time playing with a keychain. Our restricted motions demonstrate the suppressed physical activity, which include being tight and impeding our movements. When we have an abnormal audio sensory base, we overreact to every sound, and to internal voices. We are also inattentive, rambling, and guardedly reacting to verbal stimulations. When we are inarticulate, we get upset.

When our abnormality presents on the visual sensory base, we remember only unpleasant things—we have flashbacks, have visual hallucinations, and are incapable of reasonably describing what we see in front of our eyes. When we are careful and observe deviation, we do not provoke the increase of abnormality and do not trigger production of fabricated, abnormal expressions. When we observe that the movements are rapid and exaggerated, we do not want to mirror those movements. To level with abnormalities, we keep appropriate and regular movements.

Sometimes we have abnormalities in all of our sensory bases; it happens when our fragments are oversensitive to sound, visual stimulation, and movement. We get agitated and angry even at little increases in the pitch of sounds, as well as someone's accented speech or an odd sequence of words. We get angry at someone who, during conversation, looks in the opposite direction. We get upset because of many small things that make us irritable and angry. We become very nervous because everything we hear, see, touch, and smell does not satisfy us. This situation happens because we do not have the verbal ability to process our feelings.

The situation gets tricky when we have negotiations with others. We are not sure what kind of feelings nonverbal fragments express. When we are forming responses and want to have successful negotiations, we need to be sensitive to the problems of others and have understanding of their feelings. First we identify the sensory type which their fragments represent. If one of their sensory manners presents exaggerated or restricted reactions, it is a sign of an imbalance in the brain's chemistry.

We need to check our responses when we prepare for negotiations and others around us are easily annoyed. When others have abnormalities in their sensory styles, we need to adjust our responses. To help others mirror our appropriate responses or switch to a dissimilar sensory approach, we use appropriate responses in the same sensory mode. Sometimes our mimicry and our movement are more suitable to one group; one group feels better when we are verbal, and another prefers the mixed approach. When we are not sure what someone's nonverbal message expresses, we can understand it through different, domineering sensory types.

We respect the feelings of others in the same way as we respect our own feelings. To have a good guess about the feelings of others, we need to get in touch with our own fragments, which will pinpoint the appropriate manner for approaching others without hurting their feelings. We delegate responsibility to our own fragments that match others' sensory style. This is a complicated negotiation. We choose our responses according to the situation and relay our intuition and the knowledge of the art of negotiation.

EPILOGUE

We want to have a solid identity, dynamic interaction between flexible fragments, and congruency in our responses. We want our audio, visual, kinesthetic, and olfactory fragments to be in constant interactions. We are in constant dialogue and meetings with all our fragments. Inside our psyche we have the strength to achieve harmony. We also must be aware that there is utopia outside of our psyche.

Our fragmented identity is under constant threat of further splitting. This knowledge does not bring us any satisfaction or pleasantry. Our analysis of individual psyches is based on the observation of several collectives. We also see our abnormal characteristics in the radicalized collective. The fragmented identity has a resemblance to the radicalized collective; we study our unstable structure to be aware of what we need to reinforce. We have external dialogue and meetings because we want to have a solid identity. Until we have a solid structure, our dialogue and meetings with others are only intuitive.

The radicalized collective has a pathological structure. We learn a lot from pathology and ought to avoid the structures that do not allow negotiation. Radicalized society is similar to a body that suffers from the invasion of a virus: it takes over us and does not give us a chance to function in our natural way. Some of us have natural resistance to the virus, but others become casualties. We do not discuss how the collective is radicalized, but we observe how a radical collective affects us. We look at the dysfunction of the radical collective as a macro structure and learn something from it. The radicalized collective has a kinesthetic base in the form of marches and parades as an exhibit of loyalty to the collective.

The leaders with kinesthetic expression and with verbal speeches radicalize the masses. The radicalized collective and a fragmented identity have a similar structure. To survive, the radicalized collective creates psyches with fragmented identities. It has a visual base that is present in the paintings, banners, and distinctive uniforms of the members of the collective. We see the verbal part of radicalization in the visual brainwashing of movies. Actually, in movies made in the collective, the domineering fragment is multidimensional, is displayed on all sensory modalities, and radicalizes others. The audio radicalization in the collective is exhibited in songs, books, and hymns. The fixated fragment in the movies is demonstrated by a refusal to compromise and an unwillingness to negotiate.

Unlike the social collective, in our psyche we create a utopian collective. Our fragments share the same psyche, and we take care of all our fragments. We separate real people from their imprints in our psyche, because we do not have the ability to create an exact imprint of others. We do not have a complete understanding of others, and initially we have negotiations with their imprints in our psyche. We want to achieve a solid identity and have the power to be involved in dialogue and meetings with others. We are going on a voyage inside of our psyche, and that is when we are able to create our utopian psyche structure. As a result, we can be successful in connecting to others who are outside of our psyche.

BIBLIOGRAPHY

Bandler, Richard, and John Grinder. The Structure of Magic I: A Book about Language and Therapy, *Palo Alto, California: Science & Behavior Books, 1975.*

Buber, Martin. I and Thou, *second edition. Translated by Ronald Gregor Smith. Edinburgh: T. and T. Clark, 1937.*

Friedman, Maurice. Martin Buber's Life and Work: The Early Years, 1878–1923, *New York: Dutton, 1981.*

Klein, Melanie. Envy and Gratitude: A Study of Unconscious Forces, *New York: Basic Books, 1957.*

Kohut, Heinz. The Restoration of the Self, *New York: International Universities Press, 1977.*

Bowen, Murray. "Theory in the practice of psychotherapy." In Guerin, P.J. (ed.), Family Therapy, *New York: Gardner Press, 1976.*

Rogers, C. R. "A theory of therapy, personality and interpersonal relationships, as developed in the client-centered framework." In Koch, S. (ed.), Psychology: A Study of Science, *New York: McGraw Hill, 1959.*

Printed in the United States
By Bookmasters